Contents

List of figures   vii
List of maps   ix
List of tables   x
List of contributors   xii
Preface   xvi

1 **Globalization and China's new urbanism**   1
   FULONG WU

PART I
Globalization and urbanization   19

2 **Beyond the reach of globalization: China's border
   regions and cities in transition**   21
   XIANGMING CHEN

3 **Globalization and the growth of Chinese cities**   47
   CÉCILE BATISSE, JEAN-FRANÇOIS BRUN
   AND MARY-FRANÇOISE RENARD

PART II
Globalizing large Chinese cities   61

4 **Beijing as an 'internationalized metropolis'**   63
   IAN G. COOK

5 **Local and social change in a globalized city:
   the case of Hong Kong**   85
   WERNER BREITUNG AND MARK GÜNTER

6 **Globalizing Macau: the emotional costs of modernity**   108
   PHILIPPE FORÊT

  7 Cross-boundary integration of the Pearl River Delta and
     Hong Kong: an emerging global city-region in China   125
     CHUN YANG

  8 New configuration of Taipei under globalization   147
     HSIAO-HUNG NANCY CHEN

PART III
City development under globalization   165

  9 Global capital and local land in China's urban real
     estate development   167
     YOU-TIEN HSING

 10 Transplanting cityscapes: townhouse and gated community
     in globalization and housing commodification   190
     FULONG WU

 11 A globalized golden ghetto in a Chinese garden: the
     Fontainebleau Villas in Shanghai   208
     GUILLAUME GIROIR

PART IV
Globalization and urban political and
economic implications   227

 12 The creation of global–local competitive advantages
     in Shanghai   229
     ROGER C. K. CHAN

 13 Globalization and the growth of new economic sectors in
     the second-tier extended cities in the Yangtze River Delta   252
     WEN CHEN, JUNBO XIANG, WEI SUN AND SHENGJIN CHU

 14 Political and economic implications of new public spaces
     in Chinese and Asian global cities   271
     STEVEN W. LEWIS

 15 Globalization and grassroots practices: community
     development in contemporary urban China   292
     YUAN REN

     Index   311

Globalization and the Chinese City

Along with China's re-emergence on the world stage, the Chinese city is evolving into the globalized world. These changes have brought many new dimensions to Chinese urban life.

Globalization and the Chinese City introduces readers to the far-reaching global orientation that is now taking place in urban China. The contributors describe overarching globalization through examining the transformation of the built environment in detail. The contributors analyse many urban development processes like urbanization, real estate development, changing landscapes, the industrial restructuring of the second-tier city and the formation of the city-region in the context of global and local interactions. The geographical coverage of the book includes mainland China, Hong Kong, Macau and Taiwan in the Greater China region, border/frontier regions, the cross-boundary city region and the second-tier cities as well as China's globalizing metropolises, such as Beijing, Shanghai and Hong Kong. In examining city development and local practices as part of the globalization processes, the global city is treated as a collection of microcosms and concrete places, overcoming the analytical tension of the dichotomy of the East versus West. This flexible and realistic approach is particularly useful in going beyond the restrictive notion of globalization when dealing with the non-Western world.

A comprehensive and well-edited volume, *Globalization and the Chinese City* is an important reference for all those interested in contemporary urban changes under globalization and a key text for researchers and students of the Chinese economy and society.

Fulong Wu is a chair Professor in the School of City and Regional Planning at the Cardiff University. His main research areas are urban spatial structure in Chinese cities and urban housing and land development, and he received the 2001 Otto Koenigsberger Prize from Habitat International. He serves as a member of the editorial advisory board of several architectural and planning journals and is co-editor with Laurence J. C. Ma of *Restructuring the Chinese City* (Routledge, 2005).

Routledge Contemporary China Series

1   **Nationalism, Democracy and National Integration in China**
    Leong Liew and Wang Shaoguang

2   **Hong Kong's Tortuous Democratization**
    A comparative analysis
    Ming Sing

3   **China's Business Reforms**
    Institutional challenges in a globalised economy
    Edited by Russell Smyth and Cherrie Zhu

4   **Challenges for China's Development**
    An enterprise perspective
    Edited by David H. Brown and Alasdair MacBean

5   **New Crime in China**
    Public order and human rights
    Ronald C. Keith and Zhiqiu Lin

6   **Non-Governmental Organizations in Contemporary China**
    Paving the way to civil society?
    Qiusha Ma

7   **Globalization and the Chinese City**
    Edited by Fulong Wu

Globalization and the Chinese City

Edited by Fulong Wu

LONDON AND NEW YORK

First published 2006
by Routledge
2 Park Square, Milton Park, Abingdon, Oxon OX14 4RN

Simultaneously published in the USA and Canada
by Routledge
270 Madison Ave, New York, NY 10016

Routledge is an imprint of the Taylor & Francis Group

Typeset in Times New Roman by
Newgen Imaging Systems (P) Ltd, Chennai, India
Printed and bound in Great Britain by
MPG Books Ltd, Bodmin

British Library Cataloguing in Publication Data
A catalogue record for this book is available from the British Library

Library of Congress Cataloging in Publication Data
A catalog record for this book has been requested

ISBN 0–415–35199–5

Figures

3.1 The structure of administrative organization in China   51
4.1 The urban structure of Beijing in the 1990s   73
5.1 A massive campaign started in 2001 to promote Hong Kong
as 'Asia's world city'   87
5.2 Hong Kong's three air traffic networks   88
5.3 Employment by economic sectors in Hong Kong, 1971–2001   91
5.4 Change in employment structures in selected industries in
the three zones (1992, 1997)   94
5.5 Redistributed income from main employment in
Hong Kong, 1991–2001   101
7.1 Hong Kong-based manufacturing investment
in the PRD, 2002   129
10.1 (a) The gate of the 'Orange County'. (b) The design
of buildings   193
10.2 (a) The interior design of the reception area of East Lake Villas.
(b) The interior design of the Riveira   198
10.3 The distribution of prime foreign housing project in
Beijing   199
11.1 A villa of 'French aristocratic style' (*Faguo guizu shi*)   215
11.2 A villa of 'rural Dutch style' (*Helan xiangcun shi*) and
replica of an equestrian bronze statue of Louis XIV. Note
the video surveillance camera   215
11.3 The winding form of paved-alleys enable the spread of *qi*   219
11.4 Artificial mountains (*yang*) and lake (*yin*) mirror
of Taoist paradise   221
12.1 Analytical framework of competitiveness of industrial
cluster   244
13.1 The change in economic sectors in Su–Xi–Chang   254
13.2 The growth of industrial output and SOE output   260
14.1 Advertisement in Beijing about preventing AIDS   278
14.2 Advertisement in Beijing about the subway policemen   278

14.3 Advertisement in Shanghai about 'civilized behaviour'   280
14.4 Advertisement in Shanghai showing how to become
     a 'civilized person'   281
14.5 Advertisement in Shanghai about Shanghai's role in
     serving the whole nation   282

Maps

2.1	The Greater Tumen Subregion	26
2.2	The Greater Mekong Subregion	27
5.1	The three zones and the location of the CBD in Hong Kong	93
6.1	The 1926 plans of the Harbour Works Department	109
6.2	Macau in 1910	113
6.3	Macau in the 1930s	114
6.4	Macau in 2000	120
7.1	The sphere of the 'Greater PRD' region	128
8.1	High-tech industrial development corridor of Taipei	149
8.2	The proposed northern Taiwan city-region	157
8.3	The sketch plan of industrial, living and leisure axis of Taipei	160
11.1	Location of Fontainebleau Villas in Shanghai	211
13.1	Location of Su–Xi–Chang	253

Tables

1.1 The time scale of different eras: globalization from
    a temporality perspective   5
2.1 Jilin province's trade with North Korea and the
    Soviet Union (Russia), 1982–1995   28
2.2 Yunnan province's border trade with Myanmar, Lao PDR,
    and Vietnam, 1989–1995   30
2.3 Yunnan's top six prefectures and regions in border trade,
    1990–1995   31
2.4 Import and export volumes through land border crossings
    at the Yanbian ethnic Korean autonomous prefecture,
    Jilin province, China, 1993–1996   38
2.5 Cross-border flows through the major river ports and
    overland crossings of Yunnan province, 1993–1997   39
3.1 The list of the cities in the sample   52
3.2 Econometric result of the foreign investment and trade
    on urban concentration   54
4.1 Economic comparison of large Chinese cities, 2001   72
4.2 Pollutant discharge, 2001   78
4.3 Investment in anti-industrial pollution projects, 2001   79
5.1 Flight connections from Hong Kong per week (2000)   89
5.2 Regional headquarters and regional offices by country
    of mother company   90
5.3 People employed in selected tertiary industries, 1992–2002   92
5.4 People employed in selected industries in the CBD
    of Hong Kong   95
5.5 Hong Kong population by place of birth, 1961–2001   97
5.6 Foreign residents in Hong Kong, 1987–1997   98
5.7 Languages spoken in Hong Kong, 1991–2001   100
5.8 Overall income growth in Hong Kong, 1991–2001   100
7.1 Growth of cross-boundary movement of population
    and vehicles between the PRD and Hong Kong (1990–2002)   131
7.2 Comparison of consumer expenditure of Hong Kong
    and mainland cross-boundary visitors (2000–2002)   133

7.3 Frequent cross-boundary visitors between Hong Kong and
the mainland, 2001   134

7.4 Shares of the main cities in the Greater PRD, 2001   136

7.5 Operating hours of the boundary control points between
Hong Kong and Shenzhen (until July 2003)   140

8.1 Innovation and R&D centres in Taiwan (2004)   152

8.2 Comparison between Neihu Technology Park and Nangang
Software Park   153

8.3 Sector-wise comparisons between Neihu Technology Park
and Nangang Software Park   154

8.4 Taiwan's outward investment, 1993–2003   156

8.5 Taipei's cultural industry   159

10.1 Major features of 3 among the 12 surveyed foreign
gated communities in Beijing   197

12.1 Gross Domestic Product (GDP) and other investment in
Shanghai, 1990–2002   238

12.2 Indices of Gross Domestic Product (GDP) in Shanghai   239

12.3 Foreign Direct Investment (FDI) in Shanghai, 1990–2002   239

12.4 Industrial output in Shanghai, 1993–2002   240

13.1 GDP per capita in the cities of Su–Xi–Chang   254

13.2 Change in industrial sectors in local industry   255

13.3 Comparison of the high-tech industrial development   255

13.4 Comparison of producer services in Shanghai, Suzhou
and Wuxi in 2000   256

13.5 Comparison of tertiary industry between Shanghai
and Su–Xi–Chang, 2000   256

13.6 FDI by country and region in Wuxi and Suzhou   257

13.7 Options of FDI strategies and management in South Jiangsu   258

13.8 FDI and economic development in the Yangtze River Delta   259

13.9 FDI by sector in Su–Xi–Chang, 2001   261

13.10 Ranking of Chinese urban competitiveness in 2003   264

15.1 Comparisons of major urban community development
models in China   298

Contributors

Cécile Batisse is Associate Professor of Economics at the University of Auvergne (IDREC-CERDI). She has published many works on the Chinese Economy relating to economic geography, local development and trade.

Werner Breitung (PhD, Basel/Switzerland) is Associate Professor at the School of Geography and Planning of Zhongshan (Sun Yatsen) University in Guangzhou, Research Scholar of the Cultural Institute of Macao and part-time lecturer at The University of Hong Kong. He has published a book and many papers on urban spatial changes especially in Hong Kong. His main research interests are the changing border functions and the global city.

Jean-François Brun is Associate Professor of Economics in the Faculty of Economics and Management (CERDI) at the University of Auvergne. He has published papers in economic development, especially on economic growth, international trade and public finance. He has also published papers on Chinese economic policy.

Roger C. K. Chan is Associate Professor at the Centre of Urban Planning and Environmental Management, The University of Hong Kong. He has published widely on issues related to urban and regional development in China. His current research projects include hi-tech development in Shanghai and the pan-Pearl River Delta region dynamics.

Hsiao-hung Nancy Chen is Professor of Sociology at the National Chengchi University in Taiwan. She earned her PhD from the University of Pittsburgh in 1977 and has since taught in several universities at home and abroad. Her areas of interest range from the Sociology of Development, Urban Sociology, Sociology of Organization, Social Welfare Policies, to Contemporary Chinese Society. Besides newspaper columns, Dr Chen has so far published more than 150 articles and chapters/books. She has been awarded Best Teacher by the Ministry of Education and granted a Fulbright visiting scholarship to the University of Chicago and a National Science Council Grant to the University of Oxford. She serves extensively as social policy consultant to various Taiwanese governmental committees and NGOs.

Wen Chen is Professor in the Nanjing Institute of Geography and Limnology, Chinese Academy of Sciences. She has published many papers on urban economy, regional development and planning. She received, in 2001, the Excellent Youth Geographer Award from the Chinese Geography Society and the project entitled 'greening of industry and environmental pressure in the Yangtze Delta' funded by the Natural Sciences Foundation of China.

Xiangming Chen is Professor of Sociology, Adjunct Professor of Political Science and Adjunct Professor of Urban Planning and Policy, University of Illinois at Chicago, as well as a research fellow with the IC^2 Institute, University of Texas at Austin. He has been conducting comparative and transnational research on the multiple facets of global–local relations in the urban and regional contexts of China and Asia, with a recent focus on the rise of Shanghai and its surrounding region. He is the author of *As Borders Bend: Transnational Spaces on the Pacific Rim* (Rowman & Littlefield Publishers, 2005) and co-author (with Anthony M. Orum) of *The World of Cities: Places in Comparative and Historical Perspective* (Blackwell, 2003). He has also published in a number of leading international social science and urban studies journals.

Shengjin Chu is a doctoral candidate at the School of Business, Nanjing University.

Ian G. Cook is Professor of Human Geography, Programme Leader in Geography and Head of the Centre for Pacific Rim Studies at Liverpool John Moores University. Ian's main research interests are aspects of spatial transformation in China. His books include the co-edited volumes on *Fragmented Asia* (Avebury, 1996), *Dynamic Asia* (Ashgate 1998) co-authored *China's Third Revolution: Tensions in the Transition to Post-Communism* (Curzon, 2001) and *Green China: Seeking Ecological Alternatives* (RoutledgeCurzon, 2002). Ian has also contributed to a number of recent and forthcoming edited volumes and journals on such topics as the active elderly in China, Chinese TVEs and urban and regional pressures of development.

Philippe Forêt (University of Chicago PhD) is a researcher at the Institute of Cartography of the Swiss Federal Institute of Technology at Zurich, Switzerland. He has written articles on the historical geography of China and inner Asia. His books include: *Mapping Chengde* (Honolulu, University of Hawaii Press, 2000) and *The True Story of a Mountain Bigger than the Himalayas* (Paris, Breal, 2004). He is the co-author of *Inner Asia as They Saw it* (Geneva, Olizane, 2003) and *New Qing Imperial History* (London, RoutledgeCurzon, 2004). A grant from the Swiss National Science Foundation supported his work on the last three books. Forêt is a member of the editorial boards of the *Central Eurasian Studies Review* (Harvard University) and the *Bulletin of the Museum of Far Eastern Antiquities* (Stockholm).

Guillaume Giroir is Professor of Regional and Urban Geography at the University of Orléans (France). He has published many works, both theoretical and empirical, relating to a geographical approach to transition and the process of globalization in China. His main field studies include the outskirts of Chinese megacities – satellite towns, state farms, high-tech parks, theme parks and the environment, and especially gated communities (*bieshu qu*).

Mark Günter, MSc, majored in Economic Geography at the University of Bern, Switzerland. His thesis was on socio-economic developments in the global city Hong Kong. He has been working as a project manager and consultant for Martel GmbH in Gümligen (Switzerland) since 1996, where he acquired substantial experience in assisting with the management of large collaborative projects in the 5th and 6th European Research Framework Programmes. He is currently doing his PhD at the ETH in Zürich, Switzerland.

You-tien Hsing is Associate Professor of Geography at University of California at Berkeley. She is the author of *Making Capitalism in China: The Taiwan Connection* (Oxford University Press, 1998). Currently she is working on her second book on the politics of land development in Chinese cities.

Steven W. Lewis, PhD, is a Research Fellow at the James A. Baker III Institute for Public Policy, where he heads the Transnational China Project, and also Director of Asian Studies and Professor of the Practice in Humanities at Rice University. His research interests are focused on the development of privatization experiments, including mass communication organs and enterprises, and the formation of energy policy and central–local government fiscal relations in China and other transition economies. His recent publications include 'What Can I Do For Shanghai? Selling Spiritual Civilization in Chinese Cities' (in Stephanie Hemelryk Donald, Michael Keane, Yin Hong, eds, *Media in China: Consumption, Content and Crisis*, Curzon Press, 2002) and *The Media of New Public Spaces in Global Cities: Subway Advertising in Beijing, Hong Kong, Shanghai and Taipei* (Continuum, 2003).

Yuan Ren is Associate Professor in the Institute of Population Research at Fudan University in Shanghai. He has been awarded fellowships at University of Aberdeen in the UK by the British Council (2000) and at UIC in USA (2002). He specializes in urban studies and demography, is the author of *Rural Community Development in China* (Baijia Press, 2001, in Chinese), and has published many papers in such journals as *Social Science in China*, *Sociological Research*, *Chinese Journal of Population Science*, *Population and Economics*, *Population Studies*, *Chinese Population*, *Resource and Environment*, and *Market and Population Analysis*.

Mary-Françoise Renard is Professor of Economics in the Faculty of Economics and Management at the University of Auvergne, Head of IDREC (Research Institute on Chinese Economy) at CERDI and Director of the Master programme, 'Chinese Economy'. She has published papers on Chinese Economy, especially on decentralization, macroeconomic policy and international integration. She is a member of the Editorial Board of China Economic Review.

Wei Sun is a graduate student at Nanjing Institute of Geography and Limnology, Chinese Academy of Science.

Fulong Wu is a chair Professor in the School of City and Regional Planning at the Cardiff University. He has published many papers on urban spatial structure in Chinese cities, urban housing and land development. In 2001, he received the Otto Koenigsberger Prize from Habitat International and serves as a member of the editorial advisory board of *Environment and Planning A*, *Environment and Planning B* and *Journal of Architectural and Planning Research* and a member of the board of the Urban China Research Network. He is co-editor with Laurence J. C. Ma of *Restructuring the Chinese City* (Routledge, 2005).

Junbo Xiang is a doctoral candidate at the School of Architecture, Tsinghua University.

Chun Yang is Research Assistant Professor in the Department of Geography at the University of Hong Kong. She has published papers on foreign direct investment and urbanization in the Pearl River Delta, cross-border interactions and integration between Hong Kong and mainland China in general and the Pearl River Delta in particular, in *Urban Studies*, *Habitat International*, *Issues & Studies*, *Environment and Planning A* and *International Development Planning Review*.

Preface

In the late autumn of 1984, a group of students at Nanjing University carried a bucket of dark brown liquid over to the university canteen. They did not realize that this ordinary everyday scene in the early days of economic reform was as significant as their predecessors rushing out of the west gate of Beijing University campus, which marked the 'May Fourth Movement'. This bitter tasting liquid, more like Chinese medicine than coffee, symbolically indicates two themes which have been recurring over the latter two decades of the twentieth century and continuing in the new twenty-first century: globalization and marketization. From drinking coffee as a fashion to actively engaging in selling coffee, these two themes are so well integrated and 'locally initiated' that nobody at that time imagined them as imposing social changes from the outside world.

This volume originates from the RGS-IBG Annual Conference 2003 in London. More chapters have been commissioned to strengthen particular aspects that are important to the topic. Although there has been a strong presence of China geography scholarship in North America in meetings such as the Annual Meeting of the Association of American Geographers, there have been relatively few such organized sessions in the meetings of the Royal Geographical Society and the Institute of British Geographers. But the response to our call for papers to the conference was surprisingly good – this is reflected in the interesting composition of participants from Western Europe, East Asia and Great China area in addition to North America. The scholarship is also trans-local – some have received training in both Chinese and Western institutions and furthermore, as the most productive 'Western' urbanists, many have conducted extensive fieldwork in China. Coincidentally, most participants have chosen globalization as the key perspective to reveal the changing urban landscape in China. Their contribution has gone beyond the 'typical' economic analysis of foreign direct investment and explores wider political, social and cultural changes.

The primary mission of this book is to introduce readers to the far-reaching global orientation that is now taking place in urban China. The contributors describe overarching globalization through examining the transformation of the built environment in detail. As such the title of this book – *Globalization and the Chinese City* – can be interpreted in two different ways: one is more 'classical' – examining how economic globalization has been transforming the Chinese city;

and the other is slightly more 'novel' – the understanding of globalization with multiple spatial scales and 'longer temporality'; thus examining city development and local practices as part of globalization processes. This flexible and realistic approach treats the global world as a collection of microcosms and overcomes the analytical tension of the East versus West, which is particularly restrictive in the examination of the non-Western world. The contributors analyse many urban development processes such as urbanization, real estate development, restructuring the second-tier city and formation of the city-region in the context of global and local interactions. In terms of geographical coverage, the book covers the Greater China region, including mainland China, Hong Kong, Macau and Taiwan as well as the border region and cross-border areas. In sum, the book has made an interesting connection between globalization as forging 'spaces of flow' and the Chinese city as a dynamic place of change.

I wish to acknowledge the many debts that I have accumulated in the years that I have conducted research on urban China. My deepest gratitude is to Professor Anthony Gar-On Yeh at the University of Hong Kong, Academician of the Chinese Academy of Science, for enlightening me when I first stepped into the Western academic world. I thank Dr Ya Ping Wang for co-organizing the sessions on urban China in the RGS-IBG Annual Conference 2003 in London, all participants for their contributions, Professor Laurence Ma and John R. Logan for their constructive advices on the book's preparation, and Peter Sowden at Routledge for his patience, support and advice during the preparation of this volume. The contribution of over 35 anonymous reviewers has significantly improved the quality of this volume – their collegial support could not be acknowledged more personally. I thank Shenjing He for her help in proof-reading and assisting in editing. Finally, I thank the Leverhulme Trust for granting the research fellowship grant enabling me to enjoy precious study leave.

Fulong Wu
Southampton, United Kingdom

1 Globalization and China's new urbanism

Fulong Wu

'Being national is being global' (*minzu de jiushi shijie de*)

This is a common expression in China about how to become part of world culture; it emphasizes that world culture is itself composed of individual national cultures and that the more distinctively national the culture that one attempts to foster the more attractive and recognizable that national culture is in the world. Thus to become 'global', rather than imitating others, one should maintain one's indigenous cultural roots. This introductory chapter is about the emergence of China's new urbanism in the context of globalization.

Globalization has now become a 'new meta-narrative' of contemporary world changes of which the global city has been represented as the key manifestation (Sassen 1991, 2002, Short and Kim 1999, Taylor 2003, Olds and Yeung 2004). The rise of global awareness on the other hand promotes the imperative of local knowledge. Even in what is asserted as a global economy, activities rarely operate truly at a 'global' scale – more or less this globalization means transcending national boundaries or being 'trans-local' (Smith 2001). The recent proliferation of local growth research has concentrated on the scale of the city and region through which the new global economy is formed and 'negotiated' (Scott 2001, see also the special issue of *Urban Studies*, 2003). An extensive literature on global cities has been developing ever since the seminal hypothesis was developed by Friedmann and Wolff (1982) and the research by Sassen (1991, 1994) and others (Knox and Taylor 1995, Short and Kim 1999, Marcuse and van Kempen 2000). The focus on the city has begun to reveal a so-called global–local nexus (Beauregard 1995) through which globalization is no longer understood through the paradigm of 'top-down' and externally imposed processes. The critical local dimension has begun to be appreciated. It is this discovery that brings the need to address the imbalance in the literature, which is highly skewed towards Western economies. Despite some recent reflection on globalization in Asian Pacific cities (e.g. see the special issue of *Urban Studies*, 2000, Lo and Yeung 1998, Lo and Marcotullio 2000, Olds 2001) and on Third World cities, cities in developing countries have not been addressed adequately from the perspective of globalization (Smart and Smart 2003). More recently, there has been an appeal for studies to go beyond the 'Third World city' to examine the similarities and dissimilarities of urbanization in Southeast Asia and the Western world (Dick and Rimmer 1998). From studies outside the 'core' global cities, it is shown that there are indeed different typologies of 'global cities' in the making (Olds and Yeung 2004). While globalization does not necessarily lead to the 'hegemony' of Western or American institutions (Hannerz 1992, 1997), such a notion still implicitly accepts that there is an external process called 'globalization'. Our view is that globalization is built up from the local – this is particularly important to the 'developing countries', commonly regarded as the 'periphery' and hence as being subject to 'external' global forces.

Nowadays globalization is used, together with 'marketization', to capture the change in the Chinese city (Logan 2002, Ma 2002, Lin 2004, Wu and Ma 2005b). For mainland China, such a globalization process has been made possible by the 'open door' policy and the subsequent adoption of an 'export-oriented' growth strategy, following the economic growth model in the greater China region and East Asia. This opening-up has been coupled with 'economic reform'. The initial stage (from 1979 to 1992) of economic reform was perhaps more oriented towards internal institutional changes. But since 1992, especially after China joined the WTO in 2002, the pace of opening-up has quickened. While recent research has begun to pay attention to the impact of globalization on Chinese society (e.g. Lin 2000, Zhou 2002, Ma and Cartier 2003, Zheng 2004), there has been no systematic attempt to address the economic, cultural and political implications for the Chinese city. This chapter aims to rethink the concept of globalization from the point of view of a much longer time scale. The study of Chinese cities under globalization may thus bring a fresh understanding of the global city. At the same time, using the perspective of globalization to examine the Chinese city will generate a deeper understanding about changing Chinese society. This edited volume explores the intersection between globalization and local changes in the Chinese city, thus attempting to contribute in a timely way to these global and local dynamics.

Our interrogation begins by rethinking the term of 'globalization' – a hectic and overloaded term (Yeung 1998, Jessop 1999). Globalization is often thought of as a very recent phenomenon associated with transnational corporations (TNCs) and supernational organizations (Knox and Taylor 1995) which are forming the 'global economy'. Yeung (1998), however, contests the common wisdom that globalization is creating a 'borderless world' and argues that the state is important in creating necessary territorial conditions within which the global economy can operate. Now there are sophisticated views about globalization through concepts such as the politics of scale (Swyngedouw 1997, Brenner 1999) and 'glocalization' as a place-based strategy (Jessop and Sum 2000), which are superseding the old notion of global and local dichotomy. The understanding of globalization has therefore shifted towards territorially based politics.

This 'neutral' treatment of globalization as a bottom-up and trans-local process embedded in national territories is important in the context of this book, which is about the Chinese city. Here the term Chinese city is used with a collective meaning to include various cities within 'Great China' (Sum 1999). By including Hong Kong, Macau and Taipei, I attempt to highlight the cultural dimension of the 'Chinese' city. This goes beyond treating the Chinese city only as the 'post-socialist city'. Both perceptions of '(post-)socialism' and of Chinese versus 'Western' society stress their 'abnormality' as opposed to the norm seen in 'market economies' and 'democratic societies'. The study of globalization in these contexts often holds up an implicit instance to see how this abnormality is becoming normal through globalization. This instance can be seen from the use of so-called transitional economies[1] and emerging markets, as these economies and markets are often believed to be 'outliers' of the global market economy that are now returning to a 'normal' market situation. This common perception is problematic because it falls into the global and local dichotomy and because it equates the 'global' with the 'Western'.

Globalization, in its broad sense, is a process associated with increasing mobility and faster temporality driven by the changing 'regime of accumulation'.[2] In a more open-ended definition, globalization is seen as the 'stretching and deepening of social relations across national borders so that everyday activities are more influenced by events at great distances' (Smart and Smart 2003: 265), or as Appadurai's (1996) five fluid and irregular 'scapes' brought about by 'deterritorialization', which loosens connections between people, capital, ideas and space. As such, a wider spatial manifestation results: we have seen a familiar re-configuration of urban space, with the emergence of differentiated residential space, relying on consumption together with its glamorous landscapes as a driving force, the creation of spaces of globalization itself (e.g. central business districts) and contrasting spaces of people who have migrated from different places. This process cannot be separated from its material existence.

By looking at it this way, we can avoid confusing globalization with 'Westernization' – a term containing a specific meaning in the long Chinese intellectual anxiety towards the West. In 1890, Zhang Zhidong of the late Qing Dynasty proposed a compromise solution towards the overwhelming penetration of Western influence suggesting 'Chinese learning for the essential principles, Western learning for the practical application' (*zhongxue wei ti, xixue wei yong*). He speciously invoked a Song Dynasty philosophical distinction between '*ti*' (substance, the term literally means 'body') and '*yong*' (function, the term literally means 'use'). Zhang was mainly arguing for the use of Western technology without fundamentally altering the foundation of Chinese culture. Essentially what he proposed was a limited and selective 'modernization'. Rather, this chapter attempts to see how globalization is constructed from below – a process embedded in place, by arguing that the Chinese city, now at the frontier of globalization, may be one materiality of globalization. As such, I am against the convergence thesis and the licensing of specific knowledge of the 'normal' (Western) market as a universal one. This is not simply because there are geographical differences ('geography matters') but also because there are profoundly diverse materializations of globalization. This materiality is built upon historically and institutionally conditioned differences. As suggested in the special issue of *Urban Geography*

(Wu 2005a), the 'transitional city' reflects the transition of the city. The global is, therefore, no more than a constellation of multiple microcosms. Indeed there is no such distinction between 'Western' technology and 'Chinese' principle. What has been described in this book is a set of local changes, but these changes clearly show the globalization.

As shown in the table of contents, all chapter titles bear the 'catchword' globalization. However, 'local changes' are coherently argued throughout the book. This chapter sets the scene by emphasizing the central 'theme' of the book. By 'theme', I do not suggest there is just one defined and definite position. Understandably in a collection like this covering a wide range of topics, authors have different theoretical stances and hence do not produce a singular argument. But their discussions evolve around this theme. Part I of this book examines the reach and limit of globalization focusing on the relationship between globalization and urbanization: China's urban frontier in the age of globalization and the relationship between urbanization and openness (in particular foreign investment). Part II further examines China's most globally oriented cities: Beijing, Macau, Hong Kong, Taipei and the cross-boundary city region in the Pearl River Delta. Part III analyses the process of city building for global cities: city building and land rights, transplanting cityscapes and the influence of foreign built form on Chinese luxury housing estates. Part IV assesses urban political and economic implications for the high-tech industries, the new economic sector in the second-tier cities, the emergence of 'public space' and the role of the state and the grassroots practices of 'community construction'.

Globalization and temporality

Temporality is absolutely critical but under-appreciated for understanding such a fashionable term as globalization. Is globalization a new phenomenon? There are assertions from cities such as Istanbul (Keyder 1999) or Cairo (Abu-Lughod 1971) that world cities existed long before postwar episode of globalization. But the current phase of globalization does have something new. On what time scale do we observe the emergence of the so-called global city? By linking globalization (a process claimed to be recent) and the Chinese city (a place(s) in a civilization with a long history), this volume brings together a collection of reflective chapters to contribute to the understanding of the temporality of globalization. Despite the long history of Chinese cities, the city of modern industries is relatively new in China, and the city of 'postmodernity' (a term of controversy) is also in its embryonic stage. Such a contrast between different temporalities might be an ideal context for rethinking globalization.

A thoughtful governor of the late Qing Dynasty, Zhang Zhidong, deplored that the defeat of the Middle Kingdom in the Opium War symbolized an unprecedented 'great transformation' (*da bian ju*) (Hao and Wang 1993: 186); Similarly, Li Hongzhang, the premier of Qing's 'all foreign affairs', suggested in 1872 that Chinese society had experienced great transformation in the last three millennia. In short, the defeated Chinese at that time had begun to realize that the change was 'unprecedented in millennium' ('*qiannian weiyou zhibian*'). What exactly was this unprecedented millennium change? The Western force of intrusion was seen no longer as that of a foreign nation but rather as the 'force of industrialization'. The sentiment echoes anecdotally the scene of a machine-propelled boat sailing fast upstream in the river (this was reportedly said by Fei Xiaotong,[3] a Chinese sociologist). The scene is 'loaded' because it is a 'Western' boat and it is against 'natural regularity' – the regularity in the local everyday reality. Now we come to the core point: a boat is a boat, and to what extent does it become 'Western'? What China faced was surely not foreign nations but rather a more profound transformation, now known as 'globalization'. The temporal scale of globalization can be seen from Table 1.1 where the reach of the global is associated with the new information era.

At the millennium scale, we see technological change (known as the 'era' of information') and the inherent change in production, which is often thought of as 'foreign' or alien, and a fundamental change in society (to what Fei Xiaotong characterized in *Rural China* as an anonymous, heterogeneous, high-density urbanism). In fact, before globalization became fashionable in China's politics, the same thing had been called 'modernization'.[4] At a centennial scale, we see the shaped awareness of the 'nation state', a new construct different from the fated Kingdom and the resurgence of its strongest representation as state socialism. At decennial scale comes the notion of 'socialism and post-socialism', and economic reform; at the yearly scale we see 'WTO', foreign direct investment (FDI), the Asian Financial Crisis and international trade cycles. So it can be seen that the study of globalization should not be necessarily tied up with the very short episode of WTO, although it is necessarily a highlight.

Such a temporal perspective suggests that globalization, according to a narrowly defined concept, is something new; however, when judged by the source of

Table 1.1 The time scale of different eras: globalization from a temporality perspective

The era	Time unit	In relation to the human life cycle	Spatial unit	Population size	Temporality
Primary	Daily	Shorter	Tribal	Hundreds to ten thousands	Locally scattered
Agricultural	Yearly	Shorter	City-state	Ten thousands to millions	Locally scattered
Industrial	Centennial	Equivalent	Nation state	Billions	Internationally linked
Ecological/ information	Millennium	Longer	The global	Hundred billions	Globally integrated and networked

Source: Modified from Li (unpublished book manuscript).

technological advances it is not entirely new. The emphasis on the 'nation state' is however longer than this narrow 'globalization', as shown in China's bitterly resented yet fondly embraced 'Westernization'. Such a temporality also highlights that we should not see the 'national' as equivalent to the local. In academia, it has been emphasized that the nation state is still alive and well, but this is beating a straw man. Indeed, by focusing on the nation one might implicitly license the phantom of an externally existing global and confine oneself to a particular temporality. It is unnecessary to confine our radar of attention to very temporal constructs such as the WTO and FDI (but I do not suggest an immediate decease; rather, these temporal constructs will be the natural elements of the 'era'). Even 'Westernization' is too short a notion, as this millennium change has a more profound and prolonged temporality than that and this change is inherent in this civilization itself. As such, we come closer to the notion of the 'ordinary city' (Amin and Graham 1997, Robinson 2002) as the stunningly fast rhythms have become inherently 'ordinary'. From the perspective of a longer temporality, globalization is a millennium transformation in each ordinary place.

Globalizing Chinese cities: globalization as urbanization

The narrow view of urbanization refers to the increase in urban population or population living in the cities, and the decline in rural population. The broad view, however, believes that the process includes the deepening of 'urbanism' (as a particular set of behavioural norms of the society). According to this broad view, urban redevelopment and the upgrading of economic structures are also part of the urbanization process. Often, the impact of globalization on the city is assessed through the 'global city' as a distinctive category of cities; but understanding urbanization broadly will include all city building activities towards the globally oriented economy. As will be elaborated later, the globalist view tends to see globalization as more overarching. That is, building the city for the global economy is the ultimate source of urbanization (hence the notion of territorially based globally competitive strategies – 'glurbanization'). However, here I treat globalization as a more 'ordinary' scene, not confined to the global city. In fact, globalization is perhaps manifested more conspicuously in globalizing cities (see Marcuse and van Kempen 2000) than in the established command centres.

Attention to the impact of globalization on the city mainly focuses on global cities such as New York, London and Tokyo (Sassen 1991). However, there are other types of city regions that are deeply involved in globalization but have not reached the status of global city, that is, the command centres of the global economy. Xiangming Chen (Chapter 2 in this volume) analyses China's border regions as 'transborder subregions' in the mediating middle, aiming to bridge the dichotomous 'global and local'. He argues that these intermediate forms (cross-border and transborder regions) are beyond the reach of a narrowly defined globalization. They are not necessarily tied to the top of the global urban hierarchy. But these regions have a role in 'gluing' and 'lubricating' the Asia-Pacific transborder links. He shows how the Greater Tumen Subregion (GTS) and the Greater

Mekong Subregion (GMS) are influenced by an interaction of subregional economic dynamics, decentralizing state policies, cross-border ethnic ties, boundary-spanning transport infrastructure and what are portrayed as 'trans-local' milieus, suggesting the need to rethink the limitations of the globalist vision of globalization. These subregions are driven by an increasing mobility across political boundaries that was impossible in the past.

Urban growth is driven by available investment. The coastal region of China is closely tied up with the global production of manufactured products. The positive role of foreign investment on urban growth is commonly acknowledged without detailed analysis. Cécile Batisse *et al.* (Chapter 3 in this volume) show, by an econometric analysis, that although FDI does play a positive role the growth of the non-agricultural population is explained by the structural attributes of the economy (i.e. the level of development, and the size of the secondary and tertiary sectors rather than the volume of international trade). In the long term, two or three cities are becoming extraordinary cities as they undertake global functions (such as financial centres). Although we do not know the reasons for this identified relationship, it is probably related to the fact that globalization has led to the concentration of population outside the state-registered segments in the cities, that is, rural migrants moving into the urban sector. The figure for non-agricultural population might seriously underestimate the level of population size for cities like Shenzhen, which is in fact a migrant city. This notion of non-agricultural population growth is contradictory to the common wisdom that openness in general and international trade in particular has a significant impact on the growth of Chinese cities. Further exploration of the different forms of urbanization (formal versus informal) is needed to differentiate domestically driven and export-driven growth since China itself has a big domestic market.

Whereas 'globalization' has become a fashionable term in China's policy arena, it is used interchangeably with 'internationalization'. The same is true of the use of the notion of the 'internationalized metropolis' for the global city.[5] Such an interchangeable usage is not a simple linguistic confusion but rather reflects a difference in perception. To China, the global is often presented with reference to the administrated national territory. So, Hong Kong investment is treated as 'foreign investment' in essence, although the city is now a Special Administrative Region (SAR) under Chinese sovereignty. Ian Cook (Chapter 4 in this volume) provides a reflective essay on Beijing's opening up, although the intention is not really to 'benchmark' Beijing with cities such as New York and London (see Taylor 2003, where Beijing is classified as a global city). Rather, the interest here is to describe a series of changes brought about by deliberate 'internationalization', a term associated with and evolved from 'modernization'; after all, globalization in the eyes of city officials is yet another way to characterize modernity. An indigenously emerged term such as 'internationalized metropolis' creates a great gap between the global city and the internationalized metropolis. Proposing the latter is one way to 'make the city better' or 'envision the city future'. As such it would not come as a surprise that Beijing perhaps will never reach the state of a normative (and often Western-oriented) 'great city'. The fundamental question is who has the right to define the 'greatness'. Indeed, if we accept that globalization is a process rather than an end product we begin to question such a universal conceptualization. The efforts can equally be mapped as 'modernization', which is driving cities to become more global as the policies adopted are oriented towards the global economy (Walcott 2003, Wei and Jia 2003, Zhao 2003, Zhou and Tong 2003).

By contrast, Werner Breitung and Mark Günter (Chapter 5 in this volume) analyse economic and social changes in Hong Kong with close reference to the global city thesis. Built upon Hong Kong's 'globalized' infrastructure (air-traffic linkage, telecommunications) and economy (finance and concentration of headquarters), Hong Kong is transiting towards a tertiary economy and consequently seeing a spatial redistribution of employment. Further, this has led to the polarization of the labour market and, in addition to international immigration, Hong Kong has seen income polarization and spatial segregation as observed in other global cities. But what goes beyond a narrow thesis of 'economic restructuring – social polarization' in their analysis is that the social and economic changes are also due to the specific historical situation (as a British colonial city in the past and now an SAR together with the principle of 'one country and two systems') and specific local factors such as immigration policies and cultural features. What have been seen are the polarization of the labour market and the retreat of state intervention so as to enhance 'competition'. Social and economic changes are not separated from the regime of accumulation which heavily built up the 'financial-ization of real estate' (Smart and Lee 2003). Now the search for a new accumu-lation method has begun (high-tech versus financial services, see Jessop and Sum 2000). However, this new accumulation process cannot be separated from an existing regime, as illustrated by recent controversy in the media about the Cyberport project, arguing whether it has become a 'real estate' project.

Again from a broad understanding of globalization, Philippe Forêt (Chapter 6 in this volume) examines the 'emotional costs of modernity' during Macau's globalization (or modernization through a global reach). The spatial transforma-tion of Macau between 1910 and 1930 demonstrates the city's new vision to repo-sition itself as an international trade centre. Thus, the city strived to break through its image as a picturesque tourist site and embark on a journey towards a 'modern industrial city'. It is illuminating to think of the efforts of Syracuse in the United States to re-engineer its industrial past into a postmodern city (Short *et al.* 1993). Through examining tourist guidebooks, Forêt finds that unique historical land-scapes were 'hidden away' while the modernist fantasy prevailed. This shows that globalization is essentially a 'spatial concept unfolded temporally'. As mentioned earlier, very often global reach is viewed as compression of space. But as such a process proceeds in individual places, we have a strong sense of history and witness its association with a longer temporality as an emerging modernity. A similar observation is the 'return of the colonial past' to the city discourse of Shanghai. The city's global status in the past is glorified through the selective repackaging of the 1930s in Shanghai's nostalgia (Pan 2005).

Globalization is accompanied by regionalization and the development of city-regions (Scott 2001). Chun Yang describes the emergence of the global city-region consisting of the cities in the Pearl River Delta, Hong Kong and Macau. Cross-border integration started with manufacturing investment by which Hong Kong relocated manufacturing activities into the Pearl River Delta, and continues with increasing cross-boundary flows of population, goods, vehicles, consumption and services. Until now the border has not been diminishing as a result of the 'one country, two systems' principle. But the 'closer economic partnership arrangement' (CEPA) is intended to break up this trend and bring in deeper integration. Under such an arrangement, Hong Kong should no longer be considered as an external force bringing the effects of globalization to the cities in the mainland. The result is, however, more complex than simple integration. Smart and Lin (2004) emphasize the 'muddling-through' nature of regional integration. They further reveal how the politics of real estate development continues to influence the border. Moreover, different city strategies are competing with each other. With the aspiration to become a regional city with some global functions in southern China, Guangzhou receives support from its provincial government, while Shenzhen is moving towards high-tech and logistics industries. The process of regional 'integration' demonstrates the social and political construction of the 'border' and its dynamic and complex re-construction.

The new configuration of Taipei reveals a multi-scalar contention and transformation under globalization. This re-configuration process is subject to negotiated local politics rather than being a natural trajectory that has unfolded under globalization. The picture of the Chinese city would be incomplete if we missed out Taipei, an important city of China. Again, in the context of the longer temporality of Chinese civilization, the current cross-strait politics only occupies a short historical episode. Yet, such a temporality has an immense impact on the trajectory of Taipei's striving to become a global city. Nancy Chen (Chapter 8 in this volume) points out the three strategic moves adopted towards Taipei's 'internationalization': the development of a high-tech corridor, the construction of Taipei 101 – the super-skyscraper marking the new Central Business District (CBD) – and the development of cultural industries with the marketing of Taipei as a global city. However, these strategic moves are hampered to various degrees by domestic politics, in particular party politics, between the Democratic Progression Party (DPP) (the green camp) and the Nationalist Party (Guomintang (GMT) the blue camp). Strangely, the DPP for its own party interest advocates 'removing Chineseness' and the 'localization of Taiwan's identity'; however, this advocacy follows a very narrow understanding of 'globalization' and might in fact lead to a greater isolation of Taiwan, both economically and culturally. Moreover, this 'green–blue' politics has led to a systematic under-favouring of Taipei in resource allocation, though historically Taipei has enjoyed a privileged status. The discourse of regional balance is tied up with party political constituencies, which has led to a shift of favour towards southern Taiwan where the DPP has a strong political base. But in the long term this would be detrimental to Taipei and in turn to Taiwan's global status. Thus, the new configuration of Taipei is subject to cross-strait economic and political changes as well as to local partisan politics, the DPP president Chen versus the Taipei city mayor Ma, and from the perspective of a larger geopolitics, the relationship between Taiwan and the mainland and their relations with the United States (Wang, C. H. 2003, Wang, J. H. 2004). On the one hand, Taipei's re-configuration shows the strivings of the local politicians (Mayor Ma) of global cities to 'jump the scale,' where a connection is made beyond the immediate upper level. On the other hand, it stresses how deeply the global city is embedded in the milieu of locally confined perceptions and politics at different scales.

To sum up, the first two parts of the book describe the growth of different forms (cross-border and trans-border regions) and the globalizing of large cities such as Beijing, Hong Kong, Macau and Taipei.[6] All the chapters in Part I and II describe the various local and historical conditions within which the process of globalization unfolds.

Building global cities: city development

City development is a material practice or materialization of the 'space of flow' (Castells 1996). 'Location, location, location' is the law of real estate agents. When space becomes fixed in place, it is tied up with locally embedded politics and cultural norms. In Part III of this volume, three chapters explore various aspects of city development, from landed politics to symbolic encounters between different cultures. Again and again, we see that the local is not less prominent or more passive. It would be problematic to assume that the local has lower leverage, whereas the global is always powerful and pervasive.

Despite global real estate (such as the Olympia and York development in Dockland, see Fainstein 1994), real estate is the last sector that has been closely affected by local institutions (Logan 1993). In what You-tien Hsing (Chapter 9 in this volume) calls 'land-centred new urban politics', almighty transitional capitalism does not dominate. In contrast, the real giant players are work-unit land users, or 'danwei land masters' and city governments. The former are the de facto land owners, and the latter struggle to build its own real estate 'aircraft carriers' – super real estate corporations to control land resources. This complex struggle between two players and a fast-changing institutional framework (e.g. negotiated land lease in Beijing has been banned since 30 August 2004) makes it difficult for foreign investors to gain the upper hand in land development (similarly, Wu (2002a) argues that foreign capital does not contribute the most significant proportion of capital in the real estate boom). In contrast, capital valorization and de-valorization is embedded in the local politics. Hsing provides a detailed analysis of land politics. In the operation of the land market, foreign investors are 'tamed camels', constrained by local politics and unfamiliarity with institutional set-ups. Foreign investors are more like financiers of joint projects with local partners. However, in land development there is not only path-dependency but also path-breaking. The real influence comes from what Hsing calls 'cultural politics'. The leverage comes from cultural 'exoticness'. The fame of foreign designers becomes their licence to penetrate the city design market, as shown also by Cartier (2002) and Gaubatz (2005). With their eagerness to embrace 'modernity' and globalness and demonstrate their administrative achievements, city officials prefer foreign designers, as 'monks from afar can chant better'. The result is the empowerment of the latter, but this is not naturally associated with fluidity but rather is made by local administrators, and surprisingly at the symbolic (design) level rather than operational (land market) level.

In 'Transplanting cityscapes', Fulong Wu (Chapter 10 in this volume) describes the very 'dubious' or imagined 'globalization' of city landscapes, either created by local institutional constraints or used to overcome such constraints to open up niche markets. Such transplanting of cityscapes cannot be captured by the narrow definition of 'globalization' – the space motif is borrowed, dubiously imagined and indeed may have nothing to do with its global geography ('authentic' North American/classical European design). The logo of the 'Euro-classic' is a metaphor – it is a symbolic rather than a physical space. While FDI might trigger demand for expatriate housing, the clustering of rental properties giving rise to a landscape of 'foreign gated communities' is not a product of narrowly defined globalization. It is in fact a set of 'foreign housing' – housing not defined by its actual sale to foreigners but its eligibility for that, thus reflecting the degree of 'commodification' of housing. Similarly, the use of Western architectural motifs in Beijing is a conscious action by developers to exploit globalization and thereby sell the vision of the good life to the local elite.

The global and local are not necessarily antagonistic. Guillaume Giroir (Chapter 11 in this volume) argues that rather than 'civilization clash', vis-à-vis Huntington (1996), globalization means an adaptation of different cultural strands and a 'civilization mix'. What we again see in the luxury residential area is a 'playful' landscape. Only with the growth of wealth and confidence are the local elites able to pursue their life. In this sense, the gated community in China is more or less an indigenous product corresponding to the changing political economic conditions (Huang 2005, Webster *et al.* 2005, Wu 2005b). Fontainebleau becomes 'Fengdanbailou' ('the red leaves with white dew'). And thus such a typical Westernized landscape might be equally interpreted as a very 'original micro-territory' of its own. Fast temporality may lead to 'identity crisis', but this may not necessarily be so – Buddhism was first brought to China from India in the first century AD and became popular during the Five Dynasties and the Tang periods. Since then Buddhism has been part of Chinese culture and local practice. We might think so-called de-territorialization and re-territorialization (Short and Kim 1999) are not entirely accurate terms as there are no such separated steps between them.

To sum up, in city building, we see a spectrum of proactive local activities. The local is not a passive receiver – but actually can imagine, exploit and invent what the global is. In Giroir's term (Chapter 11 in this volume), in these golden ghettoes of gated communities, the locals are producers and consumers of 'dreamed Westernality'. Such a cultural mutation and mix at a global scale is globalization: such a 'Disneylandization' (see Zukin 1991 for the city as a 'theme' park) might not be an American phenomenon, and there might not even be a 'global spread' of American phenomena (for the global spread of gated communities, for example, see Webster *et al.* 2002). Linked to a longer millennium temporality, it is part of the different forms of faster rhythms and mobility.

Urban political and economic implications

Extensive urban political and economic implications have been brought about by globalization. The notion of 'competitiveness' is closely associated with global-ization, as it is globalization that brings different local economies together into an interrelated yet competitive system. Roger Chan (Chapter 12 in this volume) analyses the creation of competitiveness in Shanghai. Investigating software development, Chan argues that urban governance has experienced 'de-regulation' and 're-regulation' processes. By re-regulation the government needs to promote more market-oriented rules and indigenous entrepreneurship. Globalization does not simply diminish the imperative of governance; moreover, the need for entre-preneurial governance means more than a simple transformation of the adminis-trative system to make it more 'compatible' with the market. The imperative comes from the need to foster 'structural' competitiveness (Jessop 1998), and the government itself has to become a market agent to nurture the entrepreneurship of place, such as formulating preferential policies and incentives and the devel-opment of 'servicing and support clusters', providing the training of personnel, fostering linkage between universities, R&D centres and industries. Chan identi-fies some tangible achievements, such as industrial restructuring by closing down state-owned enterprises, the development of land markets and quasi-government agencies such as Pudong Development Corporation, and significant gaps in underdeveloped services and business support systems. Such an analysis high-lights not only the 'local dimension' of place making (Wu 2000) but also the political implications for urban governance. In order to become a market agent, the state(s) has to adopt a new set of discourses and a legitimization process.

The implication is not only for individual cities but also for the region as a whole. The Yangtze River Delta has become the major site for global commodity produc-tion, in which second-tier cities such as Suzhou, Wuxi and Changzhou are becom-ing new industrial clusters. Wen Chen *et al.* (Chapter 13 in this volume) point out the role of FDI in regional economic restructuring. The original industrial structure characterized by textile and light industries has been transformed into one of high-tech, electrical and electronic product manufacturing, accompanied by the shift from township and village enterprises (TVEs) based on collective economies (so-called southern Jiangsu model, see also Wei 2002) to a system based on economic zones and industrial parks. Even under the shadow of Shanghai, Chen *et al.* point out the significant potential for producer services and R&D. However, in order to achieve its full potential, the Suzhou, Wuxi and Changzhou region has to consider not only competition but also cooperation with Shanghai. Similarly to the Pearl River Delta, the Yangtze River Delta will see the formation of the global city region.

Steven Lewis (Chapter 14 in this volume) examines the emergence of public space, in this case subway station advertisements, as a reflective outcome and a promotional tool for the globalization of cities. These subway stations, often combined with retail trade (shopping malls), are places of consumption and social interaction. Changing visual and textual rhetoric, according to the theory of global discourse, would prompt residents to think beyond the local and identify more and more with the transnational sphere. But, in the case of Chinese cities as well as in other Asian cities such as Singapore, public service advertisements also correspond strongly with the role of the state – these spaces are interwoven with and penetrated by public service advertisements to 'educate' residents to become 'proud local citizens' – and surprisingly do not propel residents to think themselves as 'global competitors'. Although globalization brings more awareness beyond the local, the emerging public space does not seem to be dominated by transnational symbols, though commercial advertisements ask consumers to 'think of themselves as global consumers'. Whereas technology and presentation format (the use of both Chinese and English) reflect 'progression' under globalization, the content of the discourse is tied up with the continuity of the local society.

Moving from discourse to governance, Yuan Ren (Chapter 15 in this volume) argues that despite a global trend of rising civil society, pathways are different and grassroots practices vary. Community development contains a special meaning in post-reform urban China. It differs from, for example, the resort to community/ neighbourhood in the British 'Urban Renaissance' (The Urban Task Force 1999). Instead, community development might not directly result from narrowly defined 'economic globalization' or the global spread of market-based political structures. The underlying mechanism is related to the trans-local mobility of production forces and labourers, mostly domestic. The decline of the state work-unit system as the production unit for labour forces has led to the rise of municipalities. The state thus attempts to re-establish and consolidate the 'social order' by developing grassroots governance (Wu 2002b). Ren notes that 'communities' in China are deeply rooted in the earlier administrative structure (namely 'Street Offices' and 'Residents' Committees', see Wu 2002b). But there are diverse practices in different cities. The strengthening of the administrative system in local governance and the expansion of 'self-organized' social space are opposite tendencies, which are played out in the setting of the globalization of China's economy. In order to be globally competitive, 'neoliberal' policies propose reducing the state's welfare function and at the same time inevitably loosening its controls on population. The phenomenon of the shrinking welfare state is truly a global one, and perhaps that is why community development is also a globally increasing phenomenon.[7]

Bringing these four chapters together, we can see more than the 'path-dependence' often argued in post-socialist literature (Stark and Bruszt 1998, Burawoy 2001). The process of globalization generates new urban political and economic conditions and in turn new notions, discourses and practices as examined in these chapters: entrepreneurial governance, regional cooperation, responsible citizens and self-dependent communities. These new trends reveal the incompleteness of globalization and the limits of trans-local mobility: the city as a social spatial entity has to maintain order and demonstrate stability to counter such mobility.

China's new urbanism: materiality of globalization

By suggesting new urbanism as a materiality of globalization, I attempt to emphasize two different meanings. First, in order to be globally competitive, the city is a material form used by the state to launch a 'development strategy', or what Jessop and Sum (2000) describe as 'glurbanisation' strategies, referring to entrepreneurial strategies that are concerned to secure the most advantageous insertion of a given city into the changing interscalar division of labour in the world economy. This view essentially justifies the urban form as an inherent advantageous materiality through which globalization unfolds. Although this perspective captures the intrinsic 'production of space' vis-à-vis Henry Lefebvre, it tends to exaggerate the role of globalization by treating it as an externally existing force rather than a derivative result of space production.

Second, globalization is no more than a materialized (in locally diverse ways) process, more or less derived from the contradictory dynamics of places. Very much because trans-local mobility has been made possible by technological development in the new information era, city building as a local activity may or may not take an (imagined/transplanted) global form; in this situation globalization is not the ultimate purpose but rather a derivative by-product. In other words, there is no such thing as 'building the city for global capital', because viewed on a longer temporal scale (as millennium transition) the 'dominance' of MNCs is too ephemeral.

The significance of emphasizing the material aspect of globalization lies in its demystifying of 'globalization', and in the context of Chinese society, it helps to go beyond the impasse of the 'Eastern versus Western' debate, thus understanding societal changes more as a 'natural' course of its own. This rebuts the constant gaze over the façade of the central business district in selective 'global cities' such as Shanghai's Lujiazui or 'monumental' places like Beijing's Olympic site. It also prevents us from wasting too much time in counting the number of headquarters while pessimistically admitting that the Chinese city is not yet a 'global city'. The latter often assumes such a mature state of financial command centres as the destiny of the Chinese city; but such a destiny, when viewed against a longer temporal scale of civilization and its renaissance, is simply too narrowly defined.

In this final conclusion, I would argue that China's new urbanism is one of multiple materializations of globalization. Globalization is thus essentially embedded in the urbanization of various societies. Owing to the very nature of the city – high-density, complex, agglomerative, mobile, 'anonymous' and densely 'networked' – actions at a distance are materialized into this urbanized form. Increasing mobility and trans-local capacities bring together diverse activities in the local place, and it is this local place that makes such mobility a sustained, stable and 'normal' state, without evolving into chaos. This is the view of the city from complexity theory.

By contrasting and juxtaposing a process (global-*ization*) with an entity (the Chinese city), this book helps us to think about the 'virtual' nature of the former (nonetheless, really existent). While it is reasonable to think of various urban forms, such as gentrified urban neighbourhoods, as a manifestation of 'new globalism, new urbanism' (Smith 2002), what we see in this book is that there is no such thing as a looming global practice that can be copied by every city. Instead, there are multiple microcosms and multiple practices. Importing a foreign brand or transplanting a cityscape might naturally remind us of a new globalizing world; but at the very detailed level these practices are more locally rooted. On the other hand, practising Buddhist ritual in an imaginative trans-local context during China's recent reminiscent interest in 'traditional Chinese culture' is more than just preserving the local – rather, the practice itself is a material manifestation of globalization.

Acknowledgement

The preparation of this chapter has benefited from the constructive comments of Laurence Ma, George Lin and Alan Smart. I wish especially to thank Li Gongyou for his insightful discussion on changing 'time scale' and sharing with me his book manuscript entitled *The Second Transformation* to be published by Beijing University Press.

Notes

1 'Transitional economies' often refer to the economies under transition from the socialist to market economies. While the economy of mainland China has been regarded as one of these 'transitional economies', other economies in Great China can be described as 'emerging markets', because together with some Eastern and Central European cities, these markets are 'emerging' as new opportunities for 'Western' investment. Similarly to transitional economies, the term 'emerging markets' also implies that these markets once were not mature 'market economies' and now are becoming market-driven economies.
2 Wu (2003b) and Wu and Ma (2005a) use the concept of the 'regime of accumulation' to understand spatial restructuring and the 'city of transition'.
3 Li Gongyou (unpublished book manuscript), *The Second Transformation: Chinese Ecological Viewpoints*, Beijing: Beijing University Press. See also Li (1999).
4 Modernization refers to the narrow notion of changing into modernity through techno-logical advance; the term in politics refers more to the construction of the modern indus-trial system but modernist theory advocates a whole set of changes from pre-modern social norms (with ideology and politics as superstructure) to modern ones (character-ized by Western democratic society). Ironically, when the term is used in the politics of developing countries, it is often interchangeable with globalization, that is, the process of converging from pre-modern to modern (or postmodern, read Western) societies.
5 These officials have not gone beyond visions of 'modernization' to reach the more dynamic conceptual realm of globalization (*quanqiuhua*).
6 Shanghai is missing from this list as the paper on Shanghai commissioned to a 'local' researcher in Shanghai has not materialized. But there is an extensive literature on Shanghai and its globalization (e.g. Wu 2000, 2003a, Yusuf and Wu 2002).
7 I would like to thank an anonymous reviewer for bringing up this important point in Yuan Ren's chapter.

References

Abu-Lughod, J. (1971) *Cairo: One Thousand-One Years of the City*, Princeton, NJ: Princeton University Press.
Amin, A. and Graham, S. (1997) 'The ordinary city', *Transactions of the Institute of British Geographers*, 22: 411–429.

Appadurai, A. (1996) *Modernity at Large: Cultural Dimensions of Globalization*, Minneapolis, MN: University of Minnesota Press.

Beauregard, R. (1995) 'Theorizing the global–local connection', in P. L. Knox and P. J. Taylor (eds) *World Cities in a World System*, Cambridge: Cambridge University Press, 232–248.

Brenner, N. (1999) 'Globalisation as reterritorialisation: the re-scaling of urban governance in the European Union', *Urban Studies*, 36: 431–451.

Burawoy, M. (2001) 'Neoclassical sociology: from the end of communism to the end of classes', *American Journal of Sociology*, 106 (4): 1099–1120.

Cartier, C. (2002) 'Transnational urbanism in the reform-era Chinese city: landscapes from Shenzhen', *Urban Studies*, 39 (9): 1513–1532.

Castells, M. (1996) *The Information Age, Volume 1: The Rise of the Network Society*, Oxford: Blackwell.

Dick, H. W. and Rimmer, P. J. (1998) 'Beyond the third world city: the new urban geography of South-east Asia', *Urban Studies*, 35 (12): 2303–2321.

Fainstein, S. (1994) *The City Builders*, Oxford: Blackwell.

Friedmann, J. and Wolff, G. (1982) 'World city formation: an agenda for research and action', *International Journal of Urban and Regional Research*, 6 (3): 309–344.

Gaubatz, P. (2005) 'Globalization and the development of new central business districts in Beijing, Shanghai and Guangzhou', in L. J. C. Ma and F. Wu (eds) *Restructuring the Chinese City: Changing Society, Economy and Space*, London: Routledge, 98–121.

Hannerz, U. (1992) *Cultural Complexity: Studies in the Social Organization of Meaning*, New York: Columbia University Press.

—— (1997) 'Scenarios for peripheral cultures', in A. D. King (ed.) *Culture, Globalization and the World-System: Contemporary Conditions for the Representation of Identity*, Minneapolis, MN: University of Minnesota Press, 107–128.

Hao, Y. and Wang, E. (1993) 'Changing view of the Chinese towards Western relation, 1840–1895', in Z. Fei (ed.) *The Cambridge History of Chinese Late Qing Dynasty, 1800–1911*, Beijing: Chinese Social Science Publisher, 170–236.

Huang, Y. (2005) 'From work-unit compounds to gated communities: housing inequality and residential segregation in transitional Beijing', in L. J. C. Ma and F. Wu (eds) *Restructuring the Chinese City: Changing Society, Economy and Space*, London: Routledge, 192–221.

Huntington, S. (1996) *The Clash of Civilizations and the Remaking of World Order*, New York: Simon & Schuster.

Jessop, B. (1998) 'The rise of governance and the risks of failure: the case of economic development', *International Social Science Journal*, 155: 29–45.

—— (1999) 'Reflections on globalisation and its (il)logic(s)', in K. Olds, P. Dicken, P. F. Kelly, L. Kong, and H. W. Yeung (eds) *Globalization and the Asia-Pacific: Contested Territories*, London: Routledge, 19–38.

Jessop, B. and Sum, N. L. (2000) 'An entrepreneurial city in action: Hong Kong's emerging strategies in and for (inter)urban competition', *Urban Studies*, 37 (12): 2287–2313.

Keyder, C. (1999) *Istanbul: Between the Global and Local*, Lanham: Rowman & Littlefield.

Knox, P. and Taylor, P. J. (1995) *World Cities in a World-system*, Cambridge: Cambridge University Press.

Li, G. Y. (1999) 'The fourth time scale', *Twenty-First Century*, 55: 132–135 (in Chinese).

Lin, G. C. S. (2000) 'State, capital, and space in China in an age of volatile globalization', *Environment and Planning A*, 32 (3): 455–471.

—— (2004) 'The Chinese globalizing cities: national centers of globalization and urban transformation', *Progress in Planning*, 61: 143–157.

Lo, F. C. and Marcotullio, P. J. (2000) 'Globalisation and urban transformations in the Asia-Pacific Region: a review', *Urban Studies*, 37 (1): 77–111.

Lo, F. C. and Yeung, Y. M. (1998) *Globalization and the World of Large Cities*, Tokyo: United Nations University Press.

Logan, J. (1993) 'Cycles and trends in the globalization of real estate', in P. Knox (ed.) *The Restless Urban Landscape*, Englewood Cliffs, NJ: Prentice-Hall, 35–54.

Logan, J. R. (2002) *The New Chinese City: Globalization and Market Reform*, Oxford: Blackwell.

Ma, L. J. C. (2002) 'Urban transformation in China, 1949–2000: a review and research agenda', *Environment and Planning A*, 33: 1545–1569.

Ma, L. J. C. and Cartier, C. (2003) *The Chinese Diaspora: Space, Place, Mobility, and Identity*, Oxford: Rowman & Littlefield.

Marcuse, P. and van Kempen, R. (2000) *Globalizing Cities: A New Spatial Order?* Oxford: Blackwell.

Olds, K. (2001) *Globalization and Urban Change: Capital, Culture, and Pacific Rim Mega-projects*, Oxford: Oxford University Press.

Olds, K. and Yeung, H. W. C. (2004) 'Pathways to global city formation: a view from the developmental city-state of Singapore', *Review of International Political Economy*, 11 (3): 489–521.

Pan, T. (2005) 'Historical memory, community-building and place-making in neighbourhood Shanghai', in L. J. C. Ma and F. Wu (eds) *Restructuring the Chinese City: Changing Society, Economy and Space*, London: Routledge, 122–137.

Robinson, J. (2002) 'Global and world cities: a view from off the map', *International Journal of Urban and Regional Research*, 26 (3): 531–554.

Sassen, S. (1991) *The Global City*, Princeton, NJ: Princeton University Press.

—— (1994) *Cities in a World Economy*, Thousand Oaks, CA: Fine Forge Press.

—— (2002) *Global Networks, Linked Cities*, New York: Routledge.

Scott, A. J. (2001) *Global City-regions: Trends, Theory, Policy*, Oxford: Oxford University Press.

Short, J. R. and Kim, Y. H. (1999) *Globalization and the City*, Essex: Longman.

Short, J. R., Benton, L. M., Luce, W. B. and Walton, J. (1993) 'Reconstructing the image of an industrial city', *Annals of the Association of American Geographers*, 83 (2): 207–224.

Smart, A. and Lee, J. (2003) 'Financialization and the role of real estate in Hong Kong's regime of accumulation', *Economic Geography*, 79 (2): 153–171.

Smart, A. and Lin, G. C. S. (2004) 'Border management and growth coalitions in the Hong Kong transborder region', *Identities: Global Studies in Culture and Power*, 11: 377–396.

Smart, A. and Smart, J. (2003) 'Urbanization and the global perspective', *Annual Review of Anthropology*, 32: 263–85.

Smith, M. P. (2001). *Transnational Urbanism: Locating Globalization*, Oxford: Blackwell.

Smith, N. (2002) 'New globalism, new urbanism: gentrification as global urban strategy', *Antipode*, 34 (3): 427–450.

Stark, D. and Bruszt, L. (1998) *Postsocialist Pathways: Transforming Politics and Property in East Central Europe*, Cambridge: Cambridge University Press.

Sum, N. L. (1999) 'Asian "Crisis" and "Great China": the bursting of the "property bubble" and its impact on urban regimes', *The Future of Chinese Cities: A Research Agenda for the 21st Century* (28–31 July 1999, Shanghai, PRC).

Swynegdouw, E. (1997) 'Neither global nor local: "glocalization" and the politics of scale', in K. Cox (ed.) *Spaces of Globalization: Reasserting the Power of the Local*, London: Guildford Press, 138–166.

Taylor, P. J. (2003) *World City Network: A Global Urban Analysis*, London: Routledge.

The Urban Task Force (1999) *Towards an Urban Renaissance*, London: Routledge.

Walcott, S. (2003) *Chinese Science and Technology Industrial Parks*, Aldershot: Ashgate.

Wang, C. H. (2003) 'Taipei as a global city: a theoretical and empirical examination', *Urban Studies*, 40 (2): 309–334.

Wang, J. H. (2004) 'World city formation, geopolitics, and local political process: Taipei's ambiguous development', *International Journal of Urban and Regional Research*, 28 (2): 384–400.

Webster, C., Glasze, G. and Frantz, K. (2002) 'The global spread of gated communities', *Environment and Planning B*, 29 (3): 315–320.

Webster, C., Wu, F. and Zhao, Y. (2005) 'China's modern gated cities', in C. Webster, G. Glasze, and K. Frantz (eds) *Private Neighbourhoods: Global and Local Perspectives*, London: Routledge.

Wei, Y. H. D. (2002) 'Beyond the Sunan model: trajectory and underlying factors of development in Kunshan, China', *Environment and Planning A*, 34 (10): 1725–1748.

Wei, Y. D. and Jia, Y. (2003) 'The geographical foundations of local state initiatives: globalizing Tianjin, China', *Cities*, 20 (2): 101–114.

Wu, F. (2000) 'The global and local dimensions of place-making: remaking Shanghai as a world city', *Urban Studies*, 37 (8): 1359–1377.

—— (2002a) 'Real estate development and the transformation of urban space in Chinese transitional economy: with special reference to Shanghai', in J. R. Logan (ed.) *The New Chinese City: Globalization and Market Reform*, Oxford: Blackwell, 154–166.

—— (2002b) 'China's changing urban governance in the transition towards a more market-oriented economy', *Urban Studies*, 39 (7): 1071–1093.

—— (2003a) 'The (post-) socialist entrepreneurial city as a state project: Shanghai's reglobalisation in question', *Urban Studies*, 40 (9): 1673–1698.

—— (2003b) 'Transitional cities', *Environment and Planning A*, 35: 1331–1338.

—— (2005a) 'The city in transition and the transition of cities in China', *Urban Geography* (in press).

—— (2005b) 'Rediscovering the "gate" under market transition: from work–unit compounds to commodity housing enclaves', *Housing Studies*, 20 (2): 235–254.

Wu, F. and Ma, L. J. C. (2005a) 'The Chinese city in transition: towards theorizing China's urban restructuring', in L. J. C. Ma and F. Wu (eds) *Restructuring the Chinese City: Changing Society, Economy and Space*, London: Routledge, 260–286.

—— (2005b) 'Transforming China's globalizing cities', *Habitat International* (in press).

Yeung, H. W. C. (1998) 'Capital, state and space: contesting the borderless world', *Transactions of the Institute of British Geographers*, 23: 291–309.

Yusuf, S. and Wu, W. (2002) 'Pathways to a world city: Shanghai rising in an era of globalisation', *Urban Studies*, 39 (7): 1213–1240.

Zhao, S. X. B. (2003) 'Spatial restructuring of financial centers in mainland China and Hong Kong: a geography of finance perspective', *Urban Affairs Review*, 38 (4): 535–571.

Zheng, Y. N. (2004) *Globalization and State Transformation in China*, Cambridge: Cambridge University Press.

Zhou, Y. X. (2002) 'The prospect of international cities in China', in J. R. Logan (ed.) *The New Chinese City: Globalization and Market Reform*, Oxford: Blackwell, 59–73.

Zhou, Y. and Tong, X. (2003) 'An innovative region in China: interaction between multinational corporations and local firms in a high-tech cluster in Beijing', *Economic Geography*, 79 (2): 129–152.

Zukin, S. (1991) *Landscape of Power: From Detroit to Disney World*. Berkeley, CA: University of California Press.

Part I

Globalization and urbanization

2 Beyond the reach of globalization

China's border regions and cities in transition

Xiangming Chen

Introduction

One of the principal ironies of contemporary globalization is that it appears simultaneously to reach all corners of the world and affect its various parts differently. The uneven spatial impact of globalization is manifested in the dominant position and influence of a few global cities like New York, London, and Tokyo (Sassen 2001), the varied repositioning of major cities in the global air travel network (Smith and Timberlake 2001), and the rare rise of previously marginal towns to important international centers like the Chinese city of Shenzhen bordering Hong Kong (Chen 1987, 1993). Moreover, there are cities in the world that lie largely beyond the span of global influence and thus beneath the analytical radar-screen of the global or world city perspective (see Robinson 2002). As we move from spots or dots on the world map where globalization has left the strongest imprint to where its marks are much less visible, perhaps to the point of non-existence, we encounter the important question of why this is so. A more obvious answer would be that some less or hardly globalized cities and places are located in less open economies and in geographically isolated or remote regions, or both. A related explanation would be that these cities have less or unfavorable links to the global economy. A more effective way of tackling this question, however, is to identify the mechanisms that mediate the global–local nexus by either fostering favorable global ties to cities or forestalling such ties. This is key to provide a deeper account for the uneven local impact of globalization, especially for the development of cities that are difficult for globalization to reach.

Chinese urban development provides a fitting case for understanding why and how some regions and cities develop with little or no impact of or connectivity to globalization. China has the largest number of cities of different sizes and developmental stages located in geographically and economically diverse regions with uneven physical access to the outside world. Second, while Chinese cities experienced relatively limited change over a long history they have become considerably more differentiated in growth, functional influence, and international links across regions over the last two decades. Major cities along China's 'golden coast' have boomed, whereas a number of interior or remote border cities have mired in underdevelopment. Even within the prosperous coastal belt, early developers like Shenzhen and other cities in Guangdong and Fujian provinces, which were fairly small and marginal in the past, have raced ahead of the more established port cities like Shanghai and Tianjin, which have since picked up pace and regained their earlier glory (see Chen 1998). This sequence and pattern of growing inter-local differentiation stems primarily from the state's policies of targeting and favoring sets of cities in different regions for fast and focused growth in a staged and incremental fashion.

This powerful policy regime is only one component of a broader mix of explanatory factors that have contributed to the uneven development of Chinese cities across regions. However, much of the literature has focused on the prosperous Pearl River Delta in Guangdong province by emphasizing the powerful driving force of overseas Chinese investment behind rapid growth and global integration (see Hsing 1998, Lin 1997). Studies on Shanghai have highlighted the relative roles of the central and municipal government policies and foreign investment in its accelerated growth and global influence (see Yeung and Li 1999, Wu 2003, Zhang 2003). The coastal bias in the literature on urban China is only a weakly offset by a small number of studies on frontier cities from generally historical and cultural perspectives (see Harrell 1995, Gaubatz 1996), with only budding attention paid to the relationship between minority border regions and globalization (Mackerras 2003). This neglect of Chinese cities in remote border regions as opposed to near the coastal boundary may have contributed to a narrow and perhaps inflated view that global capital has simply responded to the favorable state policies for and advantaged geographic locations of coastal cities and brought about their rapid growth. By not giving sufficient attention to China's border regions and cities, we have missed out on the question of if and how foreign investors have reacted to cities of less attractive locations under equally favorable but delayed state policies to stimulate their catch-up. In addition, we have missed a chance to look at whether and how intra-regional- or trans-local-level conditions unique to border regions may severely limit the local impact of the global economy.

Keeping globalization at bay

Mediating the global–local economic nexus

While globalization may facilitate the development of border areas and cities through long-range trade and investment links, the more immediate transborder subregion in which frontier cities are embedded may have a more critical but uncertain influence. I conceptualize this influence as mediating the global–local[1] nexus. Rosenau (1997) views globalization and localization[2] as coexisting and interdependent processes in such a way that the integrating force of globalization and fragmenting impact of localization blend into *fragmegrative* (his original usage) processes that produce either complementary or contradictory outcomes. Globalization may reach or even penetrate a border city previously shielded by a national boundary. But whether that border city is directly integrated into the global economy may depend on how it is tied with other localities, especially through or near a central node in a transborder region. The latter could strengthen the integrating effect of globalization by creating direct links between the global and local economies. However, a transborder region may weaken the integrating effect of globalization by rendering global–local economic ties less direct and more territorially confined. In this scenario, a transborder region may produce some local fragmentation relative to global processes.

A transborder region provides a timely context for re-evaluating the relative role of spatial and institutional dynamics in shaping global–local ties. In a transborder region, cities and their immediate hinterlands are more likely to be both local and global at the same time and subject to the influence of multiple central and local governments as well. Economic transactions between cities on both sides of a border will remain localized if they are facilitated by short distance and other favorable conditions, but may be hampered by the lack of access to a broader transport network and the global market. These trans-local economic ties can be elevated directly to the regional level and linked indirectly to the global economy when national and local governments remove or reduce border controls and tariffs and build more cross-border transport links in the following section.

The inside and outside of the tiered state

A focus on the global–local nexus should not obscure the important role of the nation-state in shaping border regions and cities. Looking at the role of the state in this context differs from the state-centric theorizing and debate over the autonomy and power of the state versus the market in national economic development.[3] What happens to the state when it is deeply penetrated by economic globalization from outside and strongly pressured by rising economic regionalism and localism from inside? First, the state evolves and reconfigures through shifts in its boundary and capacity. Political boundaries, many of which have been arbitrarily drawn and redrawn, rarely coincide with the cultural and ethnic borders. Sassen (1996, 1997) elaborated on how the state and its territorial space are becoming partially denationalized due to the rapid growth of advanced information industries, the embedding of global dynamics in domestic local places, especially in such global cities as New York and London, and the relocation of some components of national state sovereignty and capacity onto supranational authorities and corporate systems.

Generally speaking, important decisions regarding border control, customs regulations, trade and investment, infrastructure development, and tourism in and between neighboring countries reside with the central state. As trade and investment ties between border cities and their hinterlands grow closer, the demand for more subnational and local policy-making tends to rise. This downward shift of economic action and associated policy-making raises stakes for both provincial and municipal governments because their decisions and choices have a stronger and more direct influence on the economic benefit or loss for their jurisdictions while central government interference may have an inhibiting effect. The pressure of globalization on the nation-state to be more market conforming, reinforced by the bottom-up pressure from cross-border private sector activities, has shifted decision-making power from the central to the local government (see Orum and Chen 2003).

Despite this shift in the relationship between the central and local state that strengthens the latter, how autonomously the local state acts remains constrained by varied national political contexts and is subject to the growing influence of private firms. In the Chinese context, while the central state is strong it has delegated growing decision-making power to provincial and local governments since the early 1980s, thus making them loyal but flexible agents. The enhanced autonomy of local governments in Guangdong and Fujian provinces stems from a mutually dependent and beneficial relationship between officials and entrepreneurs. While the former supports the latter through providing access to profits and protection of local(ized) entrepreneurs, both domestic and overseas, influence officials through offering payoffs, employment opportunities, and business partnerships (see Wank 1995, 1999). The spatial variation in this relationship can be captured by a comparison across border regions and cities.

Cross-border ethnic ties

Border cities often share historical, cultural, and ethnic ties across international boundaries. These ties in the Asia-Pacific region in general and China in particular were severed or weakened by competing political ideologies, military conflicts, and absent economic relations between China and Taiwan, China and South Korea, China and the former Soviet Union, and China and Vietnam at various times. They have revived and been expanding over the past two decades or so, however. Kinship and ancestral networks created and sustained by past and present migration circuits coupled with shared regional dialects have become active in the open and highly interactive border environment, which is also imbued with a strong native-place identity based on geographic affiliations.

Just as the local economy and state in a transborder context interacts with global processes in complex ways, cross-border ethnic ties could either foster or impede globalization at the local level due to its contingent nature and influence. They not only reside in but also shift with changes in local development situations and territorially based political institutions such as the local government. Under these concrete conditions, cross-border ethnic ties are capable of exerting a practical influence on border-spanning economic activities.

As I have argued elsewhere (Chen 2000), cross-border ethnic ties have a twofold role in "gluing" and "lubricating" the Asia-Pacific transborder links, albeit to different degrees. "Gluing" involves bringing multiple actors on different sides of a border together in some sort of economic cooperation through mutual investment and joint production. Just bringing economic actors across borders together is not sufficient as their cooperation may be hampered by frictions of different systems. "Lubricating" refers to ways and tendencies by which ethnic ties smoothen cross-border economic cooperation. Without lubrication, the glued seams of economic ties may strain and even come apart under the competing pressures of incompatible systems. As close and extensive ties with overseas Chinese in Hong Kong and Taiwan have "lubricated" the manufacturing machine in Guangdong and Fujian provinces, it would be interesting to see if the cross-border ethnic ties of China's border cities would make a difference to their growth in conjunction with the presence or absence of global capital and the decentralizing state.

Border effects and transport infrastructure

The effect of borders is another key to the development of cities on or near them. Borders can either block or bridge the development and integration of different border areas. Understanding this barrier or opportunity effect of borders hinges on how we conceptualize borders and their functions. The two dominant and commonly accepted views on a border are that it is either a dividing line or a contact zone. From the "line-border" perspective, a border represents a frontier territorial edge lying astride the boundary that sets the legal limit of the state. It tends to separate rather than unite border regions of two states through demarcated jurisdictions, control over crossings, and enforced customs rights. The competing perspective, however, sees a border as a contact zone or filter factor that creates a functioning membrane space for transboundary economic exchanges and social interactions and their diffusion beyond the border (Ratti 1993).

Borders have multiple barrier effects beyond the rigid legal demarcation of separate states. Rietveld (1993: 49) identified four border-related barriers: (1) weak or expensive infrastructure services in transport and communication for international links; (2) consumer preference for domestic rather than foreign products and destinations; (3) government interventions; and (4) lack of information on foreign countries. International road or rail links across borders are generally less developed than domestic links on either side of borders. This creates higher detour costs for transportation between border cities that has to be routed through other domestic cities. Government interventions that increase borders' barrier effects include rigid visa requirements, high tax levies, tight currency exchange controls, and complex registration and certification procedures for border trading companies and border-crossing products. Overcoming these obstacles, especially through improving cross-border transport infrastructure will facilitate more integration of border cities and hinterlands.

By presenting the arguments and identifying their associated factors in the following section, I intend to show that they individually or jointly are capable of deflecting or neutralizing the positive or negative impact of globalization in such a way that sets the transition of border regions and cities in China or elsewhere on a distinctive trajectory.

China's border cities in two transborder subregions

To demonstrate how the four sets of factors interact to influence the development of Chinese border cities, the empirical analysis focuses on selected cases in two transborder subregions: the Greater Tumen Subregion (GTS) in Northeast Asia and the Greater Mekong Subregion (GMS) on mainland Southeast Asia. While I have conceptualized these two transborder subregions, together with several other similar cases, and examined them in full detail elsewhere (see Chen 2005),

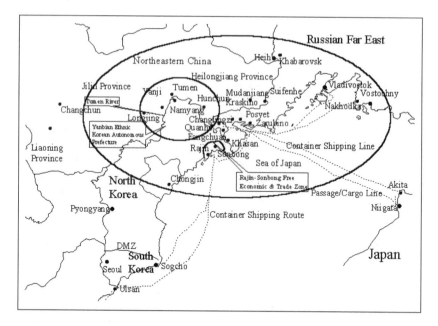

Map 2.1 The Greater Tumen Subregion.

I choose them here for two reasons. First, they contain Chinese frontier cities and areas that will contrast with the heavily studied coastal cities regarding growth patterns and external ties. Second, they serve as the crucial context in which the four sets of factors mentioned earlier operate in conjunction to foster or constrain the development of Chinese border cities largely beyond the reach of globalization.

Within the GTS, which as a whole is complicated to define due to its multiple layers,[4] I focus on Jilin province and its city of Hunchun primarily and other border cities, secondarily in the Yanbian Ethnic Korean prefecture of Jilin province bordering the riparian parts of North Korea and the Russian Far East (RFE) covered by the Tumen River (see Map 2.1). The GMS comprises Thailand, Vietnam, Lao People's Democratic Republic (Lao PDR), Myanmar (formerly Burma), Cambodia, and China's Yunnan province (see Map 2.2). To be consistent with the units of analysis in the GTS, I examine Dehong prefecture and the two cities of Ruili and Wanding in Yunnan bordering Myanmar.

Frontier cities and border trade: missing global impulses for local development

Growing trade, which is an important aspect of globalization, takes the form of mostly border trade of China's border provinces, prefectures, and cities with the neighboring countries in the GTS and the GMS. As Table 2.1 shows, trade between Jilin province and North Korea grew rapidly from a small base in 1982.

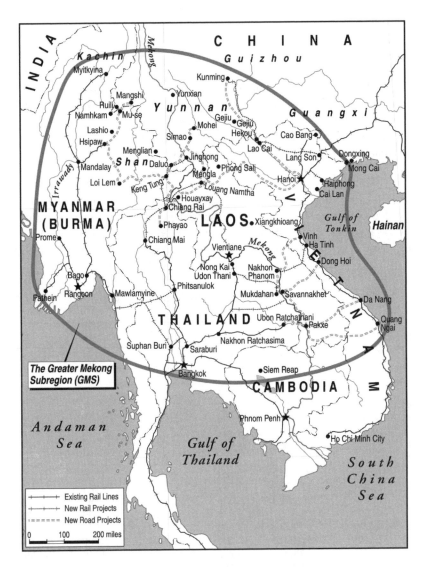

Map 2.2 The Greater Mekong Subregion.

During 1954–1970, trade between Jilin and North Korea was largely confined to small-scale bartering between the Yanbian Korean Autonomous prefecture (which is over 40 percent ethnic Korean) of Jilin and North Korea. Due to China's Cultural Revolution, this trade was suspended between 1970 and 1982 when Jilin province resumed both border trade and local barter trade with North Korea. Jilin exported mostly lumber, rice, rubber, steel, and metal products, while North Korea's exports included seafood products, fruits, steel, and fertilizer (Shi and Yu 1995).

The period 1991–1994 saw the most rapid growth of Jilin–North Korean trade, now conducted in US dollars (see Table 2.1). The number of traded items went from 8 in 1982 to 217 in 1987, and to 230 in 1994. The number of Chinese and North Korean companies involved in trade rose from 20 in 1991 to over 110 in 1994. The volume of trade between Yanbian and North Korea surged from US 75 million dollars in 1991 to US 310 million dollars in 1993. The latter figure accounted for nearly 70 percent of Yanbian's total foreign trade (Lawrence 1999) and about 60 percent of Jilin's total trade with North Korea that year (Shi and Yu 1995).

Trade between North Korea and Jilin, especially Yanbian began to contract in the second half of 1994 and dropped sharply in 1995 (Table 2.1). The floods in North Korea, coupled with economic mismanagement severely reduced the short list of commodities (e.g. rice) that could be exported to Jilin. The problem for North Korean trading companies being late in payments for Chinese exports got worse due to a severe shortage of cash. The Chinese central government also withdrew the favorable policy of the 50 percent tax on imports through local barter trade. These factors led Jilin to reduce its trade with North Korea (Shi and Yu 1995).

Table 2.1 Jilin province's trade with North Korea and the Soviet Union (Russia), 1982–1995

Year	North Korea[a]			Russia[b]		
	Total trade	Export	Import	Total trade	Export	Import
1982	103	52	51	—	—	—
1983	1,199	664	535	—	—	—
1984	4,445	2,110	2,335	—	—	—
1985	10,987	5,758	5,229	—	—	—
1986	8,656	4,472	4,184	—	—	—
1987	12,772	6,726	6,046	—	—	—
1988	15,796	7,870	7,926	1,210	687	532
	(15.5)	(10.4)	(31.5)	(1.2)	(0.9)	(2.1)
1989	22,856	11,175	11,681	8,221	5,988	2,233
1990	14,802	8,152	6,650	11,124	5,368	5,756
1991	9,271	4,843	4,428	11,478	5,890	5,588
	(6.9[c])	(4.7)	(11.7)	(8.2)	(5.7)	(14.7)
1992	23,400	11,200	12,200	16,400	1,700	14,700
		(8.6)	(19.1)		(12.9)	(22.9)
1993	47,126	22,960	24,165	—	—	—
	(15.8)					
1994	45,500	25,300	20,200	55,600	31,300	24,300
1995	11,000	7,300	3,700	—	8,000	—

Sources: Compiled from Fu (1998: 410–411), Fukagawa (1997, table 3.5), Li *et al.* (1997: 37), Liu and Liao (1993, tables 3 and 4), and Shi and Yu (1995, table 1).

Notes
a The figures prior to 1991 were in 10,000 Swiss Francs, which had a roughly 1:1 exchange rate with the US dollar. The figures for 1991 through 1994 were in 10,000 US dollars.
b Data before 1991 pertained to the former Soviet Union.
c The figures in parentheses for 1988 and 1991 are percentages of the province's total foreign trade.

By 1996, trade between North Korea and Yanbian declined to US 27 million dollars and rose slightly to US 32 million dollars in 1998 (Lawrence 1999).

The border city of Hunchun in Jilin province has emerged as an important frontier center due to its favorable location. Centrally situated at the trilateral borders of China, North Korea, and the RFE, Hunchun has the closest and most convenient access to the railroad and road terminuses near the North Korean and RFE borders and through them to all major North Korean and RFE ports.[5] Hunchun had a long history as a frontier center for trade with Japan, Korea, and Russia.[6] This prosperous ocean trade ended in 1938 when Japan unilaterally imposed a blockade on shipping on the Tumen River from Hunchun to the Sea of Japan.

From 1949 to the mid-1980s, despite being a rural county, Hunchun remained an officially classified important border post and was largely cordoned off from domestic entry unless one had a special permit. The place, where buildings of two stories or taller was banned, became economically marginalized. Hunchun entered a new era of opening and rapid economic growth in 1985 when its border crossing with the RFE was (re)opened. In 1988, Hunchun was administratively upgraded from a county to a municipality and allowed by Jilin province to build a special economic zone (SEZ). Following the onset of the United Nations Development Programme (UNDP) sponsored Tumen River development in 1992, Hunchun was chosen by the central government to be among the first group of officially designated open border cities and allowed to set up China's first Border Economic Cooperation Zone (BECZ). Bounded for 88 square kilometers and planned for 24 square kilometers, the Hunchun BECZ received infrastructure investment totaling US 150 million dollars from the state. In April 2000, the national government approved the establishment of the Hunchun Export Processing Zone (HEPZ), one of only 15 in China. In February 2001, the national government approved the Hunchun China–Russia Free Market and Trade Zone, with the construction of a huge indoor market hall. The zone offered financial incentives and procedural conveniences including visa-free entry for Russian traders and duty-free exodus of Russian goods taken out of the zone by Chinese traders.[7]

In 1992, Hunchun had a population of approximately 175,000 that grew to 250,000 by the end of the decade. Its gross domestic product (GDP) in 2001 tripled that of 1995. Since 1995, Hunchun's foreign trade has been growing almost 100 percent annually, while its GDP has been up between 16 and 20 percent a year, which is comparable to those of some coastal cities. Passenger and cargo flows through Hunchun's overland ports with North Korea and the RFE have been rising over 30 percent per annum.[8] About 80 percent of the industrial enterprises in Hunchun have received some foreign investment, most of which came from Hong Kong, South Korea, and Japan. Although the Asian financial crisis in 1997 slowed down the inflow of foreign investment, Hunchun made a relatively quick recovery by attracting 33 foreign-invested enterprises into the BECZ that involved contracted capitalization of 127 million dollars by the end of 2000.[9]

Hunchun has been trying to reach out to the global economy from a geopolitically important but politically unstable and economically underdeveloped part of Asia. While Hunchun has done better than its North Korean and Russian counterparts across the borders, it has not created very beneficial local–global economic links. One disadvantage is its concentration of extractive industries in the GTS as natural and mineral resources for extraction are fixed in space and physical isolation (Bunker 1989). The major barrier to creating global–local economic links for Hunchun and other Chinese border cities in the GTS is the lack of economic complement. This barrier is difficult to overcome because the GTS consists of the poorer and more peripheral regions and cities of three countries. It has severely limited the type and scale of foreign manufacturing investment that has turned out competitive exports from cities in southeastern China.

Yunnan province and its border cities were important trade outposts historically. Yunnan's active historical role in border trade, however, stagnated from the Cultural Revolution to the early 1980s, when coastal provinces and cities were heavily favored over inland border provinces. While Yunnan's international trade rose from US 130 million dollars in 1980 to merely US 750 million dollars in 1990 (Wang and Li 1998), higher than the national increase of 203 percent, it lagged significantly behind most coastal cities.

The 1990s saw the return of Yunnan's important role in international trade, especially in border trade. Yunnan's foreign trade grew 20 percent annually and amounted to US 15 billion dollars in 1997. Foreign trade as a share of provincial GDP rose from 1.8 percent in 1978 to 10.3 percent in 1997. Yunnan's border trade grew from a cumulative total of US 24 million dollars during 1978–1984 to US 431 million dollars in 1994 (see Table 2.2), averaging an annual rate of over 30 percent. As the table also reveals, Yunnan's foreign and border trade is heavily oriented toward the three neighboring countries. Between 1991 and 1995, Myanmar, Vietnam, and Lao PDR were the first, fifth, and tenth largest markets for Yunnan's exports, absorbing 34.2 percent of its total exports. The largest importer by far, Myanmar accounted for

Table 2.2 Yunnan province's border trade with Myanmar, Lao PDR, and Vietnam, 1989–1995 (in millions of US dollars)

Year	Yunnan's total border trade (1)	Yunnan's trade with Myanmar, Lao PDR, and Vietnam (2)	Yunnan's border trade with Myanmar, Lao PDR, and Vietnam (3) = (5) + (6)	Border trade as a percentage of total trade (4) = (3)/(2)	Border import from Myanmar, Lao PDR, and Vietnam (5)	Border export to Myanmar, Laos PDR, and Viet Vietnam (6)
1989	109	—	—	—	—	—
1990	151	141	131	92.9	43	88
1991	198	165	154	93.4	52	102
1992	274	233	228	97.8	74	154
1993	346	311	271	87.2	76	195
1994	431	431	255	59.2	110	145
1995	—	556	229	41.2	112	117

Sources: Adapted from Li and Zhao (1997: 185), State Statistical Bureau (SSB) (1998, various tables), Wang and Li (1998: 31).

77 percent of Yunnan's exports to the three countries in 1999 (Zhonghua Publishing House 2001). In 2002, Yunnan's trade with Myanmar reached US 407 million dollars, which accounted for 47.2 percent of China's total trade with Myanmar.[10]

As Table 2.3 shows, Yunnan's six border prefectures accounted for just about all the provincial border trade through 1995. Dehong Minority Autonomous prefecture had the lion's share of the total border trade due to its location. Bordering on Kachin and Shan states of Myanmar for over 500 kilometers, Dehong is close to such important Myanmar cities as Lashio, Myitkyina, and Mandalay (see Map 2.1). From the Burma Road (built as a vital supply route after Japan's 1937 invasion of eastern China) between Kunming and Mandalay at Lashio there is a road link to India via Myitkyina and rail and river (the Irrawaddy) connections to Yangon (Rangoon) and the Indian Ocean.

Key Chinese and Myanmar border towns are intensive spots for border trade. The end of Chinese support before the collapse of the Burmese Communist Party in 1989 facilitated the opening of more border trading posts between the two countries. The Myanmar border town of Muse became open for border trade in 1988. The Chinese border city of Ruili created the Jiagao Border Economic Development Zone in 1991. Thanks to Ruili's most active trading role, border trade accounted for half of Dehong county's revenue in the 1990s (Kuah 2000).

Yunnan's border trade is primarily characterized by small-scale transactions between border residents and petty traders at about border 100 crossing points of varied administrative grades along a lengthy border.[11] Local border residents and international traders cross the almost invisible and lightly guarded check points frequently to buy and sell at border trade markets that consist of rows of stalls or small store fronts. At the border trade market in Ruili, there are often close to 1,000 petty traders and dealers including some from Myanmar, Bangladesh, India, Nepal, Pakistan, and Thailand selling cotton, jade, bracelets, ivory items,

Table 2.3 Yunnan's top six prefectures and regions in border trade, 1990–1995 (in millions of US dollars)

Year	Dehong prefecture[a]	Xishuang–Banna prefecture[b]	Baoshan region[a]	Honghe prefecture[c]	Lincang region[a]	Wenshan prefecture[c]
1990	117	—	5	—	2	—
1991	159	5	8	17	4	4
1992	207	11	18	18	8	7
1993	242	27	45	19	27	14
1994	280	52	54	43	36	23
1995	255	66	54	42	30	23
Total (%)[d]	60	10	10	8.5	7	4.2

Source: Adapted from Li and Zhao (1997: 235–248).

Notes
a Bordering Myanmar.
b Bordering both Myanmar and Laos PDR.
c Bordering Vietnam.
d The figures in this row are each region's estimated share of the Yunnan's total border trade.

and aquatic products. Despite the limitations and problems of small-scale border trade, there have been some efforts to move cross-border economic cooperation in the GMS beyond the localized exchange of raw commodities or simple goods. The Ruili and Wanding municipal governments have encouraged foreign investors to utilize raw materials to manufacture products to meet both local and international demands. By 1997, imported materials for export processing (mainly jade, precious stones, and rubber) as a share of Yunnan's total border imports reached 35.5 percent. This integration of border trade and simple manu-facturing has facilitated the evolution of Yunnan's border trade, which has shifted from involving primarily local commodities to broadly sourced products, as the proportion of industrial goods from elsewhere in China and exported through Ruili and Wanding reached almost 90 percent (Economic and Trade Cooperation with Neighboring Countries Bureau 1995). The evidence suggests the possibility for Yunnan's border cities to develop through achieving broader and deeper economic cooperation in the GMS beyond border trade.

Late decentralization to the periphery: a necessary but insufficient political stimulus

As China's open policies favored the southeast coast in the late 1970s and early 1980s and the Bohai rim in the mid- and late 1980s, its northeastern and south-western border regions fell much behind. In early 1990s, however, the central government began to shift the open policy and development focus to the more iso-lated and backward inland border regions by offering them financial incentives that had been granted exclusively to the coastal areas. This policy adjustment was intended to narrow the growing regional disparities and appease leaders of the inland areas who felt that they had been mistreated.

The central government singled out specific border areas of Jilin province along the Tumen River for more favorable policies, which was also stimulated by the UNDP sponsored Tumen River development initiatives in the early 1990s. The State Council of China established a special office and a research and devel-opment team with the State Science and Technology Commission as the leading unit to handle issues concerning Tumen River development, while the State Development and Planning Commission incorporated the Tumen River project into the Ninth "Five Year Plan."[12] The central government handed out the largest favor in 1992 by designating the city of Hunchun as a top-level open border city. This gave Hunchun the privilege to implement all the favorable policies that had been granted to coastal cities. It also allowed Hunchun to set up one of China's first and few border economic cooperation zones.

Following the central government's initiative, the governments of Jilin province, Yanbian prefecture, and Hunchun municipality formed leaders' groups and special offices in charge of developing the Tumen region. The Jilin provincial government immediately adopted favorable policies to spur the growth of border cities like Hunchun. In 1992, the Jilin government shifted 10 provincial-level rights of approval in border economic cooperation and trade down to the municipal government of Hunchun and granted the latter over 20 other favorable policies. From the mid-1980s through 1993, the national and provincial governments doled out a cumulative total of US 140 million dollars to build up the infrastructure in Hunchun's energy, transportation, and telecommunications sectors (Yu 1994). Just as what happened to the key cities in the Guangdong and Fujian provinces, the central government's combined strategy of granting favorable policies, decentralizing administrative power, and capital outlays, coupled with proactive local responses, have elevated the status and the role of a border city like Hunchun in the regional place hierarchy.

Despite the weakened central control and stronger central support, local governments in Northeast China, particularly in the Tumen region have been constrained to take full advantage of these favorable conditions. Given their border locations in China's primary region of state-owned extractive and heavy industries, cities like Hunchun became heavily dependent on subsidies from both central and provincial governments. Although these local governments were permitted to provide financial incentives to foreign investors and to create and keep revenues through exports, the lack of exportable light consumer goods limited their opportunities. The government of Hunchun was not in a position to achieve fast growth and generate wealth like Shenzhen.

Despite the long-standing trade between the border peoples of Yunnan and the neighboring countries, China's central government imposed severe restrictions on border trade prior to 1978 based on the premise of its border regions being politically sensitive and militarily insecure. For example, the central government limited the purchase of goods by Chinese farmers across the border to 30 Chinese yuan (about US 4 dollars) at each transaction and the exchange boundary to a 10 kilometers stretch from the border line (Kuah 2000). This tight control and monitoring began to loosen by 1985 when it promulgated a policy that encouraged provincial governments and border residents to be more liberal in border trade. By 1992, the central government took a step further by handing over to the provincial government the rights to implement regulations and control over border trade. The central government also introduced guidelines for trade with Myanmar and designated Kunming, Ruili, and Wanding as state-level open cities and towns for border trade and investment. This was similar to the policy of granting the same status to several cities of Jilin province in the early 1990s.

The growing power of the provincial and county government has reinforced autonomous and targeted policy-making at the subnational levels. While Yunnan province unveiled its own policy for border trade as early as in 1985, which included tax concessions and bureaucratic streamlining, the early 1990s saw the acceleration of provincial independence in formulating bolder border trade policies. The provincial government, for example, would provide additional incentives to foreign investors in designated border towns and areas. It also simplified visa and customs procedures for those residents to cross the border as tourist-traders who could re-enter Yunnan multiple times on a daily basis (Kuah 2000). Although getting the "green light" from the center later than the Guangdong and Fujian governments, the Yunnan provincial government has been more aggressive than Jilin province, where state-owned industries were more dominant, in pushing border trade. The active provincial government fueled strong initiatives of the local governments of Yunnan's key border cities and towns.

The Dehong prefectural government provided the most illustrative example of effective local autonomy in line with the trickle-down of decentralized central and provincial government power. It established the Jiegao Border Economic Development Zone in the border town of Ruili that had previously been designated by the central and provincial governments as a key outpost for border trade. The zone, which covers an area of 4 square kilometers and borders on Muse in Myanmar (see Map 2.2), has attracted a steady inflow of small-scale investments from Hong Kong, Thailand, and Singapore. In addition, a China–Myanmar Street was set up between Jiegao and the border to accommodate small shops and mobile daily traders (Hong Kong Trade Development Council 1992). Other local government pro-development actions included setting up a center to provide investors and enterprises with information on border trade and introducing favorable changes in customs inspection, taxation, border control, and customs duties. These measures spurred border trade and related activities, which contributed to over 50 percent of provincial and local government revenues in the first half of the 1990s (Kuah 2000).

Revived cross-border ethnic ties: beneficial but limited

Given the historical settlement pattern of Koreans in China, China's 1990 census revealed that 97 percent of the nearly 2 million ethnic Koreans in China lived in the three northeastern provinces with 1.2 million of them residing in Jilin province. The Yanbian Autonomous prefecture, which administers the key Chinese border cities of Hunchun and Tumen in the GTS (see Map 2.1), is home to approximately 900,000 ethnic Koreans, which accounted for 41 percent of Yanbian's total population and 43 percent of the entire ethnic Korean population in China. In the city of Hunchun in 1992, ethnic Koreans accounted for 47.3 percent of the local population (Li and Wu 1998). With a more open border, cultural adaptation and linguistic similarity also have become valuable ethnic social capital that could foster economic exchanges.

The geographic concentration of South Korean investment in the Yanbian region validates the connection between cross-border ethnic ties and inflow of capital. Also spurred by the establishment of diplomatic relations between China and South Korea in 1992, South Korean investors flocked to Yanbian to set up factories in garments manufacturing, food processing, chemicals, and construction materials. Particularly, a number of small Korean food processing and cold-storage companies began to congregate here to export products back to Korean supermarkets. The 42 Korean-invested enterprises by the end of 1992 accounted for one-third of all foreign ventures in the prefecture and reached US 16 million dollars in capitalization (Peng and Yan 1994). In the city of Yanji, the capital of Yanbian prefecture, 119 (over 50 percent) of the 226 foreign-invested enterprises were financed by South Korean capital (Wang and Zhang 1998).

The city of Yanji, the heart of the Chinese Korean region, has remained the most attractive destination in northeastern China for South Korean investment and remittance. According to the local informants in Yanji whom I interviewed in 1999, a heavy influx of remittance from South Koreans boosted the local economy in the mid-1990s, especially in real estate development and the restaurant business. Some of the remittance came from the Korean Chinese working as temporary labor in South Korea. In 1996, remittance from South Korea accounted for half of the real estate investment in Yanji and helped elevate per capita income for Yanji to the fourth highest of all Chinese cities.

The onset of the Asian financial crisis in 1997 dampened Yanji's prosperity. South Korean investors quickly pulled out from their ventures and left behind stockpiles of unsold products waiting to be exported. Since the large majority of the South Korean-invested enterprises were small, collectively owned local firms, which offered no guaranteed employment (the so-called iron rice bowl), the withdrawal of South Korean capital left many local workers unemployed. The financial crisis also led to a sharp reduction of South Korean tourists, and even those who came after 1998 engaged largely in window-shopping. Nevertheless, the striking billboard for the South Korean Airline (Asiana) dominated at the Yanji Airport, despite the fact that it was not yet allowed to fly in. There was little question of the heavy South Korean presence in this Chinese border region heavily populated by ethnic Koreans.

The ethnic ties not only brought South Korean investment into Yanbian, but also brought about new types of economic exchanges (besides barter trade) across the China–North Korea border under the local governments' favorable policies toward North Korea businesses. In Yanbian, North Korea has invested in 25 businesses, mostly restaurants, sauna parlors, karaoke bars, and real estate companies on the Chinese side of the border (Chen 1995, Lawrence 1999). Illegal young North Korean girls were found to work in some of the karaoke bars in Yanji without being detained, as local informants revealed. Ethnic Korean merchants continued to do business with their North Korean counterparts, even under the unfavorable conditions of not getting paid on time and having few attractive goods to buy. Unlike the South Korean connections earlier, the Korean Chinese use kinship-based social networks under a more open policy to generate economic exchanges intended to benefit North Koreans on the other side of the border.

Yunnan province is home to 26 of China's 55 minorities. In 1996, the minorities accounted for 35 percent of Yunnan's total population and occupy about two-thirds of the area, much of which involves the border zones next to Myanmar, Lao PDR, and Vietnam (Li and Zhao 1997). Ten minorities in Yunnan's border region including the Dai, Jinpo, Miao, Yao, and Yi have settled across borders for a long time. The Dai, who reside heavily in Xishuanbanna and Simao prefectures along the China–Myanmar and China–Lao borders, are known as the Shan who are concentrated in the Shan state of Myanmar (Hsieh 1995). The Jinpo of Yunnan and the Kachin in the Kachin state of Myanmar belong to the same ethnic origin (Zhao 1997). The Hani in Yunnan are known as the Akha in Myanmar and

Thailand. In 1991, of Ruili's total population, the Dai accounted for 45.8 percent, the Jinpo 12.6 percent, while the Han Chinese and other minorities made up the remaining 41.6 percent (Liu and Liao 1993).

For decades, the old ethnic ties mentioned earlier lay dominant in their respective local areas when several wars fought on Indochina and lack of political trust among the countries preempted cross-border economic and cultural exchanges. The 1990s marked a new decade for the Mekong River region with the launch of the GMS Program and the opening of southwest China. In this more open environment, ethnic identity and linguistic capacity have become favorable factors in border trade, especially in small-scale bartering and transactions at the border free markets.

Most of the Myanmar traders crossing over the border are ethnic Chinese, many of whom originated in Yunnan, and some of them left as recently as during the Cultural Revolution.[13] They used the Chinese language for communication during buying and selling, convenient and efficient for both parties (Hong Kong Trade Development Council 1992). This ethnically mediated border trade bears remarkable similarity to border trade between North Koreans and Korean Chinese along the Jilin–North Korea border in the GTS.

Growing cross-border trade and investment has translated into new cross-border social interactions and outcomes, especially for Yunnan's border towns. In the pre-reform and pre-opening era, poverty in this remote border region forced residents in such towns as Ruili to pick tea leaves over in Myanmar to supplement their meager income. And local girls often married Burmese men. In recent years, however, many of these old trends have reversed. A large number of Myanmar border residents came to work in Ruili. Many of the former local residents who had left returned and resettled. More and more Myanmar girls preferred to marry young men in Ruili (Chinese Central Academy of Ethnology 1993).

Urban frontiers and transport infrastructure:
the challenge to bridging peripheral cities

The combination of multiple border crossings and both land and rail access to several good and geographically proximate ports has not created the kind of tight cross-border links that would help overcome the economic and political barriers to the integration of the GTS. The primary reason lies in the overall underdevelopment of transport infrastructure. The various border regions and cities in the GTS are remote and peripheral to the economic and political centers of the three countries involved. Because of this status, they have suffered from a cumulative shortage of large-scale investment for improving their transport facilities. The roads and railroads in and between these places were limited, not well connected, and had lower grades and carrying capacity. The seaports were poorly equipped with loading and storage facilities and therefore could not perform up to full capacity. For example, while the Chinese side was completing parts of a highway leading to the Quanhe border crossing in 2000 the North Korean side still used a sand and gravel track that turns into mud in the rain or snow. This poor condition makes it difficult for trucks carrying containers to cross the border (Lawrence 1999). The Hunchun government and shipping companies also were active in opening new shipping routes through and beyond the GTS, including regular container shipping from Hunchun to the Rajin port and on to Pusan of South Korea, and from Hunchun to the Posyet port of the RFE and then across the Sea of Japan to Akita of Japan (see Map 2.1).

The long-term payoffs from improved transport links are shrouded in uncertain future demand for the cross-border flow of goods, which fluctuated in the mid-1990s (see Table 2.4). Further integration and development of the GTS and greater cross-border trade flows will put more pressure on the still underdeveloped transport system across the border regions of Northeastern China, the RFE, and North Korea. While this broad scenario may turn out to be realistic, the specific demand on the various cross-border transport links may be uncertain. It is projected that the volume of China–RFE trade through the Changlingzi crossing could reach 200,000 tons by 2005, while the through volumes of China–North Korean trade at the Quanhe, Shatuozi, and Tumen crossings may approach the same level. The projection is partly based on the steadily growing exports of large quantities of grain and high-heat coal from Yanbian to meeting the shortages in North Korea and the RFE and continued demand in Japan and South Korea. In addition, the growth of foreign-invested companies in Yanbian especially in its strong lumber processing industry will stimulate greater import of timber and export of processed wood and paper products (C. Chen 1998).

Just as the Tumen River is the ecological glue for linking the border cities of China's Jilin province with the parts of the RFE and North Korea, the Mekong River supplies rich water resources[14] that bind a long stretch of Yunnan province and the neighboring riparian GMS countries. The twelfth largest and sixth longest river in the world and the sixth largest in Asia, the Mekong ranks only behind the Yangtze River of China in flow volume. During the Vietnam War, the Mekong River was known as the world's most notorious waterway – the "Iron Curtain of Asia" – which symbolized death and division (Asia Inc. 1996). By the 1990s, the mighty Mekong emerged as a major ecological corridor for subregional economic cooperation due to (re)newed inter-state arrangements such as the Mekong River Commission and the GMS Program. For goods from China's interior northwestern region to reach mainland Southeast Asia, shipping along the Mekong would shorten the distance by about 3,000 kilometers compared with going through the southeastern ports (Tang 1995). The river sometimes known as the 'Danube of the Orient' appeared poised for booming commercial use.

However, the shipping capacity of the Mekong has been limited by two factors. First, a long stretch of the Mekong is difficult to navigate. For example, the river between the China–Myanmar border down along the Thailand–Lao PDR border to Vientiane, about 1,080 kilometers long, contains dangerous shoals and shallow

Table 2.4 Import and export volumes through land border crossings at the Yanbian ethnic Korean autonomous prefecture, Jilin province, China, 1993–1996

Crossing	1993			1994			1995			1996		
	Import	Export	Total	Import	Export	Total	Import	Export	Total	Import	Export	Total
Changlingzi	65,308	10,929	76,237	16,532	15,552	32,084	3,983	7,504	11,487	3,004	4,139	7,143
Shatuozi	40,161	7,676	47,837	17,308	8,478	25,786	2,469	4,181	6,650	1,940	3,020	4,960
Quanhe	—	—	—	—	—	—	—	—	—	8,741	15,032	23,773
Tumen	217,588	287,588	505,176	144,200	100,497	244,697	186,769	186,269	373,038	32,240	40,204	72,444
Kaishantun	13,302	14,406	27,708	11,508	11,548	23,056	2,420	1,200	3,620	3,310	3,310	6,620
Nanping	14,104	1,143	15,247	15,795	12,112	27,907	4,130	2,496	6,626	16,666	6,911	26,277
Guchengli	13,905	965	14,870	12,762	473	13,235	8,872	1,172	10,040	14,042	1,000	15,024
All crossings	364,368	322,707	687,075	218,105	148,660	366,765	208,643	202,822	411,465	79,943	73,616	153,559

Source: Adapted from C. Chen (1998: 7).

beds. Second, most of the ports and docks along the Mekong, especially its upstream, are relatively small and old. Resources for upgrading them are highly limited as the Upper Mekong runs through the less developed regions of four GMS countries, namely southwestern China, northern Thailand, northwestern Lao PDR, and eastern Myanmar.

To improve the difficult navigating conditions, a number of government efforts have been made in recent years. At the beginning of 2002, China, Lao PDR, Myanmar, and Thailand reached a new agreement to improve the navigating conditions of the Mekong River, with China putting up the bulk of the funds (US 5 million dollars) and being responsible for all technical solutions and implementations. The planned projects include fixing dangerous shoals, erecting navigation marks and signs, and widening and deepening some stretches of the riverbed. The central and Yunnan governments have invested heavily in upgrading such major ports as Jinghong and Simao on the segment of the Mekong called Lancang near Yunnan's border (see Map 2.2). This investment paid off in the growing activities at several river ports (Table 2.5).

Table 2.5 Cross-border flows through the major river ports and overland crossings of Yunnan province, 1993–1997

Ports or crossings	Year	People (number)	Vehicle (number)	Cargo (ton)	Cargo value (10,000 USD)
Jinghong Port	1993	6,850	140	1,260	2.3
(bordering	1994	26,000	444	11,760	4.9
Myanmar)	1995	6,951	410	12,329	504.9
	1996	25,600	3,209	33,100	1,136.3
	1997	11,275	1,454	32,550	1,208.9
Simao Port	1993	1,990	35	700	0.4
(bordering	1994	3,800	681	1,850	0.4
Myanmar, Laos	1995	1,404	268	20,551	494.1
PDR, and Vietnam)	1996	6,100	159	10,300	606.6
	1997	680	306	15,283	147.8
Mohan Crossing	1993	98,000	16,780	10,780	1,251.7
(bordering Lao	1994	196,800	48,819	20,997	1,538.7
PDR)	1995	144,500	12,374	69,538	3,407.0
	1996	114,400	3,364	32,800	1,545.0
	1997	90,770	7,756	19,410	1,287.3
Daluo Crossing	1993	260,000	44,087	79,205	1,508.3
(bordering	1994	350,000	53,719	91,730	1,827.7
Myanmar)	1995	396,800	71,565	96,540	1,961.6
	1996	2,050,000	137,008	57,800	1,152.9
	1997	2,040,912	132,166	21,320	682.5
Menglian Crossing	1993	15,700	9,876	9,730	231.3
(bordering	1994	184,100	1,306	35,200	287.8
Myanmar)	1995	117,878	11,981	16,041	1,095.3
	1996	322,700	34,070	25,000	552.3
	1997	185,522	32,008	22,177	336.6

Source: Adapted from Wang and Li (1998: 38).

The limit of globalization and China's frontier cities: transborder subregions as the mediating middle

The extensive evidence analysis earlier has shown little impact of globalization on several Chinese frontier cities, at least not directly. Instead, their transitions, as varied as they may be, have been similarly influenced by an interaction of trans-border subregional economic dynamics, decentralizing state policies, cross-border ethnic ties, and boundary-spanning transport infrastructure. While this mix of factors may appear complex and difficult to disentangle they collectively have kept the penetrating influence of globalization at bay, so to speak. This role of theirs is clearly and closely tied to the composition of the two transborder subregions (GTS and GMS), which consist of multiple border cities and their hinterlands in geographically contiguous transnational spaces in which the Chinese border cities are embedded. Given its layered units, actors, and ties, each transborder subregion mediates global–local relations and local development in different ways. Economically, the limited complementarity among the participating units in the GTS and GMS, coupled with their marginal status, form an internal barrier to the development of China's frontier cities. The limited inflow of global capital and export-oriented manufacturing due to the peripheral location of units in the two transborder subregions have imposed an external constraint on the Chinese border cities to develop beneficial trans-local and global ties. This combination has narrowed the band of economic activities in the Chinese border cities to border trade with neighboring countries that only generates relatively weak development impulses.

Politically, while the Chinese border provinces and cities in both the GTS and GMS have benefited from decentralization and some local autonomy, decentralization was relatively late and did not go far enough to allow the provincial and local governments to develop wider and deeper links with the global economy. This is further hampered by the lack of decentralization and its unevenness among the neighboring countries and cities across the borders. The RFE has been trapped in a double bind of continued control by and dependence on Moscow, leaving the RFE with little room and resources to unleash its strength in and contribution to the GTS through economic cooperation with China. The very short leash from the totally controlling political center in North Korea has practically eliminated any chance for autonomous development of the Rajin-Sonbong Free Economic and Trade Zone that would otherwise occur with the its special status and adjacency to the Hunchun BECZ. Even as the series of decentralization measures introduced by both the central and provincial governments have boosted Yunnan and its border cities' advantages in trade with Myanmar, Lao PDR, and Vietnam, the more limited autonomy of cities in the latter countries has set limits on the scope of this trade and its extension to cross-border manufacturing activities.

While cross-border ethnic ties reflect a distinctive aspect of global cultural connections, they have had a positive but limited effect on the development of China's border cities in the two transborder contexts. Boundary-spanning Korean identity has induced some concentration of South Korean investment in the predominantly ethnic Korean cities in Jilin while historical and cultural links among various cross-border ethnic minorities have promoted small-scale border trade and tourism for Yunnan's border cities. However, lacking the massive scale of overseas Chinese ties in southeastern China, the Chinese frontier cities of Yanji and Ruili could not draw from greater outside resources. In addition, the cross-border ethnic ties in these two transborder subregions were less active under the stronger political and military control of regimes like North Korea and Myanmar, which has hampered the ways in which these ties could benefit both Chinese and non-Chinese border cities.

Finally, improved transport infrastructure in both the GTS and GMS has strengthened the opportunistic effect of geographic proximity and more open borders. This in turn has contributed to the development of Chinese border cities by facilitating greater cross-border flows of people, vehicles, and cargo between them and other border cities. However, the severe lack of large-scale financial resources needed for developing transport infrastructure has left some barrier effect of borders in place. In the meantime, limited and uneven growth of cities on or near different borders creates uncertain present and future demand for cross-border transport infrastructure.

This set of favorable and unfavorable factors, which define the dimensions and parameters of the transborder subregion context, has a greater impact on the development of Chinese frontier cities than the presumed strong and far-reaching influence of globalization present in the fast-growing coastal cities. The distinctive transition of China's border regions and cities challenges analysts to look beyond the analytical lenses of globalization and market reform to be conceptually more eclectic and nuanced and empirically more comparative and wide-ranging. By examining several frontier cities in a complex transborder subregional milieu, this study intends to open a new vista on urban China research.

Acknowledgments

I thank two anonymous reviewers for criticisms and comments.

Notes

1 The definition of what is the "global" and what is the "local" may not be precise, just as it is difficult to pin down their respective physical boundaries. While generally using the term "local" to mean localities such as cities and regions rather than nations, and the term "global" to signify worldwide processes, Amin and Thrift (1994: 6) choose to leave both terms more or less ambiguous. They highlighted the more varied use of the "local," which might refer to a small area like the rural industrial districts of Italy or a large agglomeration like Silicon Valley as a player in the world economy. In this chapter, I use the "local" to refer to the border cities or areas that are actual or potential players in the global economy. This allows me to examine explicitly the role of transborder subregions in mediating the economic relations between border cities or areas and the global economy.

2 Rosenau (1997) defines globalization as a process that compels individual and their collectives to act similarly and thus broaden boundaries or de-emphasize them, while localization is a process that narrows the horizons of individual and collective actors and heightens the limiting role of boundaries.

3 Stimulated partly by the publication of *Bringing the State Back In* (Evans *et al*. 1985, also see Block 1987), the role of the state in economic development, especially in the East Asian context has drawn sustained scholarly attention and debates. While the literature is too large to summarize here, the controversy has shifted from disagreement between the neoclassical economics view and the developmental state perspective to a debate between the latter and an institutional approach and interpretation. Representing the developmental state school, Amsden (1989) and Wade (1990) suggest that the state has guided and directed the market with a heavy hand through such policies as picking winners and losers and protecting domestic firms. For an extended summary of these policies see Henderson and Appelbaum (1992: 21–22). On the other hand, Kuo (1995) challenges the developmental state model by pointing to evidently important roles of business associations and firms in a changing clientelist or corporatist relationship with the state in Taiwan and the Philippines. Evans (1995) demonstrates that the South Korean state only became developmental when it was embedded in social networks and cooperated with important actors in civil society.

4 At the inner most core of the GTS is a small triangle anchored on the border city of Hunchun in China's Jilin Province, the border port city of Sonbong of North Korea, and the port city of Posyet in the Khasan region of the RFE, all located within a radius of 40–50 kilometers from the estuary of the Tumen River. This zones of 1,000 square kilometers was originally labeled the Tumen River Economic Zone (TREZ) when the United Nations Development Programme (UNDP) began its involvement in the Tumen River development project in the early 1990s. It was enlarged into a larger triangular region called the Tumen River Economic Development Area (TREDA) in 1994. Covering approximately 10,000 square kilometers, the TREDA is bounded at its apexes by the Chinese border city of Yanji, the North Korean port city of Chongjin, and Vladivostok and Nakhodka of the RFE, located within 80–120 kilometers of the estuary. The hinterland of the TREDA would envelope the bulk of China's Jilin and Heilongjiang provinces, the entire Hamgyong-Bukdo of North Korea (a provincial-level administrative unit bordering Jilin province), and the southern portions of Primorskii Krai (Maritime Territory), Khabarovsk Krai, and Amurskaia Oblast (all provincial administrative units) of the RFE. On a still larger scale, the TREDA and its hinterland constitute the spatial core of economic cooperation in Northeast Asia among northeastern China, North Korea, South Korea, the RFE, Mongolia (especially its eastern part), and Japan along the Sea of Japan (see Marton *et al*. 1995, Fukagawa 1997).

5 Hunchun features a unique combination of both overland opening and sea access. Its border with Primorskii Krai (Maritime Territory) of the RFE to the southeast covers 232 kilometers. Its overland border crossing is only 32 kilometers away from the RFE border town of Kraskino, which is connected to Trans-Siberian Railway through a spur line. Hunchun is located about 46 kilometers away from the small RFE port of Posyet and 140 kilometers away from the largest and most important port of Vladivostok in the RFE. Hunchun borders Hamgyong-Bukdo of North Korea to the southwest across the Tumen River along 140 kilometers. The Chinese border town of Fangchuan, the east most point of China's land border along the Tumen River, is only 2 kilometers away from the North Korean border train station at Doo-Man River Lee (an equivalent of township). The rail and land crossings connect Hunchun conveniently with the three North Korean ports of Rajin (90 kilometers away), Sonbong, and Chongjin. Finally, with the town of Fangchuan being only 15 kilometers away from the Sea of Japan, Hunchun marks the closest shipping point from Northeastern China to the west coast of Japan, with a distance of 800 kilometers from Niigata (see Liu and Liao 1993).

6 Hunchun's important role in ocean trade with Japan goes all the way back to the Tang dynasty (AD 618–907). The Hunchun–Japan shipping route earned a reputation as the "Ocean Silk Road" or the "Japan Road." Even after Russia took over a large portion of China's northeastern territory in the late nineteenth century, a Sino-Russian border treaty signed in 1886 continued to allow Chinese ships to enter the Sea of Japan from

Hunchun on the Tumen River. There were regular commercial vessels running between Hunchun and Posyet and Vladivostok. In 1906, for example, over 1,500 vessels passed through the Hunchun port with a total tonnage of 25,000. The Hunchun border customs established in 1909 was the very first such facility in northeastern China (Liu and Liao 1993). China lost the shipping right from the Hunchun port to the Sea of Japan in 1938 due to Japan's military-backed blockade of the mouth of the Tumen River during the Russian–Japanese War.

7 *Renmin Ribao* (The People's Daily), overseas edition, January 2, 2002, p. 8.
8 *Renmin Ribao* (The People's Daily), overseas edition, November 7, 2000, p. 1.
9 *Renmin Ribao* (The People's Daily), overseas edition, January 2, 2002, p. 8.
10 Reported in *Renmin Ribao* (The People's Daily), overseas edition, December 18, 2003, p. 3.
11 Yunnan's border with Myanmar, Lao PDR, and Vietnam stretches a total of 4,060 kilometers, of which 1,997, 710, and 1,353 kilometers separate the province from the three neighboring countries, respectively. Yunnan province has 17 prefectures, 8 of which, with 26 counties, border Myanmar, Lao PDR, and Vietnam. Yunnan has 8 state-level (first-grade) border crossings, 8 provincial-level (second-grade) border crossings, and over 80 third-grade crossings with check points and border street markets (Economic and Trade Cooperation with Neighboring Countries Bureau 1995). There are also hundreds of unofficial land or river border crossings between Yunnan and Myanmar (Mellor 1993).
12 Interview with the Director of Tumen River Research Institute under the Academy of Northeast Asian Studies at Jilin University, Changchun, Jilin Province, July 28, 1999.
13 From the city of Ruili alone, over 10,000 people crossed the border into Myanmar (Burma at the time) in the Great Famine of 1958. In 1969, due to the ultra leftist policy of politicizing the border associated with the Cultural Revolution, another 9,000 people left. The two exoduses drained half of the town's total population (Chinese Central Academy of Ethnology 1993).
14 With its portion in China known as the Lancang, the Mekong River originates from the northern wing of the snowy Tanggula Mountain in the Tibetan plateau, flows down through the southern part of Qinghai Province and western Yunnan, exits China at Xishuanbanna, passes through Lao PDR, Myanmar, Thailand, Cambodia, and Vietnam before emptying into the South China Sea via a massive delta known as the Dragon's Mouth. The Mekong River is 4,880 kilometers in total length, and 2,161 kilometers are within China with 1,247 kilometers flowing through Yunnan province alone (Wang and Li 1998).

References

Amin, A. and N. Thrift, (1994) "Living in the global," in A. Amin and N. Thrift (eds) *Globalization, Institutions, and Regional Development in Europe*, London: Oxford University Press, 1–22.
Amsden, A. H. (1989) *Asia's Next Giant: South Korea and Late Industrialization*, New York: Oxford University Press.
Asia, Inc. (1996) "The Mekong: corridor of commerce," special map attached to the February 1996 issue of the *Asia Inc.* magazine, Hong Kong.
Block, F. L. (1987) *Revising State Theory: Essays in Politics and Post-Industrialism*, Philadelphia, PA: Temple University Press.
Bunker, S. G. (1989) "Staples, links, and poles in the construction of regional development theories," *Sociological Forum*, 4 (4): 589–610.
Chen, C. (1998) "Yanbian diqu wuliu xianzhuang yu yuce" (The current state and forecast of goods flows in the Yanbian region), *Dongbei Ya Luntan* (Northeast Asia Forum), 2: 1–10.

Chen, X. M. (1987) "Magic and myth of migration: a case study of a special economic zone in China," *Asia-Pacific Population Journal*, 2 (3): 57–77.

—— (1993) "The Changing role of Shenzhen in China's national and regional development in the 1980s," in G. T. Yu (ed.) *China in Transition: Economic, Political and Social Developments*, Lanham, MD: University Press of America, 251–279.

—— (1995) "The evolution of free economic zones and the recent development of cross–national growth zones," *International Journal of Urban and Regional Research*, 19 (4): 593–621.

—— (1998) "China's growing integration with the Asia-Pacific economy," in A. Dirlik (ed.) *What Is in a Rim? Critical Perspectives on the Pacific Region Idea*, Lanham, MD: Rowman & Littlefield Publishers, 89–119.

—— (2000) "Both glue and lubricant: transnational ethnic social capital as a source of Asia–Pacific subregionalism," *Policy Sciences*, 33 (3–4): 268–297.

—— (2005) *As Border Bend: Transnational Spaces on the Pacific Rim*, Lanham, MD: Rowman & Littlefield Publishers.

Chinese Central Academy of Ethnology (1993) *Zhongguo Yanbian Kaifang Chengshi Touzi Maoyi Zhinan* (An Investment and Trade Guide for China's Border Open Cities), Beijing: The Chinese Central Academy of Ethnology Publishing House.

Economic and Trade Cooperation with Neighboring Countries Bureau (1995) *Zhongguo Yunnan Bianmao* (Frontier Trade in Yunnan, China), *summary statistics*.

Evans, P. B. (1995) *Embedded Autonomy: States and Industrial Transformation*, Princeton, NJ: Princeton University Press.

Evans, P. B., R. Dietrich, and S. Theda (eds) (1985) *Bringing the State Back In*, Cambridge and New York: Cambridge University Press.

Fu, Y. N. (1998), "Ershiyi shiji jilinsheng yu zhoubian guojia jingmao hezhuo zhanwang" (The prospect for economic and trade cooperation between Jilin Province and the neighboring countries), in Z. S. Liu and S. J. Wang (eds) *Dongbei Ya Dique Heping Yu Fazhan Yanjiu* (Research on Peace and Development in Northeast Asia), Jilin: Jilin University Press, 407–418.

Fukagawa, Y. (1997) "The Northeast Asian economic zone: potential for the latecomer," in E. K. Y. Chen and C. H. Kwan (eds) *Asia's Borderless Economy: The Emergence of Subregional Economic Zones*, St Leonards, Australia: Allen & Unwin, 59–88.

Gaubatz, P. R. (1996) *Beyond the Great Wall: Urban Form and Transformation on the Chinese Frontier*, Stanford, CA: Stanford University Press.

Harrell, S. (ed.) (1995) *Cultural Encounters on China's Ethnic Frontiers*, Seattle, WA: University of Washington Press.

Henderson, J. and R. P. Appelbaum (1992) "Situating the state in the East Asian development process," in R. P. Appelbaum and J. Henderson (eds) *States and Development in the Asian Pacific Rim*, Newbury Park, CA: Sage Publications, 1–26.

Hong Kong Trade Development Council (1992) *Market Report on Yunnan Province*, Research Department, Hong Kong Trade Development Council.

Hsieh, S.-C. (1995) "On the dynamics of Tai/Dai–Lue ethnicity: an ethnohistorical analysis," in Steven Harrell (ed.) *Cultural Encounters on China's Ethnic Frontiers*, Seattle and London: University of Washington Press, 301–328.

Hsing, Y.-T. (1998) *Making Capitalism in China: The Taiwan Connection*, New York: Oxford University Press.

Kuah, K. E. (2000) "Negotiating central, provincial, and county policies: border trading in southern China," in E. Grant, C. Hutton, and K. E. Kuah (eds) *Where China Meets*

Southeast Asia: Social & Cultural Change in the Border Regions, Bangkok: Institute of Southeast Asian Studies, 72–97.

Kuo, C.-T. (1995) *Global Competition and Industrial Growth in Taiwan and the Philippines*, Pittsburgh, PA: University of Pittsburgh Press.

Lawrence, S. V. (1999) "Cross–border disappointment," *Far Eastern Economic Review*, April 29: 12–13.

Li, J. and Y. Z. Zhao (1997) *Yunnan Waixiangxin Jingji* (Yunnan's Outward–Oriented Economy), Dehong, Yunnan: Dehong Ethnology Press.

Li, W., Y. M. Zhu, and Y. He (eds) (1997) *Tumenjiang Diqu Ziyuan Kaifa, Jianshe Buju yu Huanjin Zhengzhi Yanjiu* (A Study on Resource Exploration, Construction Patterns and Environmental Treatment in the Tumen River Region), Beijing: Science Press.

Li, Y. W. and G. L. Wu (1998) "Zhongguo chaoxianzu zai dongbeiya heping yu fazhan zhong de zuoyong" (The role of ethnic Korean Chinese in the peace and development of Northeast Asia), in Z. S. Liu and S. J. Wang (eds) *Dongbei Ya Dique Heping Yu Fazhan Yanjiu* (Research on peace and development in northeast Asia), Jilin: Jilin University Press, 55–66.

Lin, G. C. S. (1997) *Red Capitalism in Southern China: Growth and Development of the Pearl River Delta*, Vancouver, WA: University of British Columbia Press.

Liu, B. R. and J. S. Liao (1993) *Zhongguo Yanbian Kaifang yu Zhoubian Guojia Shichang* (China's Opening Borders and the Neighboring Countries' Markets), Beijing: Legal Press.

Mackerras, C. (2003) *China's Ethnic Minorities and Globalization*, London and New York: RoutledgeCurzon.

Marton, A., T. McGee, and D. G. Peterson (1995) "Northeast Asian economic cooperation and the Tumen River Area Development Project," *Pacific Affairs*, 68 (1): 9–33.

Mellor, W. (1993) "A border bonanza," *Asia, Inc.*, 2 (11): 38–46.

Orum, A. M., and X. M. Chen (2003) *The World of Cities: Places in Historical and Comparative Perspective*, Oxford and Cambridge: Blackwell.

Peng, S. and D. L. Yan (eds) (1994) *Zhong Han Jingmao Hezhuo Zhinan* (A Guide to Economic and Trade Cooperation between China and South Korea), Tianjin: Tianjin People's Press.

Ratti, R. (1993) "How can existing barrier and border effects be overcome? A theoretical approach," in R. Cappellin and P. W. Batey (eds) *Regional Networks, Border Regions and European Integration*, London: Pion Limited, 60–69.

Rietveld, P. (1993) "Transport and communication barriers in Europe," in R. Cappellin and P. W. Batey (eds), *Regional Networks, Border Regions and European Integration*, London: Pion Limited, 47–59.

Robinson, J. (2002) "Global and world cities: a view from off the map," *International Journal of Urban and Regional Research*, 26 (3): 531–554.

Rosenau, J. N. (1997), *Along the Domestic–Foreign Frontier: Exploring Governance in a Turbulent World*, New York: Cambridge University Press.

Sassen, S. (1996) *Losing Control? Sovereignty in an Age of Globalization*, New York: Columbia University Press.

—— (1997) "The spatial organization of information industries: implications for the role of the state," in J. H. Mittelman (ed.) *Globalization: Critical Reflections*, Boulder, CO: Lynne Rienner Publishers, 33–52.

—— (2001)*The Global City: New York, London, Tokyo*. Second Edition, Princeton, NJ: Princeton University Press.

Shi, Z. K. and W. S. Yu (1995) "Jilin sheng tong chaoxian bianjin maoyi ji difang yihuo maoyi de taishi fenxi" (A current analysis of border trade between Jilin Province and North Korea and local bartering trade), *Dongbei Ya Luntan* (Northeast Asia Forum), 1: 52–55.

Smith, D. and M. Timberlake (2001) "World city networks and hierarchies, 1977–1997: an empirical analysis of global air travel links," *American Behavioral Scientist*, 44 (10): 1656–1678.

State Statistical Bureau (1998) *Yunnan Tongji Nianjian 1998* (Yunnan Statistical Yearbook 1998), Beijing: China Statistics Press.

Tang, G. H. (1995) *Yunnan Yanbian Kaifang: Zhanglue he Cuoshe Yanjiu* (Yunnan's Border Opening: A Study of Strategy and Measures), Kunming: Yunnan University Press.

Wade, R. (1990) *Governing the Market: Economic Theory and the Role of Government in East Asian Industrialization*, Princeton, NJ: Princeton University Press.

Wang, R. and P. Li (1998) "Lancangjiang xiayou diqu kouan jianshe guihua yanjiu baogao" (A research report on the construction and planning for the crossings at the lower reach of the Lancang River), *Jingji Luntan* (Economic Forum), 107 (Special Issue): 24–50.

Wang, S. J. and D. H. Zhang (1998) "Lun difang chengshi difang zhengfu zai dongbeiya diqu jingji hezhuo zhongde diwei he zuoyong" (The status and role of localities and local governments in the regional economic cooperation of Northeast Asia), *Dongbei Ya Luntan* (Northeast Asia Forum), 4: 24–28.

Wank, D. L. (1995) "Bureaucratic patronage and private business: changing networks of power in urban China," in A. G. Walder (ed.) *The Waning of the Communist State: Economic Origins of Political Decline in China and Hungary*, Berkeley, CA: University of California Press, 153–183.

—— (1999) *Commodifying Communism: Business, Trust, and Politics in a Chinese City*, Cambridge: Cambridge University Press.

Wu, F. L. (2003) "The (post-) socialist entrepreneurial city as a state project: Shanghai's reglobalization in question," *Urban Studies*, 40(9): 1673–1698.

Yeung, Y.-M. and X. J. Li (1999) "Bargaining with transnational corporations: the case of Shanghai," *International Journal of Urban and Regional Research*, 22 (1): 2512–2533.

Yu, G. Z. (1994) "Guanyu jianli tumenjiang sanjaozhou kuaguo jingji tequ de zhonghe yanjiu baogao" (An integrated research report on the establishment of a cross-national special economic zone in the Tumen River delta), *Dongbei Ya Yanjiu* (Northeast Asian Studies), 14 (Supplemental Issue): 12–29.

Zhang, L.-Y. (2003) "Economic development in Shanghai and the role of the state," *Urban Studies*, 40(8): 1549–1572.

Zhao, G. Z. (1997) "From border trade to economic regionalism: Yunnan Province and the upper Mekong corridor in the 1990s," *Journal of Chinese Political Science*, 3(1) (Summer): 27–63.

Zhonghua Publishing House (2001) *Yunnan Tongji Nianjian 2000* (Yunnan Statistical Yearbook 2000), Beijing: Zhonghua Publishing House.

3 Globalization and the growth of Chinese cities

Cécile Batisse, Jean-François Brun and Mary-Françoise Renard

Introduction

Urban concentration is a complex phenomenon which differs greatly from one country to another and in the course of the time and, as suggested by Henderson (2000), depends on the level of development. The urbanization process that occurred in Europe and in North America during the nineteenth and twentieth centuries was quite different from the one currently observed. Some features of the present urbanization process are worth pointing out (Cohen 2003).

1   The scale of the present change is unprecedented:
   a   urbanization is occurring at a rapid pace;
   b   the number of large urban agglomerations is growing;
   c   the average size of cities is increasing;
   d   urbanization is the result not only of natural increase in population but also of the migration.
2   As in the countries enjoying high per capita income, the largest part of the population is already living in cities; urbanization concerns mainly the developing countries where most of the heavily populated cities are located.
3   The extent of urbanization depends partly on globalization. Even if globalization reduces the need for spatial proximity, it induces changes in the organization and in the location of firms.

The quest for better efficiency means to seek economies of scale and external economies. Then, the process of international integration is often seen as a reason for the agglomeration of activities and for an increasingly urbanized society. However, agglomeration and urbanization are not the same, although they are related with each other. The process of urbanization may be explained by the concentration of service activities and by external economies which are two key features of agglomeration. Besides, reclassification or redefinition of urban population is also an important component of urbanization in China.

As Cohen (2003: 37) puts it: 'Globalization has allowed individual cities to break away from the fate of their national economies. Increasingly success or failure depends on the ability of municipal governments to capitalize on the assets of the local environment and to provide the modern infrastructure, enabling environment and low-wage, flexible workforce demanded by modern businesses'. This is especially relevant for China where decentralization has given cities a noticeable political power. Furthermore, cities are important economic actors as, for instance, some of them are direct partners for foreign firms through joint-ventures agreements.

China is experiencing rapid urbanization. Since 1978, the government has implemented reforms of fundamental importance. They had many components to drive China to a market economy. One of the fundamental ideas has been to decentralize power to local governments and to cities (Dulbecco and Renard 2003). According to the 'open-door policy', another major component of the reforms, foreign investment has been allowed in Special Economic Zones (SEZs) located in coastal provinces. They have been an engine for growth, especially in cities. Cities have been gradually allowed to sign joint-ventures with foreign firms. These policy measures have been crucial to increase the efficiency of the Chinese economy and have been the core of the transition process. This has led China to evolve from an agricultural country to an industrial one.

The growth of cities is one of the major concerns for the central government in the coming years. Its goal is, as shown in the last Five Year Plan, to reduce the inequalities between provinces, and also between rural and urban areas. The government wants to develop infrastructure between and within provinces. This should help to modernize the inland provinces and also help to slow down the concentration of activities into coastal regions. With more than 379 millions city-dwellers in 1998, China has the largest urban population in the world. There is a wide consensus that the patterns of urbanization are unusual since the end of the 1970s. Some works have focused on the influence of China's confusing definitions of urban areas on the process itself (Chang 1994, Zhang and Zhao 1998). Many papers have been devoted to the 'global city' or the 'space of globalisation' in a city (see Wu and Ma 2005). The attention is paid for instance to the definition of cities as 'command centres', the impact of services activities and the transformations in the organization of the cities. However, despite all these achievements, there still remain some empirical puzzles. For instance, is urbanization linked to the opening up of China? In this chapter, we explore the assumption that trade openness and foreign direct investments (FDI) may partly explain that process during the 1990s.

The chapter proceeds as follows. In the next section, we briefly summarize the salient features of the urbanization process. Then, we use data on Chinese cities to test the impact of openness on urbanization prior to the accession to WTO. Our analysis uses different sub-samples of cities and two indicators for openness: trade and FDIs. For most sub-samples openness does not seem to exert an impact on the urbanization process. When significant, trade and FDI have opposite effects. Finally, we conclude the chapter by summarizing our findings.

Some characteristics of the Chinese urbanization process

When the communist government seized power in 1949, more than two-thirds of the urban population was located in the eastern provinces. The coast also contained close to half of the Chinese cities, including most of the largest ones. The central region was predominantly rural and was characterized by small cities. The western region was almost wholly rural, although it had some medium cities. In a decade, the urban population of the eastern provinces doubled with large centres such as Shanghai. In the central provinces, the average size of cities did not increase as much as it did in the coastal area, but the urban population increased threefold. This can be explained by an increase in the number of cities. From the mid-1950s to the beginning of the reform, the government policy of discouraging the growth of large cities appeared to have some effect.[1] In addition, the bias against coastal region stimulated the growth and the development of interior cities, including Lanzhou, Wuhan, Xian and Zhengzhou. Thus, in 1980 the central region represented one-third of China's urban population while half of urban population was concentrated in the eastern region (National Bureau of Statistics 1981).

With the reform process, China's urbanization has been proceeding along two different tracks: one is the traditional urbanization sponsored by the government and the other is the spontaneous urbanization driven by local economic development and market forces (Zhu 1999). The market forces are partly driven by openness. During the Sixth Five Year Plan (1981–1985), urbanization was still largely restricted by the Hukou system. This reflected the 'bias against urbanization and its association with capitalism, Western moral pollution, and potentially counter-revolutionary forces' (Au and Henderson 2002: 5). In the meantime, the growth of smaller cities was promoted with the possibility of transferring Hukou from rural areas to these small cities. But, owing to successful agricultural reform and a higher productivity a surplus of labourers appeared in rural areas. As a consequence migration increased and the government became less strict. The Hukou system is still in operation but the controls have been tempered and the rules have changed during the 1990s. It is possible for farmers to enter freely into cities. There is thus a large 'floating population'. Cities become more attractive with growing unemployment (or underemployment) in rural areas. Now, the Chinese government has to manage at the same time growing inequalities between rural and urban areas and negative externalities created by urbanization.

Moreover, the new urban policy has used large cities as the engine of regional growth. Cities are expected to serve as growth centres for the countryside through externalities and spill-over effects. First Guangzhou and then Shanghai and Tianjin were given the capacity and power to modernize through openness. In addition, the government recognized the advantages of the coastal provinces. The government designated other types of growth centres, in particular 5 SEZs and 14 coastal opened cities. More generally, cities and towns have had a greater autonomy to respond to market forces. Now the cities themselves contain and manage the migrant flows.

Besides, the relaxation of criteria for classifying towns in 1984 was one of the factors for the increasing level of urbanization (Lee 1989). During the Mao era, provinces were looking for autarky; as a result, they produced the entire range of manufactures and did not have industrial specialization. As China is more and more integrated in international competition it is crucial to improve efficiency. So, one of the main objectives of the open-door policy was to exploit comparative advantage to participate in international trade. The result has been a growing specialization of provinces. The globalization process now induces new constraints, and the different provinces have to look for agglomeration effects. Fujita and Hu (2001) find strong evidence for increasing agglomeration between 1985 and 1994. They interpret this phenomenon as 'self-agglomeration' induced by FDI and trade policies. But this increasing agglomeration benefited the coastal provinces, particularly Guangdong province.

Moreover, the development of township and village enterprises (TVEs) has facilitated the transformation of rural areas into urban ones. Foreign investment is an important factor contributing to the growth of spontaneous urbanization. It provides the bulk of funds needed for new urban development and contributes to the transformation of the economic and employment structures (Zhu 1999). For example, the urban development of the city of Fuqing in Fujian province has been mainly driven by intensive foreign capital inflows. As an additional incentive, China's urbanization has been propelled by local forces: the development of TVEs which provide employment opportunities. Jinjiang in Fujian province illustrates urbanization through the transformation of rural employment structures and the development of TVEs. In provinces like Jiangsu, Zhejiang and Guangdong, there are some examples of this rural–urban transformation (Zhu 1999).

Econometric analysis of the Chinese urbanization in the 1990s

Data issues

Provincial data come from the comprehensive statistical data and materials on 50 years of new China (National Bureau of Statistics 1999a,b,c). The data at the city level were obtained from Xin zhong guo cheng shi wu shi nian (National Bureau of Statistics 2001). China is divided into 27 provinces and 4 provinces having the status of municipality: Beijing, Tianjin, Shanghai and Chongqing[2] (Figure 3.1). The definition of urban areas is exceedingly complicated. Moreover, it has evolved with the course of the time. Two main concepts emerge:

1   Cities (*shi*) which have generally more than 100,000 inhabitants. The large urban agglomerations (1 million inhabitants or more) concentrate one-third of total urban population. The number of large cities in 1998 was threefold of the figure in 1978.
2   Towns (*zhen*) represent the main element of present urban strategy. In 1998, there were about 18,000 towns, a significant increase from 2,664 in 1982.

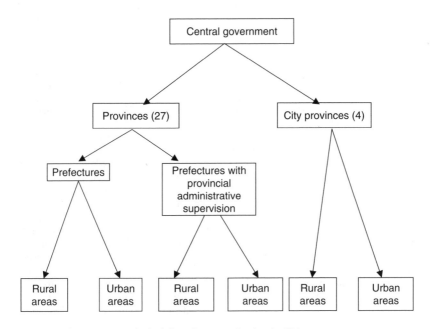

Figure 3.1 The structure of administrative organization in China.

Cities and towns include districts that are actually rural areas inhabited by farmers. According to Zhang and Zhao (1998: 331), 'cities are ranked in three levels: the first is equivalent to the authority of a province, the second is equivalent to the authority of a prefecture, and the third is equivalent to that of a county'. The Urban Statistical Yearbook, Xin zhong guo cheng shi wu shi nian, covers the first two levels officially designated as cities under a provincial administrative supervision. Rural districts are excluded.

The Hukou system classifies the population into different categories: rural/urban and agricultural/non-agricultural. The first distinction is based on a location criterion whereas the second is based on the economic activity. We consider urban population as the people living in urban districts and being non-agricultural by profession (Zhang and Zhao 1998, Chen and Coulson 2001).[3] Owing to an unrecorded migration from rural to urban areas, the data inevitably underestimate the urban population in the cities forming the sample (Table 3.1). In other respects, some inconsistencies render the data unreliable. Observations have been excluded from the sample if at least one of the following features has been noticed: (1) a legal status change has occurred; (2) the city experienced large variations in non-agricultural population which is not induced by a legal status change; (3) discontinuity is identified in time series which cannot be corrected. The sample includes 132 cities and covers the whole country except Tibet. Data have been averaged over the period 1992–1998.

Table 3.1 The list of the cities in the sample

Province	City	Province	City	Province	City
Beijing	Beijing[a]	Jiangsu	Huayin	Hunan	Changsha[a]
Tianjin	Tianjin[a]	Jiangsu	Changzhou	Hunan	Changde[a]
Hebei	Handan[a]	Jiangsu	Zhenjiang	Hunan	Hengyang
Hebei	Tangshan[a]	Zhejiang	Wenzhou[a]	Hunan	Xiangtan
Hebei	Shijiazhuang[a]	Zhejiang	Hangzhou[a]	Hunan	Zhuzhou
Hebei	Qinhuangdao	Zhejiang	Huzhou[a]	Hunan	Shaoyang
Hebei	Langfang	Zhejiang	Ningbo[a]	Guangdong	Guangzhou[a]
Hebei	Zhangjiakou	Zhejiang	Zhoushan	Guangdong	Zhanjiang[a]
Hebei	Baoding	Zhejiang	Jiaxing	Guangdong	Zhongshan[a]
Shanxi	Datong[a]	Anhui	Huainan[a]	Guangdong	Dongguan[a]
Shanxi	Taiyuan[a]	Anhui	Hefei[a]	Guangdong	Qingyuan
Shanxi	Yangquan	Anhui	Bengbu	Guangdong	Shantou
Shanxi	Suzhou	Anhui	Huaibei	Guangdong	Yangjiang
Shanxi	Changzi	Anhui	Wuhu	Guangdong	Maoming
Inner Mong	Baotou[a]	Anhui	Anging	Guangdong	Jieyang
Inner Mong	Chifeng	Anhui	Ma Anshan	Guangdong	Shenzhen
Inner Mong	Hohhot	Fujian	Fuzhou[a]	Guangxi	Nanning[a]
Liaoning	Shenyang[a]	Fujian	Quanzhou	Guangxi	Qinzhou[a]
Liaoning	Anshan[a]	Fujian	Xiamen	Guangxi	Guigang[a]
Liaoning	Dalian[a]	Jiangxi	Nanchang[a]	Guangxi	Liuzhou
Liaoning	Fushun[a]	Jiangxi	Xinyu	Guangxi	Guilin
Liaoning	Huludao	Shandong	Linyi[a]	Hainan	Haikou
Liaoning	Yingkou	Shandong	Jinan[a]	Sichuan	Chengdu[a]
Liaoning	Liaoyang	Shandong	Zibo[a]	Sichuan	Neijiang[a]
Liaoning	Fuxin	Shandong	Weifang[a]	Sichuan	Leshan[a]
Liaoning	Dandong	Shandong	Taian[a]	Sichuan	Suining[a]
Liaoning	Benxi	Shandong	Laiwu[a]	Sichuan	Mianyang
Liaoning	Jinzhou	Shandong	Zaozhuang[a]	Sichuan	Guangyuan
Liaoning	Panjin	Shandong	Rizhao[a]	Sichuan	Zigong
Jilin	Jilin[a]	Shandong	Qingdao[a]	Sichuan	Panzhihua
Jilin	Changchun[a]	Shandong	Dezhou	Sichuan	Yibin
Heilongjiang	Harbin[a]	Shandong	Jining	Guizhou	Guiyang[a]
Heilongjiang	Gigihaer[a]	Shandong	Dongying	Guizhou	Zunyi
Heilongjiang	Jiamusi	Henan	Zhengzhou[a]	Guizhou	Luipanzhui
Heilongjiang	Yichun	Henan	Luoyang[a]	Yunnan	Kunming[a]
Heilongjiang	Shuangyashan	Henan	Anyang	Shaanxi	Xian[a]
Heilongjiang	Jixi	Henan	Xinxiang	Shaanxi	Weinan
Heilongjiang	Mudanjiang	Henan	Kaifeng	Shaanxi	Baoji
Heilongjiang	Hegang	Henan	Pingdingshan	Gansu	Tianshui[a]
Heilongjiang	Daqing	Henan	Jiaozuo	Gansu	Lanzhou[a]
Shanghai	Shanghai[a]	Hubei	Wuhan[a]	Qinhai	Xining
Jiangsu	Nanjing[a]	Hubei	Yichang	Ningxia	Yinchuan
Jiangsu	Wuxi	Hubei	Ezhou	Xinjiang	Urumqi[a]
Jiangsu	Nantong	Hubei	Xiangfan		
Jiangsu	Liayungang	Hubei	Huangshi		

Note
a The cities with more than 1 million inhabitants.

Test of the impact of openness on urbanization

The following equation is estimated:

$$nonagripop_c = \alpha + \beta_1 upoc_p + \beta_2 area_p + \beta_3 gdpcap_c + \beta_4 second_c$$
$$+ \beta_5 tert_c + \beta_6 road_p + \beta_7 trade_p + \beta_8 FDI_p$$
$$+ \beta_9 TVE_p + \beta_{10} BTS + \beta_{11} cap + \beta_{12} SEZ + \varepsilon$$

where the subscript c ($c = 1, \ldots, 132$) indicates a variable at the city level and the subscript p indicates a variable at the provincial level.

The dependent variable, *nonagripop*, represents total non-agricultural population of the city excluding rural districts. The following explanatory variables are considered. First, the variables capturing openness: Openness is made up of international trade and FDI. The impact of trade openness is a priori ambiguous. If openness means giving preference to a large coastal city, then it may increase urban concentration (Henderson 2000). However, according to new economic geography trade, openness may be a factor of urban decentralization (Ades and Glaeser 1995, Fujita *et al.* 1999) as transport costs decline. Provincial trade openness, *trade*, is measured by the ratio of exports and imports to provincial GDP. FDI may increase concentration as they are located in few areas. Moreover, to get benefits from FDI, domestic firms have to be located close to these areas. The ratio of FDI to GDP, *FDI*, is supposed to have a positive effect on the non-agricultural population.

Second, the control variables: *upoc* is the urban population in the province outside the considered city. It serves as a control variable like in Ades and Glaeser (1995). The land area in square kilometres of the province, *area*, is also a potential determinant of concentration of non-agricultural population whose sign is a priori ambiguous. As is usual in the literature, urbanization is expected to grow with the level of per capita income, *gdpcap* measured as the real per capita GDP at the provincial level. A positive relationship is expected as a higher level of per capita GDP means more diversified activities and hence greater industrialization.

City growth can be connected to the industrialization process, either because there exists increasing returns in the output process (Krugman 1991) or because natural advantages may explain geographic concentration of population (Ellison and Glaeser 1999). Anyway, increasing returns and natural advantages are a complement rather than a substitute (Henderson 2000). Urban concentration is positively explained by the expansion of the secondary, *second*, and tertiary, *tert*, sectors. This expansion creates incentives for firms and workers to settle down in the city to get benefits from spill-over effects and externalities. The variable *second* is measured as the share of the secondary sector in GDP at the city level and *tert* as the share of the tertiary sector in GDP at the city level.

Road infrastructures, *road*, may have two opposite effects. By reducing transportation costs better roads may either reinforce the attraction of some cities by easing access to markets or decentralizing activities to neighbouring cities.

Table 3.2 Econometric result of the foreign investment and trade on urban concentration

	(1)	(2) (A)	(3)	(4) (A)	(5)	(6) (A)	(7)	(8) (A)	(9)	(10) (A)
UPOC	0,3231	0,5799	0,5312	0,8369	0,3256	0,5953	0,3950	0,2784	0,7463	0,9309
	(3.14)	(5.01)	(4.08)	(4.12)	(3.06)	(4.81)	(3.01)	(1.18)	(4.21)	(4.93)
Area	0,1780	0,3639	0,1638	0,9760	0,1700	0,3477	0,2903	0,1308	−3,0626	−2,7993
	(1.48)	(2.26)	(0.25)	(1.67)	(1.38)	(2.17)	(1.61)	(0.55)	(1.75)	(1.26)
GDPcap	0,2553	0,3662	0,3415	0,5357	0,2566	0,3676	0,1444	0,3454	0,3879	0,5838
	(3.16)	(2.80)	(2.63)	(2.39)	(3.13)	(2.65)	(1.24)	(2.11)	(3.05)	(2.86)
Second	1,0999	1,3681	1,0032	1,1820	1,1004	1,3746	1,1874	1,2865	0,9163	1,1689
	(5.20)	(6.11)	(3.26)	(3.83)	(5.08)	(5.75)	(3.76)	(3.12)	(2.88)	(3.66)
Tert	0,7219	0,7045	0,7092	0,6928	0,7337	0,7219	0,6474	0,6887	0,7962	0,6534
	(5.99)	(2.18)	(3.73)	(1.31)	(6.07)	(2.18)	(3.44)	(1.54)	(3.98)	(1.28)
TVE	−0,3190	−0,3378	−0,5212	−0,3043	−0,3330	−0,3756	−0,2957	−0,0421	−2,7362	−3,0082
	(2.03)	(1.89)	(1.04)	(0.72)	(2.05)	(1.90)	(1.57)	(0.13)	(2.23)	(1.91)
Road	0,0564	−0,3893	−0,0892	−1,1706	0,0873	−0,3334	−0,1737	−0,0519	2,5507	2,1190
	(0.32)	(1.80)	(0.16)	(1.98)	(0.49)	(1.48)	(0.85)	(0.18)	(1.93)	(1.35)
Trade	0,0635	−0,1282	−0,0206	−0,1366	0,0717	−0,1125	−0,0315	0,3613	−0,6072	−0,6929
	(0.64)	(0.80)	(0.10)	(0.40)	(0.73)	(0.70)	(0.13)	(1.35)	(1.98)	(1.61)
FDI	0,1429	0,2585	−0,2460	0,0889	0,1377	0,2461	0,2537	0,1500	0,0386	0,2508
	(1.26)	(2.19)	(1.37)	(0.27)	(1.19)	(2.09)	(1.37)	(0.72)	(0.22)	(0.87)
BTS	2,3921	2,7512	3,0293	3,6943						
	(8.06)	(5.90)	(3.35)	(3.73)						

	(1)	(2)	(3)	(4)	(5)	(6)	(7)	(8)	(9)	(10)
Capital	1,0376	0,6606	1,0457	0,5872	1,0388	0,6623	1,0989	0,5920	1,0043	0,6408
	(8.54)	(3.69)	(5.13)	(1.75)	(8.57)	(3.72)	(6.03)	(2.38)	(5.14)	(2.13)
SEZ	-0,7089	-0,4610			-0,7288	-0,4915				
	(2.87)	(1.36)			(2.93)	(1.42)				
Intercept	-10,2826	-11,1273	-12,1245	-13,2285	-10,6166	-11,8209	-8,5086	-7,9713	-6,9821	-8,5984
	(5.86)	(5.24)	(3.62)	(2.63)	(5.98)	(5.17)	(3.14)	(2.20)	(1.40)	(1.04)
Number of obs	132	57	65	32	129	54	67	25	62	29
F-test	53.26	75.68	22.28	63.27	34.23	44.19	23.27	34.99	14.22	83.26
R^2	0.75	0.86	0.79	0.41	0.68	0.82	0.71	0.87	0.42	0.83
Bera-Jarque	0.35	0.64	0.25	0.84	0.37	0.62	0.13	0.40	0.37	0.82
White	0.80	0.70	0.87	0.24	0.71	0.71	0.71	0.58	0.32	0.14
RESET	0.37	0.24	0.07	0.30	0.46	0.26	0.35	0.35	0.61	0.72

Notes

Column (1) all cities in the sample.
Column (2) cities with more than 1 million inhabitants.
Column (3) cities in coastal provinces.
Column (4) cities in coastal provinces with more than 1 million inhabitants.
Column (5) all cities in the sample excluding Beijing, Tianjin, Shangai.
Column (6) cities with more than 1 million inhabitants excluding Beijing, Tianjin, Shangai.
Column (7) cities in non-coastal provinces.
Column (8) cities in non-coastal provinces with more than 1 million inhabitants.
Column (9) cities in coastal provinces excluding Beijing, Tianjin, Shangai.
Column (10) cities in coastal provinces with more than 1 million inhabitants excluding Beijing, Tianjin, Shangai.

1 Dependent variable is an average non-agricultural population in the city from 1992 to 1998.
2 t-test value is within the brackets.

In China, the impact of the length of roads at the provincial level (in kilometres) is a priori unclear. This variable, the only one available for roads, gives information about the quantity but not about the quality of the infrastructure.

The share of the workers in township and village enterprises in the total provincial employment, *TVE*, creates incentives for people not to migrate in cities. TVEs are very specific to China as they contribute to transform rural areas. For instance, in the case of Fujian, Zhu (2000) argues that the TVEs change the structure of employment to industrial activities.

We also controlled for the provincial capitals, *cap*, which are the more attractive cities because they are the main industrial, commercial and administrative centre of the province. This is even true for Beijing, Tianjin and Shanghai; thus a dummy, *BTS*, controls their impact. As the status of Chongqing changed in 1997, it has been excluded from the sample. The dummy *SEZ*[4] takes into account the preferential status given to these cities. The variables, averaged over the period 1992–1998, are transformed in logarithm, and the coefficients can thus be interpreted as (constant) elasticises.

Econometric results

Table 3.2 reports OLS (Ordinary Less Squares) results,[5] with standard errors between brackets. Three tests have been conducted and the *P* values are reported under each equation. First, the Bera-Jarque test never rejects (at the 5 per cent level) the null that the residuals are normally distributed. For column (7) a dummy variable for Suzhou has been introduced into the equation. Second, the White test never rejects (at the 5 per cent level) the null of homoscedasticity. Third, the RESET test does not reject (at the 5 per cent level) the null that the functional form is correct. For column (3) the *P*-value is close to the 5 per cent level.

Regressions are conducted on two samples: the whole sample and the sub-sample of the cities with more than 1 million inhabitants. From a statistical point of view, the data available for the latter are of better quality, as they are more homogenous and coherent. From an economic point of view, they represent a large share of the total urban population and their attractiveness is higher than that of smaller cities.

For the columns (1)–(4) in Table 3.2, variables *upoc*, *gdpcap*, *second*, *tert* and *cap* are significant and positive. Several papers show that the non-agricultural population in China tends to concentrate in the wealthiest areas (Kojima 1995). Hence, the per capita GDP affects the non-agricultural population positively. As expected, the share of secondary and tertiary sectors in GDP has a large and significant effect on the concentration of the non-agricultural population. Lastly, the capital city dummy is positive and significant. Kojima (1995) shows the extreme degree of population concentration in provincial capital cities. This phenomenon is observed whichever development level of the province is considered (columns (1), (3) and (7)).

The variable *TVE* shows interesting results when we decompose our two samples according to geographic areas. Hence, we have considered cities located in coastal provinces and those located in central and western provinces. This variable appears significant with a negative impact on the non-agricultural population for the cities in the coastal region when Beijing, Tianjin and Shanghai are excluded from the sample (columns (9) and (10)). In the non-coastal region (columns (7) and (8)), first, the share of the workers in the TVEs is relatively low compared to that in the coastal region, as TVEs' products are mainly for export. Second, the TVEs are more productive and efficient in the coastal provinces (OECD 2002). If we consider the coastal provinces (columns (3), (4), (9) and (10)), the attractiveness of the TVEs on the population appears only significant when BTS are excluded.

The variable road has a significant negative impact when we consider the sub-sample of the larger cities located in all provinces (column (2)) or in the coastal provinces (column (4)). This variable has a positive influence on the non-agricultural population for cities in coastal provinces when Beijing, Tianjin and Shanghai are excluded (column (9)). These results do not really support Henderson's (2002: 100) arguments that for developing countries, 'increased infrastructure density strongly reduces urban concentration'.

FDI have a positive and significant effect on urban population, only for cities over 1 million inhabitants and *SEZ* have no impact on these cities (columns (2) and (6)). However, *SEZ* has a significant negative impact when the whole sample is considered (even if *BTS* are excluded; columns (1) and (5)).[6] These results are in accordance with Zhang (2002) who showed that driving forces behind urbanization are especially inflows of FDI.

International trade has no significant effect, except for the coastal cities without *BTS* where it appears negative (column (9)). This result supports Krugman and Livas' hypothesis. One can note that these cities are located in the most advanced provinces regarding the reform process.

Conclusion

Using data at the city level, this chapter has examined the impact of the open-door policy on Chinese urbanization. There is some econometric evidence that during the 1990s FDI had a positive effect on urbanization for the largest cities (over 1 million inhabitants). On the other hand, urban population concentration is negatively related to international trade for the cities located on the coast. For the whole sample, international trade has no significant impact.

The results seem more robust for variables not related to openness. For instance, urban population concentration appears to be positively explained by the level of development, measured by the per capita GDP, the size of the secondary and the tertiary sectors of the economy. The TVEs, a distinctive feature of the Chinese economy, have a negative impact on urban concentration, as expected.

The sample does not cover China's entry into WTO. One could expect further liberalization, a greater mobility for people and capital, and thus an increase in the concentration of activities and population in prosperous urban areas. In anticipation of this phenomenon, the central government has launched the Western Development Policy since 2000. It also tries to promote a more balanced urban development.

Notes

1 Between 1953 and 1978, the proportion of urban population fluctuated around 15 per cent (Yusuf and Wu 1997).
2 These four cities have central State administrative supervision.
3 This means that we define urban population by occupation rather than by Hukou.
4 The SEZs are Shenzhen, Zhuhai and Shantou (Guangdong) created in 1979, Xiamen (Fujian) in 1980 and Hainan Island in 1988.
5 In the Table 3.2, (A) refers to samples with cities with over 1 million inhabitants.
6 In the remaining equations, the dummy variable *SEZ* never appeared significant and so has been excluded.

References

Ades, A. F. and Glaeser E. L. (1995) 'Trade and circuses: explaining urban giants', *Quarterly Journal of Economics*, 110: 195–227.

Au, C. C. and Henderson J. V. (2002) 'How migration restrictions limit agglomeration and productivity in China', NBER, Cambridge: MA, Working Paper 8707.

Chang, K. S. (1994) 'Chinese urbanization and development before and after economic reform: a comparative reappraisal', *World Development*, 22(4): 601–613.

Chen, A. and Coulson, N. E. (2001) 'Determinants of urban population growth: evidence from Chinese cities', Mimeo, International conference on chinese urbanization, Xiamen, China.

Cohen, B. (2003) 'Urban growth in developing countries: a review of current trends and a caution regarding existing forecasts', *World Development*, 32: 23–51.

Dulbecco Ph. and Renard, M. F. (2003) 'Permanency and flexibility of institutions: the role of decentralization in Chinese economic reforms', *The Review of Austrian Economics*, 16: 327–346.

Ellison, G. and Glaeser, E. L. (1999) 'The geographic concentration of industry: does natural advantage explain agglomeration?', *American Economic Review Papers and Proceedings*, 89: 311–316.

Fujita, M. and Hu, D. (2001) 'Regional disparity in china 1995–1999: the effects of globalization and economic liberalization', *The Annals of Regional Science*, 35: 3–37.

Fujita, M., Krugman, P. and Venables, A. J. (1999) *The Spatial Economy*. Cambridge, MA: MIT Press.

Henderson, J. V. (2000) 'The effects of urban concentration on economic growth', NBER, Cambridge: MA, Working Paper No. 7503.

—— (2002) 'Urbanization in developing countries', The World Bank Research Observer, 17: 89–112.

Kojima, R. (1995) 'Urbanization in China', *The Developing Economies*, 33: 121–154.

Krugman, P. (1991) *Geography and Trade*. Cambridge, MA: MIT Press.

Krugman, P. and Livas, E. R. (1996) 'Trade policy and the third world metropolis', *Journal of Development Economics*, 49: 137–150.

Lee, Y. S. F. (1989) 'Small towns and China's urbanization level', *China Quarterly*, 120: 771–786.

National Bureau of Statistics (NBS) (1981) *Zhongguo Tongji Nianjian 1981* (China Statistical Yearbook 1981), Beijing: China Statistics Press.

—— (1999a) *Zhongguo Tongji Nianjian 1999* (China Statistical Yearbook 1999), Beijing: China Statistics Press.

—— (1999b) *Xin zhong guo cheng shi wu shi nian* (Fifty years of new Chinese cities), Beijing: China Statistics Press.

—— (1999c) *Comprehensive Statistical Data and Materials on 50 Years of New China*, Beijing: China Statistics Press.

—— (2001) *Zhongguo Tongji Nianjian 2001* (China Statistical Yearbook 2001), Beijing: China Statistics Press.

Organisation for Economic Co-operation and Development (OECD) (2002) *China in the World Economy*, Paris: OECD.

White, H. (1980) 'A heteroskedasticity-consistent covariance matrix estimator and a direct test for heteroskedasticity', *Econometrica*, 48: 817–838.

Wu, F. and Ma, L. J. C. (2005) 'Transforming China's globalizing cities', *Habitat International* (in press).

Yusuf, S. and Wu, W. (1997) *The Dynamics of Urban Growth in Three Chinese Cities*. World Bank, Oxford: Oxford University Press.

Zhang, K. H. (2002) 'What explains China's rising urbanization in the reform era', *Urban Studies*, 39(12): 2301–2315.

Zhang, L. and Zhao, S. X. B. (1998) 'Re-examining China's urban concept and the level of urbanisation', *The China Quarterly*, 154: 330–381.

Zhu, Y. (1999) *New Paths to Urbanization in China: Seeking More Balanced Patterns*, New York: Nova Science Publications.

—— (2000) 'In situ urbanization in rural China: case studies from Fujian Province', *Development and Change*, 31: 413–434.

Part II
Globalizing large Chinese cities

4 Beijing as an 'internationalized metropolis'

Ian G. Cook

For modern China, the possibility of developing the major city such as Beijing and Shanghai into an 'internationalised metropolis' was one to be earnestly desired.[1] China was reckoned by its government to be under-urbanised in comparison to international norms, and cities were seen to be key locations in the process of economic development. Although I could have used such terms as 'global city', 'world city' or 'megalopolis' for this chapter, I have decided to stick with this concept of 'internationalised metropolis' because it reflects the Chinese official view of urbanisation. The chapter focuses on how far Beijing has realised the possibility of becoming an internationalised metropolis and what lessons can be learnt from this process of transformation.

The concept of an 'internationalised metropolis'

As noted, this concept is taken from Yan Mingfu's paper in 1995. Representative of the reformers in the Chinese Communist Party (CCP), Yan Mingfu notes that it was in 1978 that the 'Central Committee of the Communist Party of China passed the Resolution to Reform the Economic Structure of China. For the first time, the leading role cities play in our socialist modernization was approved' (p. 3). Prior to this Resolution, under Mao, cities faced variable fortunes depending on the vagaries of policy at the time. Cities were seen primarily as production centres with their pre-revolutionary consumption focus severely curtailed, and although it is now recognised that policies were not anti-urban as was once thought by Western urbanists, cities were nonetheless constrained in the 1960s and 1970s especially by strict controls on rural–urban migration. Industrialisation was the prime concern of CCP policy makers during the Maoist period, and urban costs were minimised. The passing of this Resolution, however, promoted an urbanisation strategy based, on the one hand, on the 'centralizing function of cities' and, on the other hand, upon 'an open network of economic zones on various scales...supported by cities' (ibid.). As is now well known, four Special Economic Zones (SEZs) were set up in South China in 1980 and 14 coastal cities were opened up to foreign investors in 1984, while at the local level development zones proliferated especially in Guangdong province and neighbouring Hong Kong. Urbanisation became rapid, especially in China's 'Gold Coast' region along the eastern seaboard, and increased to 26.4 per cent in 1990 compared to 19 per cent in 1980.

But this speed of urbanisation was still insufficient according to Yan Mingfu, who states:

> The increase [to 26.4 per cent] was a little higher than half of the average level of urbanization in the world at the time. This indicates that the level of our urbanization failed to keep up with the national economic development. In this sense, we can say that the development of our urbanization in the near future will be a very tough job.
>
> (Ibid.: 4)

In order to tackle this 'very tough job', he notes that China needed to develop the following fourfold policy: (1) Formulate a rational policy for the development of cities to promote a coordinated development of small, medium-sized and large cities; (2) Build international metropolises and promote the development of China's export-oriented economy; (3) Pay attention to the spatial layout of cities and promote the development of urban clusters and cities in the western parts of China; (4) Pay attention to enhancing the overall quality of the established cities in China. The combination of these policies would ensure a balanced urban and regional structure across China, one fit for the twenty-first century.

For the purpose of this chapter, it is the second of these that concerns me. These international metropolises underpin the rise of China's booming export economy by functioning

> like bridges and bases for a country to take part in worldwide economic activities. They play a pivotal role in connecting domestic economy to international economic affairs and they are absolutely indispensable for a country to raise its capacity and level of participating in international competitions [*sic*].
>
> (Ibid.: 6)

These points illustrate a clear understanding among key decision-takers in China of the role of the city in contemporary globalisation. After identifying the four cities of Shanghai, Beijing, Guangzhou and Tianjin as having the potential to reach this level, Yan Mingfu continues

> [t]hese cities ought to take the opportunity to gradually perfect their international functions as internationalized metropolises, and to build an infrastructure and a service system that have reached the first-class international level so that their regional development will be brought into the greater circulation of the world economy. The formation and development of internationalized metropolises are an advanced stage of urbanization. And they are the practical necessity and the only way to carry out our policy of opening to the world. Therefore, we should attach sufficient importance to the development of internationalized metropolises.
>
> (Ibid.)

Note some of the key points in this statement: the role of 'international functions' reaching the first-class international level in infrastructure and the 'service system' so that their 'regional development will be brought into the greater circulation of the world economy'. The aim is to reach the highest global level and to interact fully with the global economy. I shall return to such points later, but will now turn to Beijing itself, a city that I have had the good fortune to research regularly via an annual field course with my students, since 1992, coupled with several additional research visits. The city has witnessed dramatic change in that period, but before addressing these it is pertinent to provide a contextual background to an understanding of the city via consideration of its development over time. The global context is important, but so too is the local situation with which globalisation interweaves.

The local context of change: Beijing's development trajectory

Beijing (northern capital, *'bei'* = north; *'jing'* = capital) occupies a historically strategic position at the northern apex of the North China Plain vis-à-vis Mongolia to the north-west, Manchuria to the north-east and China itself to the south. It was conquered many times in its history. The city has had many names during its past and at one time was called 'Nanjing' (southern Capital)! This was during the period when the northern people – the Liao or Khitan ruled the area from AD 916 to 1125 – and reminds us that location is a relative concept not an absolute one. The more important names from the past include Dadu (meaning Great Capital), which was known in the West mainly via the writings of Marco Polo as 'Canbaluc' (Khanbaliq or Khambaluk, home of the Great Khan) the names given to the city when the Mongol conquest led to Kublai Khan founding the Yuan dynasty in 1271 and making Beijing his capital. The city during this period was focused on the Imperial Palace built where Beihai Park is now, near to the Ming Forbidden City that replaced it. The Imperial Palace took 26 years to build and had a hall that according to Polo could seat 6,000 people.

It was during this period that Beijing became arguably the greatest city in the world (though Hangzhou further south is another top contender) and was to remain so for centuries. The city, for example, was the focus of the reopened Silk Road along which the goods of Asia and Europe were transported while the capital was also linked (in 1293) to the Grand Canal which ran down to the Yangtze and beyond, facilitating the import of rice and other foodstuffs to feed the urban population which grew to 500,000 inhabitants at this time. The current concern with globalisation in its many facets, while understandable, can lead to an overlooking of such long-distance linkages in the past. The time taken to traverse such distance was of course much greater than today, but it was nonetheless possible to have social and economic intercourse across the vast swathes of Asia even though few travellers actually crossed the whole extent from Asia to Europe. Peter Taylor in his recent book (2004) draws attention to Abu-Lughod's earlier work on 'a transcontinental archipelago of cities' based on overlapping regional city networks rather than a single network due to the vast travel time involved during this era. Peking occupies an important place in this 'archipelago' during the thirteenth and fourteenth centuries, and is part of 'a glimpse of a worldwide configuration of inter-city relations that presages the contemporary world city network' (Taylor 2004: 9).

The Mongol invaders were eventually overthrown by the indigenous Chinese and the Ming dynasty was established in 1368. At first, the capital was moved to the Yangtze region and the 'real' Nanjing was established. Beijing received its other great name of '*Beiping*' (often Peiping to Westerners via the Wade–Giles system of transliteration) meaning 'Northern Peace', a name that it has retained off-and-on through the centuries. The Ming Emperor, Yongle, moved the capital back to Beijing (named as such) in 1403 and the new Imperial Palace (the Forbidden City) was built during this era, from 1406 to 1420, according to the rules and regulations of Chinese cosmology with the importance of the north–south axis and the square layout representing the earth as a whole. The ornate and beautiful Temple of Heaven (with the Hall of Prayer for Good Harvests round to represent Heaven which was conceived as being round) was also built during this era as were many of the historical structures in and around the city, including the Great Wall that was renewed and the Ming Tombs for the Emperors.

For many, the Ming dynasty represents a 'Golden Age' when art and civilisation flourished, and it has left many fine monuments for the contemporary tourist visiting the city. However, the dynasty eventually became too introverted and corrupt and was overthrown by a peasant revolt with Beijing falling in 1644 only to be conquered by the Manchus 43 days later. The Manchus established the Qing dynasty but retained the Imperial Palace and the basic layout established by the Ming. The city grew further to a population of 700,000 around 1800 and the city was extended (because of the historic concept of city walls population pressures periodically forced urban authorities to either build beyond the walls or to rebuild the walls over a larger area). The Jesuits played a minor, albeit important, role during this epoch and a Catholic cathedral and other buildings owe their origin to Jesuit influence. The nineteenth century brought a less positive contact with the West, and Beijing was attacked by Western troops during the Second Opium War leading to much destruction and pillaging of the old Summer Palace. Further humiliation and destruction followed during the 'Boxer' Rebellion in 1900 when many Chinese were killed and more of the city destroyed by Western troops who relieved the siege of the foreign embassies by the Boxers. In many ways, the globalisation of the modern era can be said to be presaged in these nineteenth-century incursions by foreign powers; China would find it more and more difficult to isolate itself from the changes taking place at the global level.

The twentieth century brought further hardship to the people of Beijing. The overthrow of the Qing dynasty allowed them to cut off their pigtails but heralded an unstable period that lasted for decades until the triumph of the Communists in 1949. Notable events in the first half of this century include the May 4 Movement of 1919 when 300,000 students, intellectuals and others protested against the proposals of the Treaty of Versailles to give previously German concessions – like

Qingdao for example – to Japan, and this proposal stimulated the development of the CCP. Then in 1928 the rickshaw pullers undertook street protests against the new trams that threatened their livelihood while in 1935 there were massive anti-Japanese demonstrations in protest against their take-over of Manchuria. The Japanese invaded the city in 1937 on a pretext after an incident on the Marco Polo Bridge south-west of the city centre and controlled Beijing until 1945. After a brief interregnum under the Guomindang, the Communists took the city peacefully on 31 January 1949 and the People's Republic of China (PRC) was formally pro-claimed in front of the Gate of Heavenly Peace (Tiananmen) on 1 October 1949. A new era had begun in Beijing's vibrant history.

The modern era has brought dramatic change to Beijing. But, as the above brief sketch taken mainly from my annual field course guide indicates dramatic change has taken place before. During the Ming and Qing dynasties, the city asserted its dominant role within China, but its internationalism was reduced as barriers were erected to the outside world. The humiliations of the Western encroachments during the nineteenth and early twentieth centuries coupled with those of the Japanese in the twentieth century were symptomatic of a weakened China vulnerable to the military might of the international community. Small wonder then that Mao stated at the founding of the new PRC, 'China has stood up, it will never be humiliated again'. The Maoist era lasted with variations of policy and direction until his death in 1976 and following a brief power struggle with the 'Gang of Four' the Dengist era began in 1978 and ushered in the 'Four Modernisations' and the related 'Open Door' Policy. Since Deng's death in 1997, his policies have been continued first under Jiang Zemin and more recently under Hu Jintao. A new Beijing has arisen, but there are sharp contrasts between the outcomes of the Maoist and Dengist periods with contrasting echoes from the past in terms of the levels of closure and openness respectively to the outside world.

Under Mao, the most dramatic visible changes to the city came in the 1950s. The first draft of the Master Plan for Beijing was produced in 1952, according to Gan (1990). Soviet-style planning led to the establishment of Tiananmen Square and the building of new buildings around it, such as the Great Hall of the People one of the great buildings completed for the 10th anniversary of the PRC in 1959 (Zhou 1984). This acted as a major counterpoint to the Forbidden City and reinforced the power of the CCP, a power comparable to that of the old Imperial dynasties. The old city walls and imposing gates were mainly destroyed (the venerable Chinese geographer Hou Renzhi was reputed to have wept when this was done) and the city expanded in area and population. Its population of 1.2 million in 1949 within the old boundaries was probably 4.14 million within its expanded boundaries, including 1.76 million urban population, according to Dong Liming (1985). The 1950s and 1960s, therefore, saw much house building with high-rise or mid-rise flats replacing the old low-level *hutongs* (alleys) of the traditional city. These flats tended not to have hot water supplied nor (often) central heating. Victor Sit's (1995) chapter on Urban Housing in his 1995 book gives further details. Today, the population of Beijing municipality is officially 14 million, including 7 million in the narrower urban area excluding the surrounding sub-urban districts (there are great problems interpreting Chinese urban data because the definition of the city changed in 1984 and now usually includes the surrounding agricultural area whereas before it did not; see Chan 1994 for further details). The population has grown markedly, whichever data set is employed, and reflects much immigration to this major focal point in Chinese society.

The Maoist era ushered in an emphasis on industrial development, on heavy industry in particular, as the change was made away from the increasing consumption emphasis of the Western city towards the Socialist production city. Thus, there were 20 steel mills within the inner city, for example, as well as petro-chemical works and other noxious industries. In the outer areas the Shijingshan Iron and Steel Works (also known as Shougang or the Capital Iron and Steel Works), begun in 1920, was considerably expanded in 1958 to include a blast furnace, a steelworks, an electric furnace and other features. Until recently, it was still a major steel works, but more on this later. Dong (1985), Gan (1990) and others discuss some of the issues arising from such industrialisation and the debate over the appropriate direction for Beijing to take. The Maoist emphasis on production followed by the Great Proletarian Cultural Revolution from 1966, in which huge Red Guard rallies were held in Tiananmen, led to Beijing becoming a rather austere city which received relatively few visitors except those with socialist credentials, businessmen and/or foreign diplomats. Writing in the 1970s, Felix Greene (1978: 9) noted that only four of the city's 187 hotels were set aside for foreigners, and so,

> Peking [*sic*] is not a cosmopolitan city. There are times, quite probably, when more visitors arrive in New York or London in a week than arrive in Peking in the course of a whole year. This makes one all the more aware of the differences between the people of Peking and the visitors from elsewhere.

Greene's description of this period and his accompanying photographs make a fascinating contrast with the Beijing that I have come to know since 1992. The adults in his photos invariably wear versions of the blue Maoist uniform, although the children are brightly dressed. The factories he describes as being run by worker's committees. There is a lack of conspicuous consumption in the street scenes, with no privately owned cars, and the Beijing of that time is a far quieter and simpler city in which hard work and toil predominates. There was little nightlife, a dearth of streetlights and few people were out after 9 o'clock at night. Even in 1992 this situation still predominated, unlike today. Entertainment became focused around 'the language of the masses', and dry revolutionary productions in the fields of opera, drama and film, but

> [i]n the early 1970s, however, the Chinese themselves were beginning to complain of the lack of variety. In 1973 Premier Chou En-lai said he had received many complaints and he urged an increase in the number of productions staged. On the stage and in films there was little to see except 'model'

revolutionary dramas with their heroic poses and exaggerated language, and there was little characterization in depth. As I write (1978), it appears that fetters are being broken. Films that had been withdrawn are now being released again; artists, writers and dramatists who were ignored or silenced are again being given recognition. With this new freedom I believe we shall see a new and exciting flowering of all cultural activities in China.

(Ibid.: 129)

During this era, as these brief descriptions suggest, there was little of the global within the city. Beijing was very much a Chinese Communist city markedly different from other large cities in different parts of the world. There was, for example, a strict *hukou* registration system that limited immigration to Chinese cities, including Beijing. In material terms, the average family would aspire to own a watch, a radio and a bicycle, and there were few 'white goods' available, unless one was well connected within the CCP or a member of staff of an embassy, for example. Mao died in 1976, and the contemporary era is dominated by the quite different policies of Deng Xiaoping and his successors. The new Master Plan for Beijing was proposed and approved in 1978 (Gan 1990). Beijing became an 'Open City' benefiting from Deng's 'Open Door' policy, and the urban population has now exchanged its blue uniforms for the suits, leather jackets and bright dresses of the modern world. The debate concerning industrialisation still continues, however, and there are inherent tensions between industrial growth and the demands of a modern (post-modern?) capital city. For example, Shougang was remodelled and updated as recently as the early 1990s but is now being gradually removed from the city. Similarly, the petrochemical works at Fangshan was developed at a high cost even though this is a highly congested site in the uplands to the south-west of Beijing and lies within an area of high tourist potential.

The Chinese State played a key role in changing the climate for foreign investment gradually introducing a series of measures in the 1980s that ensured a corresponding increase in overseas investment. By 1990 alone local sources suggested that there were already 430 joint ventures with a total investment of US 1,105 million dollars, mainly in the outer areas, exports had reached US 1.32 billion dollars, 3.6 times that of 1978, and included machinery and equipment, textiles, arts and handicrafts, silk, carpets and medical and health instruments, while on the demographic side the benefits of the reform period ensured that average life-span of the population had reached 72.47 years. Tiananmen temporarily dented this period of prosperity, but following Deng Xiaoping's famous southern tour in 1992 full encouragement was once again given to opening up to the outside world.

Today, within the inner area of the city, largely as a result of the growing pressures of globalisation, the built environment is being transformed due to the rapid speed of construction of new hotels for the tourist market, new retail establishments (including one by Yaoshan, a Japanese company, Sun Dong An Plaza and Oriental Plaza run by Hong Kong developers), new road infrastructure and other features of a modern urban area. It is estimated that Beijing now contains 3 million or more floating population which has flocked into the city as the relaxation of the *hukou* restrictions combined with the immense changes in the rural areas of China (freeing up male labour especially) have led to a huge surplus in rural population (further details are in Cook and Murray 2001 or Zhang 2003, for example). The city has now changed markedly, and the last decade or so has been a period in which the pace of change has been most marked. I shall now turn to the evidence for Beijing having become an internationalised metropolis.

Beijing as an internationalised metropolis

What makes an internationalised metropolis? As Yan Mingfu noted earlier, infra-structure and service provision must reach the first-class international level. We shall be searching, therefore, for evidence that such facilities in Beijing are com-parable with the best around the world. The Beijing area must also have been 'brought into the greater circulation of the world economy'. In other words, Beijing must clearly have been brought into the 'space of flows' at the global level, in which capital information and ideas for instance flow into and out of, and interact within, the global city (Presas 2004). Beijing must be seen to be fully interlocked with global-level networks of different types if it is to be viewed as an internationalised metropolis. There are further clues to explore from the literature on World Cities, Global Cities and a recent article on 'World cities or great cities' by Ng and Hills (2003) which me and my colleagues have found to be so intrigu-ing that we have designed an undergraduate module with this focus. As the latter note, it was Peter Hall (now Sir Peter Hall) who first presented the concept of 'World City' in 1966. Cities, such as New York, London, Paris or Moscow, were major centres of political power, trade, finance, the arts and education among other features. Friedmann explored the concept further in the 1980s, noting such features as the spatial hierarchy of world cities, measurement of the level of a world city via the number of TNC HQs (Transnational Company Headquarters) or representative offices, and the role of global capital in their development. Later work by other authors such as Sassens or Castells has tended to deal more with the polarisation effect of globalisation in which on the one hand global cities are key centres for the circulation and propagation of capital by and for the rich while simultaneously acting as magnets for the poor to service the needs of the rich.

In China, large cities seem to be especially important in globalisation (e.g. Zhao and Chan (2003) and contributors to this volume). Despite great expansion in China's wealth in recent decades as a whole the country still remains a Third World Country; therefore the spatial concentration of resources within China's large cities by the Chinese State makes sense in terms of enabling a process of catching up of these cities to the global system of capital flow. There is also a major cost to this process, however. Not only are many left behind in more remote regions, as wealth concentrates spatially, but these cities themselves have a huge ecological impact, and I myself have referred to the 'concretisation of the earth' and 'ecological trampling' of China's large cities as well as summarising some of their key features (Cook 2000, Cook and Murray 2001, Murray and Cook 2002). I shall consider some of these costs of globalisation in the final section.

Beijing benefits from being the capital city of the largest nation on earth, one that has awakened from its deep slumber to attain remarkable economic success. As a centre for China's huge bureaucracy, the city has access to a sophisticated labour force of considerable wealth as Table 4.1 indicates. This official data, from the *China Statistical Yearbook*, shows that in 2001 the city's GDP was outstripped only by Shanghai while it came first in local government revenue, savings deposits, number of 'fully employed persons' and total wages. In terms of industrial output value, although the municipal authorities have been modifying the employment structure towards the tertiary and quaternary sectors, Beijing still produced more than Guangzhou albeit less than nearby Tianjin to which it is so closely linked. Nonetheless, it was the tertiary sector that contributed nearly 60 per cent of GDP by 2000 and in the decade of the 1990s produced 500,000 new jobs to become a key element in the urban economy (Huang 2003).

As regards human resources, Pannell (2002) has recently noted the focus on 'advancing knowledge-based technologies through the creative use of highly skilled human capital', and there is much investment to ensure a top-quality R&D base. Bill Gates, for example, has not invested heavily only in the United States or United Kingdom; in 1998 he announced plans to invest billions of dollars to set up a Microsoft China Research Institute in Beijing. Other major players in Beijing include Intel, who in 1999 announced that it would create its third wireless R&D centre in the capital and Nokia who also have an R&D centre (He 2003). By 2002, total utilised Foreign Direct Investment (FDI) in Beijing was just over US 5 billion dollars, compared to US 4 billion dollars in 2001. Zhongguancun Science and Technology Park (see Figure 4.1) is now known as 'China's Silicon Valley' and is in the forefront of the drive to make Beijing an IT, e-government and e-business city (Li 2003). Zhou and Tong (2003) have analysed the growth of this high-tech cluster. Their summary table details 19 Multinational Companies (MNCs) operating in Beijing, 10 of which were established in the 1980s, 8 in the 1990s and 1 (Oracle) in the 2000s. Since 1994, 14 of these companies have moved to establish R&D centres. A major attraction to outside investors is not just the brainpower of Chinese engineers; it is estimated that they cost one-tenth of their equivalent in California's Silicon Valley. Although the MNCs operate at the high end of technology they benefit from the synergies created with the Chinese companies operating at the lower end dealing with such companies and gaining from the brain drain of expertise from them. 'On the other hand, MNCs depend on local firms for marketing and servicing their products and thus have transferred considerable technical and management expertise to local firms' (ibid.:149). This ensures a win–win situation with benefits for each side from this dialectical relationship.

Zhao (2003) has analysed the location of foreign firms in China and Hong Kong, including their Pacific-Asia regional headquarters. Although Hong Kong retained a major role in this, within China Beijing had the largest share both of

Table 4.1 Economic comparison of large Chinese cities, 2001

City	Hukou population	GDP (billion yuan)	Industrial output value (billion yuan)	Local government revenue (billion yuan)	Total investment in fixed assets (billion yuan)	Savings deposits (billion yuan)	Fully employed staff and workers	Total wages (billion yuan)
Beijing	11,223,000	284.6	290.9	45.4	141.7	353.6	4,058,000	77.8
Tianjin	9,139,800	184	294	16.3	62.2	128.5	1,864,200	26.7
Shanghai	13,271,400	495	700.4	62	199.4	300.2	2,980,500	65.0
Wuhan	7,582,300	134.8	102	8.6	48.6	80.2	1,371,200	15.5
Guangzhou	7,126,000	268.6	283	24.6	97.8	260	1,678,700	38.2
Chongqing	30,979,100	175	107.2	12.6	65.7	131.7	2,038,700	19.4
Chengdu	10,199,000	149.2	70.8	7.8	53	99.6	1,186,700	14.8

Source: State Statistical Bureau, 2002.

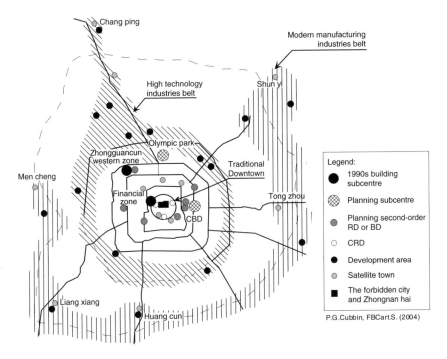

Figure 4.1 The urban structure of Beijing in the 1990s.

Source: Adapted from Huang Shizheng, 2003.

Notes
RD: Retail District, BD: Business District, CRD: Central Retail District.

foreign companies and also of their headquarters. Out of 6,238 foreign companies operating in China by mid-2000, Beijing had 2,738 or 44 per cent compared to Shanghai's 1,541 or 25 per cent (Zhao 2003: 549). Even more so, out of those 2,498 that had regional headquarters in China, a massive 1,429 or 57 per cent were in Beijing (compared to 773, 31 per cent, in Shanghai). Zhao's (2003: 555) further analysis of *Fortune 500* company headquarter location leads him to contend that 'Beijing will present a potential threat to Hong Kong as the chief financial centre for the country, even for the Pacific-Asia region'. This confirms Taylor's (2004) analysis of 'global network connectivity' with Beijing being ranked 22nd globally on 'bank network connectivity' and the city is also ranked first as a top level gateway to emerging markets. This case is due in large part to the nature of China's governance, which with its level of secrecy and lack of transparency has 'exacerbated the role of asymmetric information' (Zhao 2003: 568) and thus made it essential for businesses to be located near Beijing's policy-making units. This confirms the role of the Chinese State in Beijing's opening up. Even Zhongguancun with its high level of entrepreneurialism could not have grown without the tacit or explicit support of the State apparatus (Zhou and Tong 2003).

But globalisation is not just about connecting with the global flows of capital; it is also about connecting to the global population itself via imagery and place marketing. Thus in a different vein there are the world heritage sites of the Great Wall and the Forbidden City (see Gaubatz 1995) that attract tourists from around the globe, not just China. Traditionally, the Chinese say that 'you can't be a Great Man (sometimes suitably amended in recent years to "Great Person") until you visit the Great Wall', and this is a tourist location of truly global significance. The wall itself runs for some 3,946 miles from east to west (although barely two-third remain visible and one-third walkable) and building was begun 2,500 years ago. Initially fragmented, it was under Qin Shi Huang Di's reign as emperor more than 2,000 years ago that the wall was unified. But it was a Ming emperor, Taizu, who was the last, until recently, to have any notable work carried out on the wall when in the fifteenth century he ordered it to be strengthened by using bricks (previous to this it had been made mainly of earth). This was because it was proving too easy for the Mongols to tackle.

Most tourists visit Badaling, about 30 miles north-west of Beijing, where the Pakistan government funded the restoration of the Wall. Here there is a stone archway that carries inscriptions from many of China's ethnic communities. The wall here is 8 metres high and 7 metres wide (wide enough for seven horses to walk abreast). The experience is unforgettable, and although it may not make one a 'Great Person' to climb it, it certainly provides an unrivalled experience. Elsewhere on the Wall, however, there are growing concerns about the state of the 'Wild Wall' due to erosion and general environmental degradation. Local people often, for instance, remove stones from the wall as in many other countries where crumbling ruins such as Hadrian's Wall are 'recycled', for house building and other uses. This practice is unfortunate to say the least; there again it was probably the ancestors of local people who carried many of these stones up the hillside in the first place or chiselled them out of the mountainsides.

The Forbidden City is one of Beijing's most famous sites popularised globally through the film *The Last Emperor* and now including a Starbucks to add to the signs sponsored by American Express. It was said to have had 9,999 rooms (although only about 9,000 are now said to remain!), when it was built between 1406 and 1420 to serve as the residence of the emperors of the Ming (and later the Qing) dynasties. The city consists of the Outer Palace where the emperor attended state affairs in the three main halls of Supreme, Middle and Preserving Harmony which lie symmetrically on the North–South axis down the centre path of which only the emperor was allowed to walk, and the Inner Court which contained the residences of the emperor and his family. The Inner Court is centred on the Palace of Heavenly Purity or Qianqing Palace, Jiaotai Hall and Kunning Palace with the Imperial Garden lying directly behind it. The east section of the inner court is of particular interest as it consists of halls featuring different exhibitions. Although most of my Geography students rarely enjoy this site to the same extent as the Great Wall those with a greater sense of China's history and culture are rightly impressed with this world-class monument. Others note the problems of upkeep and maintenance of such a huge site.

But it would be wrong to imply that Beijing was all about either the might of China or the heritage of the past, important though this may be. Each of my regular visits from 1992, coincident with the designation of Beijing as one of those 6 cities (and 5 SEZs) which could encourage limited FDI (Wang and Jones 2002), shows me new construction of hotels, retail plazas, commercial centres, ring roads or subways. The city, to me, has never seemed to be quite as fast as Shanghai, in turn not as fast as Hong Kong, but the pace has quickened markedly as internationalisation via the combined effect of FDI and the policies of the Chinese State itself (Cook and Wang 1998) impacts upon the city. Already by the time of my first visit in 1992, the Lufthansa Centre in north-east Beijing and the World Trade Centre on Jianguomengwai Dajie offered first-rate global-reach facilities. In the mid–late 1990s, it was Sun Dong An plaza that exemplified the changes in Wangfujing, then came the even more massive Oriental Plaza at the junction with Chang'an. There was the new subway line, East–West along the main axis of Chang'an, and then in 2003 there was the new loop line running in a vast semicircle to the north of the city. During the preparations for the 50th Anniversary of the PRC in 1999 there were estimated to be 5,000 construction sites across the city, and I regularly experienced having to think quickly on my feet as my urban trail of the previous year was faced by a massive new set of buildings across our path.

Today, Oriental Plaza is the largest shopping centre in Asia (see www. orientalplaza.com). It also contains eight world class Grade A Office Towers and a Five-Star Grand Hyatt Hotel. Funded by the Hong Kong billionaire Li Ka-Shing, the complex contains 100,000 square metres of retail space within five shopping malls in one of the potentially most desirable retail locations on earth. I say 'potentially', for China still remains a country with many millions of poor people to balance out its growing middle class, and China has just admitted that poverty is once again on the increase after decades of poverty reduction (Watts 2004). McDonalds was ejected from its prime site on the corner of Wanfujing and Changan so that this mega-complex could be built (they are still there, a few hundred yards up Wangfujing as well as being dotted liberally around the city). The shops are comparable with top retail locations worldwide in terms of their quality, brand name appeal and high prices. Noted for their thrift and parsimony, with savings rates well above average for urban residents in China, there was growing evidence in the late 1990s from a number of surveys of Beijingers being more and more willing to increase their consumption levels, to spend today rather than to save for tomorrow. My own experience tends to support this view (but see a caveat later), with increased level of high-tech goods in the shops, for example, including DVDs, mobile phones, widescreen TVs, digital cameras and the like at the same high prices as in the West. Car ownership is increasing fast to 2.2 million at the latest count, a level not expected to be reached until 2010; there are increasing number of private housing estates in and around the city, especially in the north where houses sell for 1, 2 or 3 million yuan; while a new area of consumer investment is private education for the (usually only one) child.

Apart from consumption, other aspects of social change include the rise of the 'Little Emperors' as a result of China's population policy and the increasing worries over obesity (the first 'fat camp' opened in Beijing in 1994) and nutrition levels as more Chinese switch to a high fat, Westernised diet. With Trevor Dummer, I have reviewed such health issues across China generally (Cook and Dummer 2004), while Peng *et al.* (2002) show the links between health and air quality. By 2002, one-fifth of Beijing's children were reckoned to be overweight, a rate that had increased by 5 per cent per annum since 1995. By 2004, 27 per cent of children under 15 and 20 per cent of adults were overweight (Lan 2004). Adults are becoming prone to health problems such as obesity, diabetes and hypertension, as sedentary lifestyles and over-consumption of fatty foods increase. Stress levels in the city can be high, and there are also mental health concerns as the stress of modern urban life can prove too much for some. Divorce rates are on the increase, and increasingly it is women who are instigating divorce (more than 70 per cent by the late 1990s) usually because the husband has had an affair (Cook and Murray 2001: 165). These and other aspects of social change are familiar enough to us in the West and provide further evidence of inter-nationalisation at work.

So too does the growing underclass in the city. In Beijing, it is the 'floating population' (*liudong renkou*) who provide the services that in the cities of Japan, the United States or Europe would be provided by immigrants from overseas, legal or otherwise. Often living in 'villages' with their fellows from their home province, town or city (Gu and Kesteloot 1997, Ma and Xiang 1998), these peo-ple are those who only have access to low paid 3D jobs – Difficult, Demanding and Dangerous (Shen 2002). If you see one of the many construction sites, chances are that the workers will be from this floating population. If a taxi-driver seems to be uncertain about your destination, the likelihood is not that he (usually he) is trying to rip you off, it is more likely that he is a recent migrant who only knows a particular part of the city, the Beijingers themselves having moved on from this arduous occupation. Similarly, a few years ago when 'Silk Alley' off Jianguomenwai was under threat of closure it turned out that the original stall holders, Beijingers, had largely moved on to better things. Fortunately, for those who wish to experience this unique type of retail therapy, Silk Alley was reprieved but it was easier for the authorities to exert pressure because the Beijingers them-selves had vacated this tourist location. Now, in 2004, it seems that Silk Alley will definitely be closed soon, as the wrecking ball demolishes the buildings next door and developers eye greedily this prime site along the road from the China World Trade Centre.

Strengthening internationalisation: the Beijing Olympics

The successful bid for the Olympics of 2008 will further boost the international recognition that China's rulers crave, and a bid for the World Cup of 2010 is also under way. More than any other event, the Olympics will finally make Beijing a truly international metropolis. It will obliterate the stain of Tiananmen from the historical record and propel Beijing into the top rank of metropolises. At least that's the plan. The PRC is making a huge investment, estimated to be approximately US 34 billion dollars at the latest count, to ensure that the world's eye is turned on an attractive city fit to stand with the best. The first step was to ensure that the bid was won. This Beijing had singularly failed to do when it bid for the 2000 Olympics. At that time in the early 1990s, the time was too close to the Tiananmen deaths of 1989 and the issue of Human Rights stymied the bid, even though the city had already hosted the Asian Games. I was in Shanghai in 2001 when the successful bid for 2008 was announced, and even there the jubilation was evident. I had also been with my students in Beijing soon after the final visit of the Olympic Panel to assess the bid, near the Spring Festival of 2001. We found out that the authorities had pulled out all the stops to ensure success, including such steps as introducing a range of environmental measures over the previous year to reduce pollution levels, forcing Shougang to close for the visit, switching the visit from the rather dowdy Sports Museum at the Asian Games Village to the Millennium Park, ensuring that the city was particularly spruce and, allegedly, painting the grass green in a few key locations (it was the end of winter)! We visited the Olympic exhibition in the Millennium Park, viewed the Olympic film, and were suitably impressed, predicting that Beijing would indeed win this bid.

The main theme of the Beijing Olympics is 'New Beijing: Great Olympics', and the goal is to host a 'Green Olympics', a 'Hi-Tech Olympics' and the 'People's Olympics' (www.beijing-olympic.org). The main Olympic village is being built to the north of the city, on a green site. The first plenary session of the Beijing Organizing Committee for the Games of the XXIX Olympiad (BOCOG) was held in January 2004. The outgoing Executive President Wang Qishan noted that the first phase of development, from 2002 to 2003, was now complete. This phase involved four elements: (1) Olympic venue conceptual design and construction; (2) launch of the marketing programme; (3) official emblem solicitation and (4) unveiling BOCOG's basic organizational building.

A range of venues are already under construction, and the aim is to complete these and another 11 stadia and gymnasia in the second phase from 2004 to 2006. This will leave the period from 2007 until the Games begin for test events and fine-tuning. The importance of the Games is shown by the fact that the new Executive President is Deng Pufang, winner of the UN Human Rights Prize in December 2003 for his work as President of the China Disabled Person's Federation. He is also the son of Deng Xiaoping, and was himself disabled in an incident during the Cultural Revolution.

A range of measures designed to tackle environmental issues are being introduced or increased. For example, air pollution a bugbear in many Chinese cities, including Beijing, is to be reduced and the greening of Beijing is to continue apace. But many problems remain. Table 4.2 shows pollution discharge for three key areas, waste water, SO_2 and dust for 2001 compared to the other three municipalities run directly through the State. For all three, Beijing's levels are less than that of Shanghai, but waste water is higher than that of Chongqing and Tianjin, and SO_2 levels are higher than that of Tianjin. The emission of dust level is less in Beijing

Table 4.2 Pollutant discharge, 2001

	Waste water (million tons)	Emission of SO_2 (tons)	Emission of dust (tons)
National total	23,023.40	3,811,833	2,178,736
Beijing	686.6	74,356	46,472
Tianjin	257.9	69,098	48,585
Shanghai	1,270.20	172,641	72,906
Chongqing	453	152,640	79,945

Source: State Statistical Bureau, 2002.

than the other three. Not that the authorities have been inactive; Table 4.3 shows that environmental investment already made is already greater than for these other cities by over 200 million yuan in total. Measures already taken in recent years include use of natural gas in new buses or in domestic heating (Yang 1997), reduction in use of low quality coal with high sulphur content, extensive tree-planting, development of high-tech solutions to reduce dust such as a film which can be sprayed on construction sites and is, apparently, better than water and the banning of trucks during the day in the downtown area. But problems remain as will be shown in the final section, and along with my students I do wonder whether air pollution will pose considerable respiratory problems for Olympic athletes.

Evaluation and lessons for the future

Ng and Hills (2003: 155) cited previously want cities to be 'Great' not just global, having the following attributes.

> An enlightened mode of governance with a reinvented government working in partnership with the private sector, civil society and the third sector; An active and creative member in developing innovative technology and economic activities to further sustainable global and local development; A place not just rich in economic capital but also great in nourishing human, social, cultural and environmental capital.

This article is a welcome addition to the literature helping to redress the current imbalance in which most authors focus on the economic dimension of world cities/global cities to the exclusion of social, political and environmental criteria.

The previous sections show impressive elements in Beijing's drive to be an internationalised metropolis, especially in the second of these points, developing innovative technology and economic activities. But key issues include concerns, for example, about the intrinsic quality of new developments. In their study of Beijing's retail structure, for example, Wang and Jones (2002) note that while in retailing the city has attracted overseas capital, it 'has not necessarily obtained state-of-the-art, retail-oriented information technology, merchandising techniques,

Table 4.3 Investment in anti-industrial pollution projects, 2001

	Number of projects under way				Investment completed				Projects completed
	Total	Waste water	Waste gas	Solid wastes	Total (million yuan)	Waste water (million yuan)	Waste gas (million yuan)	Solid wastes (million yuan)	
National total	11,640	4,705	5,406	559	17,452.80	7,292.1	6,579.4	1,869.7	10,277
Beijing	134	52	65	2	476.9	132.2	327.7	6.7	125
Tianjin	447	71	320	6	262.6	122.5	121.4	3.2	419
Shanghai	227	89	111	4	264.6	130.5	61.9	21.0	174
Chongqing	234	86	136	5	263.1	60.1	199.4	2.5	214

Source: State Statistical Bureau, 2002.

and management expertise'. In my own work and that with Geoff Murray (Cook 2000, Cook and Murray 2001, Murray and Cook 2002) I have explored a range of political, social, economic and environmental limitations on China's urban trajectory, including that for Beijing itself. For example, we quoted an official with the North Star Shopping Centre who complained that expansion has been hampered by credit facilities having 'bureaucratic procedures that forces applicants to undergo strict, time-consuming personal credit evaluations as well as unappealing interest rates'. In similar vein, concerns about reforms of SOEs (State Own Enterprises) and of medical and old-age insurance, for example, combine with traditional norms of thrift to introduce a note of caution among Beijingers to limit their personal expenditure.

Meanwhile, despite the serious efforts which are being made to tackle such environmental problems as air pollution, water shortage and the impact of dust storms caused by desertification to the west of the city, there is still much to do. Beijing on overcast days remains, in 2004, a seriously polluted city. The new loop line is a health hazard not in itself but because of the heavy pollution along its route, as I found for myself in March 2003 when my students and I had to cover our mouths to avoid inhaling the worst of the pollutants. In part, this is caused by the removal of polluting industries from the city centre proper to the north of the city, but is a reminder of how far pollution levels still have to fall. The city has celebrated an increasing number of blue-sky days in the last year or two, as a result of a plethora of policies, and afforestation and greening targets are high, but in 2002 for instance two of the annual dust storms still deposited 'more than 30 tons of choking sand/grit on local streets before high winds carried it east to South Korea' (*Business Beijing* 2003a) calling the desertification/afforestation programme into serious question. Further information about the wide range of environmental issues which Beijing specifically and China generally faces is given in *Green China* (Murray and Cook 2002), while a more introductory book is now available (Murray and Cook 2004). For Chinese cities, authors such as Davies (2000) or Gutikunda (2003) summarise some of the key pollution issues while Presas (2004) notes some of the environmental opportunities afforded by globalisation as well as the problems; for example, Transnational Companies such as IBM can introduce higher standards of environmental policy within their own offices, with potential innovation to Beijing itself.

Preservation and conservation of Beijing's heritage is another area of concern (Lu 1997). In previous publications (see especially box 7:4 in Cook and Murray 2001: 171–172) I have drawn attention to the threat to Beijing's classic *hutong* areas. Hutongs were first formed 700 years ago in Dadu, the city's name during the Yuan dynasty, when they were 'Hong Tong' in local dialect, meaning 'water well' essential for building. Under the Ming, the number of hutongs soared, they increased further under the Qing and by the twentieth century there were 3,200 of these narrow lanes with their *siheyuan* (courtyard) compounds with houses around a quadrangle. Such areas do not fit the profile of an international metropolis; they are often overcrowded, with population densities that 'have grown to 580–600 persons per hectare, the number being 900–1,000 per hectare in the worst areas' (Wang 2003: 109). Difficult to access, they can be dilapidated and require renovation and they are difficult to control by the authorities. They are old-fashioned, in a word, and expensive to maintain. The city announced 25 sites (not just hutongs but also including historical monuments) increased to 30 in 2002 to be under special protection and has developed a project for 'systematic conservation of historical monuments in Beijing. However, substantial progress is yet to be made ... the whole project has become a subject for criticism' (ibid.: 107).

Wang (2003) provides clear guidelines for differentiation between historical monuments and the living environment of hutongs and siheyuan. There is no doubt that the former is easier for municipal authorities to deal with; the recent renovation of part of the Ming Wall near Beijing Railway Station is superb in quality. But the hutong issue is more intractable; demolition and resettlement is an easier option but poses different problems – the previous Mayor, Meng Xuenong noted that the municipality needs to solve 'the difficult problem of resettlement of families affected by the recent demolition of ramshackle housing, and to provide them with more affordable homes and low-rent apartments' (*Business Beijing* 2003b). The new Mayor, Wang Qishan, has been quoted as saying that the old town will continue to be pulled down to make way for the 2008 Olympics projects (*Beijing Weekend* 2004). One-and-a-half million people have been relocated during 1991–2003 and according to this brief report Wang admitted that some of these relocation projects violated the law. The debate about conservation versus development in Beijing has become fierce and will continue, as it does in many cities across the world. Gaubatz (1999) provides the example of Xiaohoucang hutong that I too have visited, as one that has been developed imaginatively and sensitively *in situ*, and there are other examples too but it is admittedly difficult to balance the needs of a modern internationalised metropolis with the dwellers of high density, low-level neighbourhoods that are relatively inaccessible for modern services, including car ownership.

Then there is the perennial question of governance and attitudes of outside investors, perhaps especially US investors, to China's one-party state with the question of human rights abuse looming large. China's governance is not always 'enlightened', to use Ng and Hill's (2003) terminology. Many investors just do not care about this question, but the shadow of Tiananmen still hangs to some extent over the city. In 2003, it was the dark shadow of SARS that reminded Beijingers and foreigners alike of the limitations of governance in a one-party system. The authorities did as they have done so frequently since the founding of the PRC: first deny that there is a problem; later admit that there is a problem but that it is minor; and then when the game is up go completely over the top sacking Beijing's Mayor and the Chinese Minister of Health, introducing a severe quarantine regime for staff and patients alike at Beijing's main hospitals and being accordingly subject to harsh criticism from the world's media, politicians and the World Health Organisation (WHO) for the abysmal way in which this crisis has been handled. Just as people like me and other critical yet sympathetic observers of China, and many Beijingers themselves, were beginning to think that governance perhaps really was improving, SARS re-emphasised that the CCP is not yet the self-reflective learning organisation that it needs to become if it wishes to remain central to the leadership of this vast country. But, to be fair, the new PRC regime of Hu Jintao and his new premier Wen Jiabao, at least apologised to an international SARS meeting in Malaysia for China's errors. This was an unprecedented step. Likewise, the crisis was handled quite well eventually, and Beijing among other Asian locations such as Hong Kong and Taiwan was withdrawn from the WHO crisis list. In 2004, at the time of writing it would seem that the Avian Flu outbreak that has affected many Asian countries is being handled better by China than was the SARS outbreak.

In all, China may well be in transition (Pannell 2002), but as far as urban China is concerned we must ask, transition to what? Beijing's transformation is dramatic and impressive. But where exactly is Beijing heading, and how far does it still have to go to become a truly international metropolis? The answer at the moment is, heading into the future with (possibly slightly shaken) confidence, and with a way to go to become a truly internationalised metropolis. Beijing governance does not always 'serve to enrich socioeconomic, human, cultural and environmental capital' (Ng and Hills 2003: 161). Internationalisation does not stop to allow laggards to catch up and the targets are always moving on so fast. Reviewing the Maoist era, a popular slogan in China is that Mao was 70 per cent good, 30 per cent bad. At first I was tempted to say that Beijing is currently (March 2004) 70 per cent internationalised, 30 per cent not. Many of the students on the field visit that had just ended voted for this option, but a few did not. As I consider more carefully this issue I am minded to say that Beijing is 65 per cent internationalised, 35 per cent not. China is progressing fast, so too is Beijing. By 2008, Beijing will hope to be 100 per cent internationalised when the Olympics are on. By then, I think that the city has a good chance of a 90 : 10 ratio, but 100 per cent is, probably, too high a target. Dust (major sandstorms hit the city again this year), water quality, health problems, poor driving standards (the 'Beijing weave' as I call it, in which cars weave on the outside or inside lane to seek best advantage), unsanitary conditions of public toilets, 'Chinglish' or nonsense translations of English, hierarchical governance and other constraints will mean that the 100 per cent target remains out of reach. But the Chinese State, Beijing's Municipal Government and Beijingers themselves are going to try extremely hard to prove that the city truly is becoming an internationalised metropolis.

Acknowledgement

Many people have helped me learn about Beijing over the years. Apologies to those I miss out for reasons of space or forgetfulness, but my colleagues and students on the field courses and Prof. David McEvoy, Geoff Murray, Dr Paul Hart, Paul White, Stuart Parkin, Profs Gu Chaolin, Ye Shunzan, Yan Chongchao, Cai Jiaoming and others have been particularly helpful over the years. Thanks also to Dr Trevor Dummer for useful comments on an earlier draft and to the three anonymous referees who also provided comments and suggestions.

Note

1 Thanks mainly to the good offices of Professor Gu Chaolin, now of the University of Nanjing. I was invited in 1995 to present a paper at China's First International Symposium on International Urbanisation in China held in one of the newly expanding cities of the Pearl River Delta, Shunde City. At this symposium, Yan Mingfu, then Vice-Minister and Head of Civil Affairs in China, presented a paper which, *inter alia*, noted that 'Shanghai, Beijing, Guangzhou and Tianjin all have the possibility to be developed into internationalized metropolises'. This paper represents an 'official' view of developing internationalised metropolises in China.

References

Beijing Weekend (2004) 'News items', 27–29 February, 2.
Business Beijing (2003a) 'Boost for Beijing – Tianjin Sandstorm Control Program', 10 February.
——(2003b) 'New mayor pledges help for low earners, jobless', 18 February.
Chan, K. W. (1994) *Cities with Invisible Walls: Reinterpreting Urbanization in Post-1949 China*, Oxford: Oxford University Press.
Cook, I. G. (2000) 'Pressures of development in China's cities and regions', in Cannon, T. (ed.) *China's Economic Growth: The Impact on Regions, Migration and the Environment*, London: Macmillan, 33–55.
Cook, I. G. and Dummer, T. (2004) 'Changing health in China: re-evaluating the epidemiological transition model', *Health Policy*, 67 (3): 329–343.
Cook, I. G. and Murray, G. (2001) *China's Third Revolution: Tensions in the Transition to Post-Communism*, London: Roultedge Curzon.
Cook, I. G. and Wang, Y. (1998) 'Foreign direct investment in China: Patterns, processes, prospects', in Cook, I. G., Doel, M. A. and Li, R. (eds) *Dynamic Asia: Business, Trade and Economic Development in Pacific Asia*, Aldershot: Ashgate.
Davies, B. L. (2000) 'Airborne particulate study in five cities of China', *Atmospheric Environment*, 34: 2703–2711.
Dong, L. M. (1985) 'Beijing: the development of a socialist capital', in Sit, V. F. S. (ed.) *Chinese Cities: The Growth of the Metropolis Since 1949*, Oxford: Oxford University Press.
Gan, G.-H. (1990) 'Perspective of urban land use in Beijing', *GeoJournal*, 20 (4): 359–364.
Gaubatz, P. R. (1995) 'Urban Transformation in Post-Mao China: Impacts of the reform era on China's urban form', in Davis, D. S., Kraus, R., Naughton, B., Perry, E. J. and Hamilton, L. H. (eds) *Urban Spaces in Contemporary China*, Washington, DC: Woodrow Wilson Centre Press.
——(1999) 'China's urban transformation: patterns and processes of morphological change in Beijing, Shanghai and Guangzhou', *Urban Studies*, 36 (9): 1495–1521.
Greene, F. (1978) *Peking*, London: Jonathan Cape.
Gu, C. and Kesteloot, C. (1997) 'Peasant immigrants and their concentration areas in Beijing', *Tijdschrift van de Belgische Vereniging voor Aardrijkskundige Studies*, 1: 107–119.
Gutikunda, S. K. (2003) 'The contribution of megacities to regional sulfur pollution in Asia', *Atmospheric Environment*, 37: 11–22.
He, X. Y. (2003) 'Multinationals reap benefits of R&D centers in China', *China International Business*, 183: 32–33.

http://www.beijing-2008.org/ (the official website for Beijing Olympics) (accessed 18 July 2003).

http://www.orientalplaza.com/en/ (the official website for Oriental plaza) (accessed 12 August 2003).

Huang, S. (2003) 'The sky is the limit: the economic globalization of Beijing', *IIAS Newsletter*, 7 July.

Lan, X. Z. (2004) 'Lazy lifestyle a weighty issue', *Beijing Review*, 12 February, 28–29.

Li, X. (2003) 'Tomorrow's world' ambition heralds IT utopia', *Business Beijing*, 79: 20–21.

Lu, J. H. (1997) 'Beijing's old and dilapidated housing renewal', *Cities*, 14 (2): 59–69.

Ma, L. J. C. and B. Xiang (1998) 'Native place, migration and the emergence of peasant enclaves in Beijing', *China Quarterly*, 155: 546–581.

Murray, G. and Cook, I. G. (2002) *Green China: Seeking Ecological Alternatives*, London: RoutledgeCurzon.

——(2004) *The Greening of China*, Beijing: Intercontinental Press (in English, French and Chinese).

Ng, M. K. and Hills, P. (2003) 'World cities or great cities? A comparative study of five Asian metropolises', *Cities*, 20 (3): 151–165.

Pannell, C. W. (2002) 'China's continuing urban transition', *Environment and Planning A*, 34: 1571–1589.

Peng, C., Wu, X., Liu, G., Johnson, T., Shah, J. and Guttikunda, S. (2002) 'Urban air quality and health in China', *Urban Studies*, 39 (12): 2283–2299.

Presas, L. M. S. (2004) 'Transnational urban spaces and urban environmental reforms: analyzing Beijing's environmental restructuring in the light of globalization', *Cities*, 21 (4): 321–328.

Shen, J. (2002) 'A study of the temporary population in Chinese cities', *Habitat International*, 26: 363–377.

Sit, V. F. S. (1995) *Beijing: The Nature and Planning of a Chinese Capital City*, London: Wiley.

State Statistic Bureau (2002) *China Statistical Yearbook 2002*, Beijing: China Statistics Press.

Taylor, P. J. (2004) *World City Network: A Global Urban Analysis*, London: Routledge.

Wang, S. (2003) 'Some insights in conservation of historic streets', *Social Sciences in China*, XXIV (1): 107–112.

Wang, S. and Jones, K. (2002) 'Retail structure of Beijing', *Environment and Planning A*, 34: 1785–1808.

Watts, J. (2004) 'China admits first rise in poverty since 1978', *Guardian*, 20 July, 11.

Yan, M. F. (1995) 'Modern civilization and China's urbanization toward the 21st century', Paper presented to the *Symposium on International Urbanization in China*, Shunde City, 28 August–1 September.

Yang, M. (1997) 'Compressed natural gas vehicles motoring towards a cleaner Beijing', *Applied Energy*, 36 (3–4): 395–405.

Zhang, M. (2003) *China's Poor Regions: Rural–Urban Migration, Poverty, Economic Reforms and Urbanisation*, London: RoutledgeCurzon.

Zhao, S. X. B. (2003) 'Spatial restructuring of financial centers in mainland China and Hong Kong: a geography of finance perspective', *Urban Affairs Review*, 38 (4): 535–571.

Zhao, S. X. B. and Chan, R. C. K. (2003) 'Globalization and the dominance of large cities in contemporary China', *Cities*, 20 (4): 265–278.

Zhou, S. (1984) *Beijing Old and New: A Historical Guide to Places of Interest*, Beijing: New World Press.

Zhou, Y. and Tong, X. (2003) 'An innovative region in China: interaction between multinational corporations and local firms in a high-tech cluster in Beijing', *Economic Geography*, 79 (2): 129–152.

5 Local and social change in a globalized city

The case of Hong Kong

Werner Breitung and Mark Günter

Background

The formation and growth of *global cities* (Sassen 1991, 1994, 2001) or *world cities* (Friedmann 1986, 1995), terms used synonymously for our purpose (compare Taylor 1997 for this), is triggered by global economic change. Friedmann, Sassen and others found that the world-wide networks of production, finance, trade, power and migration require nodal points providing the infrastructure, information and financial resources that make the networks work. Global cities are therefore mostly classified by economic criteria of which three categories can be distinguished,

- *institutions*: presence and size of stock exchanges, banks, international law firms and other producer service providers;
- *connectivity*: linkages to global networks, visitors, passenger flights, long distance calls, financial transactions and Internet usage;
- *power*: location of regional headquarters, decision-making within corporate command, and control chains and supranational institutions.

The global networks are viewed as a system of nodes and links with cities represented as the nodes and the flows and power relationships between them represented as the links (Castells 1996, Beaverstock *et al.* 2000, Sassen 2002). Nodes and links are strongly interdependent. The networks grow with the number of links, thereby at the same time nurturing the main nodes which serve as points of control and provide expertise and services in crucial fields such as international law, finance, accounting and travelling (Allen 1999, Taylor *et al.* 2002). This concept, linking the geographic notion of place with economic concepts of command and control, supply chains and producer services has been challenged from both the economic side for not being consistent with actual corporate decision-making processes (Jones 2002) and from the urban geography side for not paying sufficient attention to the individuality of places (Smith 2001). Further to this critique, Smith also rejects the economistic paradigm underlying the global city idea, as he claims that urban spatial and social restructuring is not necessarily preceded and determined by global economic processes but by political decision-making and local agency (Smith 2001).

While it is true that the concept is mainly conceived out of economic geography, the role and international contacts of global cities produce certain non-economic traits which are also recognised as characteristics for these cities: temporary *immigration*, creating an international atmosphere, a mix of cultures and lifestyles and often socio-economic polarisation; a *global city culture*, notably in the central business district (CBD), which is often described as lacking local characteristics; and a *quality of life*, at least in parts of the cities, that appeals to foreign experts, managers and diplomats.

These socio-cultural aspects have been studied elsewhere, mostly with reference to Western cities (Fainstein *et al.* 1992, O'Loughlin and Friedrichs 1996, Sassen 2001, Beaverstock 2002). We now look at them in the specific context of Hong Kong. In terms of *geographical scale*, world city research engages on three levels of examination: macro level research looking at the global networks and the role of individual cities in them, micro level approaches focusing on processes *within* global cities and between them the level of the global city region. For the latter, regional hierarchies of supporting and central functions have been identified, which in themselves are again organised in networks of nodes and links (Scott 2001, Simmonds and Hack 2001). This chapter makes references to Hong Kong's role within global networks and within the emerging cross-boundary global city region in the Pearl River Delta. The main focus, however, is on the local consequences of the global city. Our findings correspond with typical local changes observed in other global cities such as a shift from secondary to tertiary industries, a vertically and horizontally growing CBD, increasing amounts of immigrants, both highly qualified experts and cheap labour (e.g. domestic helpers, delivery men and cleaners), and social polarisation and segregation.

Friedmann (1998) has pointed to vital public policy issues raised by these changes which concern regional governance, urban planning, sustainability and migrant societies. Urban planning, for example, is being challenged by competitive constellations in the world city network and the rising power of global investors, which tend to reduce urban policy to mere city marketing. Ng and Hills, (2003: 152) comparing Hong Kong with other world cities in Asia, have also criticised the economic focus of current world city research. They advocated a focus on 'great cities' providing 'a good quality of life for all'.

Globalised Hong Kong

Although not listed among the top world cities by Friedmann (1986), Hong Kong has, since the mid-1990s, frequently been identified as a highly globalised city (Skeldon 1997, Tang 1997, Meyer 2000, Lui and Chiu 2003). To explain this development with just global economy arguments would not go far enough. There is clearly a political context to refer to. In Hong Kong, the pre-handover government invested massively in the global city infrastructure such as telecommunications, airport, port, a convention centre and land reclamation for a growing CBD. This was based on the view that a globalised Hong Kong would be better prepared to maintain a distinct character to that of the mainland. Even firms such as Jardine

Matheson and the Hong Kong Bank have been described as re-inventing themselves from colonial hongs to global players during that time (Sum 1995). On the China side, the Open Door Policy allowed Hong Kong to assume a key role for an increasingly globally integrated China and to build strong cross-border links (see Yang, Chapter 7 in this volume). Hong Kong and the Pearl River Delta have developed into a global city region (Chu 1996, Sit 2001, Cartier 2002), yet with specific characteristics due to the persisting boundary, and with a specific role of Hong Kong in this region.

While we will get back to this topic in the conclusion, the focus of this chapter is not on the reasons for global city formation but rather on the local and social consequences. The argument develops in three steps. First, Hong Kong's claim to be a world city (Figure 5.1) is verified by four major aspects of global integration (air and telecommunications connectivity, financial services, and command and control by regional headquarters). Second, we enter the local level by arguing that global integration triggered sectoral and, more importantly, spatial changes in Hong Kong's employment structure; and third the social and socio-spatial consequences are discussed referring to immigration, polarisation and segregation. The chapter is based on our research since 1997 (Breitung 1999, 2001a,b, 2002, Günter 2003). Its timeframe is the period of global city formation in the 1990s. Despite the importance of the regional scale, we refer to the territory

Figure 5.1 A massive campaign started in 2001 to promote Hong Kong as 'Asia's
    world city'.

Source: Photography by Breitung (2001).

of Hong Kong when analysing *local* consequences because of the persisting significant differences in terms of economy, society, administration and data collection and provision.

Air traffic

Passenger air connectivity is an indicator and requirement for global cities (Rimmer 1996, Shin and Timberlake 2000). It indicates the extent of integration in global networks and it is necessary for global command and control functions, since multinational firms and agencies require highly accessible headquarter locations. Accessibility is reflected in the number of flights from or to a destination. In the first half of 2000, our sample survey of departures from Hong Kong recorded 1,915 weekly passenger flights to 120 destinations (Breitung 2001a: 19). Although the connectivity to all parts of China was good, international links still dominated (78 per cent). Hong Kong's connectivity network within China was finely meshed but weak compared to a more solid international network (Figure 5.2). The top ten flight destinations from Hong Kong were other Asian hubs. The classic global cities in the West, New York and London are ranked eleventh and twelfth (Table 5.1). With 14 daily flights to Singapore and 7 to New York, Hong Kong was at least as strongly connected to these cities as to parts of its 'natural' hinterland via land connections.

The amount of contact between cities, including tourism, family and business ties, is better reflected in the passenger numbers. Since domestic flights tend to use smaller planes, the share of international passengers would even be higher than the share of international flights. However, it must be noted that transit

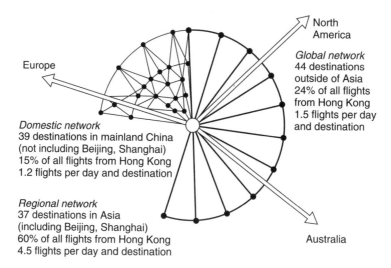

Figure 5.2 Hong Kong's three air traffic networks.

Source: Breitung (2001b).

Table 5.1 Flight connections from Hong Kong per week (2000)

Domestic		Regional (Asia)		Global (ex. Asia)	
Shanghai	71	Taipei	231	New York	49
Beijing	56	Bangkok	113	London	42
Guangzhou	31	Singapore	96	Sydney	32
Fuzhou	25	Tokyo	94	San Francisco	26
Xiamen	22	Manila	74	Vancouver	26
Guilin	18	Seoul	65	Frankfurt	23
Nanjing	16	Osaka	64	Los Angeles	22
Hangzhou	14	Kaohsiung	50	Anchorage	19
Shantou	14	Kuala Lumpur	42	Paris	18

Source: Breitung (2001a).

Notes
Based on a random choice of days in the first half of 2000. The number of weekly flights measures the accessibility better than the number of passengers. It does include stopovers but no connecting flights.

flights make passenger destinations hard to assess (for instance flights via Anchorage and, more importantly, between Taiwan and the mainland where no direct links exist).

Telecommunications

In a similar way, telecommunications connections and infrastructure are both indicator and location factor for global city functions (Castells 1996, Sassen 2002). Hong Kong's strength in this regard can partly offset the high costs for office space and wages and therefore increase its competitiveness. Already in the 1990s, Hong Kong's telecommunication services were sophisticated, convenient and inexpensive (Enright *et al.* 1997). The subsequent market liberalisation made Hong Kong one of the most open telecommunications markets in the world. Competition has substantially reduced international call rates, improved the quality of services and increased Hong Kong's external connectivity from 44 Gigabits per second (Gbps) in early 2000 to nearly 900 Gbps in early 2002. The world's biggest civil satellite teleport, 10 submarine cables to overseas and 2 terrestrial cables to Guangdong provide Hong Kong with external connectivity second only to Tokyo. A 100 per cent digital fibre-optic and co-axial telecommunications infrastructure and the broadband network cover virtually all households and commercial buildings. The mobile phone penetration rate of 91 per cent (6.2 million subscribers) is among the highest in the world (Information Services Department 2003).

Finance

The flows of money and the availability of financial services are recognised as crucial factors in turning a place into a global city. Hong Kong has been portrayed as a leading financial centre by several authors (e.g. Jao 1997, Meyer 2000).

In the 1990s, international financial interactions such as gold and currency trade, foreign loans and outward investment saw the strongest growth. The total volume of loans increased from HK 500 billion dollars (US 64 billion dollars) to almost HK 4,000 billion dollars (US 500 billion dollars) in the ten years to 1996, and the share dedicated for investment outside Hong Kong from 33 to 53 per cent (Census and Statistics Department 1997a). The destinations were mainly in Asia, increasingly China.

Hong Kong boasts more offices of international banks than Tokyo and Singapore combined (Bank for International Settlement 1999, quoted in Ng and Hills 2003) including 73 representative offices of 100 worldwide largest banks, and the second most important stock exchange in Asia (Information Services Department 2003). Since 1993, the Hong Kong stock exchange lists titles from the mainland and has become the main place for mainland companies to raise money abroad. As the financial centre of China, however, Hong Kong is increasingly facing competition from Shanghai and even Beijing (Yusuf and Wu 2002, Zhao 2003).

Regional headquarters

Next to the flows of people, information and money, regional headquarters, as transmitters of power and control, are core features of global cities. These are good indicators because their locations are more flexibly chosen according to location factors than the often historically grown top headquarters (Dunning and Norman 1987). The main functions of regional headquarters are regional market analysis and regionally specific strategic planning, organising networks and production chains, financial control, cost reduction through bulk purchase, technical support to the activities in the region, and communication between headquarters and employees in the region (adapted from Perry *et al.* 1998).

The number of regional headquarters and regional offices in Hong Kong increased steadily during the 1990s (Table 5.2). Hong Kong and Singapore were

Table 5.2 Regional headquarters and regional offices by country of mother company

Country	1991	1994	1997	2000	2003
USA	320	371	480	570	740
Japan	105	348	498	619	610
United Kingdom	100	198	214	236	282
PR of China	*	131	243	229	232
Germany	42	87	129	143	178
France	32	51	100	116	145
Taiwan	*	53	77	134	129
Singapore	*	31	62	97	103
Switzerland	49	72	67	98	101

Source: Census and Statistics Department (2004).

Note
* No record (figure too low).

traditionally fierce competitors in this field. More recently, however, as the catchment areas of regional headquarters are shrinking in size due to their rising numbers and growing importance even companies from Singapore, Taiwan and the mainland began setting up regional headquarters in Hong Kong (Table 5.2). In 1996, every second regional headquarter in Hong Kong no longer served Singapore whereas those serving Greater China alone had increased from 8 per cent in 1990 to 39 per cent in 1996 (Perry *et al.* 1998). Subsequently, the reporting method has changed, but in 2001, 83 per cent of the regional headquarters were in charge of Mainland China (Lui and Chiu 2003). For Hong Kong, competition with Shanghai and Beijing has become more important than with Singapore.

The changing employment structure

As postulated by the global city concept, global city formation has transformed Hong Kong's employment structure. Many finance, logistics and business service jobs have been created, the wage level has risen and manufacturing activities have been transferred to the extended metropolitan area beyond the city limits. With data mainly from the *Quarterly Survey of Employment and Vacancies* (Census and Statistics Department 1992, 1997b, 2002) we can analyse these changes and their spatial consequences in detail.

Becoming a tertiary city

The total number of people employed in Hong Kong remained relatively stable throughout the 1990s, despite drastic sectoral and spatial changes. The city's secondary sector, the leading sector up to the early 1980s (Figure 5.3), has been severely losing employees due to outward processing (the transfer of production units across the border), but these reductions were compensated by increasing numbers of tertiary jobs within the city (Table 5.3). Outward processing and tertiarisation are both part of a functional differentiation within the extended

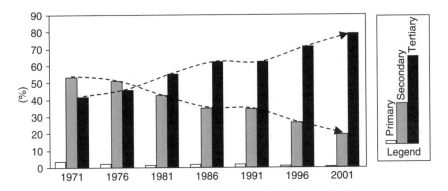

Figure 5.3 Employment by economic sectors in Hong Kong, 1971–2001.

Source: Günter (2003). Data: Van der Knaap and Smits (1997), Census and Statistics Department (2001).

Table 5.3 People employed in selected tertiary industries, 1992–2002

Industry	1992	1997	2002	1992–1997 (%)	1997–2002 (%)
Business services[a]	114,235	160,973	185,055	+40.9	+15.0
Financial services	113,431	142,070	128,478	+25.2	−9.6
Real estate	55,397	78,780	82,204	+42.2	+4.3
Communications	28,030	37,716	25,701	+34.6	−31.9
Insurances	19,674	25,030	26,639	+27.2	+6.4
Air transport	15,099	23,237	23,894	+53.9	+2.8
Total of these industries	354,866	467,806	471,971	+31.8	+0.9

Source: Breitung (2001a). Data: Census and Statistics Department (1992, 1997b, 2002).

Note

a Law firms, consulting, accounting, data processing, public relations, employment agencies, security services and others.

metropolitan area (Sit 2001). They have increased productivity and GDP in both Hong Kong and the region. While industrial employment has been diminished, Loh (2002) claims that manufacturing still plays an important role in Hong Kong's economy since companies are Hong Kong owned and significant value is added in the city. This is obscured in the statistics when manufacturing firms are re-classified as import and export firms even though they actually trade their own products, and their employees still regard them as industrial enterprises. Such re-classification may account for 250,000 of the jobs 'lost' in the secondary sector until 1996 (Breitung 2001a: 106).

Hong Kong's ascent to a global city was also a main force behind strong growth in the tertiary sector. Trade, business services and financial services gained the most jobs between 1992 and 1997, especially in global city functions such as air transport and communications. After 1997, the growth of all these industries slowed down significantly (Table 5.3) partly due to the regional crisis but possibly also due to a loss of competitiveness. This can be interpreted as Hong Kong's global role coming under threat (Balfour and Clifford 2001), but it can also be interpreted as a global city giving way to a global city region. While the growth of many producer services has come to a halt in Hong Kong it has accelerated in Shenzhen just across the border. This points to a second phase of functional differentiation within the region, now also involving some lower level tertiary activities, and not necessarily to a weakening of the region as a whole.

Spatial concentration of work places

The economic transition during the global city formation had grave spatial implications on the local level in Hong Kong. The job losses due to de-industrialisation were most severe in northern and eastern Kowloon where the employment share in manufacturing dropped from up to 60 per cent in 1991 to 35 per cent in 1997 (Breitung 1999). The growing business service and financial sectors, on the other hand, were and are still highly concentrated in the centre. In 1997, more than 320,000 out of these sectors' 520,000 employees worked in just three districts (Map 5.1), and 155,000 in the Central and Western District alone (Census and Statistics Department 1991b, 1992, 1997b).

The result of the sectoral shift has thus been a stronger spatial concentration of jobs in defiance to the government's de-centralisation policy. This is illustrated in Figure 5.4: the individual columns show growing employment shares in the New Territories in all industries (not only in manufacturing and trade, but also in finance and hotels), and a decreasing share of the centre in most industries. However, when viewing the same diagram horizontally it appears that de-industrialisation has more than neutralised de-centralisation. During 1992–1997, the growing share of highly centralised industries pushed up overall employment in the three central districts by approximately 1 per cent per annum. The three districts' share of the total employment in Hong Kong increased from 37 to 39 per cent. Employment in the New Territories grew at a rate far below the 5 per cent annual population growth, and the share of the old industrial areas located between the centre and the New Territories declined sharply.

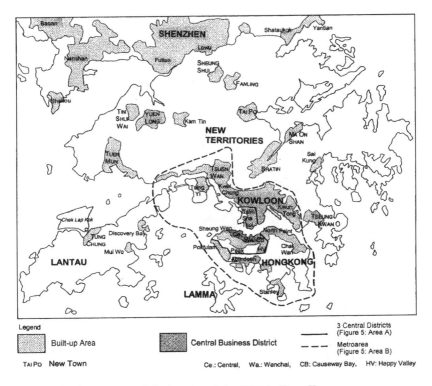

Map 5.1 The three zones and the location of the CBD in Hong Kong.

Source: Breitung (2001b).

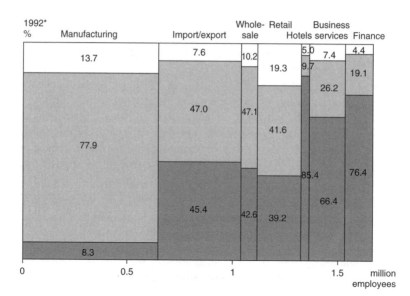

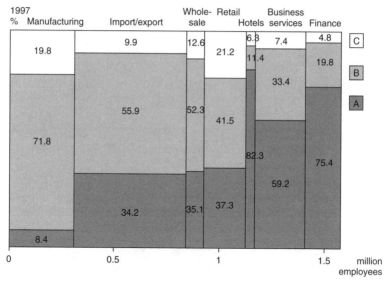

Figure 5.4 Change in employment structures in selected industries in the three zones (1992, 1997).

Source: Breitung (2001b). Data: Census and Statistics Department (1991b, 1992, 1997b).

Notes
Area A: Central and Western, Wanchai and Yau Tsim Mong Districts.
Area B: The rest of Hong Kong Island and Kowloon, Kwai Tsing and Tsuen Wan.
Area C: The new territories, excluding Kwai Tsing and Tsuen Wan (see Map 5.1).
* Manufacturing sector: September 1991 (all other sectors refer to 1992, but the secondary sector data has been collected slightly earlier).

For Hong Kong, the diverging trends of de-centralising residential patterns and centralising work patterns are causing serious planning problems. Commuter traffic is increasing dramatically especially through the cross-harbour tunnels and underground lines. In the long run, the location of the CBD on an island far from the territory's geographic centre, let alone the greater region, will definitely become a disadvantage.

Segregation in the CBD

In order to accentuate the ongoing centralisation process, we zoom in from the three most central districts (an area of 29 square kilometres) to the 3.3 square kilometres CBD between Sheung Wan and Causeway Bay (compare Map 5.1). The only significant secondary industry left in this area was printing and publishing, which is actually more a producer service and like other lower value-added services (e.g. trade and hotels) meanwhile also on the retreat. Most expanding industries were related to global city functions and the international flow of people, capital and information. Striking increases were noted in communications, air travel, business services, investment banking and stock exchange related activities (Table 5.4). These operations rely on high information density

Table 5.4 People employed in selected industries in the CBD of Hong Kong

Industry	1992[a]	1997	Change	In %
Wearing apparel[a]	870	417	−453	−52
Watches and optical goods[a]	639	207	−432	−68
Printing and publishing[a]	4,277	4,078	−199	−5
Import/export	68,164	63,918	−4,246	−6
Wholesale	8,849	8,807	−42	−0
Retail	28,726	32,075	+3,349	+12
Restaurants	29,657	30,946	+1,289	+4
Hotels	14,354	11,111	−3,243	−23
Air transport	1,552	3,350	+1,798	+116
Communications[b]	1,142	4,156	+3,014	+264
Business services[c]	56,699	71,260	+14,561	+26
Business associations	1,487	1,570	+83	+6
Banks	41,583	48,685	+7,102	+17
Finance and Investment	13,275	22,568	+9,293	+70
Exchanges and brokering	9,557	13,457	+3,900	+41
Other financial institutions	7,623	7,694	+71	+1
Financial sector (total)	72,038	92,404	+20,366	+28
Total of these industries	288,454	324,299	+35,845	+12

Source: Breitung (2001a). Data: Census and Statistics Department (1991b, 1992, 1997b).

Notes
a Secondary sector: Sept. (1991).
b Except communications in Wanchai North.
c See Table 5.3.

and agglomeration economies. As they are extremely high value added, local businesses, residential use and secondary industries could not compete with them.

The resulting processes of concentration, segregation and displacement become even more obvious when zooming further into the CBD (Breitung 2001a: 120ff): (a) The 1 square kilometres core CBD (compare Sit 1981) boasts 40 per cent of all financial sector jobs in Hong Kong and over 70 per cent of the jobs of the sector in the total CBD. The second strongest industry in the core CBD is business services. (b) Just outside the core CBD, business services rank first followed by trade. (c) In adjacent Sheung Wan and Wanchai, the same two sectors dominate but already in reversed order. (d) Towards the eastern part of Wanchai and Causeway Bay, retail and restaurants take the top rank.

This sequence from finance to business services, trade and retail, illustrates a segregation that has come about through different returns per square metre and agglomeration economies. It was both the cause and the effect of the very high property prices. By the end of 1999, the average office rents in the core CBD were about 50 per cent above other CBD locations and 72 per cent above other locations in the three central districts (Rating and Evaluation Department 2000). This price difference quantifies the agglomeration economies. Segregation and displacement of less profitable businesses in the CBD have increased notably during the 1990s. Employment in the CBD grew by over 10 per cent from 1992 to 1997, which is more than in the three central districts and much more than in the entire territory. The 1 square kilometre core CBD gained almost 15,000 jobs in the financial sector, but lost jobs in other industries. The increase in employment was stronger at the fringe of the CBD where all tertiary industries expanded displacing residential use and manufacturing.

Immigration and a changing social structure

One of the major challenges in global cities (Friedmann 1998) is their expanding immigrant population. Immigrants contribute to the cultural and demographic diversity in global cities and play a vital role in their development, both as cheap labour and as specialised professionals, but the fact that a considerable part of the population regards themselves as temporary workers rather than citizens has an impact on the civil society. In addition to this, immigration on both ends of the income scale is also contributing to the widening income gap. Hong Kong's latest population census provides remarkable evidence of these developments (Census and Statistics Department 1991a, 1996, 2001).

Diversification of immigration patterns

The total population of Hong Kong grew from 6.0 million in 1994 to 6.7 million in 2001, despite the very low fertility rate. Natural growth figures dropped from 42,500 in 1994 to 18,600 in 1999, but the migration balance jumped from 78,800 in 1994 to 150,600 in 1999 (Census and Statistics Department 2000, 2001).

The main groups of immigrants were

(a) *Expatriates*: the number of newly issued employment visas, often for employees of foreign or multinational companies, grew from 16,000 in 1986 to 47,000 in 1996 and peaked at 85,000 in 2001 (Immigration Department 2004).

(b) *Returnees*: many Hong Kong people who had previously left the city returned in the 1990s, a lot of them with foreign passports and enriched with higher education and work experience in mostly English speaking countries.

(c) *Foreign domestic helpers*: of the total net migration from 1986 to 1995 35 per cent was due to the growth by 133,252 in the number of foreign domestic helpers (Siu 1996). We will look at this phenomenon in the next section.

(d) *Mainland immigrants*: in 1980, a quota on mainland immigrants was introduced, which has been frozen at 150 persons per day since 1995 (Skeldon 1997). In 1995, mainlanders accounted for 28 per cent of the legal immigrants, almost entirely in connection with family reunions.

Hong Kong has always relied strongly on immigration (Lin 2002). Until the 1960s not even half of Hong Kong's population was born in the territory. The share has increased to 60 per cent since then and at the same time immigration has diversified towards a more international pattern (Table 5.5). Among the foreigners coming to Hong Kong, North Americans and Southeast Asians boasted the highest growth rates (Table 5.6). The world city attracted business people on the high end of the salary scale and cheap labour from the Philippines, Indonesia and Thailand on the low end.

Foreign domestic helpers

Hong Kong's biggest immigrant communities are the Filipinos and Indonesians, who mainly work as domestic helpers. During the 1990s, the number of Filipino

Table 5.5 Hong Kong population by place of birth, 1961–2001

Year	Hong Kong (%)	China[a] (%)	Others (%)	Total (%)
1961	47.7	50.5	1.8	100
1971	56.4	41.6	2.0	100
1981	57.2	39.6	3.2	100
1986	59.4	37.0	3.6	100
1991	59.8	35.6	4.6	100
1996	60.3	32.6	7.1	100
2001	59.7	32.5	7.8	100

Sources: Siu (1996); Census and Statistics Department (2001).

Note
a Including Macau.

Table 5.6 Foreign residents in Hong Kong, 1987–1997 (in 1,000)

	Philippines	Indonesia	USA	Canada	Japan	Thailand	UK	Australia	India	Total
1987	39	—	14	9	9	10	15	9	16	172
1989	51	—	16	12	10	13	18	11	17	207
1991	72	—	16	15	11	17	21	13	18	251
1993	99	15	20	20	14	22	26	17	19	321
1995	128	26	27	28	22	26	33	21	21	415
1997	134	37	22	33	21	25	36	22	22	461
1999	136	53	22	33	18	27	35	22	22	495
2001	147	75	21	32	15	29	33	21	22	527

Source: Immigration Department (for 1987–1995 from Siu 1996).

Notes
The figures are derived from immigration and emigration statistics. They represent people present in the territory on 31 December of the respective year, if they have entered it with a foreign passport.
— Indonesia was not among the top ten countries prior to 1992.

domestic helpers more than doubled to 155,450. Around 69,000 Indonesian domestic helpers, a negligible group in 1991, now comprise the second largest faction (Immigration Department 2003). Globalisation is a major force behind this influx of foreign domestic helpers (Günter 2003). On the one hand, enhanced mobility allows people from poorer countries to earn a better living in places like Hong Kong. Especially the Philippines have made the export of labour their niche 'industry' in the global economy (Tyner 2000). On the other hand, the global city is run by people with little time but enough money to support their exclusive lifestyles by employing domestic helpers.

As the high- and low-income groups expanded, employing domestic helpers and seeking double income also became a strategy for the middle-class families to maintain their status. Today, most foreign domestic helpers in Hong Kong actually work for Chinese middle-income households. The affordability of domestic help has further increased with the recruitment of Indonesians, who are more susceptible to illegal underpayment than the Filipinos.

Compared to the rigid rules enforced on immigrants from China, the policy towards temporary immigration from Southeast Asia is relatively lenient. Some claim that local domestic helpers are being pushed out of the job market, but the fact is that they tend to seek part-time work in small households while immigrants cater to the full-time market. Competing with both are the numerous illegal immigrants and female applicants for immigration from China. Since the 1970s, Hong Kong has replaced the traditional Chinese *Amahs* with Filipino maids, and currently still finds it convenient to keep recruiting them. While there are many historical, political, cultural and psychological reasons behind this phenomenon, a major factor from the economic point of view is the weak legal status of foreigners. Unlike legal Chinese immigrants, who might take up other jobs or apply for social aid when they lose their job, Filipinos have to leave the city once their work contract expires. It is commonplace in global cities that low-income immigration goes hand in hand with a low legal status, either through restrictive visa rules or illegality.

The demographic impact of immigration

The quota mentioned in the previous section keeps the influx of Mainland Chinese at a relatively low level. Although this policy is popular among the general public in Hong Kong it keeps many cross-boundary families separated, which is problematic from an ethical and demographic point of view. Hong Kong is actually denying some of its own residents' offspring the right of abode, while the local birth rate is among the lowest in the world and most foreign immigrants come without children. In 1996, only 2 per cent of the Filipinos were under 14, compared to 19 per cent of the total population. Foreign immigration therefore aggravated the lack of children. It increased on the other hand the growth of the middle-age population brackets. Twenty-eight per cent of the local Chinese were 30–40 years old, compared with 33 per cent of the North Americans, 43 per cent of the Japanese and 53 per cent of the Filipinos in the city. The median age shifted drastically from 28 in 1986 to 36 in 2001.

Another significant effect was gender specific. In the earlier days, immigrants were predominantly male but the recent influx of domestic helpers has pushed the female population over the 50 per cent mark. It is particularly high among the Filipinos (93 per cent), Thais (87 per cent) and Indonesians, and among newcomers from China and Macao (due to cross-border marriages). The foreign domestic helpers have also accelerated the increase in female workforce participation from 29 per cent in 1971 to 43 per cent in 2001. They became part of the workforce themselves and allowed more local women to seek alternative employment to housework. The foreign managers, experts and professionals working for the global city are still predominantly male, often single, and have a low and decreasing average number of children.

Socio-cultural impact: the growing importance of English

Changing language use exemplifies a cultural aspect of becoming global city. Despite the de-colonisation process, the percentage of people who speak English at home grew by about 40 per cent between 1991 and 1996, and more people claimed to be able to communicate in English (Table 5.7). Those speaking English at home include mixed families, Filipino domestic helpers communicating with their employers and returnees whose children were brought up in English speaking environments. This trend is in contrast to the general perception of declining English standards among the local population and the diminishing use of English in public following the change in sovereignty. There seems to be a widening gap between a primarily Cantonese speaking society and the cosmopolitan residents who are proficient in English. This diverging trend is detrimental to the global city development because it reduces social cohesion and makes the recruiting of locals more difficult for multinational c

Apart from English, Putonghua will increasingly be important
ment as a global city. Hong Kong people have shown great fle
pared themselves for the integration with China. The percei
speaking Putonghua at home remains low, but those who are a

official language of China have increased by almost 90 per cent from 1997 to 2001 (Table 5.7).

Socio-economic impact: income polarisation

Between 1991 and 1996, the median income in Hong Kong grew by 84 per cent per worker and by 76 per cent per household. Even in price-adjusted terms, this reflected an extraordinary growth in wealth during the global city formation (Table 5.8). This growth, however, was not evenly distributed. Those salary classes above HK 15,000 dollars monthly income enjoyed the strongest gains, which can be attributed to the social ascent of the middle-income group and to immigration. The growth of the high-income group boosted the real estate market and the general price level in Hong Kong, which was harmful to the lower income groups.

While the global city formation (1991–1996) was characterised by rapidly growing incomes and increasing polarisation, the economic slowdown (1997–2001) saw reduced income growth but a continuation of the polarisation process (Figure 5.5). The group earning around HK 4,000 dollars per month did not participate in the growth of incomes or even suffered from dropping incomes. This group comprises domestic helpers and other people with low wage jobs.

Table 5.7 Languages spoken in Hong Kong, 1991–2001

	Mainly spoken at home (%)			Can be spoken (%)		
	1991	1996	2001	1991	1996	2001
Cantonese	88.7	88.7	89.2	95.8	95.2	96.1
English	2.2	3.1	3.2	31.6	38.1	43.0
Putonghua	1.1	1.1	0.9	18.1	25.3	34.1
Other Chinese dialects	7.0	5.8	5.5	—	—	—
Japanese	0.2	0.3	0.2	1.0	1.2	1.4
Filipino/Tagalog	0.1	0.2	0.2	1.1	1.8	1.9
Indonesian	0.1	0.2	0.2	0.7	0.9	1.3
Other languages	0.5	0.5	0.6	—	—	—

Source: Census and Statistics Department (2001).

Note
— cannot be calculated from data.

Table 5.8 Overall income growth in Hong Kong, 1991–2001

	1991	1996	2001
Median monthly income from main employment in HKD	5,170	9,500	10,000
Average gross income gain in 5 years (%)		84	5.2
Inflation (consumer price index A) in 5 years (%)		48	0.2
Average net income gain in 5 years (%)		36	5.0

Source: Census and Statistics Department (2001).

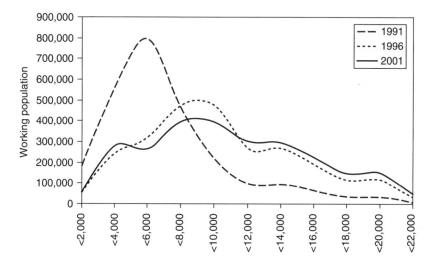

Figure 5.5 Redistributed income from main employment in Hong Kong, 1991–2001.

Source: Günter (2003). Data: Census and Statistics Department (2001).

Notes

1 In order to increase comparability and clarity, the data of different income classes have been redistributed to HK 2,000 dollars class widths and transformed into smooth graphs. The numbers on the *y*-axis refer to the HK 2,000 dollars brackets.
2 HK 2,000 dollars = US 257 dollars.

Hong Kong's Gini coefficient, an indicator for income inequality (see Lui 1997), rose from 0.43 in 1971 to 0.53 in 2001 (Wong 2002). This is much higher than in other comparable Asian cities (Ng and Hills 2003). In terms of household income, the highest earning 20 per cent of households earned 50.7 per cent of the total income in 1986, which increased to 56.5 per cent in 2001. In contrast, the lowest earning 20 per cent of households earned 5.0 per cent of the total in 1986, which dropped to 3.2 per cent in 2001. Relatively speaking, the poor suffered a further set-back. In absolute terms their nominal income was more or less stable until 1997 but dropped markedly during the financial crisis. Over the whole decade of the 1990s, it declined by 23.3 per cent while the income of the highest earning fifth of households rose by 26.1 per cent (Wong 2002). Although such data can easily be misinterpreted (see Lui 1997) – for example, household incomes in the lowest bracket fell partly due to the decreasing size of households – all data suggested growing income polarisation.

Socio-spatial impact: segregation and suburbanisation

Whereas Forrest *et al.* (2004) are right to say that there are no areas of 'ghetto-type disadvantage in Hong Kong', as in the United States or Third World cities, we argue that globalisation has indeed led to a strong and growing spatial segregation. The disparities are, however, hard to trace by quantitative analysis as

Hong Kong's society contains three distinct sub-societies with very little contact and interlinkage. These sub-societies are defined not in the first place by different levels of wealth but as socio-cultural milieus, while then internally displaying distinct social stratifications.

First, the local mostly Chinese urban population is relatively homogeneous, although social stratification and spatial segregation exist. They comprise most of the population in Kowloon and the new towns. Recent immigrants from China, concentrated in the poor areas of Kowloon have always started at the bottom of the social ladder but after some time integrated well into this society. There is no reason to believe that this has changed, especially as their number is lower now than in the past.

Second, the colonial upper class used to live quite separated from the locals, mostly around Victoria Peak and adjacent parts of Hong Kong Island. This pattern has now been filled by the global city immigrants and supplemented by emerging suburban settlements. These areas contain not only many of the territory's top-earners but also a large number of low-wage support staff such as domestic helpers. Both are predominantly immigrants. The middle-income stratum is lacking.

Third, a small group that however obscures many spatial analyses is the rural population in the New Territories. They inhabit large parts of sparsely populated land and therefore feature prominently in maps (Forrest *et al.* 2004). As some have earned well from land sales they do have a strong social stratification, but this does not always show in official statistics. Not all may report their wealth accurately to people and institutions outside their sphere. On the other hand, poverty in these areas is easy to overestimate. A less monetary society and strong social ties in the villages support life on little income.

For our purpose the third group is of little relevance, but the rising gap between the first two groups is highly significant and closely linked to global city formation. With a more internationalised pattern of immigration its spatial focus has changed. In the past, most immigrants were Chinese who settled first in Kowloon. In the 1990s, most newcomers moved to the high-class areas of Hong Kong Island. At the Peak and the south coast, almost 30 per cent of the 1996 population were in Hong Kong for less than a year. The strongest increase of recent immigrants compared to 1991 was recorded between the Peak and the inner city (Mid-Levels). Similar trends could be observed for related criteria such as foreigners, English speakers, high incomes and the 30–44-year age group. The share of foreigners, for example, has increased from 33 per cent in 1991 to 43 per cent in 1996 in the high-class areas and from 8.5 per cent in 1991 to 12 per cent in 1996 in the rural suburban areas, but stayed more or less unchanged in Kowloon (7 per cent) and the new towns (5 per cent) (Breitung 2001a: 96). Thus the spatial segregation between the local and the global city sub-societies has grown along with some income polarisation. Polarisation was highest yet among the new immigrants, in this case without any spatial segregation, as rich and poor live in the same areas – in fact in the same flats or houses.

The increase in the rural suburban areas points to a second spatial phenomenon. Hong Kong had never in the past any significant low-rise suburbanisation as in many Western countries. This is changing now with foreigners moving into villages (e.g. in Sai Kung) and immigrant enclaves being built (e.g. Discovery Bay). The increase from 8.5 to 12 per cent would be much stronger if the statistical areas in question did not contain a mix of rural and suburban population. Interestingly, the said increase pertains mostly to North American, British and Filipino immigrants. The share of most other nationalities in Hong Kong's rural areas has not changed significantly. The global city immigrants, foreigners and returnees bring with them distinct Western or Anglo-American housing ideals and have the money to realise these ideals in Hong Kong. As for the Filipino immigrants their place of residence does not reflect choice. Most of them live in their employers' places.

Conclusion

This chapter shows rather distinctive transformations in Hong Kong during the global city formation period of the 1990s. Many of the processes observed in Hong Kong confirm earlier findings elsewhere. Wherever global command and control functions are found they are highly competitive in their use of space and work force. They tend to concentrate in the most central locations where they displace other uses, thereby triggering spatial differentiation and functional segregation. They also tend to concentrate the income gained in the hands of a small group of highly competitive employees, thus intensifying social polarisation. A significant part of the high-end workforce as well as low-end support staff are recruited from a global labour market. The relationship of these two distinct groups of immigrants has been described as symbiotic and at times quite removed from the local society. Their appearance changes the ethnic, demographic and social composition of the population in global cities.

Our findings overall reaffirm the respective accounts in the global city literature. However, the Hong Kong case also illustrates the decisive role that non-economic and non-global factors can play in global city formation. These factors were mainly the different policy agendas pursued in the United Kingdom, China and Hong Kong during the period of transition. First, the *political transition* from a British colony to a Special Administrative Region (SAR) of China, which was initially perceived as a threat, gave additional urgency to Hong Kong's global integration in the view of the outgoing colonial power and the Hong Kong elite. Second, the links to the insufficiently globally integrated *mainland of China* have greatly supported global city formation. The importance of a hinterland is generally recognised, but in the case of Hong Kong in the 1990s, the growth rates in the hinterland and the degree of dependence were unique. Third, with the principle of 'one country – two systems' in place, *the border* remains as a barrier hindering interaction in the global city region but accelerating de-industrialisation and tertiarisation by upholding two different regulative regimes.

Apart from this specific historical situation there are always many local factors influencing global city formation, such as the following examples for the

Hong Kong case: First, Hong Kong's immigration policy effectively controls the labour supply from the hinterland while favouring the importation of foreign domestic helpers. Their diffusion beyond the initial foreign, upper-class employers literally carries globalisation into the living rooms of the local society. Second, as a *newly developed economy* Hong Kong had a smaller middle-class in the first place. Despite polarisation and social decline positive attitudes towards globalisation prevail due to the previous experience of development. Third, some specific *cultural features* such as Chinese values and the mixed residential structure supported social coherence and stability. These traditional forces are however weakening.

While Hong Kong shows many similarities and some distinct variations compared to global cities in the West, the same is true compared to globalising cities in the mainland. Hong Kong is quite different because of its colonial history, the well-established capitalist and globally integrated economy, the developed regulatory system (rule of law, civil service) and the lack of significant rural–urban migration. While both Shanghai and Beijing are in the process of global city formation they are far behind Hong Kong in most aspects. Hong Kong was the first global city for China and still is the most important one. But Hong Kong's observed slow-down can partly be attributed to the new competition. The rise of Shanghai and Beijing is much discussed in Hong Kong. Hong Kong is losing its exclusive role, but eventually a growing and increasingly globally integrated Chinese economy will support several world cities.

A second challenge for Hong Kong is seen at the regional level. The loss of functions to Shenzhen and the Delta is often described as another competition, but it is a matter of *spatial differentiation* and fading *boundaries*. Differentiation and the concentration of top command and control functions are, on the global level, at the root of world city formation. On the local level, an increasingly differentiated hierarchy of functions has been shown within a few square kilometres in the CBD. The same now also evolves on the regional level with top functions concentrating in central Hong Kong, the middle range in Shenzhen and Guangzhou and the rest elsewhere in the region. In this view, the shift of functions to Shenzhen is likely to raise the overall competitiveness of the global city region and thereby strengthen the centre as well.

The real challenge for Hong Kong may well lie on the local level. The social gap between the mostly immigrant 'global' sub-society and the local population is a threat to social stability. High differences in wealth can arouse conflicts and crime, especially in times of economic or political crises. A lack of social cohesion is also problematic from the governance and planning point of view when the transient elite lacks genuine interest in the place and the local population feels disempowered, yet both compete for increasingly scarce government funds. World cities can greatly benefit from the social capital of international immigrants and the hard capital gained through their global role if the material and immaterial gains are well distributed. Hong Kong's political challenge now is to integrate the different sub-societies and together become a 'great city' – apart from being a world city.

Acknowledgements

The authors want to thank Professor Victor Sit and the anonymous referees for their comments on this and earlier versions of this chapter.

References

Allen, J. (1999) 'Cities of power and influence: settled formations', in J. Allen, D. Massey and M. Pryke (eds) *Unsettling cities: movement/settlement*, London and New York: Routledge, 181–218.

Balfour, F. and Clifford, M. (2001) 'Hong Kong under siege', *Business Week*, 23 July 2001.

Beaverstock, J. V. (2002) 'Transnational elites in global cities: British expatriates in Singapore's financial district', *Geoforum*, 33: 525–538.

Beaverstock, J. V., Smith, R. G. and Taylor, P. J. (2000) 'World-city network: a new metageography?', *Annals of the Association of American Geographers*, 90: 123–134.

Breitung, W. (1999): 'The end of "Made in Hong Kong"? – De-industrialisation and industrial promotion policy in Hong Kong', *Geographica Helvetica*, 54: 242–251.

——(2001a) Hongkong und der Integrationsprozess: räumliche Strukturen und planerische Konzepte (*Basler Beiträge zur Geographie* 48). Basel: Wepf.

——(2001b) Globalstadt Hongkong – lokale Konsequenzen der globalen Vernetzung, *Asiatische Studien*, LV/3/2001: 611–648.

——(2002) Hongkong: Die Globalstadt Chinas, in R. Schneider-Sliwa (ed.) *Städte im Umbruch*, Berlin: Reimer, 73–100.

Cartier, C. (2002) *Globalizing South China*. Oxford: Blackwell.

Castells, M. (1996) *The Rise of the Network Society*. Cambridge, MA: Blackwell.

Census and Statistics Department (1991a) *1991 Population Census*. Hong Kong: Census and Statistics Department.

——(1991b) *Employment and Vacancies Statistics*, Series C (industrial sectors). Hong Kong: Census and Statistics Department.

——(1992) *Employment and Vacancies Statistics*, Series A, B, D (services and trade sectors). Hong Kong: Census and Statistics Department.

——(1996) *1996 Population by-Census*. Hong Kong: Census and Statistics Department.

——(1997a) *Social and Economic Trends*. Hong Kong: Census and Statistics Department.

——(1997b) *Employment and Vacancies Statistics*, Series A–D. Hong Kong: Census and Statistics Department.

——(2000) *Hong Kong in Figures*. Hong Kong: Census and Statistics Department.

——(2001) *2001 Population Census*. Hong Kong: Census and Statistics Department.

——(2002) *Employment and Vacancies Statistics*, Series A (service sectors). Hong Kong: Census and Statistics Department.

——(2004) *Other Economic and Business Statistics* Online. Available http://www.info.gov.hk/censtatd/eng/hkstat/fas/other/other_index.html

Chu, D. K. Y. (1996) 'The Hong Kong – Zhujiang Delta and the world city system', in F. C. Lo and Y. M. Yeung (eds) *Emerging World Cities in Pacific Asia*, Tokyo: United Nations University Press, 465–497.

Dunning, J. H. and Norman, G. (1987) 'The location choice of offices of international companies', *Environment and Planning A*, 19: 613–631.

Enright, M. J., Scott, E. E. and Dodell, D. (1997) *The Hong Kong Advantage*. Hong Kong: Oxford University Press.

Fainstein, S. S., Gordon, I. and Harloe, M. (1992) *Divided Cities: New York and London in the Contemporary World*. Oxford: Blackwell.

Forrest, R., La Grange, A. and Yip N. M. (2004) 'Hong Kong as a global city? Social distance and spatial differentiation', *Urban Studies*, 41: 207–227.

Friedmann, J. (1986) 'The world city hypothesis', *Development and Change*, 17: 69–83.

——(1995) 'Where we stand: a decade of world city research', in P. L. Knox and P. J. Taylor (eds) *World Cities in a World System*, Cambridge: Cambridge University Press, 21–47.

——(1998) 'World city futures: the role of urban and regional policies in the Asia-Pacific Region', in Y. M. Yeung (ed.) *Urban development in Asia: retrospect and prospects*, Hong Kong: Hong Kong Institute of Asia-Pacific Studies, Chinese University, 25–54.

Günter, M. (2003) *Socio-economic Developments in the Global City Hong Kong*, Master's thesis, University of Bern (Switzerland).

Immigration Department (2003) *Foreign Domestic Helpers Population in Hong Kong* (tabulation received from the Department).

——(2004) *Employment Visas Issued in Hong Kong* (tabulation received from the Department).

Information Services Department (2003) *Hong Kong 2002*, Online. Available http://www.info.gov.hk/yearbook/2002/

Jao, Y. C. (1997) *Hong Kong as an International Financial Centre, Evolution, Prospects and Policies*. Hong Kong: City University Press.

Jones, A. (2002) 'The "global city" misconceived: the myth of "global management" in transnational service firms', *Geoforum*, 33: 335–350.

Lin, G. C. S. (2002) 'Hong Kong and the globalisation of the Chinese diaspora: a geographical perspective', *Asia-Pacific Viewpoint*, 43: 63–91.

Loh, C. (2002) *Nimble and Nifty: Transforming Hong Kong*, Online. Available http://www.civic-exchange.org/03publication/HKPrimer.pdf

Lui, H. K. (1997) *Income Inequality and Economic Development*. Hong Kong: City University Press.

Lui, T. L. and Chiu, S. W. K. (2003) 'Hong Kong becoming a Chinese global city, Occasional Papers', No. 29, Hong Kong: The Centre for China Urban and Regional Studies.

Meyer, D. R. (2000) 'Hong Kong as a Global Metropolis', *Cambridge Studies in Historical Geography*, vol. 30, Cambridge: Cambridge University Press.

Ng, M. K. and Hills, P. (2003) 'World cities or great cities? A comparative study of five Asian metropolises', *Cities*, 20: 151–165.

O'Loughlin, J. and Friedrichs, J. (eds) (1996) *Social Polarization in Post-industrial Metropolises*. Berlin, New York: De Gruyter.

Perry, M., Yeung, H. and Poon, J. (1998) 'Regional office mobility: the case of corporate control in Singapore and Hong Kong', *Geoforum*, 29: 237–255.

Rating and valuation department (2000) *Quarterly market statistics*. Online. Available http://www.info.gov.hk/rvd/property/index.htm

Rimmer, P. J. (1996) 'International transport and communications interactions between Pacific Asia's emerging world cities', in F. C. Lo and Y. M. Yeung (eds) *Emerging world cities in Pacific Asia*, Tokyo: United Nations University Press, 48–97.

Sassen, S. (1991) *The Global City: New York, London, Tokyo*. Princeton, NJ: Princeton University Press.

——(1994) *Cities in a World Economy*. Thousand Oaks, CA: Pine Forge Press.

——(2001) *The Global City: New York, London, Tokyo*, updated edn. Princeton, NJ: Princeton University Press.

——(2002) 'Locating cities on global circuits', in S. Sassen (ed.) *Global Networks, Linked Cities*. New York, London: Routledge, 1–36.

Scott, A. J. (ed.) (2001) *Global City-regions: Trends, Theory, Policy*. Oxford: Oxford University Press.

Shin, K. H. and Timberlake, M. (2000) 'World cities in Asia: cliques, centrality and connectedness', *Urban Studies*, 37: 2257–2285.

Simmonds, R. and Hack, G. (eds) (2001) *Global City Regions: Their Emerging Forms*. London: Spon Press.

Sit, V. (1981) 'The changing frontiers of the central business district', in V. Sit (ed.) *Urban Hong Kong*, Hong Kong: Summerson, 78–102.

——(2001) 'Increasing globalization and the growth of the Hong Kong extended metropolitan region', in F. C. Lo and P. J. Marcotullio (eds) *Globalization and the Sustainability of Cities in the Asia Pacific Region*. Tokyo: United Nations University Press, 199–238.

Siu, Y. M. (1996) 'Population and immigration: with a special account on Chinese immigrants', in M. K. Nyaw and S. M. Li (eds) *The other Hong Kong Report 1996*, Hong Kong: Chinese University Press, 324–347.

Skeldon, R. (1997) 'Hong Kong: colonial city to global city to provincial city?', *Cities*, 14: 265–271.

Smith, M. P. (2001) *Transnational Urbanism – Locating Globalization*. Malden, MA and Oxford: Blackwell.

Sum, N. L. (1995) 'More than a "war of words": identity, politics and the struggle for dominance during the recent "political reform" period in Hong Kong', *Economy and Society*, 24: 67–99.

Tang, J. (1997) 'Hong Kong in transition: globalization versus nationalization', in M. K. Chan (ed.) *The Challenge of Hong Kong's Reintegration with China*. Hong Kong: Hong Kong University Press.

Taylor, P. J. (1997) 'Hierarchical tendencies amongst world cities: global research proposal', *Cities*, 14: 323–332.

Taylor, P. J., Walker, D., Catalano, G. and Hoyler, M. (2002) 'Diversity and power in the world city network', *Cities*, 19: 231–241.

Tyner, J. A. (2000) 'Global cities and circuits of global labor: the case of Manila, Philippines', *Professional Geographer*, 52: 61–74.

Wong, H. (2002) 'Gap between richest and poorest Hong Kong is widening', *South China Morning Post*, 19 October 2002.

Yusuf, S. and Wu, W. (2002) 'Pathways to a world city: Shanghai rising in an era of globalisation', *Urban Studies*, 39: 1213–1240.

Zhao, S. (2003) 'Spatial restructuring of financial centers in Mainland China and Hong Kong', *Urban Affairs Review*, 38: 535–571.

6 Globalizing Macau

The emotional costs of modernity

Philippe Forêt

This chapter deals with the ambiguity that political authorities feel towards culture and history when they are pressed to enlarge and modernize urban infrastructures (Yusuf *et al.* 1997, Caldeira Cabral *et al.* 1999). I will discuss the strategy followed by the Harbour Works Department of Macau as the city sought to reposition itself as an international trade centre. I examine Macau's spatial transformations between 1910, when a progressive regime came to power in Lisbon, and 1930 when the first extension phase of the Porto Exterior facilities was completed. I review the tactics used to promote a new image of the Portuguese colony and seek explanations for the contradictions found in the official discourse on the changing environment. I rely mostly on the comparison of the visual narratives provided by the tourist guidebooks published during the period (Ho 1994, Pittis *et al.* 1997). Paying attention to the omissions, repetitions and silences found in the descriptions of this unique historical landscape allows me to test the limits set by culture to the globalization processes that are transforming the southern coast of China (Cartier 2001).

From postcards in the 1910s to the public image of the 1930s

For centuries, the city-port of Macau has facilitated the exchange of goods, ideas and people between China and the rest of the world (Cheng 1999a, Pons 1999). Colonial Macau took advantage of an informal agreement between Portugal and China to develop a sense of place that brought together military and religious architecture, romantic aestheticism, and crude forms of capitalism. Beginning in 1915, engineers and urban planners infatuated with modernity cast away the image of a chic summer resort. While the port authority continued to refer to the territory's cachet until 1930, its promotional literature presented the progress of industrialization, the extension of the harbour facilities, and the assets of the colony for international commerce (Map 6.1).

In order to look at the history of progress in colonial Asia, I will examine how the greatness of Portugal, the exoticism of China, and the promises of modernity came to be jointly exalted in an unlikely forum. The attraction that Macau exerted on Europeans and Americans' imaginations was such that the first photographs

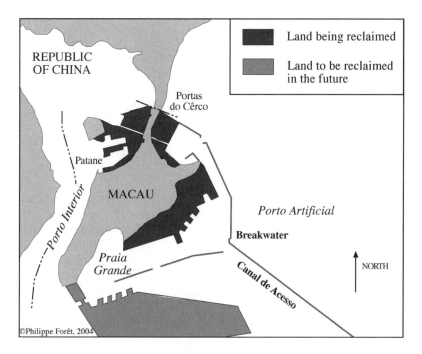

Map 6.1 The 1926 plans of the Harbour Works Department.

taken of Asia, in 1844, were those of its peninsula.[1] Seen from the stately Rua Praia Grande, the landscape of Macau yielded its own vision of global relations with values based on aesthetic contemplation, intercultural exchanges, and tolerance of vice (Pons 1999, Taylor 2002). I will draw on pictures and urban maps that enhanced the image that Macau had between 1910 when Portugal became a Republic with an empire and 1930 when work on the Outer Harbour was completed and, as a result, Macau acquired a new maritime façade. My analysis will cross several boundaries as I move between a river estuary, a reclaimed area, a Portuguese promenade, and the Cantonese low houses that extended inland behind the lofty arcades of Rua Praia Grande (Johnson 1997, Pons 1999). The geographical and ethnic boundaries that separate the littoral from downtown and Portuguese institutions from Chinese stores are easy to locate in the urban fabric. I am however interested in a much more elusive boundary, one that delineates antagonistic perspectives on Macau's past and future (Schein 2001).

I will focus on the trope of a 'charming bay', understood as the aesthetic fusion of geographical confusion (Macau as an imitation of Naples or Lisbon) and historical denial (the eighteenth-century landscape present in twentieth-century Macau) (Corbin 1995). Understanding how an image of contemplation gave way to another of action would assist in understanding how the city's uniquely complex identity changed over time (Dubbini 2002). Examining the photos taken by the administration helps in underlining the significance of contradiction and ambiguity in the cultural values of Macau's colonial elite. A geographical study of Macau's waterfront can therefore contribute to our general assessment of colonial rule and internationalism because this peculiar example directly magnifies the leading role of culture in the history of modernity (Taylor 2002).

Although often overlooked, tourist guidebooks and postcards provide an intricate insight into the interplay of globalization and colonialism (Arnold 1910). Old tourist booklets can provide evidence on the contradictory attitudes and silence policies that government agencies experienced and implemented. The landscape paintings of Macau and the photographs of the institutions located near Praia Grande (the Boa Vista Hotel, the Governor's Palace, the Sé Cathedral, etc.) reveal the resilient complexity of the colonial order (Ho 1994). The city government, while usually unable to fund them, invited architects and urban planners to prepare reclamation projects in the immediate vicinity of Praia Grande. These projects resulted in exquisite maps, lofty statements on progress, as well as new guidebooks to modern Macau (Do Inso 1930). The comparison of photographs and postcards of Praia Grande with these texts gives us an insight on concepts about mapping, collage, and disappearance that are both local and universal in significance (Mathews 1998). Instead of speaking about real places and true events, I suggest that we look at how subjective geography, one that plays with feelings of lack and loss, successively celebrated Praia Grande, divorced the bay from the Pearl River delta, and finally stopped photographing it. Such attitude changes reveal much larger issues about Macau, such as its image of self, its conceptions of modernity, or its strategy to avoid marginalization at the frontier that the Portuguese, British and Chinese Empires shared. In Macau several communities, each with its own subculture, met but never merged: Chinese and more precisely Cantonese immigrants, Portuguese bureaucrats, and Catholic Macanese residents who were Chinese looking but Portuguese speakers. The presence of a fourth group was tolerated in the city: international travellers and merchants who were welcomed for reasons we will discuss in the following paragraph.

The Colony invited international tourists to turn their backs to the Cantonese city and marvel at the muddy waters of the picturesque Praia Grande. The perception of Praia Grande changed dramatically, as the bay seemed unable to respond to the economic needs of a progressive time. A new age began in the late 1920s when the construction of Outer Harbour changed the face of Macau forever. In the name of modernity, Bahia Praia Grande – for centuries the major attraction of the Colony – came to *visually* disappear 60 years before the bay was *actually* reclaimed. I connect the disappearance of Praia Grande as a central theme to the emergence of a space of transition on the eastern shore of the peninsula. I pursue this theme through an examination of what is missing in the travel literature of colonial Macau. I deal, therefore, with the photographing policies of Praia Grande when I speculate on the absence of pictures of a bay. Bahia Praia Grande remained physically present but the tide of modernity swept away its *raison d'être*. A landscape that had acquired a dual quality since it reflected the actual Chinese and Portuguese built environments as well as visions about an idealized future thus lost its Proustian character to assume only utilitarian functions.

I will not attempt to review the especially vast scholarly literature on Macau. Richard Louis Edmonds (1993) has written a comprehensive account of the geography of Macau as well as a bibliographical introduction to the territory. Historians have been prolific on Macau taking advantage of well-documented city archives to analyse the relationship between Portugal, China and Macau. Jonathan Porter and Charles Boxer are probably the two best known scholars in Macau studies; many have enjoyed Porter's (1996) *Macau, The Imaginary City: Culture and Society, 1557 to the Present.* Austin Coates has written the semi-fictional *City of Broken Promises* on Macau in the 1780s. Academics may enjoy *Macau. A Cultural Janus* by Christina Miu Bing Cheng (1999b). The general public may consult the richly illustrated *Revista de Cultura* published by the Instituto Cultural de Macau (ICM).[2] The *South China Morning Post* and *Hong Kong Standard*, both edited in Hong Kong, are reliable sources of information on daily trivia in Macau.

The history of Macau from 1557 to 1910

Portugal officially founded Macau in 1557.[3] After Portuguese vessels defeated the pirate fleets that plagued the coasts, merchants, officers, and priests from Portugal gained residency rights on a tiny peninsula at the entrance of the most important waterway in South China.[4] Although administered by Portugal, the city paid taxes until 1848 to the Chinese government since it was part of China. In 1887, after Portugal sought to suppress the opium trade, the Qing court admitted Lisbon's occupation of the city of Macau and of the islands of Taipa and Coloane.[5] Beijing and Lisbon altered the political status of Macau in 1979, when China accepted the retrocession of a territory that post-Salazar Portugal no longer wanted to rule.[6] This agreement between the two countries over the definition of a zone for political ambiguity turned Macau into the only neutral venue that China and Europe had for four centuries (Montaldo de Jesus 1902, Ptak 2001).

International commerce had to pass through Canton and Macau until the end of China's closed-door policy and the establishment of Hong Kong in 1841 (Porter 1993). Macau became so wealthy that Sir John Bowring called it the 'gem of the Orient Earth'.[7] The Colony went through a difficult period of adjustment when it lost its lucrative monopoly as Shanghai and Canton (Guangzhou) were opened to foreign trade, and Hong Kong rose to pre-eminence in East Asia. Exports declined rapidly and were limited to tobacco, tea, silk, opium, cement and dry salt fish. The principal companies in town were all family firms: shipping and general merchants, millinery stores, printers, grocers and wine merchants, general stores, druggists, and perfumeries. Coolies transited through Macau on their way to the Americas, which provided an additional income to the Colony.[8] In 1926, 150,000 residents inhabited a 3 square kilometres wide territory; the little peninsula was entirely built over when, in 1928, the population reached 160,000. The size of the population could change dramatically according to the political conditions that reigned in China. The figure was only an estimated 80,000 in 1915 (Tetsudôin 1915: 332, MCAOP 1928: 6).

Evaluated at 50,000,000 dollars in 1926, trade was certainly not negligible but Macau had only two modern banks: the Banco National Ultramarino and the Banco Pou Seng. Seven Chinese banks were located in Rua dos Mercadores and Avenida Almeida Ribeiro. This number is small because Macao has historically been important for her speculative activities and not for her commercial activities (MCAOP 1926: 40). Since its beginnings, Macau has been known as a haven for organized crime, a springboard for illegal immigration, a centre for prostitution, and today a smuggling point for endangered species and art objects (Porter 1993).

Officially, four activities dominated the life of Macau at the beginning of the twentieth century all of them in the hands of the Chinese merchant class: importation of rice, exportation of fish, the manufacture of fireworks, and gambling:

> Macao is popularly known as the 'Monte Carlo of the Orient' – there being several large gambling establishments, conducted under Government control, the licenses bringing in a large revenue to the colonial treasury. Besides licensed gambling houses, there is a lottery conducted by the Government. The lots are drawn once a month, the highest prize being as large as $150,000.
>
> (Tetsudôin 1915: 332)

Tourism was actually a very important element of the local economy, in terms of income as well as in terms of prestige (Arnold 1910). During the second part of the nineteenth century, Macau became the summer resort of many of the wealthy residents of Hong Kong. The sea breezes that entered Macau provided a cooler summer than in Victoria City. Tourists took a refreshing bath at Bela Vista or Boa Vista early in the morning, enjoyed the pastel colours of the city buildings in the afternoon light and, before the gambling saloons opened, strolled on the well kept promenade of Praia Grande where military bands played (Map 6.2). They found the time to visit the churches of the 'Christian city' (*a cidade cristã*) as well as the Buddhist temples of the 'Chinese city' (Wangxia in Chinese or Mongha in Cantonese).

The eastern shore of Macau from 1910 to 1930

Flowing southward from Canton, the Xijiang River (Si-kiang or West River) brings alluvium to the Zhujiang delta (Chu-kiang or Pearl River). The prosperity of Macau has directly depended on port accommodations, a channel, and constant dredging (Montaldo de Jesus 1902). Silt has always threatened access to Macau because the city is situated on a river estuary. Proposals for port development were made in the 1880s but led to nothing, though everybody agreed that the biggest obstacle to economic progress was the silting of the harbour, 'a distressing, severe, (and) terrible impediment' (MCAOP 1926: 7). Foreign corporations had some reservations on the ability of the colony's government to act decisively. Made in 1915 in Hong Kong newspapers, statements like 'The Portuguese

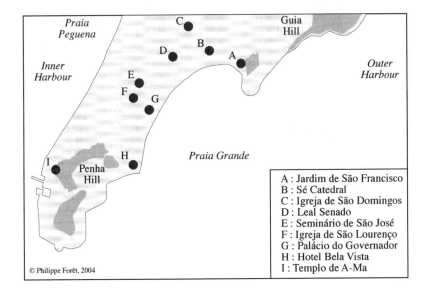

Map 6.2 Macau in 1910.

authorities are now apparently earnestly endeavouring to revive the prosperity of Macau' imply that the authorities in place before Portugal became a Republic were the major obstacle to infrastructure projects (Tetsudôin 1915: 332).

In the late 1920s, Macau decided to open itself to steamers that drew 25 feet of water because it wanted to be part of the traffic of high sea ships that sailed from Hong Kong and Canton, respectively four and eight hours away (Do Inso 1930). Until then, the city had nine wharves but none large enough for ocean-going shipping. The government first conducted construction work on the narrow Inner Harbour or Porto Interior, around Ilha Verde on the western side of the peninsula. Brick factories, cement plants, timber yards and dry dockyards occupied the reclaimed land. The development of the Outer Harbour or Porto Exterior, was the major undertaking on the eastern side of the peninsula. Work began in 1923 and was expected to last for three years at least according to the port authority:

> The plans for this portion of the work were drawn up by distinguished Portuguese engineers, ideas being adapted from some of the best ports of the world. The work of construction was adjudicated to the NETHERLANDS HARBOUR WORKS Co., in public tender in which two British, one American and two Dutch firms were bidding.
>
> (MCAOP 1926: 10)

The 'Porto artificial' project consisted of three elements: the building of breakwaters strong enough to resist typhoons, the dredging of a channel (the 'Canal de acesso') and the building of a reclamation area half the size of Macau, according to the 'Sketch of Macau'. Area reclaimed and to be reclaimed, with site of new Port' map, the project was placed within an ambitious framework that would eventually connect through landfills Coloane and Taipa Islands to the peninsula of Macau (MCAOP 1926: 12a). As the *South China Morning Post* wrote in its 19 March 1926 issue: 'The Portuguese have proceeded with their undertaking with confidence in their hearts and the hope to accomplish something, that, handed down to posterity, will be a monument of endeavour and an example of determination for ages to come' (MCAOP 1926: 12). The Outer Harbour originally included in its plans the reclamation of the Bahia da Praia Grande, where ships anchored when weather permitted, but eventually the new Porto artificial did not extend to the shallow bay (Map 6.3). We need to explain why since there were no physical, political, or technical obstacles to an expansion further south. For a while, a purely cultural and totally invisible border protected the bay from additional development.

The tourist literature on Macau around 1910

An intensively cultural cityscape developed over time that reflected Macau's unique and historical responsibility in world exchanges (Cheng 1999a). Portuguese architecture, with its impressive fortresses and churches protected the native Cantonese population that rarely knew Portuguese, almost never rebelled, and was not Catholic in its huge majority.[9] This architectural legacy

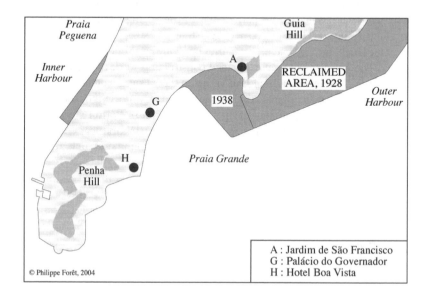

Map 6.3 Macau in the 1930s.

formed the basis needed for the construction of an image of romantic Macau as a destination for international tourism (Arnold 1910). Alfred Harmsworth, a visitor who later became the notorious Lord Northcliffe, stated in an article to *The Times*,

> [t]o me Macao appeared as a beautiful little Portuguese city. There is a certain melancholy about it; but it is the melancholy, not of solitude, but of ruins, of avenidas, of lovely gardens tended by hands long forgotten (...). The pale pink and pale green houses, with balustrades and verandahs, take one for few seconds back to the Tagus.
>
> (MCAOP 1928: 6)[10]

Left for decades without the facilities needed for industrial development, Macau allowed itself to cultivate a *metis* identity very different from the ethnic segregation enforced in nearby Hong Kong (Cheng 1999a). This ambiguity is well reflected in the travel literature on Macau, since the places of interest available for tourist consumption included both Portuguese and Chinese landmarks. The way they were described in guidebooks did not imply that colonial sites were necessarily more significant than native sites. There were exceptions of course: the guidebook to China of the Imperial Japanese Government Railways excluded all Chinese places and listed the façade of São Paulo, Fort Guia, and Camões' garden being the only sites worthy of interest (Tetsudôin 1915: 332).

The Tourist Guide to Canton, The West River and Macau proposed programmes that varied according to the duration of the stay. This guidebook became so popular that it went out of print twice. A functional division in time separated the colonial and native landscapes. Most visitors were in Macau for only two days, but a few had the leisure of staying four days or more. Suggestions to hurried travellers for their first day in Macau included Portuguese places only with the exception of the gambling saloons. The menu of the second day proposed a mixture of Chinese restaurants and factories and the touring of more Portuguese institutions. Travellers who remained for three days or more visited the Cantonese walled villages around Macau and partook of 'tiffins' while enjoying the rural scenery (Hurley 1903: 80–82).[11]

The Bahia Praia Grande (Nanwan) was called the most scenic place of the sleepy Colony. Praia Grande was more precisely the name of a fashionable promenade in summer, a kilometre long esplanade that extended along the shore of the bay. Banyan trees were planted close to the beach but protected by a granite wall. The Government House, official buildings, consulates and residential houses were lined up on the opposite side of the Rua Praia Grande:

> The Praya Grande is a fine marine drive overlooking the bay of the same name. The Governor's residence, many fine private and public buildings, and the Government Offices, are situated along this crescent shaped bay, facing the open sea, while shady banyans line this beautiful road.
>
> (MCAOP 1926: 30)

The rich *hong* merchants had their city mansions built along the promenade: 'Mr. Chun Fong has a very handsome residence on the Praia Grande near the Public Gardens in Macao' (Hurley 1903: 92). The major hotels of the Colony, too, were on Praia Grande (Arnold 1910). Such was the case with the Boa Vista Hotel which was reputed among the best in East Asia for its unsurpassed cuisine, diligent guides and grandiose panorama:

> Pleasantly situated at a slight elevation to the West of the Praia Grande and approached by a well paved road having a very easy gradient, it commands grand panoramic views over the beautiful sea dotted with many islands, the quaint old Settlement and the distant mainland.
>
> (Hurley 1903: xxxxii)

Travellers who admired it from the hotel's upper veranda reported that the Bay of the Praia Grande Seen was a modest replica of the beautiful Bay of Naples (Hurley 1903: 73).[12] Although repetitive, quoting such comments is important because they identify the bay with the geographical pivot of colonial Macau.

The tourist literature on Macau around 1930

The Harbour (or Port) Works Department of Macau ordered its Publicity Office to compile two short travel guidebooks, which were published in English in 1926 and 1927. The Department anticipated an increase in business that would have followed the completion of expansive port facilities on the eastern shore of Macau. The purpose of the first brochure was to present the new opportunities that would exist for the 'progressive business man' and to encourage international tourism:

> Macao is very interesting to the tourist, who can find in this town, beautiful gardens, Chinese temples and evidences of Portuguese occupation from early times. The Chinese quarter will always be of interest to visitors, and is quite close to the European residential centre.
>
> (MCAOP 1926: 21)

The Harbour Works Department felt it had to rectify the public image of Macau because until then the Colony was considered only as a resort where the traveller would relax from more stressful Hong Kong and Canton:

> The splendid climatic conditions (of Macau) and its salubrity, the tranquillity and natural beauty, and its picturesque scenery and historical associations make this Portuguese colony one of the most charming of ports in the Far East.[13] It is very much admired by tourists, and declared to be a splendid resort for quiet and retirement (...). Macao is the health-resort par excellence, and what it offers is not peace alone, but what is more, 'an atmosphere of peace and rest' much sought after but seldom found.
>
> (MCAOP 1926: 8)

In *Macao: The Portuguese Colony in China*, the Department insisted that the administration welcomed the entrepreneurs who would take advantage of commercial opportunities and the industrial potential of a city. Land was cheaper and labour had always been inexpensive.

In 1927, the Department published *A Visitors' Handbook to Romantic Macao*, which, although organized differently, constituted an enlarged revision of *Macao: The Portuguese Colony in China*.[14] The first edition of the *Visitors' Handbook* was quickly sold out and a second edition was printed the year after:

> The active demand for this booklet has proven the need for such a publication, and the complete exhaustion of the first edition in less than two weeks has prompted the issue of a second edition, considerably added to with new sections and much further useful information
>
> (MCAOP 1928: preface)

As the change of titles suggests, the editors had become interested in foreign tourists more than in captains of industry. This is curious because the Colony was now open to ocean traffic, the construction of the new port had been almost completed and empty space existed on reclaimed land for the building of offices and warehouses. Nevertheless, the Department issued a new booklet to help 'the adventurous spirits' in their discovery of 'Old Macau':

> There is a charm in romance that words cannot express, and romance embraces life in all its aspects, extending also to Nature, countries, and human habitations; and few are the romantic scenes left in this modern world. In Macao, however, there is romance still: the romance of history, sung and seldom forgotten, and herein lies its charm. Those who would turn from sordid commercialism to seek and appreciate the charm that underlies beauty will find Macao, in her Nature setting, soul satisfying.
>
> (MCAOP 1928: 5)

This quotation is an evidence of the tensions between two competing views of modernity in Macau – one that accepts its cultural heritage and one that rejects it. The same government agency sought to promote them at the same time as if a charming, introspective, and cultural Macau would coexist with a progressive, extroverted and industrial Macau that looked towards the future. The eastern shore of Macau was the locale where this tension became most clearly visible because it was here that the Porto artificial confronted Praia Grande Bay.

Taking pictures of the landscape of modernity

Places that symbolize modernity were scattered in the text of the Macao guidebooks of the Harbour Works Department (MCAOP 1928: 12).[15] The list included the Military Hospital near the wooded park of the Guia Lighthouse, the lighthouse itself whose lighting installations were replaced around 1900, the secluded Macau Electric Company founded in 1910, and the radio station of Macau, one of the most powerful ones in East Asia.[16] On its hilltop, Fort Guia was very conspicuous although the largest military structure was at São Paulo do Monte. Add to this list the Macau Club where physicians, lawyers, engineers and all 'the principal Portuguese residents of Macao' met. The club's reading room provided newspapers from Macau, like *A Patria* and *O Combate*, and the foreign daily papers.

The two guidebooks of the port authority had many pictures of the Colony. The illustrations in the *Visitors' Handbook* were of higher quality and selected with care to impress readers. The locations of the images in the booklet and the arrangement of the photograph series were indicative of the editors' concerns. Camões' bust and grotto, the A-ma temple, the Vasco da Gama monument, the Barrier Gate, the Pillar of Victory, the Guia Lighthouse, the Flora Gardens, the Old Protestant Cemetery, the Camões' Gardens, São Paulo Church and Santa Casa da Misericordia, were culturally significant places. One picture deserved a special mention for its original fusion of Portuguese and Chinese traditional architectures: 'In and Around Macau' was a collage of two photographs that features a Chinese garden and the Governor's residence. A Chinese reader would not have missed the symbolism of the composition: the garden forms a square while the Governor's palace lies inside a circle. In Chinese cosmology, the earth is square while the sky is round. The picture can therefore be interpreted as an allegory for Macau: a Chinese piece of land under a Portuguese canopy (MCAOP 1928: 12a). These pictures that celebrated colonial culture were immediately followed by a second series of photographs. The industrial Ihla Verde, a brick making factory, the fishing fleet, the industrial district of Patane, the dockyard of Inner Harbour, the Macao Water Works, streets scene in the Inner Harbour and Chinatown did not fit well with what travellers had read so far about picturesque Macau. This systematic but internally incoherent arrangement of illustrations must be the outcome of meetings between officials who held contradictory visions on the future development of Macau.[17]

On the other hand, pictures of a number of places were missing: photographs of the Race Course, the Victoria Cinematograph, the Riviera, Boa Vista and President Hotels, the Almeida Ribeiro and Republica avenues could have contributed to the modernity theme. Photographs of the Teatro Dom Pedro V, the Lin Fung Temple (Lin-fung miu or Lianfeng miao), the Penha Chapel, and the Sé Cathedral could have enriched the romantic theme.[18] Other places could have been photographed to illustrate the dual allegiance of the Macanese identity like the Loo Lim-yok's estate with its Portuguese-style mansion surrounded by a Chinese-style garden. The strangest omission was the absence of pictures of Praia Grande and the Outer Harbour, as if the Harbour Works Department failed to reach a consensus on how to depict Macau's new eastern shore.

The business community of Macau had some sympathy for Praia Grande, but not too much since it symbolized a long era of stagnation. The politically conservative *Macao Review* published a prophetic description of the Colony's future. An anonymous journalist wrote that the port authority was opening to

Macau 'the gates to a glorious day, after a long, long night of languid slumber'. In the same article he compared Praia Grande to an abandoned cemetery:

> No sound of activity was to be heard as the steamer slowly steamed into port, giving the visitor the impression that he had come upon a city that was dead. Proceeding down the Outer Harbour [toward Praia Grande], the feeling was further enhanced: some solitary fishing craft lay idly at anchor.
>
> (*The Macao Review* 1–2: 19)[19]

The two pictorial treatments of Praia Grande around 1930 present a strong contrast with the tourist literature and many postcards produced two decades before (Ho 1994). The depictions of the Colony put Praia Grande at the centre of the travellers' aesthetic experience in Macau, but the port authority did not show the bay. Complacent and repetitive descriptions of the promenade are present in each guidebook, but where are the photographs? Praia Grande became literally a text since no visual material accompanied its introduction to the tourists. This treatment by the colonial administration is surprising because until the turn of the century the bay was the favourite theme of many paintings and postcards of Macau. In other words, Praia Grande was transformed from a visual to a textual landscape when officials of the Republic of Portugal sought to modernize the image of the Colony.

Conclusion

Until 1910, when in Lisbon a republican regime replaced the monarchy, political isolation, economic irrelevance and the sedimentation of its port had combined to keep Macau somnolent and picturesque. The Colony survived the passage of time in the shadow of Hong Kong, while keeping a distinct identity as a Sino-Portuguese settlement that the tourism industry supported. The official guide-books to Macau nevertheless made it obvious that government agencies did not expect tourists to stay for more than a few days. The charms of the city were not supposed to last. After all, there was no reason to assume that casual visitors would fail to quickly perceive the true dimensions of the Macanese society or would find insularity, parochialism, and a *metis* culture so attractive that they would prolong their sojourns. The administration had, moreover, definite plans to cast off the image of a summer resort and turn the Colony into an industrial city with direct access to maritime trade. The building of the port facilities compelled officials to reconsider the identity of the Colony based until then on its historical relationship with Praia Grande. The Portuguese exclave extended on the eastern shore of the peninsula, around the bay: reclaiming the bay within the name of progress implicitly rejected the ways in which the Macanese elite had contemplated its territory for generations. While providing space for a ferry terminal, the massive reclamation projects linked to the creation of the Outer Harbour were both openly welcomed and secretly feared by the administration. The decision not to reproduce in the same booklets photographs of both the new harbour and the ancient bay illustrate this ambiguity felt about the emotional cost of modernity and globalization.

Like elsewhere in East Asia, in Shanghai, Seoul, and Tokyo, progress in Macau has meant erasing the past and rebuilding the urban environment (Map 6.4). Once physical limits were imposed to the scenery of Praia Grande, the destruction of the architectural patrimony of Macau could begin. Joint venture companies backed by Hong Kong and Chinese investors have built new casinos, shopping malls, apartment complexes and factory facilities since the 1970s. The once rural Taipa and Coloane islands are connected to the peninsula and Macau to the undistinguished urban sprawl of the Zhujiang delta (Porter 1993, Wong *et al.* 1997). Ferryboats loaded with tourists still ply the Hong Kong–Macau route. Every day, hydrofoil ferries make 80 trips between the two cities. Macau received nearly 12,000,000 visitors in 2003. Two-thirds of Macau's tax revenue came from the Sociedade de jogos de Macau, which is the Portuguese name of Stanley Ho's gaming empire. The construction of 20 Las Vegas-style casino resorts with 60,000 hotel rooms is being planned. Deutsche Bank (Hong Kong) and Société Générale (Asia) are the leading banks of the future Wynn Resorts project. The two ex-colonies, both run by business tycoons, are listed before Geneva and Zurich as the world's most expensive cities.

Today, the professionals of the tourism industry focus on both the economic potential as well as the historical landscape of Macau, even if locating the architectural remnants of a glorious past can be challenging. Travellers have never found so little that would be related to Macau's authentic history, either because sites have been thoroughly destroyed or because landmarks have been extensively

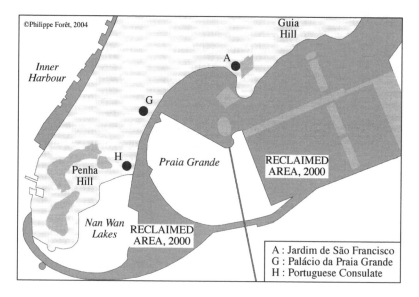

Map 6.4 Macau in 2000.

restored (Fallon 2002). Since Praia Grande Bay is now reduced to two hemispheric basins, the icon that the Tourism Bureau sells to visitors is the façade of the São Paulo church with its tombstone quality.[20] The tourism industry is quickly expanding in size, as the territory wants to position itself as a centre for international conventions and festivals (Cheng 1999a). Talks about the new airport that is supposed to end Macau's isolation and transform the city into a gateway to China may remind us of visionary discussions held in the 1920s about granting adequate transportation to the Colony (Porter 1993).

Appendix

Chronology

1845: Lisbon declares that Macau is a free port.

1863: Rua da Praia Grande is widened through the reclamation of the shore of the bay.

1864: Feasibility study for the improvement of port facilities.

1884: Submission of Adolfo Loureiro's project for the construction of an Outer Harbour.

1908–1909: Submission of Vasconcelos Porto's Outer Harbour's project.

1910: End of the monarchy in Portugal. Inauguration of the Praia Grande coastal road, which consists of Avenida da Praia Grande in the north (Nanwan da malu) and Avenida da Republica in the south (Minguo da malu).

1911: Fall of the Qing dynasty. A republic is proclaimed the year after.

1919: Creation of an Outer Harbour commission.

1923: Work on the Outer Harbour begins.

1926: Industrial fair in São Francisco gardens, Praia Grande.

1926: Military coup in Lisbon. The newly opened avenue north of Praia Grande is named after the dictator, Doctor António Oliveira Salazar who leads the *Estado Novo*, a pro-fascist corporative republic.

1927: Area reclaimed in Outer Harbour.

1928: Inauguration of the Outer Harbour and opening of a trade fair.

1931–1939: First landfill in Praia Grande. The Rua da Praia Grande is cut from the sea between the São Francisco gardens and the Government Offices.

1934: The government grants licences to casino-style gambling.

1949: Fall of Chiang Kai-shek's nationalist regime. The People's Republic of China is established.

1976: Military coup in Lisbon. Portugal becomes a democracy.

1984: Creation of a commission for the protection of Macau's architectural heritage.

1990: A new area is reclaimed to enlarge the Outer Harbour.

1993: A committee selects 'Eight Scenes in Macau' for their outstanding beauty. Praia Grande is not included.

1995: Praia Grande is closed, divided, and partly reclaimed.

1999: Macau becomes a Special Administrative Region of the People's Republic of China.

Notes

1 Both spellings, 'Macau' and 'Macao' can be found in the literature but the latter name became officially obsolete in 1955. I respect the contemporary spelling in my quotations and today's spelling in the body of my text. I apologize for the discrepancies.

2 The web site of this governmental agency is: www.icm.gov.mo.

3 The year 1557 is a conventional date. The name Macau (Macao in historical materials and Aomen in Chinese) would come from the name of the A-ma temple (Ma-kok miu in Cantonese, Make miao in Chinese), which lies at the entrance of the Inner Harbour. The temple was founded at least two centuries before the arrival of the Portuguese.

4 Piracy was still active in the 1920s.

5 The (*Luso-Chinese Treatise of Friendship and Trade*) did not delimit the borders of the territory.

6 China and Portugal established diplomatic relations in 1979. The Sino-Portuguese joint declaration announced in 1987 the return of Macau to China in 1999.

7 Sir John Bowring was the controversial governor of Hong Kong from 1854 to 1859.

8 Coolies were contract workers who replaced African slaves to (usually) work in plantations and mines. South China Shipped 250,000 coolies to Cuba and Peru during the second part of the nineteenth century, 50,000 more coolies went to Mexico between 1900 and 1920. Despite anti-Chinese riots and 'exclusion acts,' they migrated also to the USA, where they built the transcontinental railroads and toiled in the vineyards of California. Canton and Hong Kong restricted the infamous coolie trade, but the regulations of these two cities did not apply to Macau.

9 According to the 1927 census, the population of Macau numbered 157,000 out of which 98 per cent were Chinese. About 85 per cent of the population is ethnically Cantonese. Other Han Chinese communities are from Fujian and Shanghai. The Macanese community – Portuguese speakers of Sino-Portuguese ancestry – would constitute a tiny minority of 1.5 per cent. The percentage of Catholics was historically much higher than it is was in the 1920s: up to 95 per cent by the end of the seventeenth century instead of a low 25 per cent reported in 1930.

10 Lord Northcliffe was the enterprising owner of the *Daily Mail*, the *Daily Mirror*, *The Times*, etc.

11 Indian workers carry their lunch to work in metal boxes stacked together that are called *tiffins*. As they toured colonial Asia, Westerners discovered that tiffin boxes were very convenient for their picnics.

12 While the Boa Vista Hotel is situated on a cliff overlooking the bay, the Macao Hotel and The International were located centrally on Praia Grande, next to the Governor's Palace, and only 5 minutes from the steamer wharves.

13 'Salubrity' refers to the conceptions on public health that the medical doctors entertained during the Victorian period. They held oppressively warm temperatures responsible for all tropical diseases. Invigorating cool winds were supposed to hasten the recovery from malaria, hepatitis, etc.

14 To avoid confusion, I am calling *Macao Guidebook* the 1926 edition and *Visitor's Handbook* the 1928 edition of the booklet published by the Conselho de administração das obras do portos.

15 The *Visitors' Handbook* provides a comprehensive 'Suggested Itinerary' from Avenida Almeida Ribeiro, to Guia Hill, the Barrier Gate, Camões' Grotto and São Paulo's ruins, Penha Hill, and finally the A-Ma Temple.

16 Because it is the oldest lighthouse on the Chinese coast, the Guia Lighthouse has acted as the emblematic introduction of modernity to China by Portugal. A drawing of the lighthouse tower ornamented the frontispiece of the pro-business *Macao Review*.

17 This is my personal interpretation. I am not aware of archival materials about such discussions.

18 The Church of Se is traditionally called a 'cathedral'.

19 *The Macao Review* was a short-lived journal that advocated the creation of a Chamber of Commerce and a generous discussion of the peculiar problems of the Harbour Works Department. Under the title 'First Impressions of Macau, by Hongkong Boy', the journal editors wrote in 1930 an anonymous travel account in which Praia Grande was described and derided, but not even named.

20 Built in 1602, the Jesuit church was burned in 1835. Only the façade has survived the fire.

References

Arnold, J. (1910) *A Handbook to Canton, Macao and the West River*, Hong Kong: Hong Kong, Canton & Macao Steamboat Co. and The China Navigation Co. (eighth edition).

Caldeira Cabral, F. M. and A. Jackson (1999) *Macau Gardens and Landscape Art*, Hong Kong: Fundação Macau and Asia 2000.

Cartier, C. (2001) *Globalizing South China*, London: Blackwell.

Cheng, C. M. B. (1999a) 'A historical and cultural prelude', in *Macao 2000*, J. A. Berlie, (ed.) Hong Kong: Oxford University Press (China).

——(1999b) *Macau. A Cultural Janus*, Hong Kong: Hong Kong University Press.

Corbin, A. (1995) *The Lure of the Sea. The Discovery of the Seaside 1750–1840*, London: Penguin Books (translation of *Le territoire du vide*).

Do Inso, J. (1930) *Macau. A mais antiga colónia europeia no extremo-oriente*, Macau: Tipografia do Orfanato da Imaculada Conceição.

Dubbini, R. (2002) *Geography of the Gaze. Urban and Rural Vision in Early Modern Europe*, Chicago, IL: University of Chicago Press (translation of *Geografie dello sguardo: Visione e paesaggio in età moderna*).

Edmonds, R. L. (1993) 'Macau: past, present and future', *Asian Affairs*, 24 (1): 2–16.

Fallon, S. (2002) *Hong Kong & Macau*, Melbourne: Lonely Planet.

Ho, W. H. (1994) *Xi ri Aomen. Mingxinpianji. O passado de Macau. Colecção de bilhetes postais. The Past of Macau. Collection of Postcards*, Macau: Fundação Macau.

Hurley, R. C. (1903) *The Tourist Guide to Canton, The West River and Macao*, Hong Kong: R. C. Hurley (third edition).

Johnson, L. C. (1997) review of *Macau, The Imaginary City: Culture and Society, 1557 to the Present*, by Jonathan Porter, *The American Historical Review*, 102 (5): 1545–1546.

The Macao Review Illustrated, 1929–1931, 1: 1–6.

Mathews, G. (1998) 'Review of Hong Kong: culture and the politics of disappearance', by Ackar Abbas, *Journal of Asian Studies*, 57 (4): 1112–1113.

MCAOP (Macao. Conselho de administração das obras do portos) (1926) *Macao. The Portuguese Colony in China. A Handbook*, Macau: The Publicity Office, Harbour Works Department.

—— (1928) *A Visitors' Handbook to Romantic Macao*, Macau: The Publicity Office, Port Works Department (second edition).

Montaldo de Jesus, C. A. (1902) *Historic Macao*, Hong Kong: Kelly & Walsh.

Pittis, D. and S. J. Henders (1997) *Macao: Mysterious Decay and Romance*, Hong Kong: Oxford University Press.

Pons, P. (1999) *Macao, un éclat d'éternité*, Paris: Editions Gallimard.

Porter, J. (1993) 'The Transformation of Macau', *Pacific Affairs*, 66 (1): 7–20.

—— (1996) *Macau, The Imaginary City: Culture and Society, 1557 to the Present*, Boulder, CO: Westview Press.

Ptak, R. (2001) 'Review of *Um porto entre dois imperios: Estudos sobre Macau e as relações luso-chinesas*, by Jorge Manuel dos Santo Alves', *Journal of the American Oriental Society*, 121 (1) (January–March 2001): 158–161.

Schein, R. H. (2001) 'Re-placing the Past?', *Historical Geography*, 29 (special issue: *Practicing Historical Geography*): 7–12.

Taylor, J. E. (2002) 'The Bund: littoral space of empire in the Treaty Ports of East Asia', *Social History*, 27 (2): 125–142.

Tetsudôin, N. (1915) *An Official Guide to Eastern Asia. Trans-Continental Connections Between Europe and Asia. China. Vol. 4*, Tokyo: Imperial Japanese Government Railways (1924 edition).

Wong, C., Deng, H. and Huang, J. (1997) *Aomen dilituji. Atlas de Macau. Macau Atlas*, Macau: Fundação Macau.

Yusuf, S. and Wu, W. (1997) *The Dynamics of Urban Growth in Three Chinese Cities*, New York: Oxford University Press.

7 Cross-boundary integration of the Pearl River Delta and Hong Kong

An emerging global city-region in China

Chun Yang

> Every state border, every border region is unique. Their meaning and significance can vary dramatically over space and time, as regimes change in one or more of the adjoining states, as borders are 'closed' or 'opened', or as prices lurch from one side of the border to the other.
>
> Anderson and O'Dowd (1999)

Introduction

The ongoing complementary processes of globalization and regionalization have brought about the emergence of global city-regions and the proliferation of cross-border regions in various parts of the world since the 1990s (Hettne 1999, Scott *et al.* 2001, Perkmann and Sum 2002). Border regions have been the focus of increasing attention from the late 1980s onwards (Geenhuizen and Ratti 2001). However, existing analysis of cross-border regions has tended to concentrate in North America, Western Europe and recent Southeast Asia (Simmonds and Hack 2000, Perkmann and Sum 2002). Most analysis has been at either supranational or national level, and has focused on economic integration through regional institutions such as the European Union (EU), the North American Free Trade Area (NAFTA) and Asian Pacific Economic Cooperation (APEC) (Scott 1999). Relatively little has been written on the nature and process of cross-border regions in developing countries at sub-national levels particularly in transitional socialist China, with only a few exceptions on the cases of mainland China, Hong Kong and Taiwan (e.g. So *et al.* 2001, Sasuga 2002, Sum 2002).

The Pearl River Delta[1] (the PRD hereafter), one of the most rapidly growing regions in China since the opening of the Chinese economy initiated in the late 1970s, has been recognized as an emerging global city-region by both academic researchers and policy-makers (e.g. Commission on Strategic Development of Hong Kong Special Administrative Region Government 2000, Hall 2001, Scott *et al.* 2001). Previous studies on the PRD region have generally treated Hong Kong as one of the most important sources of foreign investment and mainly conducted from the perspective of cross-border regional production system (Sit and Yang 1997, Shen 2003). A detailed study of the development of the export processing industry in Dongguan, a rapidly growing industrial city in the PRD, has recently argued that a distinct 'global city-region' in which Hong Kong functions as the control and marketing centre and the PRD as the hinterland is quickly taking shape (Lin 2003). After Hong Kong's return to Chinese rule in 1997, attention has been increasingly focused on the changing patterns of the relationship between the PRD and Hong Kong (e.g. Sit 1998, Yeung and Chu 1998, Yeh 2001, Cheung 2002, Hu and Chan 2002, Smart 2002, Yeh *et al.* 2002, Shen 2003). Nonetheless, the dynamics and changing patterns of this global city-region from the point of the theoretical and practical views of cross-boundary economic integration between the PRD and Hong Kong are poorly understood, and comprehensive analysis, especially on the post-1997 situation, remains stubbornly inadequate.

Global city-regions in the era of globalization and regionalization

In line with the trend towards globalization, regionalization or regionalism has enjoyed resurgence in the past few years particularly in East Asia after the financial crisis in 1997 (Liu and Régnier 2003). Since the late 1990s, regionalism has moved from supranational to sub-national or micro-levels, that is microregionalism, which refers to those processes of growing regional interconnectedness that occur below the national level and which cut across national borders. Hence, it is imperative to avoid simply considering the nation as the unit of analysis. Despite the growing number of formal and informal micro-regionalization processes, such as sub-national economic processes of interconnectedness across national borders in Europe, across the US–Mexican border and in the 'region states' of East Asia, microregionalism remains understudied (Breslin and Hook 2002).

Globalization has brought with it a change in the scales at which strategic economic and political processes territorialize. Global cities and global city-regions have emerged as major new scales in this dynamics of territorialization (Sassen 2001). In a world characterized by simultaneous trends towards global-ization and regionalization distinctive sub-national social formations whose local character and dynamics are undergoing major transformations have occurred in global city-regions. As 'a new scale of urban organization' both in terms of its polynucleated but integrated internal structure and its privileged position within far-flung global networks of commercial, social and cultural transactions (Hall 2001) the global city-regions are coming to function as the basic motors of the global economy (Scott 2001). Although rooted in the concept of 'world cities' (Hall 1966, Friedmann and Wolff 1982) and 'global cities' (Sassen 1991) city-regions are more appropriate units or variables of local social organization in the context of the global economy. A global city-region can be defined to comprise any major metropolitan area or contiguous set of metropolitan areas together with a surrounding hinterland – itself a locus of scattered urban settlements – whose internal economic and political affairs are intricately bound up with far-flung and intensifying extra-national relationships (Scott 2000). City-region is characterized by the spatial extent of closely linked economic activity, rather than the 'city', or jurisdictional definition of the settlement. Most city-regions contain dozens, hundreds or even thousands of political subdivisions. Many of the problems which settlements face call for region-wide policies and coordinated action across many jurisdictions. At least eleven global city-regions have been identified, including Bangkok, Boston, Madrid, Randstad, San Diego, Santiago, Sao Paulo, Seattle, Taipei, Tokyo and West Midlands (Simmonds and Hack 2000).

Along with these dynamic transformations some fundamental changes have been occurring. First, huge and growing amounts of economic activity emerge in the form of cross-border relationships, including migration streams, foreign direct investment by multinationals and monetary flows. Second, multinational blocs such as the EU, NAFTA, South American Common Market (MERCOSUR), Association of Southeast Asian Nations (ASEAN) and many others have proliferated. Third, sovereign states and national economies remain prominent, indeed dominant elements of the global landscape, but they are clearly undergoing many significant changes. Some of the regulatory functions formerly carried out by the central state have been drifting to higher levels of spatial resolution while other functions have been drifting downward. Fourth, there has been a resurgence of region-based forms of economic and political organizations with the most overt express being the formation of large city-regions. In consequence, the process of worldwide economic integration and accelerated urban growth make traditional planning and policy strategies in these regions increasingly problematic, while more fitting approaches remain in a largely experimental stage (Brenner 1998, Scott *et al.* 2001).

This chapter attempts to examine the nature and changing patterns of the PRD–Hong Kong cross-boundary[2] city-region over the past two decades, with particular emphasis on the post-1997 socio-economic integration after Hong Kong returned to China's sovereignty. It argues that the 'Greater PRD' (Map 7.1), which includes the PRD within the jurisdiction of Guangdong Province together with the two Special Administrative Regions (SAR) of Hong Kong and Macao, is developing into a cross-boundary global city-region. In addition, this case provides an interesting example of microregionalism and sub-national city-region in which how two different socio-economic-political systems are applied within the same country exemplifying the 'one country, two systems' principle applied by the Chinese government to the Hong Kong and Macao SARs.

Manufacturing investment-initiated integration

Significant economic interaction between the PRD and Hong Kong began with the strategic cross-border relocation of many Hong Kong manufacturing activities since the late 1970s. The opportunity for relocation was provided by China's reform and 'open-door' policy, and it was driven largely by rising land and labour costs in Hong Kong in the early 1980s which made local manufacturing increasingly uncompetitive. The 'front shop, back factory' model was adopted

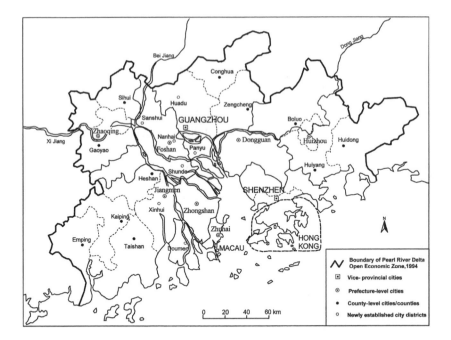

Map 7.1 The sphere of the 'Greater PRD' region.

which meant that Hong Kong remained the management and control centre while land- and labour-intensive production activities were concentrated in the PRD where they could be performed much more cheaply (e.g. Kwok 1995, Sit and Yang 1997). Most studies of the PRD have accommodated the 'front shop, back factory' model within theories of flexible regional production and regional division of labour (e.g. Eng 1997, Chan 1998, Shen 2003). Furthermore, due to the export-orientation of Hong Kong investments in the PRD investment and trade are usually treated as the major measurements of the integration between the two regions (Sung 1991, 1998).

The relocation trend established during the 1980s grew rapidly in the 1990s. According to a survey conducted by the Federation of Hong Kong Industries (FHKI) in 2002 (which updated a similar survey made a decade earlier), a total of 63,000 companies (52 per cent of all Hong Kong-based manufacturers and importers–exporters) were then engaged in manufacturing activities in mainland China. The great majority (53,300 companies) were operating in Guangdong Province, and most of those (85 per cent) were located in the cities of the PRD. The FHKI estimated that 10.3 million workers in Guangdong were employed in the manufacturing operations of Hong Kong-based companies in 2002, 3.3 times as many as in 1991 (FHKI 1992, 2003). Almost two-thirds of the factories and jobs were in Dongguan and Shenzhen conveniently located on the eastern side of the PRD close to Hong Kong (Figure 7.1).

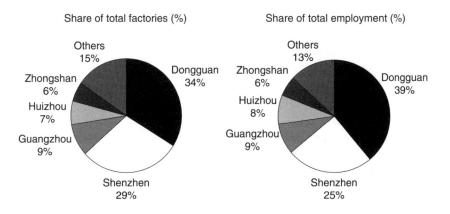

Figure 7.1 Hong Kong-based manufacturing investment in the PRD, 2002.

Source: Compiled from Federation of Hong Kong Industries (2003) *Made in PRD: The Changing Face of Hong Kong Manufacturers: Part II Full Report.*

As a result, the major part of Hong Kong's economy is now tied closely to manufacturing activities across the boundary. According to the 2002 FHKI survey, half a million workers in Hong Kong are employed in manufacturing and import–export companies with production operations in mainland China and another 1 million workers are indirectly employed in producer services-related jobs linked to cross-border manufacturing activities. For every employee engaged in Hong Kong, 24 were employed in mainland China. Furthermore, 80 per cent of the companies surveyed indicated that their Hong Kong offices were serving as regional headquarters and were performing financial management functions, 76 per cent that their Hong Kong offices were principally performing sales and marketing activities and 52 per cent that production was primarily carried out in the PRD.

Since the mid-1990s, the regional division of labour between the PRD and Hong Kong has been further defined by the relocation from Hong Kong to the PRD of low-end value-added services, such as retailing, recreation and leisure, accounting, data processing and back office operations of banks, telecommunication companies and some trade-related services. The share of factor income of Hong Kong from mainland China doubled from 7 per cent in 1995 to 14 per cent of total GDP in 2000 (IMF 2002), and this upward trend is expected to continue in the future. Although half of the FHKI-surveyed companies indicated that functions relating to regional headquarters, financial management, sales and marketing, information technology management, procurement of materials, R&D, storage and transportation and production in Hong Kong would not change in the next 2–3 years, 30–40 per cent planned to move their procurement of materials, storage and transportation to the PRD. Mainland workers had already replaced the entire engineering staff in about 50 per cent of the companies surveyed. About one-quarter of the companies indicated that mainland workers would replace all their Hong Kong employees in engineering, R&D, management, sales and marketing, and finance-accounting-legal functions within five years. About 50–75 per cent of the companies believe that mainland workers will replace all Hong Kong employees in the PRD in the near future. It is clear that manufacturing-based integration between the PRD and Hong Kong has gone well beyond pure manufacturing and expanded into services, especially services for the production of goods for export in the PRD.

Increasing cross-boundary social and economic interaction

Cross-boundary movement of population and vehicles

Growing social and economic links between Hong Kong and mainland China and the sustained rapid development of the PRD have resulted in a remarkable increase in cross-boundary travel, especially since 1997. The number of two-way daily cross-boundary passengers increased from 18,904 in 1980 to 322,192 in 2002. The rate of increase of cross-boundary passengers has quickened since 1997. The annual average growth rate between 1997 and 2002 was 12.6 per cent, compared with 8.9 per cent between 1990 and 1996 (Table 7.1). Furthermore, while most cross-border travel to the PRD during the 1980s and 1990s was business-related, personal travel has become increasingly important since 1997 and accounted for 69 per cent of total cross-boundary trips in 2002. A total of 38.4 million personal trips were made to mainland China in 2002. The vast majority of these trips were to Guangdong Province. Of the total number of trips, 45.4 per cent were made to Shenzhen and 48.2 per cent to other destinations in Guangdong Province. Only 2.5 million person-trips (6.4 per cent) were made to the rest of China (HKSAR CSD, July 2003).

At the same time, mainland has become the largest source of visitors to Hong Kong since 1997. The number of mainland visitors to Hong Kong soared from 0.5 million in 1987 to 6.8 million in 2002. Their share of total visitors increased in the same period from 9.9 to 41.2 per cent. In contrast to the free and convenient cross-boundary trips enjoyed by Hong Kong residents, trips by mainland residents to Hong Kong are hedged about with troublesome formalities. These formalities are deeply discouraging and as a result cross-boundary population flows between the PRD and Hong Kong are quite unbalanced. Over 85 per cent of trips are made by Hong Kong residents (HKSAR Planning Department 1999, 2002).

Cross-boundary trips by mainlanders were long restricted by a strict quota system. With the inter-governmental negotiation between HKSAR and Guangdong provincial government, especially the Guangdong–Hong Kong Cooperation Joint Conference established in 1998, this system was gradually relaxed and abolished altogether in December 2002. Mainland visitors also used to be required to visit Hong Kong in tour groups. This restriction is also being gradually relaxed. Under the 'Closer Economic Partnership Arrangement' (CEPA) between mainland China and Hong Kong concluded in June 2003 permanent residents with household registration of Foshan, Zhongshan, Jiangmen

Table 7.1 Growth of cross-boundary movement of population and vehicles between the PRD and Hong Kong (1990–2002)

Year	Passengers	Daily passengers	Vehicles	Daily vehicles
1990	31,614,702	86,616	4,935,775	13,523
1995	49,852,837	136,583	8,465,496	23,193
1997	64,917,374	177,856	9,508,253	26,050
2000	101,709,396	278,656	11,243,522	30,804
2001	106,637,434	292,157	11,327,857	31,035
2002	117,635,565	322,289	12,344,951	33,822
Annual average growth rate (%)				
1990–1996	9.6	—	10.4	—
1997–2002	12.6	—	5.4	—

Source: HKSAR TD (1990, 1995, 1997, 2000, 2001, 2002), HKSAR CSD (1990, 1995, 1997, 2000, 2001, 2002).

and Dongguan have been allowed to visit Hong Kong individually since 28 July 2003. Similar concessions were made to residents of Guangzhou, Shenzhen and Zhuhai on 20 August 2003, and to residents of Beijing and Shanghai on 1 September 2003. The concession is expected to extend to the whole of Guangdong Province from the mid-2004. These relaxations will certainly result in a marked increase in the number of mainland visitors to Hong Kong in the next few years. The present asymmetric cross-boundary population flows, where visits to the mainland by Hong Kong residents outnumber visits to Hong Kong by mainlanders, are likely to even out significantly. A dramatic rise in the number of mainland visitors to Hong Kong will profoundly affect the development of Hong Kong's tourism sector, and it seems clear that flows of tourists in both directions between Hong Kong and the PRD will increase significantly.

As a result of the development of export-oriented manufacturing activities in the PRD, cross-boundary movement of goods between Hong Kong and the PRD has grown rapidly since the mid-1980s. The total volume of cross-boundary movement of freight between mainland China and Hong Kong by road, rail, sea and air increased from 16.8 million tons in 1985 to 112.6 million tons in 2002, an average annual growth rate of 11.8 per cent. Cross-boundary vehicular trips increased from 0.45 million in 1981 to 12.4 million in 2002, an annual average growth rate of 17.1 per cent. The daily average number of cross-boundary vehicular trips soared from 1,220 in 1980 to 33,822 in 2002, a nearly thirty-fold increase. However, while cross-boundary population movements have grown rapidly since 1997, the growth rate of cross-boundary movement of vehicles after 1997 has been slower than before 1997 (see Table 7.1). The drop is to some extent related to congestion at the boundary crossings and the introduction of strict regulations to control cross-boundary trips, and the growth rate would climb markedly if these constraints were removed. Cross-boundary vehicular movement is strictly regulated by the authorities in both the PRD and Hong Kong. In the case of goods vehicles, for example, the so-called four up, four down (*Sishang Sixia*) regulation treats the driver, cab, box and chassis of a container lorry as a single unit and requires any vehicle allowed to cross the boundary to return with the same driver, the same cab, the same box and the same chassis. Needless to say, these restrictive requirements have raised costs and imposed delays. Meanwhile, cross-boundary trips by private cars have been subject to a quota system for more than 20 years because of infrastructural constraints. Private cars are allowed to cross the boundary if they hold licences issued by both the Hong Kong and PRD authorities.

Increasing cross-boundary activities

As cross-boundary population movements have increased there has also been a marked growth in cross-boundary trips for a range of activities including shopping, tourism, flat purchasing and daily trips for work and social services for elderly.

Cross-boundary shopping

In the wake of the 1997 Asian financial crisis, cross-boundary shopping in Shenzhen has become popular for Hong Kong residents, especially for the low price consumer goods and leisure activities. Consumer expenditure by Hong Kong residents travelling to mainland China amounted to HK 26.3 billion dollars in 2002 (HKSAR CSD, May 2003). As with cross-boundary movements of population, the pattern of consumer expenditure by Hong Kong residents in China and mainland visitors to Hong Kong is markedly asymmetric. In terms of average expenditure per person-trip, Hong Kong visitors to China spent far less than mainland visitors to Hong Kong in the period 2000–2002 (Table 7.2). There are several reasons for this imbalance. Hong Kong visitors to China tend to buy cheap goods such as Chinese tea and Chinese herbal medicines, to use fairly cheap services such as medical services and to spend little on food and entertainment (such as karaoke). Mainland visitors to Hong Kong, on the other hand, come to buy expensive products, such as jewellery, gold decoration and a wide range of clothing, cosmetics and other fashion items. This pattern is very different from the spending patterns of cross-border travellers along the border between the United States and Mexico (Timothy 1999) and the border between the United States and Canada (Di Matteo and Di Matteo 1996), even though the income gap between the United States and Mexico and the large cities on the American side of the US–Canadian border are typical of the contrasts between Hong Kong and mainland China.

Cross-boundary housing purchasing

Flats in Hong Kong tend to be small and expensive and there has been a growing tendency for Hong Kong residents to purchase flats in the PRD, especially in or near cities and towns with good road or rail links with Hong Kong, such as

Table 7.2 Comparison of consumer expenditure of Hong Kong and mainland cross-boundary visitors (2000–2002)

Year	Hong Kong visitors to mainland China		Mainland visitors to Hong Kong	
	Consumption expenditure (HKD 100 million)	Average/per person-trip (HKD)	Consumption expenditure (HKD 100 million)	Average/per person-trip (HKD)
2000	293	870	183	4,831
2001	276	770	233	5,169
2002	263	690	NA	NA

Source: HKSAR CSD, *Hong Kong Monthly Digest of Statistics*, May 2002 and 2003.

Shenzhen and Dongguan. Prices are markedly lower and the flats are often spacious and attractively located. According to a Thematic Household Survey in 2001 by the Planning Department of HKSAR government (2001b) on Hong Kong residents' attitudes to living in mainland China, 41,300 Hong Kong residents had already taken up residence in China. The vast majority of these residents (94 per cent) were living in Guangdong Province, particularly in Dongguan (34 per cent) and Shenzhen (20 per cent). The main reasons given by respondents for taking up residence in China were (i) required by work (78 per cent); (ii) a better living environment (19 per cent); (iii) reunion with spouse or children (19 per cent) and (iv) reunion with other relatives. According to the survey results 163,900 households (7.9 per cent of all households in Hong Kong) had household members who had purchased or built residential properties in the mainland while 26,300 households (1.3 per cent) rented residential properties in the mainland.

Furthermore, 25,500 households (or 1.2 per cent of all households in Hong Kong) had members who intended to take up residence in mainland China in the next ten years. The three reasons most commonly cited by this group were (i) lower cost of living (62 per cent); (ii) better living environment (33 per cent) and (iii) convenience for working in mainland China (15 per cent). The great majority of respondents who did not intend to take up residence in mainland China explained that they were (i) already employed in Hong Kong (38 per cent); (ii) unfamiliar with or unwilling to adapt to mainland attitudes (34 per cent) or (iii) did not want to be separated from relatives in Hong Kong (29 per cent).

Increasingly frequent cross-boundary trip makers

According to the cross-boundary survey conducted by the HKSAR Planning Department in 2001, 496,300 persons usually travelled at least once a week between the mainland and Hong Kong, an increase of 34.7 per cent over the 1999 figure. These frequent visitors included cross-boundary workers, students, business trip makers, leisure trip makers, home-leavers and others (Table 7.3). The number of cross-boundary workers increased from 5,800 in 1999 to 12,500

Table 7.3 Frequent cross-boundary visitors between Hong Kong and the mainland, 2001

Frequent Trip-makers	496,300	100.0%
Cross-boundary workers	19,800	4
Cross-boundary students	22,00	0.4
Frequent business trip makers	220,300	44.4
Frequent leisure trip makers	152,600	30.8
Home-leavers	49,300	9.9
Others	52,100	10.5

Source: Compiled from HKSAR Planning Department, 2002.

Note
Northbound, Southbound: Profile of Travelling between the mainland and Hong Kong based on the Cross-boundary Travel Survey (2001).

in 2001, out of which 99 per cent of them were Hong Kong residents, 95 per cent were males aged 30–49 and 97 per cent lived in Shenzhen. On the other hand, it is estimated that about 7,200 workers who lived in Hong Kong crossed the boundary to work in the mainland four times or more a week. Almost all of them were Hong Kong residents (99.8 per cent). Of them, 68 per cent travelled to Shenzhen for work purposes and about 12 per cent to Dongguan, 2.4 per cent to Zhongshan; 83 per cent of them were males aged 25–44. A total of 2,200 students travelled across the boundary daily to attend school in Hong Kong representing a big increase from about 900 in 1999. These students were all Hong Kong residents, and 92 per cent of them lived in Shenzhen close to the boundary. In addition, 203,900 persons crossed the boundary at least once a week for business, up a significant 33.8 per cent from the figure of 152,400 in 1999. A further 16,400 persons crossed the boundary at least once a week for business, up 31.2 per cent from the figure of 12,500 in 1999. In terms of frequent leisure trip makers, the number of people living in Hong Kong but travelling frequently to the mainland for leisure increased from 85,900 persons in 1999 to 145,800 in 2001, of whom 76 per cent travelled to mainland China for leisure once a week. Most of them (69.3 per cent) usually went to Shenzhen for leisure, followed by Dongguan (7.9 per cent) and Guangzhou (1.6 per cent). On the other hand, the number of people living in the mainland who travelled to Hong Kong frequently for leisure increased greatly from 3,800 persons in 1999 to 6,800 persons in 2001. Of them, 76.1 per cent travelled to Hong Kong once a week, 32.2 per cent were mainland residents and 66.9 per cent resided in Shenzhen.

The greater PRD: an emerging cross-boundary global city-region in China

Since the 1980s, Hong Kong and the PRD have been the most dynamic economies in the world. Hong Kong, as one of the Four Asian Dragons, has cut an economic dash for decades; the PRD languished until the introduction of China's reforms at the end of the 1970s but has sustained a double-digit rate of growth ever since.

Between 1980 and 2001 the annual growth rate of the PRD's GDP reached 16.9 per cent, much higher than China's total growth rate of 9.6 per cent and significantly higher than the growth rate of 13.8 per cent for Guangdong Province as a whole. The annual average growth rate of GDP during 1990–2001 of the PRD was 16.8 per cent, higher than Hong Kong's 7.4 per cent, and this robust rate of growth has narrowed the gap in the level of development between Hong Kong and the PRD and accelerated regional integration.

The PRD has been vital to the continuing growth of Hong Kong's economy since the 1980s, particularly in view of the prolonged recession in the industrialized economies. Regional integration has also promoted economic development and reform in the PRD and in Guangdong Province generally. Despite their formal political and administrative separation, the intensive interaction between the PRD and Hong Kong has transformed the HK–PRD region into a highly integrated economic region. Hong Kong's role as the largest foreign investor and entrêpot for the external trade of China, especially the PRD between the 1980s and 1990s, has made it a vital part of the region as a whole. Indeed, given its geographical position, its common Cantonese dialect, its close family and cultural ties with Guangdong Province and its leadership in regional economic development it would be reasonable to view Hong Kong as an integral part of a 'Greater Pearl River Delta' region encompassing the PRD within Guangdong Province and the Hong Kong and Macao SARs. The partnership between Hong Kong and the PRD has made Guangdong China's fastest industrializing province. Guangdong's relative share of industry value-added in China, rose from 4.7 per cent in 1978 to 11.1 per cent in 2001. More than half this share (7.8 per cent) was accounted for by the PRD. Hong Kong accounts for over 60 per cent of the Greater PRD's GDP, exports and foreign investment, although it has only 2.6 per cent of its total land area and 14 per cent of its total population (Table 7.4). For the past 25 years it has been the dominant economic engine powering the rapid expansion of the PRD, and has played a pivotal role in the PRD's foreign direct investment, trade, opening to the outside world and infra-structural development. In return, Hong Kong profits enormously from its all-out participation in the economic development of the PRD. The opening up of the PRD allowed Hong Kong to successfully transform itself from a manufacturing economy to a service economy in two decades with little or no unemployment. The contribution made by manufacturing to Hong Kong's GDP fell from 23.7 per cent in 1980 to 5.2 per cent in 2001, and its share of total employment fell from 45.9 per cent to 8.9 per cent in the same period. The services sector accounted for over three-quarters of both GDP (86.5 per cent) and employment (87.4 per cent) in 2001. In the past two decades, some manufacturing industries have almost disappeared in Hong Kong. In 2001, for example, the plastic products sector employed only 4,353 workers almost 20 times fewer than the 85,595 workers it employed in 1980.

A multi-nucleated city-region

Several studies have examined the rise of Shenzhen and Zhuhai and the decline of Guangzhou in the 1980s, and have identified Hong Kong as one of the most

Table 7.4 Shares of the main cities in the Greater PRD, 2001

Indicators	Greater PRD	HK	GZ	SZ	Share of Greater PRD (%)		
					HK	GZ	SZ
Land area (km²)	42,824	1,100	7,434	2,020	2.6	17.4	4.7
Census (PRC) or actual (HK, Macao) Population (2000, million persons)	47.93	6.73	9.94	7.01	14	20.7	14.6
GDP (2001, billion USD)	273.4	166.2	32.4	23.6	60.8	11.9	8.6
Retail sales consumer (2001, billion USD)	61.71	23.64	15.1	7.4	38.3	24.4	11.9
Exports (2001, billion USD)	282.22	189.9	11.6	37.5	67.3	4.1	13.3
Utilized foreign capital (2001, billion USD)	36.48	22.83	3.3	3.6	62.6	9.0	9.9

Source: Compiled from HKSAR Invest Hong Kong, *The Pearl River Delta: The Facts and Figures* (2003) and Guangdong Statistics Bureau, *Guangdong Statistical Yearbook 2002*.

Note
HK: Hong Kong, GZ: Guangzhou, SZ: Shenzhen.

important foreign investors in the process of urban and regional development of the PRD (Sit and Yang 1997, Weng 1998, Shen 2000, Gu *et al.* 2001). Because of the boundary between the PRD and Hong Kong, Hong Kong has usually been isolated from the PRD although it has become the de facto motor for economic growth and the leading city in the Greater PRD region.

The inter-relationships between Hong Kong, Guangzhou and Shenzhen have changed significantly in the past five years. Hong Kong has easily become the dominant metropolitan hub for the Greater PRD given its massive financial wealth, strong social and legal institutions, clean government, large pool of entrepreneurs, solid financial systems, and transparent and simple tax and regulatory regimes. Hong Kong is clearly the leading metropolitan core for the Greater PRD, and dominates the region's GDP (60.8 per cent), trade (67.3 per cent) and foreign investment (62.6 per cent). By contrast, the respective shares of the provincial capital Guangzhou are only 11.9, 4.1 and 9.0 per cent (Table 7.4). Yet due to the One Country Two Systems framework, Hong Kong is excluded from the administrative sphere of the PRD and has been mostly isolated from the PRD's regional planning. This isolation is sometimes speciously justified by the argument that Hong Kong should remain 'international' rather than becoming too 'regional' and too closely linked with the mainland. On the other hand, although Hong Kong has played a pivotal role in the rapid growth of the PRD as an economic engine the Guangdong provincial government and local level governments of the PRD are reluctant to admit Hong Kong's position as the central economic city in the region. Hong Kong has never been fully and explicitly viewed as an integral part of the regional planning and coordination for the Greater PRD. This may explain to some extent the problems of duplication and lack of regional coordination in the development of airports, seaports and other transport infrastructure in the Greater PRD region.

In the past few years the fortunes of Guangzhou and Shenzhen have seemed to offer a sharp contrast. Shenzhen has prospered while Guangzhou has been left behind. However, the story is not quite so simple and there are signs that Guangzhou could enjoy a renaissance while Shenzhen faces problems in the future. After China launched its opening and reform policies in 1978 Guangzhou did indeed lag behind burdened by the old economic system and historical baggage. But it remains the political centre for Guangdong Province, and has massive expansion potential and a strong cultural heritage. Guangdong provincial government has recently adopted measures to strengthen its central position since the late 1990s. In 1998 Guangzhou adopted a programme that would transform the city into a modern metropolitan centre within a couple of decades under the slogan 'small changes in one year, moderate changes in three years, significant changes by 2010'. The incorporation of the former county-level cities Panyu and Huadu into the city proper in 2000 enlarged Guangzhou City's total land area from 1,400 square kilometres to 3,719 square kilometres. Guangzhou's urban development plan used to envisage only expansion to the east, but now contains proposals for both eastern and southern extensions. Guangdong Province's tenth Five Year Plan (2001–2005) places Guangzhou at the core of the emerging Greater PRD rapid transit system and highway network. As a result, the cities of the PRD will be linked up by a number of highways and will be reachable within a two hour drive from Guangzhou. Guangzhou's new airport, which has come into operation in 2004, will be one of China's three aviation hubs. Historically, Guangzhou has always been a centre for light industry but the city government is now promoting and developing heavy machinery industries. Particular emphasis will be placed on the automobile industry. Guangzhou will have three vehicle plants and become China's fourth-largest national automobile production base (after Shanghai, Changchun and Wuhan). In early 2003, Guangzhou municipal government approved proposals to develop Guangzhou into an international metropolis instead of a regional centre city. The development of the coastal town of Nansha will play a major part in realizing the goal of 'significant changes by 2010'. Industrial areas along the shoreline, deepwater ports and logistics centres and high-tech industrial areas will be developed in Nansha. Guangzhou municipal government's ambitious goal is to develop Nansha into 'the Pudong of Guangzhou' (the undeveloped Pudong district was selected as the focus for investment in Shanghai's development in the early 1990s and is now a forest of glass-and-steel high-rises and the showcase for Shanghai's modernization). These projects are evidence that Guangdong provincial authorities regard the creation of a mega-Guangzhou, especially the Guangzhou-Foshan metropolitan cluster, as a major goal under the province's overall development plans.

Shenzhen is a young migrant city with substantial high-technology capacity, which hosts one of China's two national stock exchanges. Since the 1980s it has forged ahead to become one of the top three cities in the Greater PRD. Guangdong's tenth Five Year Plan indicates clearly and for the first time that both Guangzhou and Shenzhen will be positioned as the twin 'central cities' for both Guangdong Province and the mainland side of the Greater PRD (excluding Hong Kong). At the end of 1999, there was even a popular rumour that Shenzhen would join Beijing, Tianjin, Shanghai and Chongqing as China's fifth centrally governed municipality. However, the pace of Shenzhen's development has slowed down in the past three years. When Guangzhou decided to develop in new directions, such as automobile and biochemical industries Shenzhen seems to have lost its goals. Among the three pillar economic sectors ascertained by the tenth Five Year Plan two are repeated with Hong Kong including the financial centre and logistics centre (the third is high-tech city). However, due to the central government's policy of developing Shanghai into one of China's major international financial centres, financial development in Shenzhen has encountered a number of difficulties, including delay in the establishment of the second board for the listing of high-tech enterprises and the termination of the new listings on the main board. Shenzhen's advantages gained through preferential policies have ceased to exist after China's accession to the World Trade Organization. Although Guangzhou's GDP per capita of US 4,596 dollars in 2001 was lower than Shenzhen's US 5,242 dollars, and even more lower in terms of external trade and foreign investment, their development trends suggest the balance will tilt towards Guangzhou in the near future. An article entitled 'Shenzhen: Who Abandoned You?' appeared on the Internet in late 2002, which analyses the disadvantages and difficulties of Shenzhen in comparison with Shanghai and aroused quite a big response in the local society and the author with pseudonym was finally invited to have a talk with the former Mayor Yu Youjun in January 2003. Obviously, there is growing concern over the future of Shenzhen. A lack of faith in the city's future is symbolized by the move of several multinational headquarters and some private high-tech enterprises from Shenzhen to Shanghai.

Furthermore, regional competition among constituent cities within the PRD goes far beyond the three dominant city centres as the PRD contains many other ambitious second-tier cities, which may influence the dynamics of the Greater PRD as their economic identity develops. Key second-tier cities include Zhuhai, Dongguan, Foshan (including Nanhai and Shunde, former county-level cities which became city districts of Foshan in 2002), Jiangmen, Huizhou and Macao. Most of the second-tier cities are located along the western corridor of the Delta. The western corridor does not have a developed transport infrastructure as the eastern corridor, which contains the two most promising second-tier cities, Dongguan and Huizhou.

In summary, the multinucleated pattern of the Greater PRD is consistent with the assertion that the 'city-region' represents a new scale of urban organization both in terms of its polynucleated but integrated internal structure and in terms of its privileged position within far-flung global networks of commercial, social and cultural transaction (Hall 2001). Some of these regions may sometimes spill over beyond conventional national boundaries. This has happened on the border between Mexico and the United States with the growth of the San Diego and Tijuana global city-region (Stepner and Fiske 2000). The Greater PRD offers an excellent example of a cross-boundary global city-region, although the application of the 'One Country Two Systems' formula has tended to limit the extent of integration between the Hong Kong and Macao SARs and the rest of the PRD region.

Boundary effects in the regional integration

Although social and economic interaction between the PRD and Hong Kong has become more intensive, the boundary between Shenzhen and Hong Kong continues to resemble the international border as it was before 1997 (Cheung 2002). The physical landscape, management, operation and planning of the boundary area remain much as they were before Hong Kong's return to Chinese rule. Although substantial urban development has taken place on the Shenzhen side of the boundary a security zone immediately to the south of the boundary on the Hong Kong side is still maintained as a 'frontier closed area'. Only limited and authorized access is permitted to this area, just as under British rule (Shiu and Yang 2002).

At present, there are four land control points along the boundary between Hong Kong and Shenzhen: Huanggang/Lok Ma Chau, Lo Wu, Man Kam To and Sha Tau Kok. Lo Wu is the northernmost Kowloon–Canton Railway (KCR) station in Hong Kong and the Lo Wu control point serves only train-bound cross-boundary passengers. These account for more than 85 per cent of cross-boundary passengers. The other three crossing points handle cargo and passenger vehicles and account for the remaining 15 per cent of cross-boundary passengers. Because the vast majority of cross-boundary passengers choose to travel by rail and pass through Lo Wu the railway station is nearly always congested. There are particularly long queues for customs formalities at weekends and public holidays. While most international border crossings are open 24 hours a day, the Hong Kong–Shenzhen boundary crossings only operate between certain set hours and are open from between 15 and 18 hours only every day (Table 7.5). Although hours of operation have been extended several times after the Hong Kong–Guangdong Joint Conference they still fall far short of 24-hour operation.

In response to the increasing cross-boundary flows of goods and people, government officials from Guangdong and Hong Kong have met to develop plans to improve cross-boundary flows. The operating hours of the Lo Wu and Lok Ma Chau checkpoints were extended in 1998 and again in 2002, and the operating hours of the Sha Tau Kok and Man Kam To checkpoints were extended in 1999. Although many businessmen in Hong Kong have demanded that the border crossings be kept open 24 hours a day the two governments have announced that 24-hour operation would be a 'long-term goal'. This probably reflects fears in Hong Kong that 24-hour operation of the boundary crossings would result in a decline of Hong Kong property, wholesale and retail, catering, entertainment, professional services and logistics industries. There was massive congestion at

Table 7.5 Operating hours of the boundary control points between Hong Kong and Shenzhen (until July 2003)

Control points	Operation period for goods	Total hours per day	Operation period for passengers	Total hours per day
Lo Wu	—	—	6:30–24:00	17.5
Lok Ma Chau/ Huanggang	0:00–24:00	24	0:00–24:00	24
Man Kam To	7:00–22:00	15	7:00–22:00	15
Sha Tau Kok	7:00–20:00	13	7:00–22:00	15

Source: Compiled according to HKSAR government, *Cross-boundary Traffic*, http:info.gov.hk/info/ boundary.htm, accessed on 12 November 2003.

the Lo Wu boundary crossing point during the Ching Ming festival in 2000 and calls for 24-hour operation of boundary control points between Hong Kong and Shenzhen have since become increasingly strident. The Shenzhen authorities have been more eager for 24-hour operation than the HKSAR Government. However, no consensus has been achieved on the issue between the two sides except an agreement to extend the operation period to midnight in 2001, except the 24-hour opening in Lo Ma Chau/Huanggang from January 2003.

A comprehensive study on the social and economic impacts of 24-hour operation of the boundary control points was commissioned by the HKSAR Government's Central Policy Unit and conducted by the One Country Two Systems Research Institute (OCTSRI) and Marketing Decision Research Technology (MDRT) Limited in 2001 and completed in June 2002. It consisted of a household survey of 5,573 households and an enterprise survey of 1,598 firms. These surveys suggested that the overall economic impact of 24-hour opening might well be positive and that fears that such a relaxation would disrupt the local economy and exacerbate social problems were much exaggerated. The import and export, transport, communication, banking, financial services and business service sectors, which employed 34 per cent of Hong Kong's total workforce in 2001 and contributed 46 per cent of the territory's GDP in 2000, believed that they would profit from a 24-hour opening. The sectors that expected to lose out (mainly the retail, catering, hotel and entertainment sectors) accounted for only 19 per cent of total employment and 13 per cent of GDP. Both surveys suggested that the impact on the property sector would be limited and some property developers felt it would be better for the property market if the uncertainty factor is removed as soon as possible. About 33 per cent of retail operators believed that their profits would suffer as did a little more than half the catering operations (in particular restaurants, bars, karaoke lounges, massage parlours and billiard halls). There was general concern that 24-hour opening of the land boundary control points could result in an increase in drug abuse problems in Hong Kong, though the household survey findings suggested that border crossing arrangements were not a serious factor in this problem.

There is no evidence that Hong Kong consumers will flock to mainland China in large numbers if the control points operate 24 hours a day. Indeed, most survey respondents (86.7 per cent) said that they did not consider 24-hour opening of the control points would be useful. However, the survey identified a group of frequent travellers to mainland China (visiting at least once a week) who were much better disposed to such an arrangement. The group generates an estimated 46.8 million trips a year and accounted for 45 per cent of all cross-boundary trips in 2001. Most of their visits are work related (66.3 per cent). Nearly half of this group (46.8 per cent) considered that 24-hour operation of land boundary crossings would be useful compared to 12.5 per cent for the general public as a whole. However, 'reducing congestion during peak hours on weekends, public holidays and weekdays' was ranked above 'opening control points round-the-clock every day', and opening the control points for 24-hour operation will not necessarily provide relief from congestion during peak hours (MDRT 2002, OCTSRI 2002). This is probably also a factor in the caution so far displayed by the governments on both sides of the boundary.

The unbalanced cross-border flows and operating restrictions on the boundary control points represent a potential loss of economic opportunity for Hong Kong, the solution to which lies in the hands of the HKSAR Government. If the HKSAR Government relaxed restrictions on mainland travel, investment and immigration to Hong Kong, a more balanced flow of economic activities would occur between Hong Kong and mainland China, and the economic benefits thus derived could help to mitigate losses that certain local business sectors (e.g. the retail and entertainment sectors) might suffer arising from 24-hour opening of the control points. The 24-hour operation of control points is normally discussed from the point of view of Hong Kong residents only but there are also a number of cross-boundary travellers who do not carry Hong Kong ID cards. The survey indicated that an increasing number of foreign businessmen going to the PRD for business deals and inspection had stopped using Hong Kong as their business base because of the tiresome queues in Lo Wu. Perceptions of Hong Kong by foreign and mainland travellers are important, and if this class continues to encounter difficulties at the boundary, Hong Kong's role as an international trading platform will be tarnished and its attraction for tourists diminished (OCTS 2002).

Conclusions

Since the 1980s there have been numerous studies on the emerging processes and spatial patterns of urban changes as a result of globalization. As a complementary process of globalization, cross-boundary regional integration has revived since the 1990s. So far most of the documentation on globalization and regionalization and their induced spatial formations have concentrated on the cases of North America, Western Europe and (more recently) Southeast Asia. Although numerous case studies have been done, the primary unit of analysis has tended to be either the entire region or an individual country in the region. Comparatively, microregionalism remains an inadequate investigation. This chapter has attempted to fill a gap in the literature on sub-national global city-regions of cross-border nature in developing countries during the period of transitional economic development and has taken the PRD and Hong Kong in the context of China as an example.

Cross-boundary integration between the PRD and Hong Kong has expanded from manufacturing investment and outward processing in the 1980s into a wide range of cross-boundary transactions in the past decade with increasing cross-boundary flows of population, goods, vehicles and services. Ironically, while pressure for an open boundary has continued to grow the existing boundary crossings remain open for only limited periods resulting in congestion at all boundary control points. This restriction on the cross-boundary movement of population, goods and capital, especially from mainland China into Hong Kong, has constrained the pace of the regional integration between the PRD and Hong Kong. The Greater PRD does not yet enjoy the 'four freedoms' (a free flow of goods, services, capital and labour) required for complete integration. If restrictions on crossing the boundary are lifted the regional integration of the PRD and Hong Kong will become more substantial and deeper.

The intensive interaction between the PRD and Hong Kong over the past two decades took place despite boundary controls and in the absence of institutional support for regional integration. It was driven almost entirely by market forces. However, the conclusion of the CEPA between mainland China and Hong Kong in June 2003 marks a break with this trend. For the first time China and Hong Kong, as two separate WTO members, have signed a bilateral free trade agreement. This is significant not only for economic restructuring in Hong Kong in general but also for the deeper integration between the PRD and Hong Kong in particular. The fundamental impacts of the integration of Hong Kong and the PRD are a fruitful topic for future research particularly in comparison with similar experiences elsewhere in the world.

With the emergence of the Greater PRD global city-region, the study of the PRD and its interplay with Hong Kong should now move on from previous analysis which considered Hong Kong as an external driving force and should instead deploy an integrated conceptual framework recognizing Hong Kong as an entity within the Greater PRD. This transition does not only have significant theoretical implications but is also important for the prospects of the Greater PRD's regional development in the future, as it faces keen competition from other global city-regions notably the Yangtze River Delta. Sooner or later, if there is to be long-term and rapid growth in the PRD region all concerned parties must recognize the paradigmatic transformation and the emergence of the Greater PRD global city-region of cross-boundary nature. The sooner this paradigm is accepted and put into implementation the better the consequences both for the Greater PRD and China's regional development as a whole.

Acknowledgements

This research is supported by the 'Seed Funding for Basic Research' (10205230/20373/04500/301/01) from the University of Hong Kong. I wish to thank two anonymous reviewers and David Wilmshurst for their constructive comments and suggestions. An earlier version of this chapter was presented at the RGS-IBG Annual Conference 2003 in London, 3–5 September 2003, which was funded by grants obtained from the Committee on Research and Conference Grants (CRCG) of the University of Hong Kong.

Notes

1 The administrative sphere of the PRD is composed of the Pearl River Delta Economic Zone (*Zhujiang Sanjiaozhou Jingji Qu*), which was designated by Guangdong Provincial government in October 1994 (Guangdong Provincial Planning Committee and Office for the Planning of the Pearl River Delta Economic Region 1996). The existing PRD region includes two vice-provincial level cities (Guangzhou and Shenzhen), seven prefecture-level cities (Zhuhai, Foshan, Jiangmen, Zhongshan, Dongguan, Huizhou and Zhaoqing), nine county-level cities (Zengcheng, Conghua, Huiyang, Taishan, Kaiping, Enping, Heshan, Gaoyao and Sihui), two counties (Huidong and Boluo), and a number of city districts under the jurisdiction of the prefecture-level cities and above (see Figure 7.1).
2 The term 'border' (*bianjing*), widely used before 1997 to denote the frontier between the British colony of Hong Kong and Guangdong Province, has been replaced by 'boundary' (*bianjie*) in official documents since Hong Kong's return to Chinese rule, perhaps because the former term was felt to imply an international frontier. The terms 'border' and 'boundary' are therefore used respectively to reflect pre-1997 and post-1997 conditions in this study.

References

Anderson, J. and O'Dowd, L. (1999) 'Border, border regions and territoriality: contradictory meanings, changing significance', *Regional Studies*, 33: 593–604.

Brenner, N. (1998) 'Global cities, global states: global city formation and state territorial restructuring in contemporary Europe', *Review of International Political Economy*, 5 (1): 1–37.

Breslin, S. and Hook, G. D. (2002) *Microregionalism and World Order*, New York: Palgrave Macmillan.

Chan, R. C. K. (1998) 'Cross-border regional development in southern China', *Geojournal*, 44 (3): 225–237.

Cheung, P. T. Y. (2002) 'Managing the Hong Kong–Guangdong relationship: issues and challenges', in Yeh, A. G. O., Lee, F. Y. S., Lee, T. and Sze, N. D. (eds) *Building a Competitive Pearl River Delta Region: Cooperation, Coordination and Planning*, Hong Kong: The Centre of Urban Planning and Environmental Management, the University of Hong Kong, 39–58.

De Matteo, L. and De Matteo, R. (1996) 'An analysis of Canadian cross-border travel', *Annals of Tourism Research*, 23 (1): 103–122.

Eng, I. (1997) 'The rise of manufacturing towns: externally driven industrialization and urban development in the Pearl River Delta of China', *International Journal of Urban and Regional Research*, 554–568.

Federation of Hong Kong Industries and The Hong Kong Centre for Economic Research (2003) *Made in PRD: The Changing Face of Hong Kong Manufacturers: Part II Full Report*.

Federation of Hong Kong Industries, Industry and Research Division (1992) *Hong Kong's Industrial Investment in the Pearl River Delta: 1991 Survey Among Members of the Federation of Hong Kong.*

Friedmann, J. and Wollf, G. (1982) 'World city formation: an agenda for research and action', *International Journal of Urban and Regional Research*, 6 (3): 309–44.

Geenhuizen, M. V. and Ratti, R. (2001) *Gaining Advantage from Open Borders: An Active Space Approach to Regional Development*, Aldershot and Burlington: Ashgate.

Gu, C., Shen, J., Wong, K. Y. and Zhen, F. (2001) 'Regional polarization under the socialist-market system since 1978: a case study of Guangdong province in south China', *Environment and Planning A*, 33: 97–119.

Guangdong Provincial Planning Committee and Office for the Planning of the Pearl River Delta Economic Region (1996) *Study on the Planning of the Pearl River Delta Economic Region*, Guangzhou: Guangdong Economic Publishing.

Guangdong Provincial Statistics Bureau (2003) *Statistical Yearbook of Guangdong 2002.*

Hall, P. (1966) *The World Cities*, London: Weidenfeld and Nicolson.

—— (2001) 'The global city-region: global city-regions in the twenty-first century', In Scott, A. J. (ed.) *Global City-Regions: Trends, Theory, Policy*, New York: Oxford University Press, 59–77.

Hettne, B. (1999) 'Globalization and the new regionalism: the second great transformation', in B. Hettne, A. Inotai and O. Sunkel (eds) *Globalism and the New Regionalism*, Macmillan and St. Martin's, 1–24.

HKSAR (Hong Kong Special Administrative Region) Government, Census and Statistics Department (CSD) (1990, 1995, 1997, 2000, 2001, 2002, 2003) *Hong Kong Monthly Digest of Statistics.*

HKSAR Government, Invest Hong Kong (2003) *The Pearl River Delta: The Facts and Figures.*

HKSAR Government, Planning Department (2001a) *Survey on Cross-boundary Travelling Between the Mainland and Hong Kong 2000* (Executive summary).

—— (2001b) *Thematic Household Survey: Hong Kong Residents' Experience of and Aspirations for Taking up Residence in the Mainland of China* (Executive Summary).

—— (2002) *Northbound, Southbound: Profile of Travelling Between the Mainland and Hong Kong Based on the Cross-boundary Travel Survey 2001.*

HKSARG, Commission on Strategic Development (2000) *Bringing the Vision to Life: Hong Kong's Long-Term Development Needs and Goals.*

HKSAR Government, Transport Department (TD) (1990, 1995, 1997, 2000, 2001, 2002) *Monthly Digest of Transportation Statistics.*

Hong Kong Trade Development Council (2002a) 'Hong Kong as a service platform for Taiwan companies investing in the Mainland', *Trade Watch*, October.

—— (2002b) 'Why Hong Kong? – a survey of Japanese firms in the Pearl River Delta', *Trade Watch*, November.

—— (2003a) 'Why choose Hong Kong as a service platform: a survey of EU companies in the Pearl River Delta', *Trade Watch*, June.

—— (2003b) 'Why Hong Kong as a business platform: a survey of US companies in the Pearl River Delta', *Trade Watch*, July.

Hu, Y. and Chan, R. C. K. (2002) 'Globalization, governance, and development of the Pearl River Delta Region', *The China Review*, 2 (1): 61–83.

International Monetary Fund (2002) People's Republic of China-Hong Kong Special Administrative Region: Selected Issues.

Kwok, R. Y. and So, A. Y. (eds) (1995) *The Hong Kong-Guangdong Link: Partnership in Flux*, Armonk, NY: M. E. Sharpe.

Lin, G. C. S. (2003) 'An emerging global city-region? Economic and social integration between Hong Kong and the Pearl River Delta', in So, A. Y. (ed.) *China's Developmental Miracle: Origins, Transformations, and Challenges*. Armonk, NY: M. E. Sharpe, 79–107.

Liu, F. and Régnier, P. (eds) (2003) *Regionalism in East Asia: Paradigm Shifting?* London: Routledge.

Market Decision Research Technology Limited (2002) *Household Survey on 24-Hour Passenger-Clearance at Land Boundary Control Points (Executive Summary)*, prepared for the Central Point Unit, HKSAR government.

One Country Two Systems Research Institute (2002) *Socio-economic of 24-Hour Operation of Land Boundary Control Points on Hong Kong (Executive Summary)*, submitted to the Central Point Unit, HKSAR government.

Perkmann, M. and Sum, N. L. (2002) *Globalization, Regionalization and Cross-Border Regions*, Palgrave Macmillan.

Sassen, A. (1991) *The Global City*, Princeton: Princeton University Press.

Sassen, S. (2001) 'Global cities and global city-regions: a comparison', in Scott, A. J. (ed.) *Global City-Regions: Trends, Theory, Policy*, Oxford: Oxford University Press, 78–95.

Sasuga, K. (2002) 'Microregionalization across Southern China, Hong Kong and Taiwan', in Breslin, S. and Hook, G. D. (eds) *Microregionslism and world Order*, New York: Palgrave Macmillan, 66–94.

Scott, A. J. (2000) 'Global city-regions and the new world system', in Yusuf, S., Wu, W. and Evenett, S. (eds) *Local Dynamics in an Era of Globalization: 21st Century Catalysts for Development*, New York: Oxford University Press, 84–93.

—— (eds) (2001) *Global City-Regions: Trends, Theory, Policy*, Oxford: Oxford University Press.

Scott, A. J., Agnew, J., Soja, E. W. and Storper, M. (2001) 'Global city-regions', in Scott, A. J. (ed.) *Global City-Regions: Trends, Theory, Policy*, Oxford University Press, 11–32.

Scott, J. W. (1999) 'European and North American context for cross-border regionalism', *Regional Studies*, 33(7): 605–618.

Shen, J. (2002) 'Urban and regional development in post-reform China: the case of Zhujiang Delta', *Progress in Planning*, 57: 91–140.

—— (2003) 'Cross-border connection between Hong Kong and Mainland China "under two systems" before and beyond 1997', *Geografiska Annaler* (Series B, Human Geography), 85: 1–17.

Shen, J., Wong, K. Y. Chu, K. Y. and Feng, Z. (2000) 'The spatial dynamics of foreign investment in the Pearl River Delta, south China', *The Geographical Journal*, 166 (4): 312–322.

Shiu, S. P. and Yang, C. (2001) *A Strategic Study on the Hong Kong-Shenzhen Border Zone*, One Country Two Systems Research Institute. (In Chinese).

—— (2002) 'A study on developing the Hong Kong-Shenzhen border zone, in A. G. Yeh, F. Y. Lee, T. Lee, and N. D. Sze (eds) *Building a Competitive Pearl River Delta Region: Cooperation, Competition and Planning*, Hong Kong: Centre of the Urban Planning and Environmental Management, the University of Hong Kong, 245–270.

Simmonds, R. and Hack, G. (2000) *Global City Regions: Their Emerging Forms*, London and New York: Spon Press.

Sit, V. F. S. (1998) 'Hong Kong's "Transferred" industrialization and industrial geography', *Asian Survey*, 38 (9): 880–904.

——(2001) 'Economic integration of Guangdong province and Hong Kong: implications for China's opening and its accession to the WTO', *Regional Development Studies*, 7: 129–142.

Sit, V. F. S. and Yang, C. (1997) 'Foreign investment-induced exo-urbanization in the Pearl River Delta, China', *Urban Studies*, 34: 647–677.

Smart, A. (2002) 'The Hong Kong/Pearl River Delta urban region: an emerging transnational mode of regulation or just muddling through?', in J. R. Logan (ed.) *The New Chinese City: Globalization and Market Reform*, Blackwell 92–105.

So, A. Y., Lin, N. and Poston, D. (eds) (2001) *The Chinese Triangle of Mainland China, Taiwan, and Hong Kong: Comparative Institutional Analysis*, Greenwood Press.

Stepner, M. and Fiske, P. (2000) 'San Diego and Tijuana', in R. Simmonds and G. Hack, (eds) *Global City Regions: Their Emerging Form*, London and New York: Spon Press, 80–94.

Sum, N. L. (1991) *The China-Hong Kong Connection: The Key to China's Open-Door policy*, Cambridge: Cambridge University Press.

——(2002) 'Globalization, regionalization and cross-border modes of growth in East Asia: the (re) constitution of "time-space" governance', in M. Perkman and N. L. Sum (eds) *Globalization, Regionalization and Cross-Border Regions*, New York: Palgrave, 50–76.

Sung, Y. W. (1995) 'Economic integration of Hong Kong and Guangdong in the 1990s', in R. Y. Kwok and A. Y. So (eds) *The Hong Kong-Guangdong Link: Partnership in Flux*, Armonk, N Y: M. E. Sharpe, 224–251.

——(1998) *Hong Kong and South China: The Economic Synergy*, Hong Kong: City University of Hong Kong Press.

Timothy, D. J. (1999) 'Cross-border shopping: tourism in the Canada–United States borderlands', *Visions in Leisure and Business*, 17: 4–18.

Weng, Q. H. (1998) 'Local impacts of the post-Mao development strategy: the case of the Zhujiang Delta, Southern China', *International Journal of Urban and Regional Research*, 22 (3): 425–442.

Woweiyikuang (Pseudonym of Wo Zhongxiao) (2002) 'Shenzhen: We Abandoned You?' (*Shenzhen: Ni Bei Shui Pao Qi*), available on the internet on 16 November 2002, http://home.donews.com/donews/article/3/36569, accessed on 10 April 2003.

Yeh, A. G. O. (2001) 'Hong Kong and the Pearl River Delta: competition or cooperation?', *Built Environment*, 27 (2): 129–145.

Yeh, A. G. O., Lee, F. Y. S., Lee, T. and Sze, N. D. (eds) (2002) *Building a Competitive Pearl River Delta Region: Cooperation, Coordination, and Planning*, Hong Kong: Centre of Urban Planning and Environmental Management, The University of Hong Kong.

Yeung, Y. M. and Chu, D. K. Y. (eds) (1998) *Guangdong: Survey of a Province Undergoing Rapid Change*, Hong Kong: The Chinese University Press.

8   New configuration of Taipei under globalization

Hsiao-hung Nancy Chen

Three major endeavours with regard to Taipei's development under globalization are treated in this chapter. First, just like Taiwan's overall development the economic structure has shifted from a manufacture-based to a high-technology and service-based one. Old and polluted factories have either closed down or moved away from the city. Taipei municipal government in recent years has put much of its efforts into developing the so-called high-tech corridor to ensure high value-added industrial development on the one hand and keep abreast with the trend of economic globalization on the other. Second, being the global city of Taiwan that is anxious to realize the goal of becoming the 'Asia-Pacific Trans-shipment Centre'[1] launched by the previous Kuomintang (KMT – the ruling party of Taiwan (1949–2000) founded in 1991 by Dr Sun Yat-Sen, China's National Father government ever since 1995), Taipei has completed the construction of the tallest building in the world – Taipei 101 – and formed the Sinyi new Central Business District (CBD) which, in a way, can be taken as one step forward towards making Taipei an Asia-Pacific financial centre. Third, being proud of better preserving traditional Chinese culture side by side with Western culture, in comparison with mainland China, Hong Kong and Singapore, the city of Taipei hopes to be able to excel in being the Asia-Pacific culture and media centre with relatively more creative manpower and a free environment.

Viewing from a regional point of view Taipei's high-tech corridor has not only established some kind of network with the Hsinchu Industrial Park and Taoyuan high-tech corridor within the northern region of Taiwan, but also created strong ties with Suzhou and Shanghai Industrial Parks across the Taiwan Strait. However, whether or not the so-called two golden Information Transport (IT, referring mainly to mobile phone, 3D camera, and TFT-LCD screen industries) triangles will continue to flourish in the years to come will, to a great extent, rely upon the strength of further effective industrial differentiation between the two sides of the Taiwan Strait. Thus, the Taipei municipal government desperately hopes to see the launching of the 'three-links' policy.[2] Besides, the overall economic situation of Taiwan and Taipei's ability to attract foreign/world-class investors will determine whether Taipei 101 and its surrounding new CBD will become the Asia-Pacific 'financial centre'. As to the development of Taipei into the Asia-Pacific culture and media production centre, the irony seems to lie exactly in the fact that traditional

Chinese culture and history are confronting the challenge of the 'removing Chinese-ness' or 'promoting indigenousness' policy adopted by the Democratic Progressive Party (DPP) government which has been in power ever since May 2000.

On the other hand, along with globalization, Taipei has witnessed some demographic changes in the past few years. Statistics show that up to now there are about 30,000 foreign labourers, 20,000 mainland brides, nearly 10,000 foreign brides (coming mainly from the South-east Asian countries) and many more foreign investors, professional workers living in the city adding approxi-mately 80,000 foreigners to Taipei's total population. In the meantime, there is a growing number of emigrants to other countries from Taiwan. Many of them own two homes, one in the receiving country the other in Taiwan. The so-called commuting family appeared not only across the country border but also took place within the country and across cities. Through interviews, this study has found out that for foreign investors or professionals the lack of adequate business hotels is one of their major concerns. Moreover, the city of Taipei has also expe-rienced some structural changes. Ageing population has hit a record as high as 10 per cent of the total population coupled with the decreasing fertility and increasing numbers of single-headed and single families. In addition, in terms of working and leisure patterns, part-time, flexible working hours and small office/home office (SOHO) are growing. Night activities have also been flourishing due to changes in life style. It is believed that these newly emerging phenomena will create new demand and bring about different degrees of impacts on the future development. The municipal government is thus required to adopt some new governing strategies.

This chapter, besides elucidating the aforementioned three main strategies of development of the city, will try to assess the possibility of realization against both impinging local, regional and international factors. It is envisaged that local poli-tics in terms of the relationship between the central and the local government perhaps can best explain the dynamics and dilemmas of the city's development. This research is based on the literature of globalization and global cities (Friedmann 1986, Castells 1989, 1996, Fainstein *et al.* 1993, Castells and Hall 1996, Lo and Yeung 1996, Sassen 1998, 2001, 2002, Hill and Kim 2000, Shih and Timberlake 2000, Scott 2001, Smith and Timberlake 2001) in addition to a series of materials on Taiwan and Taipei (Department of Urban Development 1992, 1996, 2004, Department of Culture 2002, Department of Construction 2003, Feng 2003, Hsia 2003, Wang 2003, Yuan 2003, Chen 2004, CEPD 2004a,b, Wang 2004).

Strategies towards internationalization

When examining Taipei's development, we cannot overlook the strategies towards 'internationalization' or globalization (Wang 2003, Wang, J. 2004). Since 1995, Taiwan has engaged in the development of the 'Asia-Pacific Trans-shipment Centre'; the goal was later modified and renamed as the development of the 'Asia-Pacific Logistics Centre' in 2000 due to the change of government.[3] To cope with this strategic goal, Taipei has set the goal of developing into an

'Asian business city' targeted specifically at the formation of Asia-Pacific financial, trade, manpower, technology, communication, information and research centres. Concrete strategies include (a) strengthening transnational linkages, (b) promoting attractive urban life, (c) constructing an internationally competitive infrastructure, (d) creating a profitable business environment, (e) enhancing effective governance and (f) building up an intelligent city.

In addition, International Affairs Committee and Economic Development Committees were established in the Taipei municipal government. From the perspective of planning, the most important strategies in Taipei's recent development plan include the establishment of the high-tech industrial development corridor (see the following section), the construction of the skyscraper of Taipei 101 and the adjacent Sinyi new CBD, and the promotion of cultural activities as well as cultural industries. Now, I discuss them, in turn, in detail.

High-tech industrial development corridor

Since Taipei is no longer suitable for traditional manufacturing industries it is imperative to develop a knowledge-based high-tech industrial development corridor from Neihu, Nangang, Shihlin, Beitou to Quangtu (Map 8.1). In fact, Hsia (2003)

Map 8.1 High-tech industrial development corridor of Taipei.

Source: Department of Urban Development, Taipei Municipal Government.

reveals that the Silicon Valley, the Hsinchu Science Park, Taipei and the Yangtze River Delta have formed some kind of cross-border production networks in terms of Information Communication (IC, referring mainly to computer-related industries) and IT industries. In addition, Taipei's Mayor Ma Ying-jun believes that the transportation system adjacent to the Neihu–Nangang–Shihlin corridor ought to be greatly improved, especially the links between the industrial parks and Sungshan domestic airport. It is so hoped that once the policy of 'three-links' is approved by the Taiwan government vertical differentiation between Taipei and mainland China, especially the Yangtze River Delta, can be greatly strengthened, which will bring about economic prosperity to the city of Taipei.

One survey targeted at those enterprises with the capital asset over NT 1 billion dollars conducted by the Department of Construction, Taipei Municipal Government (2003), found out that 67 per cent of interviewees agreed that Sungshan domestic airport should be used for 'three-links'. More than 58 per cent felt that their companies would benefit from this change. About 45 per cent admitted that their willingness to stay in Taipei would be enhanced should the Sungshan domestic airport be adapted into the 'three-links' airport. More than 70 per cent of the interviewees acknowledged that if Sungshan domestic airport were converted into a 'three-links' airport, Taipei's international competitiveness would be greatly strengthened.

Experts like Feng (2003) point out that 'three-links' will not only save time (for instance, it can save 7 hours 10 minutes from Taipei to Beijing, up to 9 hours and 7 hours 50 minutes, respectively, from Taipei to Shanghai and from Taipei to Xiamen) but also increase economic efficiency, especially after the high-speed railroad went into operation in October 2005, which is estimated to take away at least 33 per cent of the domestic air traffic volume. Nevertheless, if the airport is designated to perform such a function, hardware and software improvements of the airport will definitely be required. Thus, it is important for both the city government and the Taiwan government to make a commitment.

Taipei 101 skyscraper and the Sinyi new CBD

Sinyi new CBD had been planned as a subcentre since the 1970s. However, it had not been a subcentre until the Taipei municipal government moved to the area. Consequently, there has been the construction of a number of business headquarters, department stores and entertainment facilities (cinemas and theatres) and especially the Taipei 101 skyscraper – the tallest building in the world built by private developers. Since then, the image of the new CBD has been created.

According to Sassen (2001), one of the major indicators of being a global city is that whether the city is flocked with producer services.[4] The Sinyi new CBD, as a subcentre with 508 feet tall Taipei 101, not only wishes to claim Taipei as the 'financial centre' of the Asia-Pacific region but also enshrines the whole area with the name of 'the Manhattan of Taipei'.[5] Taipei 101 with its independent electricity supply system, satellite communication facilities and multiple disaster prevention design is undoubtedly considered as one of the best architectures in the world. Compared to Hong Kong, Shanghai and Singapore it is nevertheless contended that more appropriate systems of law, taxation and manpower are required before the whole area can be qualified as the Asia-Pacific financial centre. Mr Lin Hung-ming, the general manager of Taipei 101, indicated during my interview on 19 March 2004 that 'it looks like that there is no problem to attract enough investors to fill up the building; however, it will be quite a challenging task to convert Taipei into the financial centre of the Asia-Pacific Region'.[6] It has been reported by the *United Daily* (1 November 2004) that the Taiwan Stock Exchange Market decided to move into the newly constructed building with a rent much lower than originally thought of.[7] Whether this is because of the pressures from the newly appointed DPP Director or due to other considerations remains to be further explored.

Culture and city marketing of Taipei

Since balanced commercial, technological and cultural developments have been set up as one of the city's development goals, a number of hardware and software cultural developments, such as the renewal of some old buildings and conversion into cultural activities' centres inviting world-class cultural figures to the stage in the city, as well as initiation of all kinds of cultural activities, have taken place in the past three years. The Harvard graduated mayor together with his cultural department director, who happens to hold a long-term European living experience, wish to market Taipei through a series of city cultural exchanges with neighbouring countries and areas. Taipei–Shanghai colloquium and Asia-Pacific Cultural Convention are a few examples.[8]

Factors impinging upon Taipei city's future development

In recent years, scholars have propounded the idea that 'urban competitiveness, in a sense, is an equivalent to national competitiveness'.[9] It is exactly in this vein that when discussing Taipei City's future development one has to picture Taipei in a broader spatial context. To be more specific, one has to bear in mind at least the following four dimensions: (1) The overall economic development trend of Taiwan, (2) the proper positioning of Taipei in the northern region of Taiwan, (3) the possibility of launching 'three-links' within the realm of regionalism and the feasibility of transforming Taipei as the centre for economic/industrial headquarters and (4) the proper positioning of Taipei into the Asia-Pacific urban hierarchical system under globalization. These aspects by themselves are all intertwined with each other, which I deal with in detail as follows.

Economic development of Taiwan and the Taipei high-tech corridor

According to the 2008 Taiwan's national development plan (CEPD 2002, 2004), technology-intensive, capital-intensive, high value-added knowledge-based industries will be the foci of Taiwan's economic development in the next few years (Table 8.1). As a matter of fact, to transform Taiwan into a 'green Silicon island'[10] has been one of the development goals of DPP government for the past two to three years. The Ministry of Economic Affairs even organized a massive scale business promotion convention in October 2003. Moreover, in order to streamline the idea of making Taiwan a 'world logistics centre' the government approved Kaohsiung and Keelung Harbours' application as the free trade ports in March 2004.[11] In addition, cultural and innovative industries and digitalization aimed at improving the quality of life of the Taiwanese people have also been promoted. Statistics showed that by March 2004 there were in total 21 multinationals that have set up innovative R&D centres in Taiwan (CEPD 2004a) and another 66 innovative R&D centres have been established by domestic industries (see Table 8.1 for details). Both the public and the private sectors are striving to transform Taiwan from her original equipment manufacturing (OEM) stage to an original design manufacturing (ODM) stage, and hopefully in the future may enter their own brand manufacturing (OBM) stage. In fact, Trend, Asus, Acer, MasterKong, Cheng Shin Rubber, Giant, BenQ, ZyXel, Synnex and Via have successfully developed their

Table 8.1 Innovation and R&D centres in Taiwan (2004)

Multinationals	*Domestic enterprises*			
21 innovation and R&D centres set up in Taiwan	*66 innovation and R&D centres set up in Taiwan*			
HP	Hon Hai Precision	BenQ corporation	Au optroalcs	Acctos technology
Sony (2)	FIC (First international computer)	Chinei optoelectronics	Compal Electronics	Realtek semi-conductor
Becker Avionics				
Aixtron	Chunhwa Picture Tubes	Lite-oil it corporation	VIA Technologies	United Microelectronic
Dell				
IBM (3)	Micro Star International	ETERNAL CHEMICAL	Dbtel Incorporate	Quanta Computer
Microsoft				
Intel	E-Lead Electronic	HannStar Display	Delta Electronics	GIANT MFG
Ericsson	Wisron Corporation	Cheng Shin Rubber	Acer	Advantch
Broadcom	Matsuhits Eletric	Everest	TSMC-Taiwan	Quanta display
Pericom	(Taiwan)	Textile	Semi-conductor	
Honeywell	Macronic International	Ultralife Taiwan	D-Link	Media Tek
Motorola	Toppoly Optelectronics	Compal Communications	Shlakong Synthetic Fibers	Tatung company
Atotech				

Source: CEPD 2004: 12.

Notes
1 Two or more centres that approved signing of agreement are not included above.
2 Only a partial list of the domestic enterprises and pending is provided.

own brands over the years. These industries not only own their factories in Hsinchu Science Park but hold their headquarters in Taipei. Many of these headquarters are either situated in Neihu Technology Park or Nangang Software Industrial Park. How to keep these industries and headquarters to continue to prosper in Taiwan/Taipei will certainly affect the proper positioning of Taipei both in Taiwan and the Asia-Pacific Region as well.

Tax incentives such as 006688[12] have been provided by the central government. Adequate transportation networks in both Neihu and Nangang industrial parks' surrounding areas have also been constructed or connected by the Taipei municipal government. However, the interviews with investors in both parks suggest that there is still room for improvement. For instance, in the case of Neihu Technology Park, since most buildings were built through BOT the lack of open space, parking lots[13] and lack of overall landscape design coupled with not so convenient public facilities provisions, such as eating places, downgrade its world-class industrial park image. Besides, Neihu Technology Park was originally designed to materialize Taiwan's goal of becoming the 'Asia-Pacific Trans-shipment Centre' of which the Asia-Pacific Media Centre is an integral part. Even though we may be able to locate some media industries such as Apple; newspapers from Hong Kong, for example, *China Times*, *Free Times*; and Chungtein TV, etc. in the area, the kind of cluster effect is literally non-existent because the whole plan was substituted by the 'Asia-Pacific Logistics Centre' after DPP stepped into power in 2000. The whole area remains quite diversified in its industrial composition so far, although it contains mainly IC and IT-related industries (Tables 8.2 and 8.3).

Table 8.2 Comparison between Neihu Technology Park and Nangang Software Park

Item	Neihu Technology Park	Nangang Software Park
Management body	Department of Construction, Taipei Municipal Government	Bureau for Industrial Development, Ministry of Economic Affairs
Founding time	1987	1992
Opening date	1995	1999
Area	82.44 hectare[a]	8.2 hectare
Business promotion body	None	Service Centre under Nangang Software Park
One-stop service Window	Service Centre, Neihu Technology Park	Service Centre, Nangang Software Park
Total factories	1,524[b]	203
Total employees	56,832[b]	15,000 (estimated)
Total yearly productivity (NT$)	769.1 (billion)[a]	Approximately 120 (billion)

Source: Compiled by the author.

Notes
a According to plan, the area of Neihu Technology Park will be expanded to that of 231.59 hectares, three times bigger than the existing one soon.
b Denotes data for 2003.

Table 8.3 Sector-wise comparisons between Neihu Technology Park and Nangang Software Park

Industry	Neihu numbers	%	Nangang numbers	%
Total	1,524	100	203	100
Industrial sector	347	22.77	45	22.17
Manufacturing	306	20.08	40	19.70
3C Industries	88	5.77	19	9.36
Electronic-related industries	46	3.02	12	5.91
Electronic appliance manufacturing and repair industries	23	1.51	4	1.97
Optical, medical watch and other delicate manufacturing industries	18	1.18	2	0.99
Water, electricity and gas industries	1	0.07	—	—
Construction industry	40	2.62	5	2.46
Service sector	1,177	77.23	126	62.07
Wholesale and retail	685	44.95	25	12.32
Lodging and restaurant	30	1.97	2	0.99
Transportation, communication and Warehouse	45	2.95	2	0.99
Finance, insurance and real estate	60	3.94	11	5.42
Leasing	2	0.13	4	1.97
Professional, scientific and technical services	259	16.99	81	39.90
Professional design services	51	3.35	2	0.99
Information services	139	9.12	75	36.95
Condo management services	—	—	1	0.49
Public security industry	—	—	2	0.99
Medical and health care services	2	0.13	—	—
Culture, sport and leisure services	42	2.76	—	—
Publishing	21	1.38	—	—
Broadcasting and video	14	0.92	—	—
Other services	52	3.41	—	—
Bio-tech industry	22	1.44	24	11.82
R&D sector	—	—	8	3.94

Source: Compiled by the author.

Nangang Software Industrial Park, on the other hand, being under the direct jurisdiction of the Bureau of Industry and Ministry of Economic Affairs, enjoyed much more generous incentives from the Taiwan government with regard to lower rent, better overall planning and development, and relatively high-quality public facilities. Some industries have already moved from Neihu to Nangang just to take advantage of the lower rent. In fact, many investors in Nangang have bought the space rather than rent it.[14] Given the fact that the total area of Nangang is just a bit more than 8 hectares, it therefore leaves much doubt as to whether it would be sufficient to accommodate all necessary software companies towards fully-fledged software development for Taiwan.

During the interview with the manager of Nangang Software Industrial Park it was indicated that besides the second-phase park construction, Nangang trade centre was planned to be built soon. The trade centre is so designed as to provide a modern exhibition hall, five star hotels, department stores, and office buildings to link with the high-tech corridor crossing from Neihu, Nangang, Shihlin, Beitou, to Quangtu. In the summer of 2003, the vice chair of the Council for Economic Planning and Development, Mr Chang Ching-sen, announced unnoticeably that the government decided to give up the idea of building the already approved trade exhibition hall in Nangang Industrial Park. This aroused heated debates not only between the city mayor and the Taiwan government officials but also public opinion antagonism. The government eventually had to yield to the media pressure. Nevertheless, in the name of balanced development, the total exhibition seats in Nangang Park were somewhat cut and another exhibition hall was planned to be located in Taoyuan County. The worry, however, lies in how bright the overall economy of Taiwan will be in the future, as well as what should be the optimal size of business (in terms of overall office floor area space) in the whole city, especially given the fact that Taipei 101 and Sinyi new CBD have just been completed and are currently seeking investors too. In other words, are there any likely competitions between the two?[15]

Cross-border industrial differentiation and 'city-region' development ethos

From the 'production chain' point of view, most high-tech industries are concerned with agglomeration effects. It is exactly in this vein that to broaden the planning and development scope of Taipei incorporating its hinterland becomes necessary. In other words, Taipei's future development has to embody Northern Taiwan into its picture. In fact, taking only high-tech industries into account, Taipei county, Tuaoyuan county and Hsinchu city/county have formed a sort of high-tech industries corridor which in a sense has even extended its networks to Silicon Valley on the one hand and the Yangtze River Delta with Suzhou and Shanghai in particular on the other. Recognizing this fact, for the first time in Taiwan's city history, Mayor Ma travelled to the States in summer of 2003 to promote investment opportunities of Taipei with Northern Taiwan in his mental map. He not only wished to persuade potential investors to come to Taipei but also did not mind accommodating those who considered Taipei as headquarters only and were ready to locate their factories in northern or other parts of Taiwan. In order to play the key 'node' or 'investment platform' role (Table 8.4) Taipei is fully aware of the importance of convenient transportation networks, especially given the fact that business and trade ties between Taiwan and China have been increasing rapidly. This perhaps can explain why 'three-links' with China has been so much valued by Ma and his key advisors in recent years.

Many cities in the Asia-Pacific region such as Hong Kong, Singapore, Shanghai and Beijing have all emphasized 'headquarter economy'[16] lately. There are also studies that propounded the idea of the 'city-region'.[17] In the case of Taipei it is forecasted that by the end of 2005 when the high-speed railroad is completed and put into operation the 'living circle' of the western part of Taiwan will confront some drastic changes. Northern Taiwan, just like the central and the

Table 8.4 Taiwan's outward investment, 1993–2003 (unit: US 1,000 dollars)

Year	China	Hong Kong	Singapore	Thailand	Malaysia	Indonesia	Philippines	Vietnam
1993	3,168,411	161,918	69,473	109,165	64,542	25,531	6,536	158,396
1994	962,209	127,284	100,732	57,323	101,127	20,571	9,600	108,378
1995	1,092,713	99,555	31,649	51,210	67,302	32,067	35,724	108,146
1996	1,229,241	59,927	164,978	71,413	93,534	82,612	74,252	100,479
1997	4,334,313	141,593	230,310	57,546	85,088	55,861	127,022	85,414
1998	2,034,621	68,643	158,176	131,186	19,736	19,541	38,777	110,078
1999	1,252,780	100,318	324,524	112,665	13,700	7,321	29,403	34,567
2000	2,607,142	47,512	219,531	49,781	19,406	33,711	12,971	54,046
2001	2,784,147	94,901	378,301	16,287	45,516	6,124	46,200	30,911
2002	6,723,058	167,064	25,760	5,959	31,956	9,163	82,833	55,192
2003	7,698,784	641,287	26,403	48,989	50,215	12,751	2,374	157,368

Source: Department of Statistics, the Ministry of Economic Affairs.

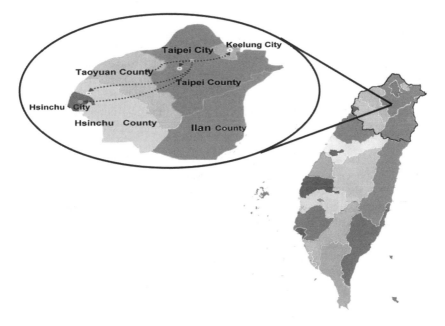

Map 8.2 The proposed northern Taiwan city-region.

Source: Department of Urban Development, Taipei Municipal Government.

southern parts of Taiwan, will form three distinct 'living regions' (Map 8.2). It is calculated that the northern region constituting different cities and counties (Taipei city and county, Taoyuan city and county, Hsinchu city/county, Keelung city and Ilan County) will cover a region of more than 9.74 million population and 80 per cent of Taiwan's total electric-related industrial products. In the light of the growing trend of regionalism, it is believed that at this scale the northern region of Taiwan, to which Taipei is an integral part, would then be able to compete with other regions such as the Pearl River Delta and Yangtze River Delta. In fact, some measures such as devising efficient and integrated tourist, industrial, and transportation plans and schemes were undertaken to avoid duplicate and wasteful investment. However, it still remains to be seen as to how far the 'city-regions' concept can be applied, not just because the city or county mayors come from different political parties, but also because Taiwan has had elections of one kind or another almost every year during the so-called political democratization processes ever since 1986 after the Martial Law was lifted. The then Taipei County Mayor Mr Su Tsen-chang (now Chairman of DPP), for instance, was the only one who failed to attend the meeting and thus did not sign the 'Northern Taiwan Region' agreement.

There are two issues related to the development of the 'city-region': first, the links between the city (Taipei) and the (Taoyuan) international airport, and second, the future of Sungshan domestic airport. Most global cities in the world own two airports. Taipei is no exception. The problem is that up to this point there has been no subway linking the city to the international airport, although the construction plan had been worked out for some time and it is under construction now. One of the main reasons is that the exact route connecting the city and the international airport has not been settled due to land speculation along the originally proposed planned areas. The other reason is related to the rampant financial constraints that occurred during the past few years. It is exactly because of this that the Ministry of Transportation opted for 'above-the-ground' construction, whereas Taipei municipal government insists on an 'under-ground' project which will be more costly and is going to postpone the completion schedule from 2009 to 2010 or 2011.

Second, there is a controversy about whether the Sungshan Domestic Airport should be connected or closed down. A more serious problem has been that Mayor Ma wishes to convert the city's domestic airport into a direct flight airport with the mainland, once the 'three-links' policy is put forth. It is felt that the industrial differentiation between Neihu Technology park, Nangang Software Industrial Park and the high-tech parks in mainland China can truly be generated if the plan can be materialized. Unfortunately, it seems that so far this idea has not been wholeheartedly shared and embraced by the Taiwanese government, which belongs to a different political party. As illustrated above, during the last mayor campaign, Mayor Ma's opponent Dr Ying-yuan Li of DPP even proposed to close down the domestic airport and convert the land into building slots for high-income residential use. Given the ideological rifts that exist between the two parties[18] it still remains to be seen whether the 'three-links' with China will be carried out soon. Although the policy adopted by DPP towards doing business with China – 'positive deregulation and effective management' – seems to be milder than their predecessor, President Lee Teng-hui's 'go slow, no haste', the Chinese side still has a doubt about whether the current government led by Chen Shiu-ben did mean what it said about opening-up for 'direct transport links'. Comments such as 'China is our enemy country', 'China is not our country' and 'Dr. Sun Yat-sen is a foreigner' etc. once again created not only mistrust but also tensions across the Strait. Therefore, few hold optimistic views towards 'direct transport', at least for the foreseeable future.

Culture and marketing Taipei

In the past three and half years, Mayor Ma and his Culture Department Director Dr Lung Ying-tai have been devoted to lifting the city's culture image (Table 8.5). As indicated, a series of domestic and international cultural activities have been promoted. For instance, well-known writers of Nobel-Prize class such as Mr Kuo Hsin-chein have been invited to station in Taipei, famous artistic groups have performed here, art and cultural facilities have been constructed, old and historic sites have been remodelled and conserved, and businessmen have been involved in contributing to cultural activities through donation or other types of support. It is hoped that the city can balance its business and technological as well as artistic and cultural activities. Since Taiwan, especially Taipei, is considered as the

Table 8.5 Taipei's cultural industry (unit: the number of organizations)

Industry	Taiwan	Taipei
Advertisement	7,375	2,567 (34.81%)
Publishing	2,357	1,552 (65.85%)
Movie	304	158 (51.97%)
Broadcasting and video	1,450	878 (60.55%)
Performing arts	163	76 (46.63%)
Artistic services	44	29 (65.91%)

Source: Directorate General of Budge, Accounting and Statistics.

place that conserves the best of Chinese culture, the city also expects to play a key cultural role in the Asia-Pacific region. As a matter of fact, Taipei's residents can enjoy *Phantom of the Opera, Cats, Mama Mia, The Sound of Music, West Side City Story* and *Chicago* just as their counterparts living in London and New York can; residents can also attend musical shows featuring Elton John and Diana Ross aside from watching cable TV with more than 100 different channels. Better still, compared to their Western counterparts one may also have the pleasure of indulging oneself in oriental arts and cultural activities, such as watching Chinese opera and talk shows, etc. Yet Taipei seems to have lost its competitiveness to Japan and South Korea in terms of the production of soap opera, comic stories and computer games and in cartoon production. Taipei is also facing keen competition from mainland China and Hong Kong when these two have worked together with regard to movie and TV programme production (the collaboration of capital and technology plus actors). Worse still is the ideology of 'removing Chinese-ness' or 'promoting localization' adopted by the DPP government, which in a way segregates and even isolates Taiwan from global or regional competition in terms of expanding the culture market in which Taiwan originally held a comparative advantage.

Concluding remarks

To summarize, Taipei has come a long way since the 1970s after the subway network reached its near completion. Today Taipei owns not only Taipei 101 (the tallest building in the world) but also the status of being ranked as one of the top five cities by *Asia Week* since 1997. The city was even elected as the most liveable city in Asia-Pacific in 2000. From what has been illustrated so far, one may say that there are three main directions for Taipei's development (Map 8.3): (a) the development of high-tech industries with IC and IT as the key sectors; (b) the emphasis of 'producer services' with the hope to mould Taipei 101 and the adjacent area into financial centres of Taiwan as well as in the Asia-Pacific region; (c) stressing cultural investment with the hope of improving the quality of life and marketing Taipei, based on its capability to blend modern amenities with traditional Chinese culture.

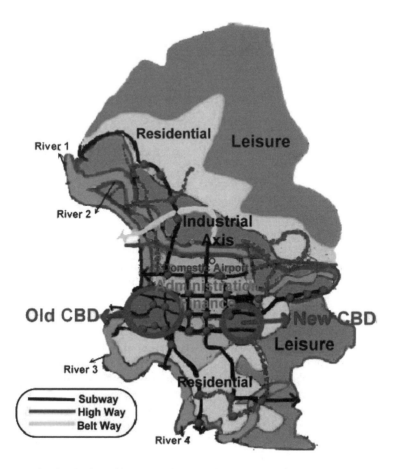

Map 8.3 The sketch plan of industrial, living and leisure axis of Taipei.
Source: Department of Urban Development, Taipei Municipal Government, 2004.

However, to assess whether these three endeavours can be successfully materialized the following considerations ought to be scrutinized carefully. First of all, on the high-tech industrial park development many scholars and experts tend to be disenchanted with the Taiwanese government's policy to develop simultaneously three science parks in Taiwan, although it is said that there exists some kind of differentiation among them (the northern Hsin-chu Science Park focuses mainly on IC, IT industries; the southern Tainan Science Park is planned to develop the TFT-LCD, whereas the central Taichung Science Park is meant to develop electricity-related industries). It is held that with limited resources and given the small size of Taiwan, the government should concentrate on a few industries and regions in which Taiwan enjoys comparative advantage because even a large country like the United States has so far set up only two main industrial parks – Silicon Valley in San Jose and Route 128 along the east coast.

Mr Miao Fong-chian, the owner of a multinational computer company (Mitac), during a recent newspaper interview, has stressed the fact that provided high-tech industries care for the 'cluster effect' very much, the majority of Taiwanese high-tech industries will sooner or later relocate into the mainland to take advantage of China's position in the world economic system, as well as the high-calibre technical and managerial manpower in which Taiwan is gradually losing its competitiveness, even when 'three-links' is being implemented. In fact, it is estimated that at least 1 million Taiwanese have already migrated into the Shanghai area seeking either job or investment opportunities there. Loosening immigration policy for Chinese high-tech personnel has been discussed for some time among Taiwanese government circles and yet mainly due to political considerations, concrete and flexible policies have not been promulgated. In the meantime, rising wages and deteriorating local labour-force-working attitudes have driven out more and more domestic industries.

Furthermore, without 'three-links' with China, Taiwan is indeed losing its position as a business and investment platform for both domestic and multinational corporations. UPS has moved its Asia headquarters from Taiwan to the Philippines. Recently, the Taipei American Chamber of Commerce and European Chamber of Commerce Annual Report's complaints about Taiwan's continuing delay of the 'three-links' schedule could be regarded as an evident example. Statistics revealed that in 2003 Taiwan lost one-third of its foreign investors. Many have gone to mainland China. My interviews with major banks and insurance companies indicated that if China relaxes the restrictions on such businesses then they would not hesitate to move. Big multinationals, domestic and foreign companies have seemingly sensed that Taiwan is internationally marginalized in both economic and political terms.

Huge capital outflows coupled with declining economic growth undoubtedly have made it quite difficult to develop the financial sector for which Taipei 101 was originally opted. Worse still is the fact that much relatively well-to-do and skilled manpower has migrated out of Taiwan and contrarily about 300,000 spouses (mainly brides from China and the South-east Asia) and 300,000 foreign labours (mainly from the South-east Asia) have flown into the island over the past 10 years. Since the majority of these people are composed of the low socio-economic stratum, a concern is that they could create new social welfare pressure which may drain the already scarce financial resources.

On the score of cultural industries, recent controversial arguments on the differences between Chinese versus Taiwanese history and culture have created not only hatred among different ethnic groups but also a destructive environment for cultural industries. It is commented that while China is striving for economic prosperity Taiwan is indulging in political and ideological struggles one after another.

Against this background, it seems that the local governments, especially Taipei as a capital city, has been caught in a quagmire as to how to cope with what the Taiwan government policy direction is on the one hand and finding a way to live with the global trends on the other. Converting Taipei into an information city, emphasizing ecological and liveability and occasionally debating or negotiating with the Taiwan government on what ought to be done responding to the globalization tide therefore become the few areas that Mayor Ma can manoeuvre. The future function of 'Sungshan airport' and the world-class football gymnasium are beyond the city's capacity, mainly due to the Taiwanese government's financial resource allocation, evidently favouring the south which constitutes the majority of DPP's supporters. It is thus often all too easy to observe that while other cities/countries in the region are busy with developmental goals Taipei/Taiwan is wasting energies on ideological issues which can hardly find a compromise and consensus at present. If such a trend continues, not only Taipei's competitiveness is at stake, but also the whole country's future would be seriously affected.

Notes

1 The 'Asia-Pacific Trans-shipment Centre' promulgated by KMT government in 1995 was originally composed of six centres – the manufacturing centre, air and freight hub/centre, financial centre, telecommunications centre and media centre. The whole plan was narrowed down and renamed as the 'Asia-Pacific Logistics Centre' in 2000 after the DPP obtained political power.
2 The 'three-links' policy implies direct trade, direct postal services and direct transport – both by air and freight across the Taiwan Strait. The idea of 'three-links' was proposed by mainland China to Taiwan as early as mid-1979. As of today, since direct trade and direct post services have been put forth, the policy now is therefore targeted strictly at direct transport between the two sides.
3 Many observers and researchers commented that KMT's 'Asia-Pacific Trans-shipment Centre' is an all-encompassing development plan whereas the DPP's 'Asia-Pacific Logistics Centre' represents a less ambitious attempt in both economic and political terms. 'Timing' undoubtedly is one important factor. The lack of experience in dealing with economic development could be another. Many people even believe that the latter contains only the name without substance, as very few constructive national development plans have been worked out since DPP stepped into power in 2000.
4 Producer services denotes mainly four sectors: financial services, advertisement services, legal firms and accounting firms.
5 Many high-rise luxurious apartments and condominiums have been built surrounding the newly developed Sinyi CBD; the average real estate price in the area is about NT 600,000 dollars/ping (1 square metre = 3.3 pings).
6 The reason provided by Mr Lin with regard to why it is not difficult to fill in the spaces of Taipei 101 is mainly because those key investors of Taipei 101 are big tycoons of Taiwan such as Hsin-kuang and Kuo-tai Insurance Company, Taiwan stock exchange, Taipei, Chaotung, Chinatrust, Tai-hsin, Shihhwa, Hungtai, Chungkuo Banks, China telecommunications, Hwahsin-lihwa, etc. It would not really be a problem should they find the necessity to locate all their branch offices in the building. As to the reasons why Taipei 101 may not be able to achieve the goal of becoming the financial centre of the Asia-Pacific Region, there are many explanations. Two outstanding factors among other things include, first, the 'timing' and second, the rising competition among Hong Kong, Singapore, Shanghai and Beijing who have opted to become some kind of financial centres in the region in recent years (*Economic Reporter*, 2003).
7 The settled rent is that of NT 2,000 dollars/ping, much lower than the originally set up NT 3,200 dollars/ping.
8 The Taipei–Shanghai Colloquium has been held a couple of times; Mayor Ma until now has not had the chance to visit Shanghai mainly due to political considerations which

prohibits the Taiwanese government. Besides, when the Asia-Pacific Cultural Convention took place in Taipei, Mayor Hsieh of Kaohsiung (now the Premier of Taiwan), who happens to be a DPP member, even tried to boycott the activity for political reasons.

9 Many scholars and experts have propounded this idea; Mr Nee, Peng-fur of the Academy of Social Sciences in Beijing, among others, has edited one book on 'City competitiveness: annual report on urban competitiveness' which briefly touches upon this subject.

10 Using DPP's terminology, the government is vigorously promoting the so-called 'Two Thousand Billion and Two Stars Plan', meaning that IC and IT industries are expected to create 2,000 billion GNP for Taiwan.

11 Dr Richard R. Vuylsteke, the Executive Director of the Taipei American Chamber of Commerce, told me during my interview that even with the 'free trade ports', it would be 'too little and too late'.

12 Plan 006688 is adopted to provide incentives for investors. It meant that for the first two years it is tax free, for the third and fourth year only 60 per cent of the tax will be levied, and for the fifth and sixth year 80 per cent of the tax will be charged.

13 Since BOT was adopted during the process of the construction of the Neihu Technology Park, many buildings did own quite a number of parking spaces, however, 95 per cent of the private-owned buildings have not opened their parking lots to the general public thus making parking one of the major complaints in the area. It is anticipated that parking will become an even more serious problem in the future when the Park grows to three times bigger than it is now.

14 According to our understanding, it was under economic recession when Nangang Software Industrial Park was first publicized in order to attract investors to the Park, the Government thus adopted the policy of allowing investors to buy rather than rent the site.

15 I posed this question to Mr Hung-ming Lin, the General Manager of Taipei 101, during my interview with him; he answered that even with a higher rent, but better services, Taipei 101 is still perhaps able to attract a number of companies to relocate their offices into the building.

16 The idea of 'headquarter economy' denotes here the idea that major cities in the Asia-Pacific region today are aiming at attracting world 500 enterprises to set up their headquarters in their respective localities. For a rather succinct description please see the editorial of *Economic Reporter* (2003).

17 The concept of the 'city-regions' has become popular in recent years; for a comprehensive introduction of the concept and its applications see Scott (2001).

18 There are quite a number of differences between the KMT and DPP parties with regard to China. The former recognizes that given the growing interdependencies between the two sides of the Strait under globalization, closer ties with each other is a must and should be handled skilfully to maximize profits for both sides. The DPP party, on the contrary, wishes to remove Chinese-ness and thus to cut off all possible relationships with China in order to be more independent from China.

References

Castells, M. (1989) *The Informational City: Information Technology, Economic Restructuring, and the Urban-Regional Process*, London: Blackwell.

—— (1996) *The Rise of the Network Society*, Oxford: Blackwell.

Castells, M. and P. Hall (1996) *Technopolis of the World: The Making of 21st Century Industrial Complexes*, London: Routledge.

CEPD (Council for Economic Planning and Development) (2004a) '*Challenging 2008: National Key Development Plans' Formulation & Implementation*, Taipei: The Executive Yuan, p. 12 (in Chinese).

CEPD (Council for Economic Planning and Development) (2004b) *Taiwan's Economy: Current Situation and Future Perspectives*, Taipei: The Executive Yuan.

Chen, H.-H. N. (2004) *The Revised Taipei Comprehensive Development Plan – Urban Governance under Demographic, Life Styles and Behavioral Changes*, Taipei: Department of Urban Development, Taipei Municipal Government (in Chinese).

Department of Construction (2003) *A Preliminary Analytical Report on Factories Survey of Taipei's Neihu Technology Park*, Taipei: Taipei Municipal Government (in Chinese).

Department of Culture (2002) *One Thousand Days of Taipei Culture*, Taipei: Taipei Municipal Government (in Chinese).

Department of Urban Development (1992) *Taipei Comprehensive Development Plan*, Taipei: Taipei Municipal Government (in Chinese).

—— (1996) *The Revised Taipei Comprehensive Development Plan – Development Goals and Strategies of Sustainability of Taipei*, Taipei: Taipei Municipal Government (in Chinese).

—— (2004) *Northern Taiwan's Metropolitan Governance under Globalization*, Taipei: Taipei Municipal Government (in Chinese).

Economic Reporter (2003) Cover story: Beijing, Shanghai and Hong Kong and 'Headquarter Economy', Vol. 2842, October 20, Hong Kong: 10–16 (in Chinese).

Fainstein, S., I. Gordon and M. Harloe (1993) *Divided Cities: Economic Restructuring and Social Change in London and New York*, London: Blackwell.

Feng, T.-M. (2003) *A Study of Integration between Taipei City and Sungshan Domestic Airport*, Taipei: Department of R&D, Taipei Municipal Government (in Chinese).

Friedmann, J. (1986) 'The world city hypothesis', *Development and Change*, 17: 69–84.

Hill, R. C. and J. W. Kim (2000) 'Global cities and developmental states: New York, Tokyo and Seoul', *Urban Studies*, 37 (12): 2167–2195.

Hsia, C.-J. (2003) *The Revised Taipei Comprehensive Development Plan – The Spatial Strategies for Globalizing Taipei*, Taipei: Department of Urban Development, Taipei Municipal Government (in Chinese).

Lo, F.-C. and Y.-M. Yeung (eds) (1996) *Emerging World Cities in Pacific Asia*, Tokyo: The United Nations University.

Sassen, S. (1998) *Globalization and Its Discontents: Essays on the Mobility of People and Money*, New York: New Press.

—— (2001) *The Global City: New York, London, Tokyo*, 2nd edn, Princeton, NJ: Princeton University Press.

—— (2002) *Global Networks*, London: Routledge.

Scott, A. J. (ed.) (2001) *Global City-Regions: Trends, Theory and Policy*, Oxford: Oxford University Press.

Shih, K.-H. and M. Timberlake (2000) 'World cities in Asian: cliques, centrality and connectedness', *Urban Studies*, 37 (12): 2257–2285.

Smith, D. and M. Timberlake (2001) 'Cities in global matrices', in Sassen, S. (ed.), *Global Networks/City Links*, New York and London: Routledge.

Wang, C.-H. (2003) 'Taipei as a global city: a theoretical and empirical examination', *Urban Studies*, 40 (2): 309–334.

Wang, J.-H. (2004) 'World city formation, geopolitics and local political process: Taipei's ambiguous development', *International Journal of Urban and Regional Research*, 28 (2): 384–400.

Yuan, E. (2003) *The New Ten Big Construction Projects*, Taipei (in Chinese).

Part III

City development under globalization

9 Global capital and local land in China's urban real estate development

You-tien Hsing

In a typical report on the investment environment of China, as the one cited by Stanley Lubman (2004) in a report prepared by the European Commission, China is not yet a genuine market economy because of its 'inconsistencies among laws, weak and inconsistent or arbitrary enforcement and the weak capacity of the judicial system'. The weak capacity of the judicial system in turn has produced higher investment risks for investors. Another frequently cited source of investment risks is the strong yet arbitrary and often negative state intervention in the market, which is considered as the basis for corruption. While many of these complaints could be well founded it is unclear how exactly these elements contribute to the 'investment risks' in China, and how such risks work against investors from abroad.

In this chapter I will try to decode the term 'investment risks' with my study of the real estate industry in Chinese cities in the last 25 years. I propose that the 'risks' are to be understood within the framework of the new urban politics in Chinese cities that foreign capital, especially those involved in the highly localized real estate sector, have encountered. The risks are considered high when the investors are not in the dominant position in the process of investment. The lack of control over the key resource – the low-cost and well-located urban land – inevitably produces the unpredictability, therefore the sense of risks for foreign investors. The highly localized character of real estate has forced the transnational capital to act much more passively than they would in other sectors such as micro-electronics. In China's real estate markets, transnational capitals respond to, instead of shaping, the agenda of the local market. This chapter also shows that in the interaction between the local and the global it is not just the logic of the almighty transnational capitalism that dominates. The interface of the global and the local is a dynamic zone in which multiple logics under various conditions work to shape the process and results of such interactions. The institutional factors, including the legal system and the state's relationship with the market, are crucial in terms of the level of predictability of the investment, but they are not sufficient explanations of the 'investment risks' that foreign capitals have encountered in different markets in China.

What is the logic of China's land market and what is the new urban politics in Chinese cities, then? China's new urban politics emerged in the early 1990s at the time when China was experiencing an unprecedented pace of urbanization in which urban population grew from 20 per cent of the total population in 1980 to 36 per cent or 456 million by 2000 (Lin 2002). The dramatic pace of urbanization took place during China's radical economic and political transformation characterized by administrative and political decentralization, economic marketization and commodification without privatization.[1] Decentralization, featuring the increased fiscal autonomy of the local state, has motivated and compelled local states to expand their revenue base. Marketization has facilitated the local states to accelerate local accumulation through directing and participating in the market. The market of commodified yet not privatized urban land is a major venue of local states' intervention in the market as well as the answer to local state's needs for rapid local accumulation. It is in this process of local political and economic restructuring that we observe the emergence of the land-centred new urban politics in Chinese cities played out by two major players that I will discuss in the following section. Foreign investors' involvement in China's real estate market, therefore, is a process of encountering and responding to the dynamism between these players in the land and real estate markets.[2]

Danwei land masters: the 'real estate alligators'

The first set of players in the real estate market come from the socialist legacy of state land tenure. State ownership of land, among other major resources, has defined China's planned economy. According to the Constitution, 'Urban land belongs to the state. Land in the countryside and in suburban areas is under collective ownership unless the law stipulates that the land is state-owned. Residential land and family plots belong to the collective. No organization or individual is allowed to occupy, sell, lease or illegally transfer land in any way' (article 10). Under this system land did not have a market value. Numerous urban land users, including the state-owned enterprises, hospitals, universities, research institutes, military units and governmental agencies, were allocated land through administrative channels on the basis of capital investment plans. These state institutions have long held the use and managerial rights over the land that they have occupied. In other words, the nominal state ownership of land has coexisted with a highly fragmented system in which land parcels were actually used and controlled by numerous state institutions that are all parts of the state.

This paradoxical situation of urban land was less of a problem when the demand for urban land was low and land parcels were rarely transacted for profits. But rapid industrialization, urban expansion and economic diversification since the mid-1980s have changed all that.[3] As investors demanded more land, uncoordinated and underground land conversions and transactions grew rapidly. In 1988, the Chinese central government responded to the pressures and opportunities of urban expansion by formally establishing a leasehold market of land. The land use rights and ownership rights were separated under this scheme. Land use rights can now be legally sold or transferred and land leases have become commodities that are tradeable in the market by negotiation, tender or open auction (article 10, clause 4).[4]

The emergence of land leasehold markets has led to another paradox in China's land rights reform: commodification without privatization. Commodification of land has created market-like competition for land rents. These users of state-owned urban land, as mentioned above, started to expand their use rights to the rights of transfer and profit, and sold their land use rights to developers of various kinds. Such derived rights of transferring land have challenged the state's nominal ownership rights. But these derived rights are neither formally recognized nor actively denied by the state. In other words, we see the separation between the state's nominal ownership rights and the various state entities' explicit use rights from which the implicit rights of transfer and profit can be derived. The ambiguity of land rights has set the stage for contestation over land. But this is only the beginning of the story.

The newly established land use rights (LURs from now on) market did not automatically replace the system of administrative allocation of land. Instead, the two systems have coexisted since the late 1980s. The difference between these two systems of land supply in the primary land market is obvious. Administratively allocated land continues to be available at low costs for mostly non-profit users without time limits. Certain types of non-profit users such as those in public health, education and defence sectors also enjoy significant land tax exemptions. On the other hand, LURs for profit-making purposes are leased for much higher fees.[5] Such leases also carry a fixed time period which is usually 70 years for residential use, 50 for industrial and 40 for commercial use.[6]

Realizing that differences in prices and lease conditions between the two systems of land supply in the primary land market will create huge loss of state assets and an increase in the possibility of corruption the central government has imposed restrictions on the transaction of land between them.[7] Land users are not allowed to sell the LURs of administratively allocated land at negotiated prices for commercial purposes unless compensation fees and land value appreciation taxes are paid to the government. In spite of such measures, however, commercial transactions involving administratively allocated land take place through informal channels that bypass official approval procedures and evade taxes and fees (Li and Isaac 1999, Ho 2001, Ho and Lin 2003). Developers also take advantage of the blurry line between non-profit and commercial projects. Developers often disguise commercial projects as non-profit ones in order to avoid higher compensation fees and land appreciation taxes. For example, a for-profit hotel in Nanjing may have a sign on the front door that says 'government employee education and recreation centre' (Po 2001). A Karaoke singing bar could be attached to a youth activity centre to avoid the fees, surcharges and taxes.

Another loophole in the urban land leasing system involves the transfer of LURs. According to the constitutional amendment, LURs can be transferred through negotiation (*xieyi churan*) by public tender (*zhaobiao*) or open land auctions (*paimai*). Tenders and auctions are rarely used in practice. It is estimated that in Shanghai, one of the most active land and real estate markets in urban China, as much as 95–98 per cent of all land transaction cases take place between the lessee and lessor through direct negotiations (Ho 2001). Although city bureaus are responsible for categorizing, grading and pricing urban land parcels for LURs sales the actual sale prices of LURs are negotiable and secretive. A city government official admitted that the official price charts were established as a baseline for bargaining.[8]

Because negotiation is the primary method of LURs transfer and because much land is still subject to administrative allocation many buyers are excluded from the local urban land market. Those with connections and access to low cost and well-located land enjoy great advantages in the land market. Extreme price differences between the land supplied through these two channels become the impetus for the emergence of a black land market or to use the Chinese term a 'hidden' (*yinxing*) land market. The land market is 'black' or 'hidden' in the sense that most of the transaction activities do not comply fully with the government regulations or follow proper licensing procedures. Thus, many administratively allocated land parcels were transferred to commercial developers in the secondary market without government approval or with insufficient compensation fees to the government; land use conversion is not formally approved or properly registered with the land management bureau.

What should be noted is that this 'hidden' land market is no small business, and the descriptor of 'black market' hardly conveys the prevalence of such land transactions.[9] It is estimated that at least two-thirds of urban land in China is administratively allocated as of late 1990s. Of the administratively allocated urban land, 30–40 per cent of it was occupied by industrial state-owned enterprises or the SOEs. The rest were used by government entities, public institutions and military units. Physically, individual danwei compounds mixed the life and work of their employees and their families who had developed strong attachments to their own danweis and equally strong exclusive attitudes towards other danweis (Lu and Perry 1997). Such cell-like isolation of individual danweis was also exhibited in the physical layout of a danwei compound: '...when a danwei is started, wall-building is the first step in construction, not the last as in common in North America. Buildings relating to it are faced inward rather than outward.... Such spatial arrangement created a protected area within, a boundary effect, and a means of excluding outsiders.... It excludes those who are not members, while at the same time it provides a basis for integrating those within it into an effective social, economic and political unit' (Bjorklund 1986: 21). What's interesting, though, is that this mixture of land use and the community-like integration of work and life is hailed by Western liberal urban designers and planners. In a danwei compound there is little commuting problem because most people live and work in the same or nearby neighbourhoods. Workers of the state-owned factories could go home for lunch and nap before they resume their work in the afternoon. On the way home, they could pick up the kids from the danwei-run day care centres and some groceries from the danwei-run produce shops.

These state units, or danweis, that used the land also defined the urban land.[10] Land use categories are defined by the primary identity of danwei land users, instead of the function of the land. For example, for a state-owned textile factory its land was usually categorized as industrial land regardless of other types of land use on site. Similarly, 'commercial land' refers to the lots occupied by the danweis under the administration of the financial or commercial system (Huang 1997). This danwei identity-based classification of land use reflects the nature of urban land ownership in the planned economy.

As the LURs markets grew rapidly in the 1990s, LURs sales became an important source of revenue for state danweis. Danwei land owners began to play an active role in the land market. This happened at the time when the 'factory director responsibility' system cut off most of the SOEs from state price protection and made SOE managers responsible for their own profits and losses. Indebted and failing SOEs began to sell their premium land in the city cores and moved to the outskirts of the city. They used the profits from LURs sales to rejuvenate their enterprises and to compensate their employees who had lost jobs during enterprise restructuring. Large and more profitable SOEs as well as military government agencies and institutions did the same, only with more resources under their control. They began to establish development companies for developing the land they occupied. Some danweis used the land as their equity share in new joint ventures with established developers. They built apartment complexes, offices and commercial buildings for rent or sale. Military units and universities did the same.

Many danweis and their development companies would start with housing projects. The old socialist cities neglected housing, which led to deteriorated housing stock and overcrowding by the 1970s (Bian *et al.* 1997: 225). The central government's answer to the urban housing crises was to encourage the state danweis, especially the SOEs, to build housing for their employees. The role of danweis as the primary housing provider in Chinese cities continued in the 1980s and 1990s. Cheap, administratively allocated land enabled the danweis to build affordable housing for their employees at one-fifth the cost of commercial housing. Some of these housing units would later be leased out to those that were not affiliated with the danweis at higher prices, violating the applicable rules.[11] By the end of the 1990s, more than half of the new housing stock in major cities was developed by state danweis. In Shanghai, danwei-built housing increased from less than 40 per cent of the total housing units to 86 per cent between 1980 and 1990. In comparison, the Shanghai municipal government built about 14 per cent of all new housing units during the same period (Z. Zhang 2002: 34).[12]

Much to their advantage, the state danweis also occupied some of the best quality land in the heart of the cities. This came about because, motivated by the idea of the city as the production rather than consumption centre, the socialist planners allocated centrally located land to the industrial SOEs in the 1960s and 1970s (Chen and Willis 1999: 47, Wu 2002). For example, by the 1970s, the urban core of Beijing, about 5 per cent of the total area of Beijing city, hosted 55 per cent of state-owned factories in the entire municipality (Dong and Sun 1998, Xu *et al.* 1998). In Shanghai, nearly 60 per cent of the SOE factories and almost 70 per cent of the industrial workers worked and lived in the central part of the city in 1982. This pattern of land allocation continued into the 1990s. According to a 1998 survey of 17 major cities in China industrial land still occupied 22 per cent of total urban land (Cao 2002: 105–107).[13]

Enterprises in the pre-reform command economy also operated under soft budget constraints (Kornai 1992). Most danweis had bargained for more land than they could actually use because land came with little cost attached during the socialist era. So the danweis had sought land before they were ready to use it, and they requested land not only for building factories or office structures but also for building supporting facilities. Such facilities included maintenance shops, employee housing compounds and service areas (e.g. health clinics, dining halls, day care centres and schools for the children of the employees). Consequently, many danweis had accumulated large land reserves on the eve of the reform, which would eventually turn them into large land 'masters' in urban China in the 1990s. In Shanghai, ten bureaus in the industrial system controlled 28 per cent of Shanghai's land and became super land masters in Shanghai (Huang 1997: 31).[14] Besides the enterprises, government institutions and military units have been other primary danwei land users in urban cores. These centrally located land parcels turned out to be highly valuable in the LURs markets in the 1990s. Even those danweis that were located on the urban fringe prior to the market reform have seen the value of their land increase because of rapid outward expansion of the city, transforming these areas from 'semi-rural' to urbanized areas.

Many danweis then established land development companies, taking advantage of the land they occupied and their tax exemption status. Owing to their large land reserves, they did not have to engage in high-risk land development projects themselves. Danwei-based development companies simply transferred their LURs to other commercial developers in the secondary land market and reaped huge profits. By 2001, only 1,200 out of the 4,000-plus land development companies in Beijing were engaged in actual development projects (W. Zhang 2002: 41). The rest were mostly active in the secondary land market, selling their LURs to other commercial developers who did not have the connections. There began to emerge an active network of land brokers to facilitate land circulation from the primary to the secondary market, and within the secondary market.

Among the successful land brokers were some of the former managers or officials of the land-owning danweis. They had the connections to government agencies charged with the authority of approving development projects or the information of the availability and ownership entanglement of land lots.[15] Through the work of these land brokers, premium danwei land parcels went to commercial developers. Individual pieces of land were assembled by large development companies, or made into large parcels for large-scale projects.[16]

Individual danwei land master's influence is buttressed by the xitong behind it. Each danwei belongs to a vertically organized, functional state bureaucracy that originated in the planned economy. These vertical bureaucracies – called xitong or tiao in Chinese – intersected with the horizontally organized territorial governing system (*kuai*) to form the infamous tiao–kuai matrix in China's governing system. Land lease sales in the hidden land markets are carried out by the danweis but backed by their supervising bureaucracies within the xitong. Some of the most powerful xitongs, such as telecommunication, finance and railways, held authority over the city government in resource allocation. The leaders of these xitongs, usually the ministers at the central level, are ranked higher than the directors of the planning and land management bureaus of the city.

In short, in China's large cities, the centralized state ownership of urban land has coexisted with a highly fragmented pattern of land use control in the core areas. This paradox was created in the planned economy but intensified in the early 1990s. Large danwei-based development companies took advantage of their access to land and their political connections to buy more land from other state danweis. Xitong-based development companies consolidated the parcels occupied by various subordinate units within the xitongs to establish large development companies with large land reserves. Their large land reserves and financial support, as the result of a two-decade-long consolidation of resources, has made state danwei-originated large developers one of the most formidable players in the urban land market. Even at a time of strict policy control of land and real estate development these 'real estate alligators' continued to enjoy their prestigious positions as the 'aristocracy of the market'[17] in China's real estate sector and continued to expand.

City governments: struggling to build real estate 'aircraft carriers'

But the urban land, especially those located at the urban core areas, was too valuable in China's new political economy to be left to the state danwei-originated real estate alligators alone. Since the late 1980s Chinese territorial governments at the provincial, municipal, district and county levels were granted greater authority in urban land management. A new institution, the Ministry of Land Management, was established in 1986. The bureau of land management at each level of local government is given the authority to coordinate the allocation and use of state-owned urban land. For the first time in the People's Republic of China's (PRC's) history, there is a clearly designated state institution for the task of land management (Huang and Wen 1998). Land allocation is no longer just attached to the overall economic development plans and controlled by individual functional ministries but an important resource to be managed under a specified state agency. The responsibilities of the land management bureau include preparing annual land use plans, allocating quotas of converting farmland for non-farm uses, issuing permits for land conversion, monitoring LURs sales and collecting taxes on the transactions of land.

By 1998, city governments were granted the exclusive authority to lease urban land. An important stipulation is that all administratively allocated land in the primary land market should be transferred to city governments before they can be leased in the secondary market. The law further provided that the title of the land has to be formally transferred from individual danweis to city governments before the LURs can be transferred to commercial developers (Wu 1998: 265). In other words, under the new land management regime, the city governments have not only the regulatory authority over urban land but also represent the state in exercising the proprietary rights over the urban land.

For city leaders, the new regime of urban land management and their newly granted proprietorship over urban land is a much needed endorsement of the overall territorial authority of the local governments. Reversing the vertically oriented, socialist commanding system it is an official recognition of the importance of a territorial approach to urban governance. What's more important about the new urban management regime is that it provides the base for local governments to expand their revenues. Many cities face real fiscal pressures and look to land control as a source of revenue for city treasuries. Owing to fiscal decentralization since the 1980s, city governments now enjoy greater fiscal autonomy. But along with fiscal autonomy came responsibilities for taking care of the city's fiscal liabilities. With central revenue transferred down, locally generated revenue has to be stretched to cover urban infrastructure constructions, social welfare, education and much of the governmental overhead. So far, most cities have relied on local industrial and commercial development for more tax yields, but land-related revenue stream is impossible to ignore by the city officials as it makes a direct and immediate contribution to the local coffer. According to Ho and Lin (2001: 15), land-related revenues accounted for 30–70 per cent of total revenue of local governments at the county and district levels in the 1990s.

The formal administrative and legal regime provides the city government with a solid base for consolidating its control over the urban land. The financial autonomy makes it both an incentive and imperative for the city government to exercise the new authority. In practice, however, formal institutional arrangements do not guarantee the actual exercise of such power. As mentioned earlier, the leaders of the xitong, usually the ministers at the central level are ranked higher than the directors of the planning and land management bureaus of the city. Consequently, the city's land managers and regulators have to confront powerful danwei backers in the state bureaucracy if they want to intervene in the latter's decisions on LURs transfer or commercial development. This is especially the case in cities like Beijing, the nation's capital, where there is a high concentration of large and powerful state danweis. A Beijing planner complained that there were too many 'popo-mama' ('mothers-in-law and mothers') in Beijing making it very difficult, if not impossible, for the city government to implement its urban development plans without much compromise.[18] The official recognition of city governments' authority over urban land did little to reduce the political risks for the city government to intervene in the plans of powerful danwei-originated developers.

But city government leaders are motivated enough to strategize and fight back. They devote themselves to large-scale urban redevelopment and public infrastructure projects to claim the land parcels that are not under the control of the 'alligators', and sell the land to developers of their choice. Redevelopment and infrastructure projects have the legitimacy of building a modern city and of public interests, giving the city government a higher moral ground. City governments and their young urban planners also launch ideological campaigns that promote the idea of efficient land use, which rejects the socialist pattern of allocating central locations to state-owned factories and schools. History is on their side, too. After Deng's historical visit to Shenzhen in the spring of 1992, a wave of 'development fever' swept the country. As the land battle in the urban cores became increasingly rigorous, the conversion of farmland in the urban fringe areas for non-farm development started to take off. The large amount of LURs sales and commercial projects in the urban cores built in the first half of the 1990s in turn created property over-supplies. Vacancy rates of Shanghai's commercial and luxurious residential projects went as high as 24 per cent. By 1994, Premier Zhu Rongji announced his austerity policy package, and real estate finance was severely affected. Many cities, especially those along the coast, were left with skeleton hotels, office towers and half-finished condos. A large number of land parcels were leased out and cleared but not developed, so they were being 'baked in the sun' (*shai taiyang*). It was estimated that 30–50 million square metres of built floor areas were vacant and about 50,000 hectares of land were cleared yet not developed (Dong 2000, Hong and Bourassa 2003, Ren 2003a,b,c). The crisis of the real estate market in 1994 created an excellent opportunity for city governments to launch a new campaign to consolidate their control over the urban land. City government officials openly blamed the excessively fragmented urban land market (and the land masters behind it) for creations and bursts of real estate bubbles. City officials argued that the oversupply of land and development projects was the result of 'too many suppliers in the market without a central coordinator'.[19]

As the newly designated urban manager and state property representative, the city governments assumed the role of the coordinator of urban land markets. City governments believe that the key to coordinating the market is to centralize land supplies, and a super landlord is the most effective market coordinator. In 1996, Shanghai's municipal government pioneered to establish the Centre for Land Development which now functions as a land bank of the city. The land bank functions as a clearing house between the primary and the secondary land market. It negotiates profit-sharing schemes with the original land users and purchases the LURs from them, and then resells the LURs in open land auctions.[20] Through the process of reclaiming and selling land parcels through the land bank, the city government hopes to establish a systematic bookkeeping of urban land as the basis for land management and tax and fee collection. The open land auctions through the land bank also means an opening up of the existing primary land markets reserved for the insiders. If successful, the city government may monopolize the primary land market and become a super land master in its jurisdiction. It can also control the sale prices of land and reap a much larger share of the profits.[21] It is to become an 'aircraft carrier' of land, according to media commentators.

In 2001, the land bank was made a national policy by the State Council's announcement of the 'reinforcement of state landed assets management' policy. The policy was widely supported by city governments. By 2002, more than two thousand land banks were established nationwide. In 2002, The Ministry of Land and Resource Management also announced a national policy (No. 11 Ordinance) stating that open land auctions are mandatory instead of optional for commercial development projects. But most developers were not impressed. Open land auctions made it possible for the city government to scrutinize land transactions more closely than before. Developers now pay higher official rates for land transaction and relocation compensation for the residents (Cheng 2003, Zhao 2003). Developers also have to comply with official development regulations, especially the floor–area ratio, or FAR, which is always lower than the level at which developers consider it profitable. The floor prices of land parcels set in open land auctions are invariably higher than prices set in individual negotiations. While LUR transfer fees through individual negotiations can be paid in instalments scheduled for many years auctioned land parcels require a much larger initial investment at the time of lease signing (Z. Ren 2003). Overall, commercial developers complain that open land auctions add a premium to the total cost of land transactions. They saw open land auctions as options only for those outside developers who did not have access to well-located low-cost land in the city. Most well-established local land masters and developers still preferred the option of negotiating with individual land owners in the primary land market. Large local developers and land masters did not feel pressed by the new policy also because they still had large land reserves after ten years of aggressive purchasing.

In the meantime, there have been great pressures on the local government in their implementation, or non-implementation of No. 11 Ordinance. In Beijing, the city government is forced to leave four '*kouzi*' ('openings' meaning exceptions to the policy) in the local regulation concerning open land auctions. The local implementation allows the following types of land to continue to be leased out through individual negotiation instead of open land auctions. These exceptions include the construction land that is within the green belt zone of the city,[22] the land for 'small town construction' projects, the land for 'dangerous housing reconstruction' projects and the land for high-tech industrial development. The last three categories are considered projects for public interests and rural development, and therefore more favourable policies should be granted to developers. As it turns out, most development projects can fit into one of these four ambiguous categories therefore do not have to obtain the land from the open land auction. Up till the summer of 2003, few bidders were seen in the open land auctions in China's major real estate markets. By 2004, a new national policy was announced. It threatened to reclaim the land parcels that were bought, but not paid or used by developers. The land banks of the city would then put these reclaimed land lots in the open land auctions. The deadline for the city government to reclaim the unused and unpaid land parcels was set for 31 August 2004. In an interview that took place on 2 September the director of Beijing Centre for Land Reserves (Beijing's land bank) admitted that it was still difficult for the city government to reclaim these land parcels. It was because the reclaim involved tremendous amount of work to clear the reclaimed land. If the land was cleared but not built, the city had to compensate the developers who did the preliminary work of compensating and removing the residents from the sites, levelling the land and installing the power and water. It was also difficult to reclaim parcels that were controlled by the danwei-backed developers. It took administrative and financial capacity and political weights for the city government to undertake the tasks. Neither of which, according to the director of Beijing's Centre for Land Reserves, was in abundant supply in the Beijing municipal government.[23]

Also there are internal constraints for the city government to consolidate its control over urban land. The city government itself is hardly an integrated organization with a coherent set of agenda. There are numerous bureaus, committees and offices in the government, in addition to a parallel party system in the city. Financial pressures have forced many agencies of the city government to establish their own profit-making operations, including development companies. For example, Beijing municipality had 623 development companies in 1995, among them 108 were owned by state danweis and 485 were owned by various government agencies (Wong 1996: 147). Nanjing had 309 development companies in 1997, two-thirds of which belonged to urban government agencies. The operation and profits of these development companies were mostly controlled by individual agencies, known as '*xiaojinku*' ('mini-coffer'), and were inaccessible to the financial management bureau of the city government. These fragmented endeavours of property development by individual city government agencies in turn weakened the overall capacity of the city government to control the urban land. Profit-amassing government agencies run small-scale projects and development companies and get in the way of the consolidation of land control by the city government. To consolidate scattered land and financial resources within the city government, the Shanghai municipal government announced the establishment of the Shanghai Real Estate Group Company in November 2002. It was to be the largest development company in Shanghai. The Group Company is established by the core governmental organs of the city: the municipal government headquarters and the Communist Party Committee of Shanghai. It has consolidated the municipal land bank with most of the development companies set up by individual city government agencies and incorporated all the public land reserves in their possession. A press report called the newly established Shanghai Real Estate Group Company 'the super aircraft carrier' in Shanghai's property market (Li and Ren 2003). The Shanghai government hopes to compete more effectively with the establishment of this super real estate aircraft carrier. It is too early to tell whether this strategy will finally put the municipal government at the commanding heights in one of the largest and most active property markets in China. But the establishment of an 'aircraft carrier' development company does indicate a new strategic orientation of the city government. The city leaders no longer rely solely on public institutions like the land bank to exercise their state-granted proprietorship of urban land. The city government has shifted its approach of land management and hopes to gain an upper hand with the market logic. It is using the strategy of building aircraft carriers in their battle against the real estate alligators.

Foreign investors: 'tamed camels'?

In the land struggle between the alligators and aircraft carriers, where do foreign investors and developers fit? Real estate development is a highly localized business. Developers' knowledge of the local market and communities and the connections with local politicians are crucial in gaining the competitive edge. The immobility of land and the direct and long-lasting impact of construction projects on a place make real estate projects the focus of conflicts among different local interests. The conditions and locations of individual land parcels, including their current uses and future prospects, make each parcel highly unique. In order to adequately estimate the availability, value and profitability of each parcel, developers need to have extensive local knowledge and information of land rights entanglements and commercial possibilities of each parcel. In the meantime, landed-property has always been one of the most heavily regulated commodities, even in capitalist economies. Land-related regulations, including urban development plans, zoning and planning and building codes are some of the most important aspects of state intervention in the market (Singer 2000). These codes and regulations are also highly localized. As a result of these characteristics of localization and heavy state intervention, most real estate developers, including those in the advanced capitalist economies, are constrained by places where they have deeply rooted and widely extended social and political networks.[24]

In China, localization of real estate has found its extreme expression. The barriers for outsiders entering individual local land market are high. Only a handful of the largest Chinese development companies have enjoyed commercial success in their cross-regional operations within China. When they are directly involved in cross-regional real estate projects, they have to find well-connected local partners to facilitate the development process. For foreign development firms, the barriers of entering China's property development market are even greater. The commodified but not privatized land system worries many foreign investors. The dominance of state daiwei-originated land masters and large developers with large land reserves, as mentioned earlier, have effectively created an enclosed land market. Only those with connections and insider information are able to obtain low cost and well-located land parcels. In addition, the local government-based development companies take advantage of their access to the best located land lots for landmark projects. As a result, the growth of foreign direct and indirect investment in China's real estate market in the past two decades has been slow. From 1997 to 2001, the percentage of FDI in China's real estate development decreased from 9 to 1.3 per cent. Total foreign capital, including the indirect investment in the sector, also decreased from 12 to less than 2 per cent.[25]

But China's real estate market is too large and lucrative to be ignored by international investors, especially in the new millennium when the share of the real estate industry in China's total GDP continues to grow. It was estimated that in large cities like Beijing and Shanghai net return of real estate investment reached 20–50 per cent in the last five years. Another report estimated the return in Shanghai's real estate, interest payment excluded, to be as high as 75–85 per cent in 2003 and 2004[26] compared to the average net return on real estate of 6.7 per cent in the United States and 4 per cent in Japan and Singapore.[27] The Chinese real estate market is too lucrative to pass. A major set of national credit control policies also has changed the environment of real estate investment in China since 2003. The credit control policies, represented by the so-called No.121 Document issued by the People's Bank in June 2003, imposed a set of stringent conditions on bank loans to real estate development and construction companies, and individual buyers. The domestic credit control policies have made the developers look more seriously for foreign financial resources.

Foreign involvement in China's real estate market can be categorized into two groups. The first group is composed of Hong Kong-based giant developers like The New World Group and Li Ka-Shing's Hutchinson–Whampoa Group. Equipped with long experiences in property development in rapidly growing cities of high density like Hong Kong and with sound connections with the central and local governments in China's major cities, they were the first ones to be directly involved in developing hotels and office buildings in the early 1980s. They also started to build luxurious housing complexes and public infrastructure projects in the 1990s. After operating in China for 25 years large Hong Kong developers have accumulated sufficient political capital and large land reserves in major cities like Beijing, Shanghai, Guangzhou, Shenzhen and more recently in the so-called second line cities like Wuhan, Nanjing and Chongqing.

Other foreign investors, unlike the Hong Kong developers, have been taking a more indirect approach to China's real estate market. The Singapore-based development groups Keppel Land and Capital Land[28] and a few American and European companies have had much stronger interests in buying and managing commercial projects that are already built, or establishing Real Estate Investment Trust (REIT) to be sold to international investors. However, the development of such less risky, indirect investment by foreign financial operators in China's real estate market is still in the beginning stage, and the Chinese government's control over foreion direct investment (FDI) and foreign commercial loans to China's real estate industry is still tight. Although the most entrenched and high profile Hong Kong developers have been able to develop a few landmark projects in the most visible parts of the major cities, most overseas developers, within and outside of the Greater China, still feel that they have a serious disadvantage in the head-to-head competition against the local Chinese real estate alligators and aircraft carriers.

The natural solution of the dilemma is to collaborate with large Chinese developers. In 2004, as credit control over real estate finance was tightened by the central government, one of the largest Chinese developers, Vanke, announced a joint venture project with German investor, Hypo Real Estate Bank International (HI), to develop a luxurious housing complex in the Pearl River Delta in Guangdong province. While HI has a majority share in the joint venture, which qualified it as an FDI project encouraged by the Chinese government, the main role of the German bank is in fact that of a financier rather than that of a partner in the actual development and management of the project. In the contract, Vanke is obligated to buy back the shares, with interest, from HI after the project receives a set percentage of return. This was the method employed to avoid government regulation on foreign commercial loans to real estate, and to reduce the risks for the German bank. The real estate community has called this financial manoeuvring 'indirect foreign loans' (*quxian daikuan*).When asked to comment on this high profile 'joint project' the general manager of Vanke admitted that the limited role of its German partner in the project is conditioned by the same old concern that most foreign investors have had, that is, the high risks in China's real estate market. And Vanke's task is to convince HI that these risks can be taken care of by Vanke, while using the credibility of HI to connect to the international circle of real estate finance.[29] Since mid-2004, there has been an increase in media coverage of growing foreign direct and indirect investment in the real estate market in large cities like Beijing and Shanghai. But my interviews show that the overall contribution of foreign capital in China's real estate is still limited. Experienced Chinese developers and investment consultants suggested that most of the media reports were just hot air. They pointed out that foreign funds demand very high return rates and impose rigid conditions for investment, while only putting in US 10–20 million dollars in each project as a way of reducing and spreading the risks, which only 'helps little'.[30]

Moreover, there were conflicts between Chinese domestic developers and foreign investors in terms of the purpose of loans. Chinese developers were more interested in getting foreign loans for operational purposes (e.g. purchasing the sites and construction costs), and retaining the ownership of the built project. But foreign investors' aim was predominantly obtaining a share of the built project while not getting involved in the complicated and lengthy building processes. In the meantime, while securitized real estate in the United States and other market economies has traditionally been focused on office and commercial space the most profitable segment in China's real estate has been residential projects. These residential projects, with their numerous home owners and residents, are often entangled with the issue of ownership rights and community property management that is beyond the capacity of most foreign investors and their local representatives.[31] The importance of foreign capital in the Chinese market, therefore, is more of a symbolic gesture of internationalization of China's real estate development. For large players like Vanke, it is also a first step towards connecting its operation with the international capital market.[32]

Indeed there is nothing new about the cautious investment strategies of foreign capital in the tempting yet volatile real estate market. What's interesting about the foreign involvement in China's real estate is the coexistence of a pair of seemingly conflicting sentiments in China regarding foreign influence in Chinese cities. First of all, there has been a nationalistic sentiment against foreign capitals' control of China's land, one of the defining elements of China's sovereignty. In the fierce competition for urban land, the government-backed development companies often have ideological legitimacy in gaining access to the best located land. For landmark projects of political significance, the sentiment of keeping foreigners' hands off the Chinese land is particularly strong. Most developers, even those top Hong Kong developers that have developed long-term political connections in large cities, complain about the Chinese governments' partial treatment of local developers when it comes to negotiation for well-located land. A Beijing-based, ambitious Chinese developer, who used to be the general manager of the largest development company in China, Vanke, told me that one of the main reasons for him to get into the development industry in the late 1980s was that real estate is one of the few fast growing sectors in China in which 'foreigners cannot beat the Chinese so easily'.[33]

Most of the urban redevelopment projects involve relocation of existing residents on the site. Relocation negotiation has been another focus of social and political conflicts. By the early 2000s, increasing numbers of residents from dismantled neighbourhoods protested the unjust relocation compensation and the corruption of government officials involved in the land lease sales. Redevelopment in urban cores for commercial projects, especially the foreign invested ones, has become a highly charged political issue. In short, the enclosed land market, the highly localized politics around the urban land, as well as the nationalistic sentiment towards foreigners' control over China's land has contributed to the low profile of foreign developers in China's booming property market. Although there has been increasing interests, most of foreign investment in China's property industry has been indirect and limited. A high ranking official in the Ministry of Construction, therefore, referred to the foreign developers and real estate investors in China as 'tamed camels'.[34] Many large and even medium-sized developers that I talked to did not seem to see foreign developers as real competitors either. A developer told me that 'the water of Beijing's real estate is too deep for foreigners to take a dip. We can make good use of their capital, but they need us more than we need them'.[35] For the majority of the Chinese developers that are small and have limited amount of land reserves they feel that they are not candidates for partnerships with foreign investors anyway. To minimize the risks, foreign investors would team up only with the largest companies – public companies that have strong government connections, professional management and large land reserves – and only the largest companies meet the criteria.[36]

In contrast to the nationalistic sentiment towards foreign capital controlling China's land is the embracing of Western modernist urbanism in China. Western urbanism has been introduced to China in full speed coinciding with the post-socialist pursuit of consumerism and modernity of Chinese cities.[37] The collective imagination of China's modern urbanity is reflected in the names of residential and residential–commercial mix projects in Chinese cities, such as Park Avenue, Vancouver Woods, Orange County, Boulevard of Windsor, Venice Garden and so on (see also Giroir Chapter 11 in this volume). It is not just the names that trigger the fantasy. These names are associated with a different lifestyle. A suburban residential complex near Beijing is named 'Californian Town'. In the advertisement that features pitched roofs against a sky of Caribbean blue, Californian Town promises a 'Californian-style happy life'. Another low-density luxurious housing project is named 'Napa Valley'. A Beijing developer told me that he was building an American style suburban housing complex of 10,000 homes near Beijing, inspired by Long Island of New York.[38] The availability of large pieces of land and the trend of large-scale residential development, which easily house tens of thousands of people in one project, has allowed the developers to build not only individual homes but to create new cities and to promise a new lifestyle. This new lifestyle, nested in the periphery of the rapidly sprawling cities, features single family homes and is often cast by the image of North American low-density suburbs and gated communities in which private cars become a must for the residents.

Various styles of Western architectural designs are found in governmental and commercial buildings. Foreign architects are active in the process of creating the new urban imagery in China. Big name agencies, consultants and architects from the United States, Western Europe and Japan are invited to plan and design landmark projects in large cities. The Swiss team of Jacques Herzog and Pierre de Meuron, laureates of the most prestigious Pritzker Prize, who designed London's Tate Modern, was responsible for the National Stadium for Beijing's 2008 Olympics. French architect Paul Andreu, Chief architect of Aeroports de Paris, who has also worked on airport terminals in Jakarta, Cairo and Seoul as well as the Grande Arche de la Defense of Paris, designed the futuristic-styled Opera house in Beijing alongside Tiananmen Square. The famous American design firm, Skidmore, Owings & Merrill (SOM), designed the tallest building in China (and the fifth tallest in the world), Jin Mao Tower, along the most prestigious Shi Ji (meaning 'century' in Chinese) Avenue, the central axis in the financial district of Shanghai's Pudong New Area. The Hyatt Hotel is one of the main tenants of the Tower which claims to contain the world's highest hotel rooms. Rotterdam-based Rem Koolhaas, another Pritzker Prize-winning designer, gave up the opportunity to design ground zero in New York City and chose to design the headquarters of China Central Television (CCTV) in Beijing.[39]

The list goes on. Many international architects see China as a great place to experiment with new design ideas which would not be realized easily anywhere else in the world.[40] The main elements of such great opportunities for architectural experiments include China's booming economy, local professional collaborators that can convert foreigners' designs to fit local construction and regulation conditions, cheap construction labour, government leaders who are eager to build monumental projects without much concern of budget constraints and the national aspiration to build modern and global cities quickly by borrowing the fame of established designers. The designers have not been predominantly American either, unlike the argument that 'globalization equals Americanization' has suggested. European and Japanese designers have won many major governmental and commercial projects, including those mentioned earlier. The diversified sources of foreign cultural influence in China's new cities also means that China's new urbanity is not just a binary choice between the Chinese 'tradition' and the Western 'modernity' but has become a more complex dynamics in which designers from various aesthetic traditions have trespassed cultural boundaries in the process of rebuilding the Chinese cities. In this process, the Chinese clients, mainly the government leaders and property developers, have strengthened their cultural legitimacy by borrowing the international fame of foreign designers; while foreign designers have also rode on the Chinese nationalistic sentiment to legitimize their own works. Many of these international designers claim that they follow the Chinese design tradition in their work. While SOM called their 88 floor tall Jin Mao Tower in Shanghai 'Oriental Revivalism'[41] the French architectural firm, Jean Marie Charpentier et Associes, emphasized that while its design of Shanghai's centrally located Opera House, 'stands out as completely different from the surrounding buildings', it 'falls into a well-defined polarity between Le Corbusier's modernity and the symbols and history of Chinese tradition'.[42]

Many less famous and less expensive foreign designers are active in smaller projects and in other cities. In the race to erect monumental projects that demonstrate their administrative achievements, or 'zhengji gongcheng', city mayors and party secretaries adopted the established symbols of progress, modernity, 'newness' and 'global-ness', represented by non-Chinese architects. Foreign firms' models and development plans, as well as events like blue-eyed architects making presentations in front of local government leaders, always attract media coverage, help and to sell the city even before the projects are built. Many Chinese architects and urban planners complain about the government leaders that are obsessed with the idea that 'yuanlai heshang hui nianjing' (monks from afar can chant better) who give the high-profile, most visible projects to foreign design and planning firms at a price that is ten times or more than what a domestic design firm could charge.[43]

In the fall of 2002, I was invited to serve on a jury to evaluate the development plans for the new city centre of the capital city of a northern province in China. Six design firms were invited to submit their proposals. These firms were from Singapore, Hong Kong, Boston, Paris, Tokyo and Beijing. The review meeting, held in the tallest and newest hotel in town, was much publicized and received large media coverage in local and provincial TV and newspapers. In the review meeting, the Parisian architect presented two 50-storey tall office towers for the new centre of the city that has had limited growth in commercial activities and service economy to fill the towers. The Boston-based architect presented pictures of the waterfront in San Francisco and Paris as possible models for the future of this northern city. He proposed a large artificial lake on the site. I asked the architect how he planned to resolve the problem of severe water shortage in northern China with the artificial lake. He looked surprised by the news of water shortage in the region. His young assistant, a China-born Harvard graduate, did not have an answer either. After the meeting, the director of the city planning bureau thanked me for raising the question in public. I asked him why he invited the foreign firms that did not spend enough time in the city and the site before they came up with plans for the city. The director said it was the idea of the city and provincial leaders that they got foreigners involved. As a matter of fact, he admitted, I was invited to join the otherwise all China-based Chinese jury because I was a professor from the United States. 'But thank god you speak Chinese, and we can talk to you directly,' he added.

Conclusion

The investment risks in China's real estate market are related to the capability of dominating the market. The local politics of the urban land market played out by the state danwei-originated land masters and the city governments has made it difficult for overseas capital to dominate. While the dainwei land masters took advantage of the socialist legacy of administratively allocated land, the city government used its newly gained legitimacy in urban management to consolidate its control over the land within its jurisdiction. These two major players and their development agencies were made powerful, and the politics of their struggle for urban land was fierce at the time of rapid urbanization and increasing fiscal decentralization. For foreign developers, this structure of land control and the conflicts generated from the deeply rooted tiao–kuai matrix in the city has made it difficult for outsiders to gain access to low-cost and well-located land. The advantage of multinational property and investment firms, such as commercial property management and marketing, as well as securitization of real estate, has not been fully developed in China either.

As a result, FDI in China's real estate has been concentrated in the enclaves of a few expensive office buildings, luxurious hotels and service apartments in the largest coastal cities. Most of them have been excluded from the fastest growing market, that is, the medium–low priced residential complexes in cities of various sizes in both coastal and some inland regions. The foreign camels have been tamed by the local alligators and aircraft carriers (and the aircraft carriers-to-be) in the real estate market in which the control of land reserves is the key to dominance. As the foreign developers can only passively respond to instead of actively shaping the politics of the local land market the 'investment risks' for overseas capital in real estate are inevitably higher than they are in sectors like telecommunications and automobiles that are more dependent on foreign technologies. In other words, the level and the type of investment risks are related to the possibilities of controlling the key components of the industry. I therefore second what Logan (1993) suggested in his analysis of globalization of real estate that global investment in highly localized real estate, however institutionalized and 'securitized', only blurs the risk taken by investors, but 'it does not erase the risks'. The ability of global developers to invest 'anywhere' is 'more apparent than real'.

In this chapter, I also propose that the analysis of the new urban politics in Chinese cities should go beyond the political economy of land. The story of land as a focus of resource struggle can hardly be separated from that of the built environment as the site for the contestation over the meaning of the place. In the process of creating and defining China's new urbanity, established foreign designers have been using Chinese cities to experiment with their new and untested ideas. Their cultural dominance has lent legitimacy to Chinese government leaders that are obsessed with new-ness and are eager to bring global-ness to Chinese cities. This collaboration between local government leaders and foreign professionals has, in turn, generated heated debates among Chinese designers about China's new urbanism. The question of foreign capital's involvement in China's real estate market, therefore, has merged with that of cultural transnationalism in China's new urban space.

Notes

1 See Ho (2001), Ho and Lin (2003)
2 The main source of information for the chapter comes from my field work in Beijing between 2002 and 2004, with supplementary information collected from other major

Chinese cities, including Shanghai, Guangzhou, Chengdu, Changsha, Zhengzhou and Chongqing since 1996.

3　China's urban population grew from 191 million in 1980 to about 456 million in 2000, and its share of total population rose from 20 to 36 per cent. But the urban growth has happened mostly in the coastal region and a few select interior areas. For a detailed analysis of China's urban growth see Lin (2002).

4　For the analysis of Hong Kong's land leasehold market that the Chinese land market is modelled after, see Hong (1999). For regulations on land lease transfers see the 'Provisional regulations on the conveyance, granting and transferring of the state land's use rights in cities and towns, 1991', enacted by the State Council in May 1991.

5　The administratively allocated land users would pay land use taxes, the highest of which cannot exceed 200 yuan per square metre, but the highest premium is more than 10,000 yuan per square metre (Li *et al.* 1999: 21)

6　'Interim regulations of the People's Republic of China on granting and transferring the rights to the use of state owned land in cities and towns', article 12.

7　The primary land market refers to the LURs transactions from the users of administrative allocated land to the commercial developers. The state and its agents are the only land suppliers in the primary market. Once the land enters the circle of transactions between commercial actors, it is in the secondary land markets. The main difference between the primary and the secondary market is that between the administratively allocated land and commercially transacted land. The land in the primary market is much cheaper. For a detailed explanation of the primary and secondary land markets in urban China, see Ho and Lin (2003).

8　Interview in China, 2002. He said it is important to make the buyer of the land parcel be aware of how big a bargain he/she gets. The official price chart serves as a baseline for measuring the favour given to the buyer.

9　See Ho and Lin (2003) for figures of China's land markets. The authors divided Chinese land market into the primary, secondary and black markets based on the official records. In the meanwhile, in their qualitative analysis, which was presented in an informative diagram, almost all directions of LUR transfers in the primary and secondary market have both legal and illegal components. In other words, few transactions were totally legal or totally illegal. Therefore, the authors correctly placed the entire land market within the box of black market. Within the box of 'black market' there are both legal and illegal transaction activities.

10　User as de facto owner of state assets is also found in socialist Eastern Europe. See, for example, Marcuse (1996).

11　By 2003, some cities started to legalize the commercial transaction of danwei built and subsidized housing.

12　Privatization of danwei housing has been the most recent trend since the early 2000s, especially in major metropolitan areas like Shanghai. This is seen as the beginning of the end of danwei influence on urban land development. Shanghai's land market has been the most frequently studied one in China. It is often seen as the trendsetter. However, whether privatized housing is an indicator of weakening danweis is debatable.

13　Urban land used for industrial use was 25 per cent of Shanghai, 17 per cent of Beijing, and 28 per cent of Suzhou. Indeed the definition of 'industrial land' and 'urban land' in this survey was not clear. It could be that the factories have moved out of the inner city core, but stayed within the greater metropolitan area of the cities.

14　This includes Bureau of Petrochemical Industry, Metallurgical Industry, Textile Industry, Light Industry, Building Materials, Suburban Industry, etc.

15　China interview 2003.

16　One of the largest development group companies in Beijing, Capital Land (Shouchuang), has seven listed companies. One of them is listed in the Hong Kong Stock Exchange. The general manager of Capital Land is the former vice chair of Beijing's Economic Planning committee that holds the key position in approving land development projects. Capital Land claimed to have a land reserve of 450,000 square kilometres by 2003. A commentator called this an era of land re-concentration (Re 2003a,b,c).

17 Real Estate Industry Competition Information, New Real Estate, June–July, 2004, no. 24, p. 34.

18 China interview, 2002

19 China interviews, 2002.

20 Although open land auction was one of the three officially recognized methods of LURs transfers since 1988, only less than 5 per cent of LURs transfers were conducted in the open land auctions towards the end of 1990s, the rest were transferred through individual negotiations (Huang 1997). My interviews support this observation. Land transfers through negotiations were still predominant until the end of the 1990s (China interviews 1999, 2002).

21 Interview of director of Land Use Department, Ministry of Land and resource Management, quoted by Z. Ren (2003).

22 The green belt zone allows only low density residential projects. Low density usually means low returns for the developers. Therefore, the land transaction could be negotiated for lower prices. But an experienced developer told me that in the low density area, they can build luxurious single family homes that are marketed as 'villas' for premium prices. Beijing interview, 2003.

23 See Cao and Lu (2004).

24 For some of the most vivid descriptions of the real estate-centred urban politics in the United States, see Robert Caro (1974) on New York, Douglas Frantz (1991) on San Francisco, and Bernard Frieden and Lynne Sagalyn's (1989) general account. For stories of large developers in North America, see Sobel (1989) on Trammel Crow and Foster (1986) on Olympia and York, also Teaford (1986), Weimer (1997).

25 Statistical Yearbook of China Real Estate Market (2001–2002).

26 Xu, Xouson, 2004, 'yingen yu digen xuangsou, shanghai fengdi qiye kaishi chongxin xipai' (credit and land supply tightened, (causing) restructuring of Shanghai's real estate). Xinhua News Network. http://bj/house/sina.com.cn/08–29–2004

27 Chen Ming, 2004, 'haiwai zijin weihe kaihao zhongguo fengdichan' (why overseas capital is optimistic about China's real estate?). New Real Estate. No. 24. p.115.

28 Compared to the American and European firms, the Singaporean firms are more involved in the local scene. Although they have not been involved directly in project development until very recently, they are concentrated on managing and marketing hotels and serviced apartments for foreign business communities.

29 China interviews, August 2004. And Gong, Zhigong, 2004, 'Vanke jingwai quxian daikuan chenggong' (Vanke's successful indirect foreign loan), New Real Estate, No. 25, August 2004. Yang Liping, 2004, 'jingwai zijin ranzhi kaifa daikwan' (Foreign capital getting involved in real estate development finance). The 21st Century Economic Report, 7 July 2004.

30 China interview, 2004

31 China interviews, 2003, 2004.

32 China interview, 2004. Li, Xiaogong, 2004, 'Shanghai lushi jinru panzheng jieduan, haiwaijijin nanyijiushf' (Shanghai real estate market entering consolidation period, overseas funds can not save the market). International Finance News, 26 July 2004.

33 China interview, 2004.

34 Interview of the vice director of the Research Centre, Ministry of Construction, Wang Yulin. (New Real Estate, 2004, No. 24, p. 146.)

35 China interview, 2003.

36 China interviews, 2003, 2004. Yang, Liping, 2004, 'jingwai zijin ranzhi kaifa daikuan' (foreign capital gets involved in development loans), 21st Century Economic Report, 26 July 2004.

37 See Wu (2004) and Olds (1997, 2001) for excellent examples of such studies on Beijing and Shanghai.
38 China interview, 2002
39 Susan Jakes, 2004, 'Soaring ambitions: the world's most visionary architects are rebuilding China. Inside the aesthetic evolution.' *Time Asia*. 3 May 2004, Vol. 163, No. 17.
40 See note 28.
41 http://www.emporis.com/en/wm/bu
42 http://www.floormature.com/worldaround/articolo.php/art224/3/en
43 China interviews, 1999, 2001, 2002.

References

Bian, Y., J. Logan, H. Lu, Y. Pan and Y. Guan, (1997) 'Work units and housing reform in two Chinese cities', in X. Lu and E. Perry (eds) *Danwei: The Changing Chinese Workplace in Historical and Comparative Perspective*. Armonk, NY: M. E. Sharpe, 223–250.

Bjorklund, E. M. (1986) 'The danwei: social-spatial characteristics of work units in China's urban society', *Economic Geography*, 62 (l): 19–29.

Cao, J. (2002) *Zhongguo tudi gaoxiao liyungyenjiu* (Efficient Use of Urban Land in China), Beijing: Jingji guanii Publisher.

Cao, S. and S. Lu (2004) 'Hepingli beijie rehao: nanyi kaizhang de chaoshi?' ('# 2 of Hepingli North Street: a "land supermarket" that could not have a Grand Opening'), *Economic Observer News*, 12 September.

Caro, R. A. (1974) *The Power Broker: Robert Moses and the Fall of New York*. New York: Alfred A. Knopf.

Chen, J. J. and D. Willis. (eds) (1999) *The Impact of China's Economic Reforms upon Land, Property and Construction*. Aldershot: Ashgate.

Cheng, G. (2003) 'Zhi chaiqain zhitong' (Curing the Pain of Relocation), *Nanfang Zhoumo*, 31 December.

Dong, L. and Y. Sun (1998) 'Tudi shiyong gaige yu Beijing chengshi diyujiegu de yuhua' (Reform of Land Use System in Beijing), in X. Xu, F. Xue, and X. Yan (eds) *Zhong-guo xiangcun chengshi zhuanxingyu xie tiaofazhan* (China's Rural–Urban Transformation and Coordination), Guangzhou: Zhongshan University.

Dong, P. (2000) 'Shiqu tudi' (Losing the Land), *Caijing*, 27.

Foster, P. (1986) *The Master Builders: How the Reichmanns Reached for an Empire*. Toronto: Ekey Porter Book Limited.

Frantz, D. (1991) *From the Ground Up: The Business of Building in the Age of Money*. California: University of California Press.

Frieden, B. and L. Sagalyn. (1989) *Downtown. Inc.: How America Rebuilds Cities*. Cambridge, MA: MIT Press.

Gao, X. (2002) 'Housing demolition in Beijing: disagreement, negotiation and Justice', unpublished master thesis, Department of Sociology, Beijing University.

Ho, P. (2001) 'Who owns China's land? Policies, property rights and deliberate institutional ambiguity', *The China Quarterly*, 166: 394–421.

Ho, S. and G. Lin (2001) 'China's Evolving Land System', working paper, Center for Chinese Research, Institute of Asian Research. Vancouver: University of British Columbia.

Ho, S. and G. Lin (2003) 'Emerging land markets in rural and urban China: policies and practices', *The China Quarterly*, 175: 681–707.

Hong, Y. (1999) 'Myths and realities of public land leasing: Canberra and Hong Kong'. *Land Lines*, 11 (2), Cambridge, MA: Lincoln Institute of Land Policy.

Hong, Y. and S. C. Bourassa. (2003) *Leasing Public Land: Policy Debates and International Experiences*. Lincoln Institute of Land Policy.

Huang, X. and C. Wen. (1998) 'The new trend of BJ's rural–urban integration', in Xu, X., F. Xue and X. Yan (eds) *Zhong-guo xiangcun chengshi zhuanxingyu xie tiaofazhan* (China's Rural–Urban Transformation and Coordination), Guangzhou: Zhongshan University, 177–182.

Huang, Z. (1997) 'Urban land development and urban space restructuring in Shanghai during economic reforms', unpublished master thesis, Department of Urban Planning, Tongji University, Shanghai, China.

Kornai, J. (1992) *The Socialist System: The Political Economy of Communism*. Princeton, NJ: Princeton University Press.

Li, L. and D. Isaac (1999) 'Development of urban land policies in China', in J. Chen and D. Wills (eds) *The Impact of China's Economic Reforms upon Land, Property and Construction*. Aldershot: Ashgate, 16–25.

Li, S. and P. Ren (2003) '*Shanghai tudi chubeizhi zhuanxing*' (Transformation of Shanghai's land reserve system), *Caijing*, 76, January 20.

Lin, L. (1999) *Urban Land Reform in China*, London: McMillan Press.

Lin, C. S. G. (2002) 'The growth and structural change of Chinese cities: a contextual and geographic analysis', *Cities*, 19 (5): 299–316.

—— (2004) 'Towards a post-socialist city? Economic tertiarization and urban reformation in the Guangzhou metropolis, China'. *Eurasia Geography and Economics*, 45 (1): 18–44.

Logan, J. (1993) 'Cycles and trends in the globalization of real estate', in P. Knox (ed.) *The Restless Urban Landscape*, Englewood Cliffs, NJ: Prentice Hall: 35–54.

Lu, X. and E. Perry (eds) (1997) *Danwei: The Changing Chinese Workplace in Historical and Comparative Perspective*. Armonk, NY: M. E. Sharpe.

Lubman, S. (2004) 'Law of the Jungle', *China Economic Review*, at: http://www.chinaeconomicreview.com/subscriber/articledetail.php?id=303

Marcuse, P. (1996) 'Privatization and its discontents: property rights in land and housing in the transition in Eastern Europe', in G. Andrusz, M. Harloe and I. Szelenyi, (eds), *Cities after Socialism: Urban and Regional Change and Conflict in Post-Socialist Societies*. Oxford: Blackwell, 119–191.

Olds, K. (1997) 'Globalizing Shanghai: the "global Intelligence Corps" and the building of Pudong', *Cities*, 14 (2): 109–123.

—— (2001) *Globalization and Urban Change: Capital, Culture and Pacific Rim Mega-projects*. New York: Oxford University Press.

Po, L. (2001) 'The socialist transition and urban transformation: a case study of Nanjing, China', unpublished PhD dissertation, UC Berkeley, Department of City and Regional Planning.

Ren, P. (2003a) '*Chengshi tudizhimi*' (The secret of urban land), *Caijing*, 76, 20 January.

—— (2003b) '*Chaiqian zhisu*' (Demolition law suites), *Caijing*, 87, 5 July.

—— (2003c) '*Xinquandi yundong molu*' (The end of the 'new land enclosure') *Caijing*, 90, 20 August.

Ren, Z. (2003) '*Ruhe nadi*' (How to obtain land?), *Jingji guanchabao* (The Economic Observer), September 24.

Singer, J. (2000) *Entitlement: The Paradox of Property*, New Haven, CT: Yale University Press.

Sobel, R. (1989) *Trammel Crow: Master Builder. The Story of America's Largest Real Estate Empire*. New York: John Wiley and Sons.

Teaford, J. (1986) *The Twentieth-Century American City*. Baltimore, MD: The Johns Hopkins University Press.

Weimer, D. (ed.) (1997) *The Political Economy of Property Rights: Institutional Change and Credibility in the Reform of Centrally Planned Economies*. Cambridge: Cambridge University Press.

Wong Z. (ed.) (1996) *Beijingfangdi chan* (Beijing Real Estate). Beijing: Hangkonggongye Press.

Wu, F. (1998) 'The new structure of building provision and the transformation of the urban landscape in metropolitan Guangzhou, China', *Urban Studies*, 35 (2): 259–272.

—— (2002) 'China's changing urban governance in the transition towards a more market-oriented economy' *Urban Studies*, 39 (7): 1071–1093.

—— (2004) 'Transplanting cityscapes: the use of imagined globalization in housing commodification in Beijing', *Area*, 36 (3) 227–234.

Xu, X., F. Xue, X. Yen (eds) (1998) *Zongguo xiangcun Chengshi zuanxingyu xietiao fazhan* (Rural-Urban Transformation and Coordinated Development in China), 177–182.

Yeh, A. G. and Wu F. (1996) 'The new land development process and urban development in Chinese cities', *International Journal of Urban and Regional Research*, 20: 330–353.

Zhang, W. (2002) 'Beijing *tudiye chushi*' (Emerging Land Masters in Beijing), *Caijing*, 1: 38–43.

Zhang, Z. (2002) 'Shanghai *Xintiandijuqu gaizaojihua gean yanjiu*' (A case study of New World Urban Renewal Project in Shanghai), unpublished master thesis, National Taiwan University, Taipei.

Zhao, L. (2003) '*Chaiqian shinien beixiju*' (Ten years of relocation drama), *Nanfang zhoumo*, 4 September.

10 Transplanting cityscapes

Townhouse and gated community in globalization and housing commodification

Fulong Wu

Foreign/Western building styles are becoming 'popular' cityscapes in Chinese cities. These 'transplanted cityscapes', especially in residential buildings, such as 'continental European style' (*'ou lu shi'*, see also Giroir Chapter 11 in this volume), are applied to the homes of China's rising middle class as well as those of multi-national expatriates. Another striking building form is the 'gated community' (see also Huang 2005, Wu 2005, Hsing Chapter 9 in this volume, Webster *et al.* 2005), which is similar to low-density sprawling American suburbs. In a sense, these 'exotic' building forms are becoming 'ordinary' cityscapes under China's new urbanism. To what extent do these transplanted cityscapes reflect the globalization of city building or even 'homogenization' and the global spread of the archetype of postmodern urbanism (for global spread of the gated community, see Webster *et al.* 2002; for the archetype of postmodern urbanism and the 'LA school' that promotes the concept, see Dear and Flusty 1998, for a critique see Beauregard 2003)?

The aim of this chapter is to explore how globalization unfolds in the process of urban development. Rather than examine the impact of globalization on the city, as if the former were independent of and superimposed on the latter, I attempt to address how globalization can be imagined, pursued and exploited in the process of local growth. Through examining the emergence of Western architectural motifs and gated foreign communities in a late-socialist capital, Beijing, it is shown that transplanting cityscapes is a conscious action by developers to exploit globalization and thereby overcome the constraints of local markets. By associating themselves with globalization, the development elite hope to sell the vision of the good life in the era of globalization. The creation of 'foreign gated communities' should be attributed not only to robust demand for high-quality expatriate housing but also to the local (historic) institutional constraint that requires a specific procedure for 'foreign housing' construction.

Transplanted cityscapes

Besides the literature on China's urban land and housing development (e.g. Yeh and Wu 1996, Logan *et al.* 1999, Wang and Murie 1999, Ho and Lin 2003) there has recently been a growing literature on the social and cultural consequences of post-reform urban development.

Hsing (Chapter 9 in this volume) observes that, in the pursuit of consumerism, fantasy names such as Orange County and Venice Garden remind one of a different lifestyle. Here there is more than the transplanting of a particular built form, but rather the dream of an American (Californian) happy life in sprawling suburbs characterized by single-family homes. Western architectures are welcomed in the design of landmark projects and trespass across cultural boundaries in the process of rebuilding Chinese cities. As this enthusiastic process proceeds, the driving forces of urban land development go beyond the political economy of land and include 'contestation over the meaning of the place'.

In a related study of residential segregation in Beijing, Huang (2005: 210) finds that wealthy neighbourhoods comprising villas and townhouses are located in the 'north near the Asian Game Village and Olympic Forest Park, Xiaotangshan Warm Springs, in the northeast along Jingshun Road near Wenyu River and Chaobai River, in the north-west along Jingchang Express, and in the south-east next to Beijing Economic and Technology Development Zone'. Superb housing compounds like Purple Jade Villas and Near-Forest Garden clearly distinguish themselves in terms of landscape from other affordable housing complexes such as Dragon-Turn Vista (Huilongguan). The social composition of these compounds is characterized by a high concentration of entrepreneurs, managers of joint ventures and people with higher education. These properties are expensive: for example, in Purple Jade Villas, the unit housing price reached up to US 3,000 dollar per square metre and the unit price ranges from US 450,000 to 1.8 million dollars (Huang 2005: 214).

In what Giroir (2005; also Chapter 11 in this volume) calls 'golden ghettos', globalization is perhaps most prominently experienced through the appearance of diverse architectural styles. These privileged residences include Purple Jade Villas and Yosemite Villas in Beijing and Fontainebleau Villas in Shanghai. Even within the same compound, there is a mélange of different styles such as the American Victorian, Royal Dutch, Portman and the Mies (Giroir Chapter 11 in this volume).

This chapter describes two cases: the use of foreign architectural motifs in residential buildings, especially so-called townhouses, and the emergence of clustered so-called foreign gated communities (*waiguoren shequ*), very often based on expatriate rental housing and thus developing into 'noble communities' (*gaoshang shequ*). All these are apparently related to globalization; transplanting cityscapes can be understood as part of globalization namely the globalization of culture. Globalization is frequently understood as an imposed process through which the core transforms the periphery. Such a hegemonic convergence is typically known as 'Americanization' (Hannerz 1997). On the other hand, transplanting cityscapes facilitates 'cultural affinities' which in turn pave the way to deepened globalization:

> When the peripheral cultural absorbs the influx of meaning and symbolic forms from the center and transforms them to some considerable degree into something of their own, they may at the same time so increase the cultural

affinities between the center and the periphery that the passage of more cultural imports is facilitated.

(Hannerz 1997: 127)

But a detailed investigation of these built forms in Beijing reveals a more 'translocal' nature (Smith 2001). Globalization only provides the possibility of relocating/copycatting alien landscapes. The imperative of transplanting city-scapes must be understood in the local context. Transplanting cityscapes is a socially constructed process, which envisages globalization as the core of social change. This reveals the action of property developers in the manipulation of urban images in a similar vein to the efforts seen in entrepreneurial governance in the West (Short *et al.* 1993, Hall and Hubbard 1998).

Townhouses in Beijing

In a northern suburb of Beijing, 16 kilometres north of the Asian Games Village, is located an 'exotic' and luxury estate. Its name, like its original North American neo-traditional design, is 'Orange County'. The external design is typical of the fashionable style of up-market housing in Beijing: the 'townhouse' style and the internal decoration of show homes are equally impressive among emerg-ing townhouse 'gated communities' (Figure 10.1a and b). The project boasts of '100 per cent authentic design' drawn from the same project in the United States. The original design, according to widely distributed brochures, won a prize for new homes in the United States in 1999. Under the title of 'Beijing's pure European and American villa', another source emphasizes its authenticity: 'adopting the original American style, the Orange County project uses a blueprint that won the 1999 California Gold Medal' (Wang 2000: 14).

It is claimed that the project was the first to be jointly designed by three gen-uine American architectural firms, who 'inject many brand new and advanced international design *linian* into the project'. The word '*linian*' is indeed a selling point employing jargon fashionable in property development in China nowadays. The word *linian*, coined from '*lixiang*' (ideal) and '*gainian*' (concept), can thus be best translated as 'visionary concept'. It represents a stark departure from the outdated idealism (communist utopianism). The emergence of such discourse thus suggests a profound transformation of cityscapes in the late-socialist era. According to the article, the design uses a new visionary concept that helps to maintain an atmosphere of 'community', which indeed 'mimics a French town on the River Seine'. Therefore, it fully 'presents exotic characteristics of the foreign country', and the construction materials, including doors, windows and ventilation systems, are in fact imported from overseas.

This place, however, is not for 'ordinary' people. The total floor space of the project amounts to 120,000 square metres and 100 of the 300 units are designed in the 'townhouse' style (Zhang 2001). The first phase was released to the market in December 2000 and sold out at an average price of 7,800 yuan per square metre. Since the average per capita annual disposable income in Beijing is 11,577 yuan

Figure 10.1 (a) The gate of the 'Orange County'. (b) The design of buildings.

(Beijing Statistical Bureau 2002), this is equivalent to less than 2 square metres per person.

The concept of the 'townhouse' has been imported into Beijing since 2000. Unlike most imported foreign words 'townhouse' is not translated according to its meaning causing a great difficulty for local people in understanding it. Because the word is pronounced as '*tanghao zhi*' meaning 'mouse in the soup' in the literal pronunciation of Chinese characters the term creates curiosity, sensation and cynicism.

There is, however, a reason behind the preservation of the English word in Chinese text, as a local journalist explains:

> [i]f we want to understand the townhouse, we should first learn a bit of English. We should first understand that it is a popular term just like SOHO, CLD, Loft, CBD, and then try to appreciate its international origin.... Townhouse targets the white collar office worker and successful people. Their English is not bad. They are naturally fond of these terms. Those who cannot understand foreign languages generally respect foreign words. Therefore, developers do not waste their efforts on translating the jargon into Chinese words.
>
> (Tang 2001: 2)

The townhouse is in fact a terraced or semi-detached house designed to high standards. Thus, local property agents explain that townhouses are 'terraced villas' or 'economic villas'. Most townhouse projects are located in the suburbs. The townhouse is called a villa because it is built at low density, in contrast with high-rise commodity housing. Because land prices dictate very high building density in Chinese cities, developers cannot afford to build low-density estates in the central area (e.g. the area within the third circular road in Beijing).

In 2001 about a dozen townhouse projects were constructed in Beijing. They are mainly distributed in the northern suburbs. Their names reflect the nature of transplanted cityscapes: 'Cambridge', the 'Asian-Olympic-Games-Garden', 'Lushan Small New Town', 'Times Manor', 'Foreign Villa' and 'Orange County'. The most expensive one is Asian-Olympic-Games-Garden, located between the fourth and fifth circular roads. The price is well above 10,000 yuan per square metre. The main housing type has a floor space of 300 square metres, and the price for one townhouse is about 3 million yuan. In general, however, the price of townhouses ranges from 800,000 to 1 million yuan, lower than those of detached houses and villas. Even this price, however, is not affordable for ordinary people.

The emergence of the townhouse in Beijing should first be understood as product innovation, according to a senior real estate consultant (Interview, June 2001). In the pre-reform period the dominant form of housing was the flat in multi-storey matchbox-style buildings. In the 1980s (the early stage of reform), high-rise high-density commodity housing estates began to emerge. These build-ings are developed in the form of residential districts (micro-regions), a concept originating in Soviet residential planning (French and Hamilton 1979). While the 'modern' large housing estates developed in the 1980s are better than the workers' villages built in the 1950s, market reform has raised expectations of higher standards of living among those who benefit from marketization.

As discussed earlier, the driving force for commodity housing lies in stratified demand. 'Fully commodified housing' (i.e. those sold on the open market to private purchasers) results from a demand for higher standards rather than a need for basic accommodation. Demand is driven by the desire for lower density, green space and private automobile ownership. In short, it is the demand for a new lifestyle which has not been seen previously in China.

The customers for townhouses belong to the upper middle class. Many buy a townhouse as a second home in addition to their apartment in the city. This social group is at the stage of wealth accumulation and expects an increase in income. The townhouse is designed for those 'who want to own a plot of land under the feet and a piece of sky overhead', and the ownership of the townhouse will bring them 'land, sky, garden, and garage'.

The emergence of the townhouse in fact fills a gap in the niche market for high-quality properties. After its emergence in 1990, Beijing's villa market experienced a frenetic boom in the early 1990s. The market collapsed in 1994 in response to the government tightening of bank loans. Since 1995 no new villa project has been approved. Thus the total supply of villas began to decrease in the late 1990s. Moreover, the design concept of villas developed in the early 1990s could not meet the rising demand. In 1999, the villa market began to recover. The townhouse in fact emerged as an 'economic villa' to fill the gap between luxury properties and ordinary commodity housing.

The profit margin on townhouse projects is very high. Although the actual cost of construction ranges from 4,000 to 5,000 yuan per square metre, the average selling price of townhouses stands at 7,500 yuan per square metre. With an average floor space of 200 square metres, the total price ranges from 1.35 million to 1.8 million yuan. Because the townhouse occupies a large area of land, with a plot ratio controlled at 0.5–0.7, it is crucial to acquire cheap land. The difference between the construction cost and the selling price has led to a profit rate well above low-market commodity housing.

From 'foreign housing' to 'foreign gated communities'

Foreign housing is literally 'housing approved for foreign sale' (*waixiao fang*). The residential market for foreigners has been separated from the local housing provision system through special approval for sale. Real estate developers must apply for permits to sell in the overseas market before they can develop foreign housing. Foreign passport holders as well as overseas Chinese were required to live in approved residences in Beijing until September 2002. Foreign housing projects had to be approved by the public security bureau, besides the normal approval procedure for commodity housing. Foreign housing is generally of high quality and is more expensive than the domestic commodity housing, but the real distinction lies in the separate route of housing production and consumption. Foreign housing represents the most thoroughly 'commodified' housing segment.

Demand for foreign housing is triggered by economic globalization. As the capital, Beijing has attracted over 10,000 joint ventures and regional headquarters (see also Zhao 2003, for Beijing's status in the financial sector). Beijing has also seen the concentration of high-tech industries (Zhou 2002). For example, Beijing has 73 headquarters among the 500 corporations with the largest import and export volume in 1995, while Shanghai has only 44 regional headquarters. The actual utilized foreign capital grew from US 177 million dollars in 1987 to US 4 billion dollars in 2001. Foreign tourism has also brought an important source of foreign exchange. China's recent WTO membership has also benefited Beijing. The preparations for hosting the Olympic Games in 2008 provide an unprecedented chance for Beijing to play a role in international affairs. Foreign workers come to Beijing from all over the world, especially North America, Western Europe, Japan and Australia. Recently, there has also been an increase in the number of overseas Chinese, and those from Hong Kong and the rest of the Asian countries. In 2002, it was estimated that there were 40,000 foreigners living in Beijing, and a significant proportion of them were middle and high-rank managers and professionals working in accountancy, law, banking and management of the offices of overseas companies. To promote the development of high-tech industries, the municipal government promulgated a proposal in the Tenth Five-Year Plan period to recruit 5,000 foreign experts working in Beijing. The growth of the expatriate community has led to a robust demand for high-quality housing. For a British or American company, housing allowances range from at least US 4,000 to 5,000 dollars per month, and all the other benefits. For example, Phillips Petroleum sent about 30 people in 2001, all of whom are on housing budgets from US 6,000 to 12,000 dollars per month, per person or per family. This is equivalent to US 3 million dollars per year of rental expenditure in Beijing. This strong spending power has stimulated the growth of expatriate housing.

Both gated and foreign housing have developed into two types: apartment complexes, which offer high-rise living, and villa compounds which are low-rise, spacious and usually contain individual gardens. For a location within the Third Ring Road, villa projects command premium prices as they have almost all the benefits of a suburban living but with the centre's locational advantage. These secured residences are surrounded with walls, with 24-hour closed-circuit television and patrolling guards. In some residences, security cards are required for entering the compound or buildings, and sometimes even the elevator and the apartment. Table 10.1 shows the listed amenities of three gated communities among 12 surveyed in Beijing. In general, they are built to a higher standard than ordinary commodity housing and the residences compete on their aesthetic character, ambience, location and distance to amenities in the city. Other facilities such as international school, international hospital and medical centres, shopping centres and Western supermarkets such as Carrefour (a French-based supermarket chain) are also considered relevant. In general the building standard is high, as shown in the interior design of reception area of East Lake Villas apartment complex in Beijing (Figure 10.2a and b).

Foreign housing projects are concentrated in a few areas such as the CBD area in the cross-section between East Third Ring Road and the Janguo Meiwai Avenue, the Third Embassy area and the Asian Games Village. The distribution of prime foreign housing projects is skewed towards the East (Figure 10.3). In addition, villas are concentrated in Shunyi, Beijing's northeast suburban county. This generally corresponds to the distribution of best quality housing areas

Table 10.1 Major features of 3 among the 12 surveyed foreign gated communities in Beijing

Name of residence	River Garden	Riveira	East Lake Villas
Type of development	Villa	Villa and apartments	Villa and apartments
Price to buy (USD) Rent (USD/month)	3 bed rooms 260.3 m²: 7,000 285.7 m²: 7,500	568,000 2 bed apartment: 2,200	2 bed apartment:149 m²: 4,200–5,380
Size (m²)	3 bed: 260.3 m² or 285.7 m²	Apartment: 120 m²	Apartment: 118, 137, 149 or 157 m² Villa: 209 m²
Facilities	Swimming pools, tennis court, squash, gym, hair salon, kids playroom and playground, school ('Montessori')	Indoor/outdoor swimming pool, gym, sauna, tennis courts and tennis coach, sports hall, basketball, squash, golf range, cinema, restaurants, supermarket, post office, beauty salon, video arcade, kids play area	Gym, indoor swimming pool, squash court, tennis court, squash, billiards, table tennis, aerobics class, sauna, post office, bank, beauty salon, 2 restaurants, supermarket
Residential/office/retail Grade of development	Residential A	Residential A	Residential A
Security	Gated, guards, CCTV	Full CCTV, gated, guards	Gated, guards, CCTV. Phase 2: security card to enter building, elevator, and apartment. Video monitors in apartment
The living environment	Spacious roads and villas, clean air and ground, quiet. Villas ageing slightly	Landscaped gardens, spacious roads and villas. Villas modern and luxurious, come fully furnished. Some villas have drive-ways, roof terraces, steam baths and jacuzzi	Landscaped Chinese garden, fairly spacious, buildings ageing slightly; Relatively quiet. Villas: relatively low density development. Apartments: relatively high density development
Additional information	No 2 bed available. Rent includes use of facilities	80% occupancy rate, shuttle bus to town and back every hour	Phase 1 built 1989, Phase 2 completion due August 2001. Phase 1 occupancy rate: 100% with waiting list. Rent includes use of facilities and utility fees (water, electricity, gas, central air conditioning)

Source: Wu and Webber (2004), originally compiled from the fieldwork in Beijing.

Figure 10.2 (a) The interior design of the reception area of East Lake Villas. (b) The interior design of the Riveira.

Source: From Wu and Webber (2004).

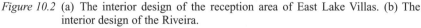

(Hu and Kaplan 2001). The uneven distribution of foreign gated communities is attributed to the historically uneven orientation of the north-east and south-west areas of Beijing. Dating back to the late nineteenth and early twentieth century, the Qing Dynasty designated the eastern part outside the Forbidden City for foreign embassies; foreigners have consequently located there. The post-1949 urban development did not eliminate this east–west spatial differentiation. Government office buildings have been built in the west, for example, in Sanlihe and Banwanzhuang, and the new Embassy area was built between the Altar of the Sun and Jianguomen (Sit 1995). Subsequent plans such as the 1982 and 1993 master plans continue to develop this division and determine the urban layout and

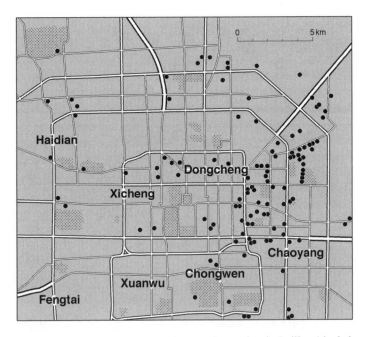

Figure 10.3 The distribution of prime foreign housing project in Beijing (shaded areas are green space).

Source: Wu and Webber (2004), originally compiled from Jones Lang Lasalle real estate leaflet; reproduced with permission.

morphology (Gaubatz 1999), and the construction of Beijing's CBD in the Chaoyang District continues to drive the area towards global and economic functions (Gaubatz 2005). Proximity to the Capital International Airport enhances accessibility in the eastern part, and the location is close to international schools, offices, hotels and entertainment facilities.

However, in-depth investigation of these landscapes shows the adaptation and imagination of alien landscapes in the host environment. They are even invented by the local developers, in the local milieu, for local consumption (a large proportion of 'foreign housing' is owned by local Chinese and rented to foreigners). How can we relate the production of alien landscapes to local institutions?

Local institutions and housing commodification

In this section, I try to probe into local institutions to see how hybrid forms of foreign housing and gated communities are created by progressive housing commodification and in turn how they pave the way for the promotion of housing markets. It is argued that the historical process of housing commodification had led to clustered distribution of 'foreign housing' and that the disjuncture between demand and supply for expatriate housing becomes a practical reason for creating a segregated sector. The spread of this building form is also promoted by developers as an imaginative way of gaining an advantage in the competitive market. In order to appreciate the local dimension of these 'global' building forms, we have to understand that the housing market in China is a highly differentiated one, created by progressive reforms.

Conditioned by progressive commodification

Foreign housing is a transitional housing form. Its creation is conditioned by progressive commodification. Before the 1990s, foreigners had experienced varying degrees of difficulty in finding accommodation. Most of them were accommodated in hotels, hotel-style apartments or the compounds purposely built for diplomats. The cost of accommodation was high, as no alternative was available. Such demand could not be accommodated within the pre-reform housing stock: the quality was either too poor or the housing was not private property but rather a social welfare benefit tied up with the entitlement to employment. For foreign teachers or students living in purposely built buildings in a university campus might be an option. The residual private rental sector was totally out of consideration for expatriate housing because of the poor housing quality and inadequate services.

Although the domestic housing system itself has been experiencing commodification, because of the nature of progressive reform, various hybrid approaches combining market and non-market measures have been invented. Foreign housing has been created by the requirement for fully market-based housing supply and in turn the foreign housing sector has been created for foreigners who were restricted from accessing ordinary commodity housing, for which various subsidies and the administrative allocation of land were still available during the process of gradual reform.

The commodification of housing provision and the establishment of the land leasing system have made it possible to establish a market for foreign housing. The sector was in fact the first one that was introduced under the market approach, and thus is recognized as having full property rights. In Beijing, the earliest foreign housing project among the fully commodified housing estates was 'Overseas Chinese Town'. The development of foreign housing has also led to a change in the way properties are marketed. International real estate agents began to bridge demand and supply. Prior to the 1990s, there was no opportunity for real estate companies to operate. The role of real estate services has since grown, with international companies entering the market to target foreigners. This is because many of the local companies still do not quite understand the level of service that large multinationals require, although local consultants have been around for a long time. Foreign companies perceive that the local firms do not have the necessary international knowledge or experience of market conditions to be as aware as international firms of their needs. The international firms understand what foreigners want, meanwhile familiarizing themselves with local knowledge.

With so many similarities in the building form, it is natural to suggest there might be a global spread of gated communities (Webster *et al.* 2002). But the actual reasons for creating China's gated foreign housing are more complex and depend upon the specific conditions. First, fear (Davis 1992), or more precisely the 'discourse of fear' (Low 2003), is often behind the construction of secured residences. As a result, property developers provide good security to attract customers. Similarly, the need for high security is understandable as many foreign residences contain embassy employees. But the crime rate is low in Beijing, and crime is not an issue in the sense that it is in the West, although there is an increasing concern as Chinese society is now much more mobile than it was before, and the disparity of income levels is becoming higher. The government, together with developers and residents, see 'gating' as a popular solution to the potential problem of social discomfort and division rather than as a response to real threat. For the government, the secured compound helps to reduce crime rates, maintain good public order and produce the image of a safe living environment, which are important for foreign investment. Recent crimes against foreign investors have been tackled swiftly by the local police, indicating the priority of ensuring the safety of foreigners. In a sense, the gated community is a sort of 'enforced' public safety standard for valuable customers – foreign investors and sojourners.

Second, as elsewhere, gated communities also constitute a status symbol. The formation of foreign gated housing is attributed to differentiated social status; but this division is displayed between expatriates and local residents. As mentioned earlier, expatriates earn a much higher income than local employees in general and also have various allowances. Housing and schooling allowances are generous so as to maintain expatriates' quality of life. As a result, foreign housing has a much higher building standard than ordinary domestic commodity housing. In fact, the notion of 'foreign housing', at the beginning of housing commodification, was almost synonymous with high-quality housing. Some projects even solicit international architectural design. Most compounds include leisure facilities such as a swimming pool, tennis court, restaurant and landscaped gardens, even a golf simulator, bowling alley or cinema. Some residences provide organized activities, a business centre, apartment cleaning service, medical services and landscaped gardens. This requirement for special services brings us to the next reason.

Third, special requirements are also probably common in gated communities known as 'common interest developments' (CIDs) (McKenzie 1994). The gated community is an efficient way of organizing services because of the high concentration of customers. But for foreign housing in China, this should be understood in the context of a particular need for international schools. The international school is an almost indispensable factor for expatriates with young children when choosing a residential location. In Beijing, these are concentrated outside the Fourth Ring Road and along the airport highway, including the International School of Beijing, the Western Academy of Beijing, the German School and the Japanese School.

Fourth, as elsewhere, the gated community is often argued to be facilitating 'community development'. Despite the diversity and transient nature of expatriates, the gated form offers the environment a way to develop a sense of 'community'. In Beijing as well as in other large cities, the Han constitute the predominant majority. While the Chinese culture is tolerant and the recent worship of the Western lifestyle welcomes foreigners from developed Western economies, the linguistic and cultural barriers prevent foreigners from forming deep relationships with local residents. Although the members of expatriate community themselves come from different ethnic backgrounds, the economic barriers to enter into these gated communities makes them more homogenous in terms of socioeconomic status. Consequently, they create similar market niches for high-end services and lifestyles. The gated communities organize various social occasions such as dinners, theatre, fashion shows, membership acquaintance parties, charity golf tournaments, ladies' luncheons and residents' association meetings. These activities are organized through the club or property management companies, which are more experienced and professional than those activities organized outside the gated communities by voluntary workers.

Fifth, the gated community in China depends upon the specific form of grass-roots governance, while the creation of the gated community in the United States has been driven by the retreat of regulation and rise of 'private governance' (McKenzie 1994, Webster *et al.* 2005). In the traditional Chinese neighbourhood, the residents' committee is the basic social organization. Defined as a mass social organization under 'self-organization, self-regulation and self-education', the residents' committee is under the control of the sub-district government agency for consolidating local governance (Wu 2002, see also Ren Chapter 15 in this volume). However, for foreign communities, these grassroots organizations are virtually meaningless. Instead, the homeowners' association is more relevant, and foreigners are keen to have the property management company to 'secure' their living environment instead of directly contacting government agencies. In some extreme circumstances, it is reported that security guards refuse to allow the police to enter the complex, as the guards are answerable to their employers – the property management company – who in turn want to please the homeowners as their clients.

In summation, the creation of the gated community is subject to seemingly similar trends, but investigation of the detailed conditions shows that it is more dependent upon local institutions and particular social cultural conditions than upon economic globalization.

Promoted for housing commodification

There are various hybrid forms of residential properties, ranging from municipal public housing to quasi-privatized work-unit housing to fully 'commodified housing' without housing subsidy or discounted land input. The fully commodified housing market is very competitive. Property developers in this segment are forced to find a selling point to 'brand' their products, as housing demand is becoming diversified and differentiated. Under market-oriented urban development housing, construction is no longer driven by the need for basic accommodation as defined in the socialist era but rather by demand for the ownership of lifestyles. Faced with an increasingly saturated market, developers need to exploit the scope of niche markets by inventing new and ostentatious housing estates. Different tactics are used one of which is to depict the high quality of the living environment. Fraser (2000: 53) examined advertisements for luxury housing and unpacked the 'romanticized discourse of oasification' by suggesting, 'the trees and flowers of the urban housing estate also mark the commodified borders of enhanced domesticity and the boundaries of a more private lifestyle for those who can afford it and those who can dream of it'.

While the emerging middle class is looking for the good life, what constitutes the good life is not an easily definable subject in the late-socialist era. In the socialist era, the concept of a 'good life' was defined by communist utopianism. The overwhelming task was to combat material deprivation and, in housing consumption, the shortage of basic shelter. Now that this seems irrelevant to the upwardly mobile Chinese, consumers begin to look elsewhere for their vision and aspirations. In this sense, globalization becomes particularly relevant as it provides a new source of imagination to foster suppressed desires. Szelenyi (1996) argued that in Eastern Europe the major transformation in post-socialist cities is the re-emergence of diversity and greater 'urbanism', defined by the Chicago School as the 'way of life'. Alongside the highly controversial effect of the polarized labour market in the global city (Sassen 1991) – whereby the new white collar work in foreign companies attracts salaries that enable some Chinese to join the new rich – globalization helps to define different lifestyles and to differentiate consumption levels. But this does not occur automatically without conscious social action undertaken by local actors.

The claimed global reach allows the developers to sell a new vision of the good life. Basing their imagination on Western lifestyles seems a more effective way to open up the niche market. To boost authenticity, developers adopt various innovative measures including employing global architects, mimicking Western design motifs, naming roads and buildings with famous foreign names that are familiar to the Chinese and even forging a relationship with sister communities in foreign towns.

Transplanting the townhouse into Beijing's suburban residential landscape is, on the one hand, driven by globalization and the demand for high-quality properties and, on the other, results from the contradictions of housing commodification. The emphasis on market development and stratified housing demand has inevitably led to the diversification of built forms. While the majority of urban residents still live in the traditional style of courtyard housing or workplace compounds, the rising upper middle class has begun to search for foreign lifestyles in this late-socialist era.

Conclusion

Globalization, rather than existing independently outside local territories, is a socially constructed process. This chapter examines transplanted cityscapes – townhouse and gated community – as a result of the conscious action of local developers, which is further rooted in the contradiction of late-socialist housing commodification. As shown in the development of 'foreign housing', economic globalization triggers the demand for expatriate housing; however, the sector is created as a distinct one separated from domestic housing by the institutional hurdles regarding housing production and consumption. Foreign housing represents the fully commodified housing sector and thus contributes to the overall process of housing commodification. Although foreign housing was once almost exclusively sold to foreigners, overseas Chinese with foreign currencies and local households with foreign remittances, wealthy domestic buyers have gradually entered the foreign housing market. In Beijing, just before the lifting of housing restriction on foreigners, local homeowners accounted for 70 per cent of the total sale of foreign housing (Da 2001). Foreign housing has thus become equivalent to high-quality commodity housing because of clearly defined property rights. Moreover, the spatial distribution of foreign housing reveals clustering in particular locations, with the building form being predominantly that of the gated community. Nonetheless, this spatially skewed distribution of foreign housing is also attributable to very local cultural conditions. In contrast with the predominant concern for safety and security (Davis 1992, Low 2003), the foreign gated community is more a result of the unusual manner of regulating housing production and organizing exclusive amenities (such as international schools and the desire for the affinity of their own expatriate communities within a relatively homogenous Chinese Han population). With the abolition of foreign housing restrictions, the gated form is likely to continue. But it will be to a lesser extent attributable to the identity of foreigners than to quality differentials, as luxury commodity housing accommodating the new rich Chinese is also being built into the gated communities (Wu 2005).

Rather than study the monumental urban projects financed by foreign investment (Olds 2001), I have chosen to depict the 'ordinary' cityscapes of residential developments for local or 'translocal' consumers. These are not the typical cases in the study of globalization in the sense that the developers are not multinationals and do not themselves operate at the global scale. The portrait of developers' global reach is at the least dubious and at the most extreme forged as a commercial marketing tool; the motifs of classical European architecture and townhouse landscaping are selective and imagined. But the phenomena are really existent as part of globalization.

What is significant is the suggestion generated by these cases that globalization is not simply imposed but is rather something that can be imagined, solicited and exploited. The global discourses here are manipulated to overcome market constraints by more effectively exploiting the niche market of the upwardly mobile urban rich. Such imaginative and selective use of globalization suggests that the globalizing city is bound to be 'unavoidably incomplete' (Beauregard and Haila 1997), as in this context of transitional economies. In fact, the notion of 'transitional economies' is problematic as some believe that these economies are transformed by some external (global) forces to converge into a standard/Western market model. Wu and Ma (2005: 276) argue that restructuring the Chinese city 'suggests that "transition" should not be regarded as a once-for-all convergence towards some universal model – often implied to be the "market economies." This prototype of "market economies" ignores that the capitalist world itself is changing'; 'many spatial forms may be similar to those seen in the Western world but the underlying process does not have a purely global logic'; and the 'restructuring of the Chinese city is a local process that exploits and constitutes global processes'. In the study of 'restless' formation and reformation of landscapes, Knox (1993) emphasizes that new architectural styles and new forms of residential development must not be abstracted from the broader sweep of socio-spatial changes. By exposing this idea in the context of the globalizing Chinese city, we can further argue that a greater flexibility of landscape production, such as transplanting cityscapes, does reflect these broader 'socio-spatial changes' but that these changes are multi-scalar processes and are not detached from the local milieu.

Acknowledgements

This chapter draws extensively the materials from Wu (2004) (reproduced with permission from Blackwell Publishing) and Wu and Webster (2004) (reprinted with permission from Elsevier). The writing of these papers has benefited from constructive comments from anonymous reviewers. Support from the British Academy on project 'socio-spatial segregation and neighbourhood change in urban China (SG-33836) and the Leverhulme Trust (RF&G/7/2001/0090) are gratefully acknowledged. I would like to express my thanks to Klaire Webber, a graduate from the University of Southampton, who conducted the fieldwork on 'foreign housing' and co-authored the paper (Wu and Webber 2004) to Dr Ya Ping Wang who enlightened me with his insights on recent housing development in China and to Dr Deng Qing who assisted the fieldworks. I am solely responsible for any remaining errors.

References

Beauregard, R. (2003) 'City of superlatives', *City & Community*, 2 (3): 183–199.
Beauregard, R. and A. Haila (1997) 'The unavoidable incompleteness of the city', *American Behavioral Scientist*, 41 (3): 327–341.
Beijing Statistics Bureau (2002) *Beijing Statistical Yearbook 2002*, Beijing: Chinese Statistical Publisher.
Da, J. (2001) *Studies on Beijing's foreign housing*, China Business Management, 6 April.
Davis, M. (1992) 'Fortress Los Angeles: the militarization of urban space', in M. Sorkin (ed.), *Variations on a Theme Park: The New American City and the End of Public Space*, New York: Noonday Press, 154–180.
Dear, M. and S. Flusty (1998) 'Postmodern urbanism', *Annals of the Association of American Geographers*, 88 (1): 50–72.
Fraser, D. (2000) 'Inventing oasis: luxury housing advertisements and reconfiguring domestic space in Shanghai', in D. S. Davis (ed.), *The Consumer Revolution in Urban China*, Berkeley, CA: University of California Press, 25–53.

French, R. A. and F. E. I. Hamilton (1979) *The Socialist City*, Chichester: John Wiley and Sons.

Gaubatz, P. (1999) 'China's urban transformation: patterns and processes of morphological change in Beijing, Shanghai and Guangzhou', *Urban Studies*, 36 (9): 1495–1521.

—— (2005) 'Globalization and the development of new central business districts in Beijing, Shanghai and Guangzhou', in L. J. C. Ma and F. Wu (eds), *Restructuring the Chinese City: Changing Society, Economy and Space*, London: Routledge, 98–121.

Giroir, G. (2005) 'The Purple Jade Villas (Beijing): a golden ghetto in red China', in C. Webster, G. Glasze and K. Frantz (eds), *Private Neighbourhoods: Global and Local Perspectives*, London: Routledge.

Hall, T. and P. Hubbard (1998) *The Entrepreneurial City: Geographies of Politics, Regime and Representation*, Chichester: John Wiley.

Hannerz, U. (1997) 'Scenarios for peripheral cultures', in A. D. King (ed.), *Culture, Globalization and the World-System: Contemporary Conditions for the Representation of Identity*, Minneapolis, MN: University of Minnesota Press, 107–128.

Ho, S. P. S. and G. C. S. Lin (2003) 'Emerging land markets in rural and urban China: policies and practices', *The China Quarterly*, 175: 681–707.

Hu, X. H. and D. Kaplan (2001) 'The emergence of affluence in Beijing: residential social stratification in China's capital city', *Urban Geography*, 22: 54–77.

Huang, Y. (2005) 'From work-unit compounds to gated communities: housing inequality and residential segregation in transitional Beijing', in L. J. C. Ma and F. Wu (eds), *Restructuring the Chinese City: Changing Society, Economy and Space*, London: Routledge, 192–221.

Knox, P. (1993) *The Restless Urban Landscape*, Englewood Cliffs, NJ: Prentice Hall.

Logan, J. R., Y. J. Bian and F. Q. Bian (1999) 'Housing inequality in urban China in the 1990s', *International Journal of Urban and Regional Research*, 23 (1): 7–25.

Low, S. (2003) *Behind the Gates: Life, Security, and the Pursuit of Happiness in Fortress America*, London: Routledge.

McKenzie, E. (1994) *Privatopia: Homeowner Associations and the Rise of Residential Private Government*, New Haven, CT: Yale University Press.

Olds, K. (2001) *Globalization and Urban Change: Capital, Culture, and Pacific Rim Mega-projects*, Oxford: Oxford University Press.

Sassen, S. (1991) *The Global City*, Princeton, NJ: Princeton University Press.

Short, J. R., L. M. Benton, W. B. Luce and J. Walton (1993) 'Reconstructing the image of an industrial city', *Annals of the Association of American Geographers*, 83 (2): 207–224.

Sit, V. F. S. (1995) *Beijing: The Nature and Planning of a Chinese Capital City*, New York: John and Wiley.

Smith, M. P. (2001) *Transnational Urbanism*, Oxford: Blackwell.

Szelenyi, I. (1996) 'Cities under socialism – and after', in G. M. Andrusz, M. Harloe and I. Szelenyi (eds), *Cities after Socialism: Urban and Regional Change and Conflict in Post-socialist Societies*, Oxford: Blackwell, 286–317.

Tang, L. (2001) 'Talking about Beijing's townhouse', *Beijing Evening*. Online. Available http://www.bjhouse.com.cn/townhousemore.htm (accessed 18 June 2001).

Wang, H. B. (2000) 'Beijing's pure European and American villa', *Housing and Real Estate*, 6: 14–16 (in Chinese).

Wang, Y. P. and A. Murie (1999) 'Commercial housing development in urban China', *Urban Studies*, 36 (9): 1475–1494.

Webster, C., G. Glasze and K. Frantz (2002) 'The global spread of gated communities', *Environment and Planning B*, 29 (3): 315–320.

Webster, C., F. Wu, and Y. Zhao. (2005) 'China's modern gated cities', in C. Webster, G. Glasze and K. Frantz (eds), *Private Cities: Global and Local Perspectives*, London: Routledge.

Wu, F. (2002) 'China's changing urban governance in the transition towards a more market-oriented economy', *Urban Studies*, 39 (7): 1071–1093.

—— (2004) 'Transplanting cityscapes: the use of imagined globalization in housing commodification in Beijing', *Area*, 36 (3): 227–234.

—— (2005) 'Rediscovering the "gate" under market transition: from work-unit compounds to commodity housing enclaves', *Housing Studies*, 20 (2): 235–254.

Wu, F. and L. J. C. Ma (2005) 'The Chinese city in transition: towards theorizing China's urban restructuring', in L. J. C. Ma and F. Wu (eds), *Restructuring the Chinese City: Changing Society, Economy and Space*, London: Routledge, 260–286.

Wu, F. and K. Webber (2004) 'The rise of "foreign gated communities" in Beijing: between economic globalization and local institutions', *Cities*, 21 (3): 203–213.

Yeh, A. G. O. and F. Wu (1996) 'The new land development process and urban development in Chinese cities', *International Journal of Urban and Regional Research*, 20 (2): 330–353.

Zhang, J. (2001) 'Explore Beijing's townhouse'. Online. Available http://www.focus.com.cn (accessed 5 July 2001).

Zhao, S. X. B. (2003) 'Spatial restructuring of financial centers in mainland China and Hong Kong: a geography of finance perspective', *Urban Affairs Review*, 38 (4): 535–571.

Zhou, Y. (2002) 'The prospect of international cities in China', in J. R. Logan (ed.), *The New Chinese City: Globalization and Market Reform*, Oxford: Blackwell, 59–73.

11 A globalized golden ghetto in a Chinese garden

The Fontainebleau Villas in Shanghai

Guillaume Giroir

Introduction

The large Chinese cities, notably in eastern China, form territories with the most numerous and deepest demonstrations of globalization. Globalization sometimes takes particular forms in terms of urban landscape, such as skyscrapers or the omnipresence of multinationals in advertising and trade. But it also strongly appears in much more reduced and hidden territories through the golden ghettos on the outskirts of megacities like Beijing and Shanghai. Not only has the process of transition and openness since 1978 represented the change from communism to capitalism but it has also completely disrupted the whole of Chinese space and society. It entails a true 'transition of civilization' (Giroir 2004a), notably in the metropolises. Indeed, the globalization of Chinese space has an important cultural dimension.

Nonetheless, China, as a great civilization, is not a passive gathering place of external influences. It re-interprets these exogenous influences according to its own traditions, values and representations, and from them a complex combination of Chinese and Western civilizations results. An observation of this phenomenon of 'civilization mix', on the scale of a type of micro-territory such as the golden ghettos, will be proposed. One may assume that these housing enclaves composed of luxury villas, recently revealed by several field investigations and put in a theory perspective (Giroir 2002, 2003, 2004a,b, 2005, Wu 2004), are privileged fields of observation for studying globalization in China. The constructed micro-territory of one of these golden ghettos – the Fontainebleau Villas – situated in the east of Shanghai will be particularly stressed and analysed.

First, this chapter aims to examine how private and secured estates could be privileged fields for studying globalization in China, especially the phenomenon of 'civilization mix'. The notion of 'civilization mix' will be discussed from both a theoretical and a geographical perspective. The chapter will also demonstrate that the Fontainebleau Villas offer a rare and paradigmatic case of this blending of civilizations.

Second, this study will examine in detail the various features of this hybrid cultural form in the case of Fontainebleau Villas; the analysis will be mainly focused on the Western architecture of these luxury villas and the Chinese cultural elements of local micro-territory. Finally, this culturally mixed and constructed micro-territory will give way to divergent, even opposing, interpretations.

From globalization to 'civilization mix'

Golden ghettos as privileged fields of investigation for globalization

The present study is one of various research works carried out by this author into Chinese gated communities. Since June 2000, field studies have been conducted in several gated communities situated around Beijing, Shanghai, Nanjing, Suzhou and Wuxi. The data are drawn from direct field observations, discussions with sales managers or sometimes residents and advertising booklets. This empirical method emphasizes the development of a specifically geographical approach to the phenomenon. Therefore, one aim is to show the great spatial differentiation of this kind of micro-territory at various scales. Whilst representing a real estate micro-market they offer real diversity according to numerous factors: location, social and ethnic backgrounds of the residents, size of the complex, nature of the architectural styles and relationship with the metropolis; hence, the case studies of Purple Jade Villas (Beijing) (Giroir 2005), Yosemite Villas (Beijing) (Giroir 2004b) or Fontainebleau Villas (Shanghai). The gated communities in Beijing show their own particular features and internal differentiation. A general typology of villa complexes in the whole of China has thus been developed. Another objective is to reveal the multidimensionality of these private housing estates. Each case study has been analysed according to a specific perspective but always in relation to the globalization process. For example, the Purple Jade Villas were analysed as a segregated, transitional, cultural and metropolitan phenomenon. The approach to Fontainebleau Villas mainly focuses on cultural geography, particularly the blending of Western and Chinese civilizations. The study of Yosemite Villas is based on the geography of representations; it reveals some aspects of current emerging capitalism in China and of the dream of China's elite. Finally, from a more theoretical perspective, these housing estates are analysed according to the notions of urban governance and public and private realms. The economic theory of clubs (Buchanan 1965) is employed to examine this phenomenon in addition to a geographical and systemic point of view, showing that it has been possible to describe these gated communities and their related micro-territories (international schools and golf course) as the 'clubs in a club system' (Giroir 2003).

These private and secured residential enclaves are among the most globalized places in China. They represent a particularly relevant field of analysis for studying the process of globalization currently taking place in China. But, as in other countries, their features are more or less modified by the local context. The degree of variation of these fairly universal phenomena may depend greatly on local singularities. So, the title of the study on the Purple Jade Villas is 'Golden ghetto in red China'. Here, the use of the notion of 'golden ghetto' is of course metaphoric. It does not refer to poor and often ethnic residential enclaves. In fact, the term itself is not recent: in the 1870s, the neighbourhood of the German Jews in Chicago received the cognomen of 'the golden ghetto' (Giroir 2005). But in the late 1970s, the phrase 'golden ghetto' was coined in reference to Carmel's American affluent household enclave and then became quite common to designate up-market gated communities in social geography as a form of urban segregation. In 1997, it received great popularity thanks to the book of a therapist, Jessie O'Neill (1997), who describes the pathologies (defined as 'influenza') of the rich, their causes and symptoms. The use of this term for China seems to be appropriate because of the widespread fascination with gold (see the common expressions of *huanjin dadao* 'golden street' or *jincheng* 'golden city' to suggest rich places). Likewise, this kind of neighbourhood contrasts sharply with the general level of social development and the present regime. Considering the Marxist–Leninist regime still in force today, these luxury villa compounds may be qualified as anti-communist or even post-communist micro-territories in terms of ideology. Therefore, they are places in the most advanced stage of transition towards capitalism and globalization in China.

The gated communities as 'globalized golden ghettos'

At the scale of megacities such as Beijing and Shanghai, the recent increase in the number of luxury villas compounds offers rich material for the study of this phenomenon. In Shanghai, this globalization process reveals not only general aspects but also some singularities. Although the estate sector of large Chinese cities seems to be clearly dualist, analysis of the actors in this market of luxury villas shows that it has been very internationalized. There are some famous names of large international estate companies, such as Jones Lang Lasalle or Hutchinson Whampoa, for instance. Hong Kong and Taiwan property developers play a major part in the construction of these luxury housing complexes, whether as isolated investors or within the framework of joint ventures with mainland Chinese firms. Thus, the Tomson Golf Villas in Pudong are funded by the Tomson Group from Taiwan run by the former *kung fu* actress, Hsu Feng, who became the principal film producer in China and then moved into the estate sector with her rich husband, Tong Cunlin.

The location of private estates greatly depends on other globalized areas. In Shanghai, most of the luxury villas are concentrated in the Hongqiao airport area to the west of the city. The close links between gated communities and airports appears clearly through the migration of new luxury villa programmes from Hongqiao airport, now only used for domestic traffic, to Pudong new international airport. Thanks to a vast land reserve, two large luxury gated communities are being built there: the Huamu Villas and the Tomson Golf Villas (95 hectares). While the gated communities in Beijing are concentrated near the capital airport, in Shanghai the geographic distribution has been modified by the recent creation of Pudong airport. Most of the luxury housing districts have close relationships with international schools. In some cases, they are situated within the gated

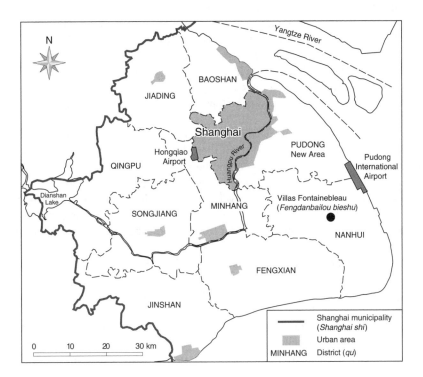

Map 11.1 Location of Fontainebleau Villas in Shanghai.

communities like the Shanghai Links Villas or Four Seasons in Pudong. But they are very often accessible by mini-bus shuttle.

The Fontainebleau Villas are situated 10 kilometres south-west of Pudong international airport in Nanhui district near the local zoo (see Map 11.1). More than 30 kilometres from the centre of Shanghai they make a housing complex of relatively limited size. Out of the 170 planned villas only 48 have been built so far, on a total surface of more than 400 hectares. It is clearly a ghetto for very rich people; hence the phrase 'golden ghetto' used in the title. The villas have a floor space varying from 300 to 500 square metres for the largest one. Hence, 70 per cent of the park land is for the whole golden ghetto. The villas cost from 1.8 to 5 million yuan. Twenty or so guards and a network of surveillance cameras constantly assure the security of the place. The majority of the residents are of Chinese origin; some are overseas Chinese.

Beyond the 'cultural globalization'

All the gated communities embody the progress of globalization in China. However, globalization is a multi-sided phenomenon. It is made up of economic, social, political and also cultural features. Therefore, one essential question concerning the gated communities is to discover the foreign cultural influence on this kind of micro-territory. Owing to the concession past, the villa complexes of Western style in Shanghai offer a greater architectural continuity with the rest of the urban fabric of Shanghai. The new private compounds in Shanghai do not follow Chinese models but rather mainly Western ones (e.g. American: Green Villas, Sunland Villas; Canadian: Donghu Villas; French: The Château and Fontainebleau Villas).

The rich Chinese (from mainland China, Hong Kong or Taiwan) who live in such luxury villas can afford to fulfil their dreams. In these secured and gated housing enclaves they also escape from the ideological constraints of the regime of which they mainly constitute the economic and often political elite. They are a minority of businessmen who have very often travelled abroad and are aware of the lifestyle of their foreign counterparts. For their part, the villa property developers and architects, generally coming from Hong Kong, are very well informed about foreign models of architecture and endeavour to propose the best of the international market for a demanding clientele eager to obtain an out-of-the-ordinary product. For all these reasons, the golden ghettos reveal part of the imaginative view of the Chinese elite, and this is shaped by Western models and representations, much more than among ordinary people.

But, if the architecture is mainly exogenous some other elements refer to China's past and to its culture. Often, the latter is reduced to the place name. So, we commonly find many references to imperial China in the names of gated communities. Some of them in Shanghai bear the names 'Dynasty Villas', 'Emerald Court' or 'Mandarin Garden'.

While the Communist Party rewrote history by making 1949 the break with the feudal period many luxury villa complexes bear names evoking old imperial China confirming once more that the transitional process is both in line with the commitment of the country on the way to modernity and a resurgence of the past. The gated communities with their rich inhabitants, new mandarins of a China torn between future and past, may also be interpreted as a demonstration of a sort of 'neo-feudalism'. They reproduce a means of separation between the elite and the people, witness to the significant social and mental scheme of the Forbidden City in China.

In very few places, the villas themselves look like castles; while alluding to the European culture they are a general symbol of feudalism. One of the best examples (apart from the Fontainebleau Villas) of this resurgence of feudalism, at least on the level of representation, is given by the most expensive complex in Shanghai (units with rents of 15,000 dollars per month), called 'Le Château' and situated near Hongqiao airport. It is a lot with sixty 600 square metres castles, built in the classical style of the former French colony in Shanghai with a high wrought-iron gate, large garage, fireplace and cellar. In this kind of up-scale housing estate it is possible to observe some elements of interaction or interpenetration between globalized culture and local civilization; hence the notion of 'civilization mix'.

However, from this point of view, the Fontainebleau Villas offer a far more significant example of the blending of Western and Chinese features, insofar as the forms of Western influence (notably, the name of the housing complex, the villa architecture and the statues) are placed in a setting that in many aspects is related to Chinese civilization. The scenery itself is designed according to the Chinese principles of the art of gardens and *fengshui* (Ji 1634, Siren 1949, Stein 1987, Latouche 1992, Gournay 1993, Berque 1998). The Chinese Taoist conception of nature plays a great role in the landscape design. There are also many references to the history of ancient China. Before going into detail, it is necessary to state some considerations of theory in order to put the present subject into perspective.

The notion of 'civilization mix'

The concept of 'civilization mix' is interpreted in a geographical perspective. It refers mainly to material forms and their non-material signification, which define the identity of a territory. They produce a 'constructed territory', which comprises various elements: areas (cultivated land and green spaces), volumes (residential units), lines (network of communications) and points (sculptures). The place name itself also has an important role in the identity of this constructed territory. The architecture is certainly the most visible and important even though not the sole element of this territorial system. However, the term 'architecture' itself as used in this chapter does not refer only to the aesthetic or technical design; it has a broader significance which includes many dimensions. It is both a residential unit type, an aesthetic style, an element of a constructed territory and a material container of multi-dimensional contents.

According to this approach, how does the presence of foreign architecture in a determined area mean globalization? The relationship between imported architecture and globalization, in general and particularly in China, can be shown at three different main levels. First, from a general point of view the transplanting of architecture from a country (or area) to another country always reveals a kind of globalization. This chosen or imposed foreign influence led to the modification of the local identity. It is part of a long-term but non-linear worldwide trend to increase the mobility and criss-crossing of persons, goods and ideas.

Second, the level of relevance of this phenomenon in terms of globalization largely depends on the historical and geographical contexts. The signification of foreign architecture is given not only by its own features but also by the territorial framework in which it takes place. This is the reason why it requires an integrated analysis. Therefore, in China a huge cultural area with its own foundations, high self-consciousness of its identity and historical propensity for autarky, the importation of foreign influence has never been neutral. The transplanting of foreign cityscapes is not merely an aesthetic phenomenon.

Third, the relative importance of this extra-aesthetic signification in terms of globalization also greatly depends on each period. Each one creates a specific socio-territorial system. More than a century ago, Western architecture was built in the Bund and foreign concessions. So this phenomenon is not new at all.

But it occurred in a semi-colonial era. The foreign architecture was mainly limited to some intra-urban buildings, offices and garden residences of prominent figures. This early stage of forced globalization was ended by the Maoist period when the housing sector was based on a strict egalitarianism, an exclusive domination of collective buildings and a rejection of aesthetic quality, then considered as bourgeois. Therefore, villas were almost non-existent.

In comparison with that period the recent importation of a Western model of the individual villa has a rich signification. Their peri-urban location, geographical concentration of affluent people and size itself are very new. This phenomenon clearly shows the progress of transition and globalization in China since 1978, but also their contradictions with the ideology of the present regime. Beyond this apparently merely architectural phenomenon it reveals the multi-sided transition process as economic, sociological, political, geopolitical and cultural. It highlights what I have called a real 'transition of civilization' which deeply modifies China and its territory.

The 'civilization mix' in the Fontainebleau Villas

Demonstration of Westernization

The Western influence is above all French. Among the golden ghettos on the outskirts of Shanghai some are directly inspired by the France of the Ancien Regime (Kong 2001). Fraser (2000), when analysing advertisements for diverse luxury villas around Shanghai, noted that the romantic image of France was very fashionable. He also described the Wutong Villas, a true piece of the France of Louis XIV, composed of very luxurious villas.

There are other housing enclaves of the same type, notably one named Le Château, near Hongqiao airport. The luxury villas are fully in line with this context, clearly claiming this French influence through their names. Fontainebleau is chosen as a reference to the France of the Kings. The Château de Fontainebleau, before the construction of Versailles, had been attached to the monarchy for nearly 700 years. As a result, these villas in the French style follow 'the French aristocratic style' (*Faguo guizu shi*) according to the architects of the complex (see Figure 11.1).

Other symbols of France of the Ancien Regime are particularly visible in the scenery of the housing enclaves, notably a replica of the equestrian bronze statue of Louis XIV, and there is another bronze sculpture representing a group of stags while a wrought-iron entry gate separates the two parts of the villa area. The monumental entry reminds one of the impressive horseshoe stairs in the Château de Fontainebleau. The Fontainebleau Villas' advertising booklet claims this historical influence and refers to the France of the Ancien Regime to Paris and to French culture. It is obvious that the memory of the French concession of Shanghai, where many private villas and mansions were built, sustains the luxury image of France.

Despite its name, the Fontainebleau Villas is not exclusively inspired by French architecture. Other architectural models are prevalent. Numerous monumental villas are inspired by the Mies (van der Rohe) (*Misi shi*), Portman (*Boteman shi*), American Victorian (*Weiduoliya shi*), rural Dutch (*Helan xiangcun shi*) (see Figure 11.2) or modern German styles (*Deguo xiandai shi*). The whole villa complex is accessible through large geometrical asphalted lanes, which allow cars to pass through.

Figure 11.1 A villa of 'French aristocratic style' (*Faguo guizu shi*).

Figure 11.2 A villa of 'rural Dutch style' (*Helan xiangcun shi*) and replica of an equestrian bronze statue of Louis XIV. Note the video surveillance camera.

Reinterpreting the foreign elements

However, the observation of these demonstrations of omnipresent Western influence in the Fontainebleau Villas should not substantiate the simplistic idea of a Chinese territory passively absorbing the numerous forms of globalization. As the heirs of a rich and ancient civilization, the Chinese are very aware of their identity. They reinterpret and select foreign contributions according to their own values and traditions. In this respect, the speech of Youshen Ruan (no date), the property developer of this housing complex, could not be clearer:

> [This villa lot] is not a mere copy of the French Château de Fontainebleau, but it is a clever re-creation, an everlasting work of art! ('*Ta bushi faguo fengdanbailou de fanban, ershi chongman zhihui de chuangxin, shi yongheng er dianya de yishu zuopin!*').

Actually, taking up elements of the architectural heritage is in no way a faithful and realistic transposition. It aims to catch a spirit and an atmosphere, and elaborates a review of exogenous influences according to a very Chinese conception.

The Château de Fontainebleau: source of inspiration more than a model to imitate

The villas in the French style do not appear at all like a reduced model of the Château de Fontainebleau, which is reinterpreted most freely. Some essential details were omitted, for example, doing away with the red bricks, so characteristic of Fontainebleau, resulting in bicoloured instead of tricoloured villas. The subtropical climate of Shanghai meant that the chimneys have been removed. Other elements have been added. The equestrian statue of Louis XIV, commissioned from Le Bernin by the King, is not in the Château de Fontainebleau but nearby in the front yard of the Louvre, not far from the pyramid. Likewise, the villas are endowed with a long covered alley shaped like a Greek temple. Other elements have been taken up, but only in part. The statue representing stags is directly inspired by the fountain of Diana the Huntress situated in the park of the Château de Fontainebleau, but there again it is no longer a fountain and Diana as well as the four dogs at her feet have disappeared.

Thus, the Fontainebleau Villas seems to be less a collection of Western architectural style than an imaginary museum of the best of the Western aspects, seen through the eyes of property developers and rich Chinese. Furthermore, asserting that the villa style may be in accordance with the classifications of the history of architecture is very relative. Calling it 'French aristocratic style' suggests the existence of a specifically unique and easily definable French type of architecture. It is obvious that the architecture of French châteaux went through many variations under the Ancien Regime. Even if the French architectural style is reduced to the classical style of the sixteenth and the seventeenth centuries, it corresponds to various architectural realizations of detail. It is clear that the designer of the Fontainebleau Villas did not seek precision when imitating these models.

The French influence as such should not be overestimated. The Fontainebleau Villas name suggests that the villas have been built in the Château de Fontainebleau style, while in fact this is not the case. The majority of villas are not in the French aristocratic style. They are only represented by a few models. It seems obvious that they are only impressive villas dressed up as châteaux. The marketing process is crystal clear emphasizing the villas' prestige by giving a common aristocratic place name and consists of making each villa benefit from the Château de Fontainebleau's prestige.

Dreamed Westernality

In fact, the property developer wished especially to restore the atmosphere of refinement and elegance conveyed by the Châteaux in the French style of the Ancien Regime, and more generally of certain Western architectural styles. He tried to meet the aspirations of purchasers for distinction. In this sense, the foreign elements are used to set up luxury. Their essence has to be understood beyond the material aspects of the villas' architecture. The point is not to aim at their morphologic similarities (*xingsi*) but to try to grasp their spiritual similarities (*shensi*). Resorting to foreign models is motivated by several reasons. To some degree it deals with an obliged borrowing, insofar as Chinese tradition does not have a true housing type associating luxury and comfort. Moreover, since 1949, the communist regime has discredited any forms of enrichment whatsoever and, by definition, prohibited the notion of luxury.

The role of a specialized press should not be denied, which in the realm of architecture is mainly present in large bookshops (like that of Xinhua, for example). It has been widespread for some years and has made the Chinese elite acknowledge that their country is seriously behind in matters of individual architecture. Therefore, the spreading of Western architectural models is part of the modernization process in China and is undeniably a fashion phenomenon. As the Chinese were not allowed to travel for a long time they have built an idealized representation of certain countries like the United States, France, Australia or Italy. Everything that comes from abroad is a means for escapism and dreams. Implanting foreign elements enables one to have at hand everything that does not exist in China.

In this respect, one of the best examples is represented by the bronze statue of stags, which, together with that of Louis XIV, is strongly reminiscent of the France of the Kings. As such, these wild animals are seen as totally exotic on the outskirts of Shanghai where forest massifs and wildlife (if they ever existed) have been giving way, for centuries and indeed millennia, to a meticulously domesticated countryside. The images of stags and more generally of hunting on horseback refer (except for the practices of nomads) to a very ancient China.

Turning Western styles into Chinese features

Nonetheless, the foreign architectural styles are subject to a subtle process that aims to make them more Chinese. They are modified and reinterpreted according to the Chinese conception of architecture and more generally of space. For example, the roof of the French-style villas is not covered with slates as they should be, but with a blue colour analogous to that of the palaces of Imperial China. In the presentation of the villas of Portman type, the exotic feature of this architecture is in fact not stressed, but rather what may correspond to Chinese taste in this style: the booklet highlights the zigzag corridor and a small river flowing beneath a small bridge. It puts a stress on the vast picture window of the villa, which allows interpenetration between inside and outside.

According to the villa booklet, the villas built in the style of Mies van der Rohe are very much appreciated by purchasers not only for being block-like but also for having a central shaft that spreads natural light. The penetration of this light at the heart of the house 'therefore gives an impression of a miracle (*qimiao*), like when, after climbing a mountain, another mountain looms up …' The architects specify that in the American Victorian style, the whole villa scheme has the shape of a well (*jingzi* making allusion to the form of the Chinese character meaning 'well'). The covered galleries on the ground floor adjoin the house, but only on the southern side, as in traditional Chinese houses. As for the rural Dutch style it is characterized by its age and half-timbering, so much appreciated for the contrast between the black wood and the white walls, as if it were the *yin* and *yang*. The three dormer windows on the roof correspond to the opening of three shower rooms, but also enable one to 'speak to heaven' (*changtian duihua*). On the ground floor, a very large open room allows air and vital energy to circulate freely.

A territorial system marked by Chineseness

If the luxury villas in a Western style prevail and constitute a largely globalized territory at the gates of Shanghai, the scenery is deeply marked by Chinese identity. First, it would be proper to indicate that although the architecture of the Fontainebleau Villas is mainly inspired by foreign styles some of them follow typically Chinese features. They are presented in two principal forms, that is 'modern Shanghai style' (*Xiandai Shanghai shi*) and 'modern Jiangnan style' (*Xiandai Jiangnan shi*). Both these architectural elements remind us of the integration of a villa with a particular territory. They restore a part of its specifically Chinese and particularly regional identity in this housing enclave. Above all, the Fontainebleau Villas are far from being simply reduced to the constructed environment and especially to Western-style villas.

Ideal return to nature

The villa lot is completely integrated into 'natural' scenery, which was largely recreated according to Chinese taste. This recreated nature tempers the pride and ostentation of impressive villas. It aims to reintegrate these buildings into the order of nature. These demonstrations of individualism, standing out as such through the villas' luxury, are in this case offset by the ideal of a simple life handed on by a tradition in which both Confucian moderation and the Taoist taste for harmony with nature and Buddhist principles of retreating from the world are mixed. Thus, the natural scenery of a Chinese type counterbalances the Western-style constructed scenery. It displays the traditional ideal of a return to nature (*huigui ziran*). Manufactured elements are swamped by natural elements (water, stones, vegetation). But this scenery is not disorganized at all. On the contrary, this nature in the Chinese style forms a true territorial system on different scales.

Fitting together of frameworks and networks, the circulation of vital energy

The whole housing complex is criss-crossed by an eight-sided network of canals. These are one of the emblematic elements of the traditional urban scenery in the lower Yangtse region, and more particularly in the city of Suzhou. The canals supplied by Weixingang river turn this luxury villa lot into a true lakeside city where there is an increase in stone bridges, wood bridges, pontoons and small boats. The foreign housing is hemmed in by these elements in a typically geometric Chinese framework. They reassert the role of liquids in Chinese thinking and represent the line of strength of the scenery, like arteries through which vital energy (*qi*) circulates. The area, which is in accordance with *fengshui* principles (geomancy), is supposed to guarantee its inhabitants health, prosperity and longevity.

In the eyes of the Chinese, luxury would not be enough if the place did not assure the conservation of vital energy. On a smaller scale, the paved alley network links the villa areas to each other, their winding forms enabling *qi* to spread in harmony (see Figure 11.3). They correspond to 'winding paths leading to a remote place' (*qujing tongyou*), so dear to men of letters, and given by the above

Figure 11.3 The winding form of paved-alleys enable the spread of *qi*.

four character phrase. The geometry of the gardens as straight as a die with their white borders contrasts with a network of circulation, like veins in a human body. All these closely fitting together lines (canals, lanes, streets) are bordered with flora, notably with local trees like *Liquidambar formosana* (*feng*), willows, pines or bamboos. This wooded vegetation is not only a reference to the local bio-climatic context, but also to poetic references in Chinese culture.

A patchwork of scenes, reflection of the universe

Like a patchwork, the scenery of the Fontainebleau Villas is punctuated by diverse scenes (*jing*) aiming to amaze walkers, to fragment the scenery and to reduce its surface. One of them is constituted by a 28,000 square metres 'biological garden of four seasons' (*siji shengtai nongzhuang*) composed of a tangle of fruit trees (kiwis, citrus fruit), a tiny kitchen garden (gourd, maize) and even a henhouse with hens and geese. Far from being designed for physical exercise or true productive activity this countryside spot is used as a place for meditation and contemplation. There, the rural and rustic aspects follow a so-called field and garden (*tianyuan*) poetic genre, a sort of bucolic poetry evoking a peaceful and remote life in a recreated and idealized farming world.

Small wooded pavilions with wooded or thatched roofs, balustrades or red Chinese lanterns are fixed here and there along a canal, near a bridge or next to a *Liquidambar formosana* thicket. They are designed to create fixed points for observing the changing scenes of nature. Some are birdhouses whose birds can help the escapism of the mind. A part of this micro-territory is occupied by one of the most recurrent patterns of Chinese gardens: the artificial mountain of rocks (*yang*), which, in perfect balance, is opposed to a lake (*yin*) (see Figure 11.4). The construction of a mountain of rocks in a garden pond refers to the Taoist representation of paradise as symbolized by five mountainous isles where the Immortals live. The paradise for rich local residents not only consists in enjoying the comfort and luxury offered by the Western-type villas but also in contem-plating this scenery (*shanshui*, literally in Chinese: 'mountain and water'), microcosm in the image of macrocosm.

Rocks, recurrent patterns of details in the scenery

The scenery of this golden ghetto is strewn with numerous marks of Chineseness, notably stones and rocks. As in most Chinese gardens, they bear extracts of classical poetry, artistic calligraphies. Three rounded rocks are covered with characters painted in black. One bears the *xian* character, while on another *qing* is engraved. Associating them gives *xianqing* ('peaceful, quiet, idle'). They are combined with a third rock where a wavy musical stave is inscribed. The whole means that the calmness of this countryside place gives peace of mind favourable to singing, and more generally to a good mood. It is an allusion to the men of letters in ancient China who, after failing the imperial exams, gave up any career ambitions in order to retire and live in harmony with nature. This practice

Figure 11.4 Artificial mountains (*yang*) and lake (*yin*) mirror of Taoist paradise.

especially concerns Tao Yuanming, a famous poet (Tang dynasty). This retirement was in fact accompanied by cultural and recreational activities, such as singing either alone or with some close relations. The residents of these luxury villas are like these old men of letters, although most of them are former city-dwellers (sometimes retired), who find there a retreat from the chaos of the metropolis.

A small teapot made of terracotta set on another rock reminds them that the gardens used to be a privileged place for the tea ceremony. Elsewhere, the lawn – such a remote Chinese element – is dotted with rocks of anguished shape. Considered as true works of art they play a part like statues in Western gardens. They remind the educated walkers of the aesthete emperor Huizong (Song dynasty), the very one who established in Suzhou a service in charge of collect- ing exceptional stones, sometimes large-sized ones, to dispatch to the court of Kaifeng.[1] On the lawn borders, long slim stones can be found. In China, one does not plant a garden but constructs it. Furthermore, the master-gardeners are also called 'raisers of stones'. The raised stones are the symbol of the osmosis between Earth, Heaven and Man, the three components of the Universe.

The Liquidambar formosana *and the theme of seasons*

Choosing the name of 'Fontainebleau' to designate this golden ghetto at the gates of Shanghai is a symbol of the rich Chinese features of the place. It is linked to the theme of seasons, omnipresent in the Chinese art of gardens. Indeed, this name is not a way of enhancing the aristocratic feature of the place and its inhabitants. The transcription into Chinese characters follows a poetic conception in which Fontainebleau becomes *Fengdanbailou*, that is, 'the red leaves of the *Liquidambar formosana* and white dew'.

The historic and geographic distance of the place of reference, the Château de Fontainebleau, gives way to a typically Chinese type of tree. Instead of only representing a piece of globalized territory the Fontainebleau Villas are made endogenous and rooted in a bio-climatic but also aesthetic, cultural and familiar context. The *Liquidambar formosana*[2] was chosen not solely for a decorative purpose. Its yellow and red blossom, exceptional colours in autumn, is favourable for observing the periodical metamorphoses of nature. It is the demonstration in plant form of what is ephemeral and fleeting, and while the Western villas embody continuity and duration it is in the image of the constantly evolving universe.

'Civilization mix': syncretism or acculturation?

The Fontainebleau Villas reveal a scenery characterized by the close mix between Western and Chinese features. Nonetheless, if one tries to go beyond the stage of reporting in order to make a value judgement several diverging and even opposite interpretations appear clearly. The present study will be limited to two readings about the cultural mix of this micro-territory, without however opting for either, insofar as both are legitimate.

A harmonious synthesis between Western and Chinese tradition

If one sticks to the representation conveyed by the property developers' views, the Fontainebleau Villas represent a successful combination of the best of Western and Chinese traditions. It may be interpreted as one expression of multiform postmodern urbanism. Truly exceeding each other, they may be a favourable synthesis between the Western art of building and the Chinese cosmological conception, between Western individualism and Chinese metaphysics (Cheng 2002). By taking the essence of each other's conception they may make a full artistic creation. The residents themselves are likely to subscribe to this representation. Indeed, if according to the property developers' views, the villas, through their aristocratic features and refinement, are the ideal living environment for individuals, the natural re-created scenery embodies a true centre of vital energy. The Fontainebleau Villas may gather, within the same place, the best of society and nature, an ideal place on the social and cosmological level.

Beyond these aspects, they may embody, in their own way and scale, China's ability to use Western models without imitating them. China, in its own interest, may be able to recycle Western modernity so as to link it to Chinese traditions. The dual signification of the place name, on its own, demonstrates this capacity to manage two cultures with different identities. In a synthetic way, the Fontainebleau Villas/*Fengdanbailou* reflects this duality: the French term flatters the rich residents while its Chinese transcription arouses in them emotion before nature. For the rich Chinese, their pride in the impressive Western dwellings is tempered by the necessary humility of their relation with nature. If they seek to show their social success they do not forget the modest condition of man within the universe. Villas retain from the West the satisfaction of the needs of individuals in society, but these villas are inserted in a garden that places man in a poetic and cosmological relation with nature, in accordance with an Eastern conception.

Demonstration of an identity crisis

Yet it is possible to give an opposing interpretation of these luxury villas. The luxury villas are made up of diverse architectural styles, but this diversity does not present any coherence. In them, styles and times are mixed as well as the level of luxury: the rural traditional Dutch architectural style, French aristocratic architecture from the sixteenth and seventeenth centuries or Anglo-Saxon architecture. The name of the housing complex, clashing with the nature of the architectural style, the absence of a dominant model of villas and a patchwork scenery on a micro-scale sustain deep confusion and result in a true palimpsest. Moreover, it can be easily assumed that owning a villa for rich Shanghai men does not mean knowing, even superficially, the history of France. Therefore, the Grand Siècle-like equestrian and animal statues, and more generally foreign architecture, are reduced to just a decorative pattern, a mere form without true historical content. The sometimes excessive simplification of architecture may lead to the production of substitutes or even denatured forms. The whole lot is part of the general trend of the 'disneylandization' of urban forms.

The Fontainebleau Villas are based on a dual amnesia. Enhancing the image of France makes one forget the colonial past, present in the French concession for a long time. Likewise, the reference to the France of the Ancien Regime is politically incorrect in a Marxist–Leninist context based in part on the break with feudalism. In their own way, the Fontainebleau Villas testify to the crisis of communist ideology in China. This true hotchpotch of Western and Eastern elements might lead one to conclude that there is an identity crisis in China. A few decades later than Japan, China may have difficulty in reconciling its own civilization with Western modernity, and may be subject to a deep process of acculturation.

Conclusion

Gated communities significantly modify the representation of post-Maoist China, a China where the disparities are much deeper than what the official views may claim, where the modernity of housing types also seems unexpected, even if only a small minority benefit from it. While further investigations turn out to be necessary for some aspects (sociology of residents, ways of development, shareholding, relations with the urban environment), it is now clear that the phenomenon may be looked on as multi-dimensional: economic, social, political and cultural. Thus, such new housing areas associate the influence of a transitional process towards globalization with a more long-term influence, in line with Chinese civilization. The Fontainebleau Villas gives some precious indications on the specificities of the imaginative views of rich Chinese. The economic elite dream about Western-like luxury, and their housing choice is clearly a demonstration of a total rejection of communism. Luxury villas in a Western architectural style are doubtless the most extreme yet localized territorial form of the transitional process. Although the rich Chinese residents of luxury villas remain imbued with the values of Chinese civilization, owning material goods is not considered to be enough to guarantee happiness. Luxury should be completed by a harmonious relationship with the universe, and from this a singular and incompatible mix of ostentation and humility, materialism and poetry results.

From a geographical point of view the Fontainebleau Villas show how complex are the ways of interpenetration between Western and Chinese civilizations. In them, these two great civilizations have created a very original micro-territory. The geographical approach developed here has allowed us to go deeper into the general question of the mode of interbreeding of global and local influences. It has shown that this blending phenomenon, rather than consisting in a mere dualistic juxtaposition of two different realms, has created a real territory where all the elements, with their own features, scale and cultural identity, shape an integrated but complex and problematic micro-system.

Acknowledgements

This field study was supported by the CEDETE, research laboratory of Department of Geography of the University of Orléans (France). I would like to thank anonymous reviewers and the editor, Fulong Wu, for useful revision and suggestions. All remaining errors are the sole responsibility of the author.

Notes

1 Some rocks remain on the spot like the Guanyunfeng in the Liuyuan garden in Suzhou.
2 The *Liquidambar formosana* belongs to the family of the *Hamamelidaceae*, which has three great varieties: American, Middle Eastern and Chinese. The *Liquidambar* is found high in the Xing'an mountains (Heilongjiang). The red and yellow colour of its leaves is similar to that of maple. The American variety discovered by the Spanish in Florida was introduced into Europe in 1681.

References

Berque, A. (1998) *Les raisons du paysage, De la Chine antique aux environnements de synthèse*, Paris: Hasan.
Buchanan, J. (1965) 'An economic theory of clubs' *Economica*, 32, February, 1–14.

Cheng, F. (2002) *Le Dialogue*, Paris: Desclée de Brouwer.

Fraser, D. (2000) 'Inventing oasis: luxury housing advertisements and reconfiguring domestic space in Shanghai', in D. S. Davis (ed.) *The Consumer Revolution in Urban China*, Berkeley, CA: University of California Press.

Giroir, G. (2002) 'Le phénomène des *gated communities* à Pékin, ou les nouvelles cités interdites' (The gated communities in Beijing, or the new forbidden cities), *Bulletin de l'Association de Géographes Français*, Paris, December: 423–436.

—— (2003) 'Gated communities, clubs in a club system: the case of Beijing (China)', Proceedings of the International Conference of Gated Communities, September 2003, Glasgow. Available on the website of Department of Urban Studies of the University of Glasgow, Centre of Neighbourhood Research: www.gla.ac.uk/departments/urbanstudies/gated/gatedpaps/gatedconfpaps.html

—— (2004a) *Transition et territoire en Chine. Le cas des périphéries de Pékin* (*Transition and Territory in China. The Case of Outskirts of Beijing*), University of Orléans (unpublished manuscript), 405 pp.

—— (2004b) 'Yosemite Villas (Peking): an American-style gated community, a reflection of representations of the rich and emerging capitalism (*zibenzhuyi hua*) in China', Proceedings of the First Symposium on Chinese Studies, August 2004, Shanghai: Shanghai Academy of Social Sciences (forthcoming).

—— (2005) 'The Purple Jade Villas (Beijing), a golden ghetto in red China', in K. Frantz, G. Glasze and C. Webster (eds) *Private Cities: A Global and Local Perspectives*, London: RoutledgeCurzon.

Gournay, A. (1993) 'L'aménagement de l'espace dans le jardin chinois', in F. Blanchon (dir.), *Aménager l'espace*, Paris: Presses de l'Université de Paris-Sorbonne.

Ji, C. (1634) *Yuanye* (*Le traité du jardin chinois*); trans. Che Bingchiu (1997), Besançon: éd. de l'Imprimeur.

Kong, S. (2001) *Haipai Bieshu Xinchao. Villa Progress* (*Villas à la mode de style étranger*), Shanghai: Shanghai Renmin Meishu Chubanshe.

Latouche, S. (1992) *L'occidentalisation du monde*, Paris: Agalma/La Découverte.

O'Neill Jessie H. (1997) *The Golden Ghetto: The Psychology of Affluence*, Minneapolis, MN: Hazeldon Press.

Ruan, Y. (no date) *Pali-Shanghai. Fengdanbailou bieshu* (*Paris–Shanghai. Les Villas Fontainebleau*) (advertising booklet).

Siren, O. (1949) *Gardens of China*, New York: The Ronald Press Co.

Stein, R. A. (1987) *Le monde en petit: jardins, miniatures et habitations dans la pensée religieuse d'Extrême-Orient*, Paris: Flammarion.

Wu, F. (2004) 'Transplanting cityscapes: the use of imagined globalization in housing commodification in Beijing', *Area*, 36(3): 227–234.

Part IV

Globalization and urban political and economic implications

12 The creation of global–local competitive advantages in Shanghai

Roger C. K. Chan

The launching of Pudong Development in 1990 aims to revitalize Shanghai's economy as well as the Yangtze River Region through re-positioning Shanghai into the global economy. Shanghai has since experienced remarkable transformation under the interplay between the forces of market and government and between the forces of local and global. China's accession to World Trade Organization (WTO) will undoubtedly intensify and complicate the interaction and even conflict between these forces, which means both an opportunity and a challenge to Shanghai. Reviewing its development strategy and the role of government in creating competitive advantage at such a turning point are thus of vital importance for this city to grasp the opportunities and tackle the challenges.

This chapter begins with an explanation of why some nations can achieve a higher niche in the International Division of Labour. It then examines what a government can do and how it interacts with a market in a nation's economic upgrading process. After identifying Shanghai's current position in the global hierarchy and analysing the benefit and cost of the role that Shanghai government played in 1990s, some suggestions about the appropriate role of government in creating competitive advantage against the background of globalization are given. The case of software industrial development will be discussed based on field surveys and interviews. It is argued that government is the key actor in providing a proper business environment and nurturing entrepreneurship.

Introduction

The process of economic transformation in China since the 1980s has to be evaluated in the light of the New International Division of Labour (known as NIDL hereafter). Dicken (1998) argued that transnational corporations are relocating their production bases to the so-called Newly Industrialized Countries (NICs) in order to search for cheaper and more economical production sites outside the industrial heartland of Europe and North America. Foreign Direct Investment (FDI) has almost been used as a universal proxy indicating the extent of integration with the global economy of a particular state. At the same time, as is demonstrated in China, nation-state's action is still influential in determining national development strategy.

Among all the big cities in China, Shanghai is always a hot research area because of its glorious history, its strategic location and its leading role in China. The prime strength of Shanghai is based on its location. Situated at the connection node of Yangtze River and the east side of the north–south coastline of China the city provides a gateway to a market of some 400 million people (Zhao and Zhang 1998) and, concurrently, an outlet for their produce to the Asia Pacific Region and beyond. Shanghai's modern development can be traced back to 1842 when it first became a treaty port and was opened to the outside world. Through providing the window between central China and the outside world Shanghai developed rapidly since then from a small village into one of the world metropolises. Up to the 1930s, Shanghai became the premier trading centre, transport and industrial venture, and also a financial centre for bankers both internationally and domestically.

The fate of Shanghai changed dramatically after the liberation of China by the Chinese Communist Party. It paid a heavy price under the centrally commanded economy, the 'self-reliance' policy and the ideology of transforming it from a 'consumptive' city into a 'productive' one. Shanghai has had to accommodate to a narrower focus centred on heavy industry and lost its leading position in the global urban hierarchy.

China's economic reform and opening to the outside world ushered in a new era for Shanghai and China. Since 1979, the central government has introduced reform policies to liberalize gradually the highly commanded economic system, increase the role of market in the circulation of goods, services, capital and labour force, and re-open China to the outside world. From then on, China's economy is rapidly integrating with the world economy. FDI, in the form of joint venture, cooperative projects, and wholly foreign owned enterprises has increased rapidly. In the end of 1995, China became the second largest destination for FDI in the entire world after the United States (Chan 2000, Wu 2000a). Its total export value in 1997 reached more than US 200 billion dollars, which makes it the eighth largest exporting country in the world (Chai 2000).

As China is playing an increasingly important role in the world economic system it ushered Shanghai into a new development stage. In 1990, the central government decided to open Pudong, the eastern part of Shanghai, and declared that

> we should open more cities along the Yangtze River, while concentrating on developing and opening the Pudong Area of Shanghai. We want to make Shanghai one of the international economic, financial and trade centers as soon as possible and to bring about a new leap in economic development in the Yangtze Delta and the whole Yangtze Basin.
>
> (Chai 2000: 130)

Shanghai has witnessed great development since then, which is the focus of the economic reform and development of the entire country throughout the 1990s. Its GDP in 2001 was six times more than that in 1990, with a yearly average growth rate of about 20 per cent. In the coming decade, according to its development proposal, Shanghai will catch up with other global cities in Asia, like Hong Kong and Singapore.

Re-examining Shanghai's development process in the 1990s, it can be found that the most marked characteristics shaping its urban transformation are the interplay between the forces of government and market and the interplay between the forces of local and global. First, China's economic transition from a centrally planned economy to a market-oriented one undoubtedly underlies all of the processes effecting urban change in Chinese cities today. Market forces are becoming an indispensable part in decision-making and shaping Shanghai's economic and spatial transformation. On the other hand, the liberalization of state control makes the local government more self-determinant, contrasting with the pre-reform situation when they were the passive agents of central government. The continuous reform and economic liberalization raise two fundamental questions: What would be the proper role of a government and a market? How should they interact with each other to revitalize Shanghai's economy? Second, through revitalizing its role as a node connecting the Yangtze River Delta and the outside world Shanghai is taking a new function and a new responsibility in the urban system in both local and international terms. Internationally, the impact of Transnational Corporations (TNCs) and FDI on Shanghai's economy has been becoming more and more significant. Mayor Han Zheng in his address to the '2005 Houston Shanghai Business Forum' remarked that the accumulated FDI in Shanghai has reached US 86 billion dollar from 1990 to 2004 (www.Chinesetv.US). The contribution to industrial output of foreign or Sino-foreign joined enterprises rose from 12.7 per cent in 1993 to 58.2 per cent in 2003. The global forces, however, should be seen as a triggering factor rather than a determinant of urban change in Shanghai (Wu 2000a). Its industrialization process before the 1990s mainly relied on domestic markets. Such a local connection continues to influence its development from 1990 onwards. Eng (1997) argued that Shanghai is different from the cities in the Pearl River Delta where external influence is predominant. Instead, both global and local forces are imperatives for urban change in Shanghai. Then, what would be the proper strategy for Shanghai to participate in the new International Division of Labour? What can the government do to create and sustain its competitive advantage in the international competition?

This chapter begins with a probe into the fact as to why some nations can achieve a higher position in the global urban hierarchy. It then examines what the government does and how it interacts with the market in the process of upgrading a nation's position in the hierarchy. The earlier discussion is then applied to Shanghai's software industrial sector concluding with some policy suggestions and planning implications about the role of the government in creating competitive advantage in the global economy.

The global context[1]

Globalization

The most significant development in the world economy during the past few decades has been the increasing globalization of economic activities (Dicken 1998). Major cities in the world are being integrated into a global network through the flow of commodities, information, capital and people. The specificity of any particular territory as unit of production and consumption is thereby being undermined as world economy becomes increasingly interconnected and interdependent (Borja and Castells 1997). At the heart of globalization lie the technological innovation and the change of international trade pattern. First, the past two decades of the twentieth century have witnessed an undeniable technological revolution mainly based on information technologies. While facilitating the flow of resources technology becomes the vital element deciding a country's competitive advantage and then its position in the New International Division of Labour (Castells 1989, Porter 1990, Dicken 1998, Mascitelli 1999).

Second, the lowering of national barriers through international trade agreements, the formation of trading blocs and interregional alliances, and the deregulation of markets within and between nations are other driving forces which will further increase the competition between cities by providing goods and services for the world market (Brotchie *et al*. 1995). TNCs become main players in the globalization process, by locating their production activities outside their home base to tap into cheaper land, labour force and market place.

These two driving forces push the process of economic integration ahead and also intensify the international competition. As a result, the relative importance of cities in the global hierarchy is changing rapidly. Cities, which can achieve and sustain competitive advantage in the international competition, are reinforced as new global or regional centres, or they ascend in the urban hierarchy, overtaking others in the course of transition.

The New International Division of Labour

Globalization of competition implies the emergence of a New International Division of Labour which reflects a change in the geographical pattern of specialization at the global scale (Dicken 1998), and also reflects a shift in global hierarchy (Evans 1995). Storper (1998) observes that there are three tiers in the International Division of Labour: Core Areas (those where high technology and knowledge, high value-added are generated and mastered); Routine Production Regions (concentrated site of branch plant, subsidiaries and assembly lines of TNCs), and Excluded Regions (those who do not enrol in the international production circuits in an important way). Core area is a creator of market and technology and maintains sustainable economic development, while routine production site can only enjoy limited and uncertain developmental possibility in limited industrial sector, and expects possibility of being substituted by other production sites. Excluded regions, of course, will be excluded from global economic development circles and remain at the lowest level in global hierarchy of industrial production. The economic activities of every modern nation are unavoidably articulated in this hierarchy, their places in production for global market have significant implications for its economic developmental possibility and the welfare of its citizens (Evans 1995).

National competitive advantage

The Recardian's theory of comparative advantage is a classical explanation on national competition. All countries will be better off if each concentrates on what it does best. Production activities compatible with its natural resources and factor endowments are most rewarding for each country, and are the sectors that its comparative advantages lie in. As a consequence, a nation's comparative advantage based on its given natural factor endowments decides inherently its niche in the International Division of Labour. As manufactures and services become increasingly 'tradable', this theory cannot explain why the value-added process happens in certain location. Evans (1995) argued that this theory only applies to a place where international trade in that location consists of unprocessed raw materials. Hechscher and Ohlins opined that the comparative advantage of a nation were so-called factors of production such as land, labour, natural resources and capital. However, as more and more industries have become knowledge-intensive and globalization process has made access to factors of production increasingly less important in the value-added process, factors of comparative advantage cannot explain sufficiently why certain nations become the home base of international headquarters while others are the base of assembly lines.

Porter (1990) substitutes the concept of comparative advantage with competitive advantage. He argues that competitive advantage of a nation is based upon the advantages of its firms in particular industry. Firms, not owned by the government, are usually on the front line of international competition. To achieve competitive success, government-owned firms must possess a competitive advantage in the form of either lower production costs or differentiated products that command premium prices. To sustain the advantage, firms must achieve more sophisticated competitive advantage over time through providing higher-quality products and services or by producing more efficiently. Differences in national economic structures, values, cultures, institutions and histories etc. contribute profoundly to competitive success of its firms. The unique characteristics of a nation that allow its firms to create and sustain competitive advantage in particular fields are the competitive advantage of nations. Porter further pointed out that there is a three-tier hierarchy of sources of national competitive advantage in terms of sustainability, in which innovation-driven advantage is at the highest level, investment-driven advantage becomes the second and the third one is basic-factor-driven advantage. Upgrading in an economy is the movement from basic-factor-driven level towards the more sophisticated sources of competitive advantage.

Explaining the International Division of Labour

Porter's concept of competitive advantage offers us a convincing way to explain what decides a nation's position in the International Division of Labour. At the initial stage, a nation draws its advantage solely from basic factors of production, whether they are natural resources, or abundant and inexpensive semi-skilled labour force. Indigenous firms in such an economy compete on the basis of price in industries that only require basic technology and knowledge. More advanced product design and technologies are obtained from other countries rather than created. Foreign firms provide most access to foreign markets. With access to abundant factor endowments becoming less important in many industries than the technologies and skills, such economies are fundamentally vulnerable to changes in markets, technology and the loss of factor advantage to other countries. 'Today's low labour cost country is rapidly displaced by tomorrow's' (Porter 1990: 15).

Nations may upgrade their economy to the investment-driven stage, in which their national competitive advantages are based on their ability to invest or attract foreign investment. Through local and foreign investment, they construct modern infrastructure and acquire complex technology, which will allow these nations to compete in more sophisticated industries. Their economies thus become less vulnerable to external environment and more sustainable. However, since their technology and skill capability are mainly acquired from foreign suppliers, who generate and master the high value-added process and command large part of the investment, investment-driven economies remain fragile and can only serve as routine production sites in the International Division of Labour (Porter 1990, Storper 1998).

On the other hand, innovation-driven economy pushes the skills and technology level in production and marketing to another platform. Such capacity to upgrade the industries in which the nation's firms can successfully compete allows firms to locate less sophisticated routine production activities into other nations to tap into cheaper natural resources and labour forces. Nations at such an economic development stage then serve as headquarters, which influence and even command the global economy, and thus achieve a niche in the core area in the International Division of Labour. As more and more industries become knowledge-intensive in the post-war period, the innovation-driven characteristic of a nation gives its firms the power to circumvent scarce factors through new products and processes, and thus sustain long-term economic prosperity (Porter 1990). These processes of transformation underpinning the creation of competitive advantage at the local/global level, on the one hand, and the role initiated by the government and other related agencies, on the other.

The role of government in creating competitive advantage

Firms and business environment

Business firms provide the organizational context for most business activities as discussed earlier. Firms, rather than nations, now compete in the international market. As such, it can be assumed that an economy's fortunes are tied up with the success of business firms; the competitive advantage of firms determines the status of a nation's economy and its ability to compete at the global market. Firms should not be conceptualized as economic machines responding to external market and cost condition in a 'borderless' world. They are inescapably embedded in the external environment, which comprises an array of issues: economic, demographic, social, political, legal and technological (Buchholz 1992, Hayter 1997, Yeung 1998, Worthington and Britton 2003). Such an external environment is referred to as 'business environment' within which a business firm's long-term planning and daily operations are facilitated and constrained.

A review of business management literatures indicates the importance of business environment for a firm according to both business strategy and organization theory perspective (Pounder 1991, Buchholz 1992, Worthington and Britton 2003). From the perspective of business strategy, scholars emphasize the importance of business environment to a firm's long-term planning and decision-making. From the perspective of organization theory, however, scholars stress the need for overall organizational adaptation to the environment as the determination of a business firm's daily operation. Business organizations must interact with and adapt to their environment in order to survive.

Geographers and urban planners illustrate the importance of external environment for business organizations in terms of 'spatial attractiveness', 'locational advantage' and 'place embeddedness' (Storper 1992, 1998, Markusen 1996, Schneider and Kim 1996, Yeung 1999). Although advancement in technology has greatly facilitated the flow of information, capital, commodity and people throughout global space, the uneven geography of productivity in the International Division of Labour and the increasing trade specialization manifest the importance of location. Storper (1992) observed that technology and knowledge-intensive outputs of the world economy continue to be produced in relatively few core places, while routine production activities spread globally. Such a process of 'territorialization' of high technology and knowledge-level activities and 'deterri-torialization' of routine production activities give rise to a 'globalized–localized system of production' (Storper 1998).

The underlying reason for the 'territorialization' and 'place-embeddedness' of high technology and knowledge-level activities is that particular economic struc-tures, values, cultures, histories and institutions of certain area provide the basis for innovation (Porter 1990, Evans 1995, Dicken 1998, Storper 1998). Dicken (1998) argues that the most important functions of location are its role as a con-tainer of distinctive business practices and its role as a regulator of economic activ-ities within its territorial basis. As all economic activities are embedded in certain territorial basis, the locational distinctiveness means that 'ways of doing things' tend to vary across national boundaries. Porter's (1990) national competitive advantage theory stated that the locational differences determine the extent to which an area is economically competitive. 'Competitive advantage is created and sustained through a highly localized process; the home nation is the source of the skills and technology that underpin competitive advantage' (Porter 1990: 19).

Apart from the fundamental importance of business environment for firms, a point needed to be emphasized is that although firms are often able to exercise some degree of control over their internal activities and processes it is often very difficult, if not impossible, for them to control the external environment in which they operate (Worthington and Britton 2003). Thereby, it is vital that firms, especially small- and medium-sized enterprises (SMEs), have the proper conditions to survive and flourish to achieve the competitive advantage of certain economic sector in a nation.

Government–firm relationship: business environment as an interface

While the business environment of a firm is related to every aspect of our society, the most important environmental influences obviously come from the intervention from the government (Buchholz 1992). The need for government involvement in the day-to-day working of economy is generally accepted (Worthington and Britton 2003). Economists have traditionally pointed to the problem of 'market failure' as the reason for government intervention in the economy: government intervention can be portrayed as the attempt to deal with the problems inherent in the operation of a free market. Scholars of global political economy examine the role of government through studying the relationship between economy and government involvement and argue that economies are always embedded in the nation as well as market (Evans 1995, Yeung 2000). Such an opinion rejects a conceptual separation between economy and the nation. It insists, however, that economy is necessarily a combination of markets and government action. The role of government is to intervene in market operation to 'beat' 'structural imbalance' inherent within capital accumulation (Yeung 2000).

The critical question, therefore, is what role should it be and where the boundaries should be drawn between private and public. Countries like the United States and Great Britain tend to prefer limited state influence towards improving the operation of the free market. In contrast, direct intervention is the key instrument deployed by the developmental states in Asia to regulate their domestic economies (Yeung 2000). Either way, the actions of the state in the economy are the most important influence in the macro and micro level and shape fundamentally the business environment in which enterprises function. Government can be even seen as the biggest enterprise at national or local level (Worthington and Britton 2003). We would argue that government is the most important influential actor in a business environment in which firms survive and grow. In other words, business environment serves as an interface in the process of government–firm interaction. The role of government in achieving national competitive advantage can be thus defined as providing appropriate business environment in which business activities especially in higher level activities and innovation are facilitated and promoted.

The role of government in creating competitive advantage in Shanghai

The role of government in creating competitive advantage

Generally, government may exert its influence on business environment directly or indirectly. It may act as a controller and producer directly. As a controller, government sets up and enforces rules aimed at providing restriction and stimulation. As a producer, it takes direct responsibility for delivering certain types of goods, such as public goods which private capital cannot provide successfully. However, in an indirect way, it acts as a guide or assistant and responds to market in a different way. Instead of replacing private producers, government assists in the emergence of new entrepreneurial groups or guides existing indigenous into new production activities, and helps local entrepreneurs to tackle global challenge.

The options available for government's intervention and to nurture a favourable business environment varies over time and place. First, diversified social, economic, institutional, cultural backgrounds decide that governments should respond distinctively to facilitate their firms' operation in international competition. Second, even within the same national territory, the economic development is a dynamic process in which the economy will go through several stages. The way of government involvement should change in order to achieve higher-order competitive advantage. The point is that the proper role of government in a certain development stage reflects the sources of its competitive advantage.

At the formative stage, a nation draws its competitive advantage mostly from basic factors of production or investment. Foreign firms provide technology and access to global market. Government becomes the leading force in education and training, R&D, infrastructure construction, providing information and capital allocation. Some direct intervention, such as subsidy, technological assistance and tariff protection would be needed to promote and stimulate the development of entrepreneurs. The role of governments in the industrialization process in the 'Newly Industrialized Countries' (NICs) serves as a good case, in which government acts as a 'bureaucratic entrepreneur' and facilitates directly the economic upgrading (Hong and Chan 2003).

The appropriate role of government will be differently marked in a higher development stage due to philosophy of intervention and types of intervention changes (Porter 1990). Allocation of capital, protection, licensing controls, export subsidy and other forms of direct intervention may lose relevance or effectiveness in innovation-based competition. As the economy broadens and deepens, it is hard for the government to keep track of every existing and new industry and all the linkages among them. Increasing prosperous and international firms are also less amenable to guidance. Instead, firm operated by private sector is the source of the impetus and skills to innovate, and guide its own development directions. Government's efforts are mainly spent in indirect ways such as stimulating the creation of advanced factors and encouraging new business formation. Although the role of government is embedded it is not static. Such a dynamic perspective can, maybe, explain why neo-liberalism countries are mainly the most developed countries in the world, since indirect involvement is a proper way for government to intervene in their development stage. We will examine the different stages of development in Shanghai in the next section.

The development of Shanghai in 1990s

Shanghai achieved great accomplishment in its development since the launching of Pudong Project in 1990. The GDP in 2004 was 745.03 billion (in Renminbi RMB), which is nearly ten times of that in 1990, 75.63 billion (Table 12.1).

Table 12.1 Gross Domestic Product (GDP) and other investment in Shanghai, 1990–2002

Year		1990	1991	1992	1993	1994	1995	1996	1997	1998	1999	2000	2001	2002	2003	2004*
GDP	Amount (billion in RMB)	75.7	89.4	111.4	151.2	197.2	246.3	290.2	336.0	368.8	403.5	455.1	495.1	540.9	625.0	745.0
	Growth rate (%)	8.6	18.2	24.7	35.7	30.5	24.9	17.9	15.8	9.8	9.4	12.8	8.8	9.3	15.5	19.2
Investment on fixed assets (IFA)	Amount (billion in RMB)	22.7	25.8	35.7	65.4	112	160.2	195.2	197.8	196.5	185.7	187.0	199.5	218.7	245.2	308.4
	Growth rate (%)	5.7	13.7	38.4	83.0	71.8	42.6	21.9	1.3	-0.6	-5.5	0.7	6.7	9.6	12.1	25.8
	IFA/GDP (%)	30.0	28.9	32.1	43.3	57.0	65.0	67.3	58.9	53.3	46.0	41.1	40.3	40.4	39.2	41.4
Investment on infrastructure (II)	Amount (billion in RMB)	4.72	6.14	8.4	16.8	23.8	27.4	37.9	41.3	53.1	50.1	45.0	51.2	58.3	60.4	67.3
	Growth rate (%)	30.1	30.0	37.5	98.9	41.9	14.9	38.3	9.0	28.7	-5.6	-10.2	13.8	13.9	3.6	11.3
	II/GDP (%)	6.2	6.9	7.6	11.1	12.1	11.1	13.1	12.3	14.4	12.4	9.9	10.5	10.8	9.7	9.0
Investment on real estate (IRE)	Amount (billion in RMB)	0.82	0.76	1.27	2.2	11.7	46.6	65.8	61.4	57.7	51.5	56.7	63.1	74.9	90.1	117.5
	Growth rate(%)	—	-7.3	67.1	73.2	433.6	297.1	41.1	-6.6	-6.0	-10.7	10.1	11.3	18.7	20.3	30.4
	IRE/GDP (%)	1.1	0.9	1.1	1.5	6.0	18.9	22.7	18.3	15.6	12.8	12.5	12.7	13.8	14.4	15.8

Source: *Statistical Yearbook of Shanghai* (2004), * *2004 Shanghai Statistical Bulletin* (2005).

An account of the recent development reveals that Shanghai has experienced evident industrial restructuring. The contribution of tertiary industry to the whole urban economy rose from 18.6 per cent in 1978 and peaked at 50.6 per cent in 2002 (Table 12.2). Along with industrial restructuring, the urban spatial structure transformed significantly. Within the inner ring, the total area of the buildings for the secondary industry dropped by 11 per cent while that of office, commercial building and housing increased by 120, 70 and 50 per cent, respectively (Tang and Luan 2000, *Statistical Yearbook of Shanghai* 2003).

The impact of TNCs and FDI on Shanghai's economy is becoming increasingly prominent. Between 1990 and 2002, the accumulated FDI in Shanghai reached US 40.42 billion dollars with the annual ratio of the FDI to GDP being on the increase every year (Table 12.3). The contribution to industrial output of foreign or Sino-foreign joint enterprises rose from 15.5 per cent in 1993 to 59.1 per cent in 2002 (Table 12.4). By 1997, there were 55, from world's largest 100, industrial enterprises locating their regional headquarters or production branches in Shanghai.

Table 12.2 Indices of Gross Domestic Product (GDP) in Shanghai

Year	GDP		Primary sector		Secondary sector		Tertiary sector	
	Billion (RMB)	%	Billion (RMB)	%	Billion (RMB)	%	Billion (RMB)	%
1978	0.27	100	0.01	4.0	0.21	77.4	0.05	18.6
1990	75.6	100	3.3	4.3	48.3	63.8	24.1	31.9
1991	89.4	100	3.3	3.7	55.1	61.7	30.9	34.6
1992	111.4	100	3.4	3.1	67.7	60.8	40.3	36.1
1993	151.2	100	3.8	2.5	90.0	59.6	57.3	37.9
1994	197.2	100	4.9	2.5	114.3	57.8	78.0	39.6
1995	246.3	100	6.7	2.5	141.0	57.3	99.1	40.2
1996	290.2	100	7.2	2.5	158.3	54.5	124.8	43.0
1997	336.0	100	7.6	2.3	174.4	52.2	153.0	45.5
1998	368.8	100	7.9	2.1	184.7	50.1	176.3	47.8
1999	403.5	100	8.0	2.0	195.4	48.4	200.1	49.6
2000	455.1	100	8.3	1.8	216.4	47.6	230.4	50.6
2001	495.1	100	8.6	1.7	235.6	47.6	251.0	50.7
2002	540.9	100	8.8	1.6	256.5	47.4	275.6	51.0
2003	625.1	100	9.3	1.5	313.1	50.1	302.7	48.4
2004*	745.0	100	9.7	1.3	378.8	50.8	356.5	47.9

Source: *Statistical Yearbook of Shanghai* (2004), * *2004 Shanghai Statistical Bulletin* (2005).

Table 12.3 Foreign Direct Investment (FDI) in Shanghai, 1990–2002 (billion US dollars) (actually utilized)

Year	1990	1991	1992	1993	1994	1995	1996	1997	1998	1999	2000	2001	2002	2003	2004*
FDI	0.18	0.18	1.26	2.32	3.23	3.25	4.72	4.81	3.64	3.05	3.16	4.39	5.03	5.85	6.54

Source: *Statistical Yearbook of Shanghai* (2004), * *2004 Shanghai Statistical Bulletin* (2005).

Table 12.4 Industrial output in Shanghai, 1993–2002

Year	Industrial output (IO) (billion yuan)	Output of foreign-related enterprises (OFE)	
		Billion yuan	OFE/IO (%)
1993	332.7	42.3	12.7
1994	425.5	91.5	21.5
1995	454.7	129.6	28.5
1996	512.6	173.3	33.8
1997	565.0	211.9	37.5
1998	576.4	259.8	45.1
1999	621.3	286.8	46.2
2000	696.8	349.2	50.1
2001	765.7	396.3	51.8
2002	847.6	468.0	55.2
2003	1126.7	655.8	58.2
2004*	1401.7	—	—

Source: *Statistical Yearbook of Shanghai* (2004), * *2004 Shanghai Statistical Bulletin* (2005).

Shanghai in the International Division of Labour

Although Shanghai is a latecomer in the international competition, the great changes in the role it plays in both domestic and international hierarchy makes it one of the much discussed growth regions in China and also within the Pacific Rim. Shanghai in the last ten years has attracted vast international capital (see Table 12.4), and most of it came from TNCs. Rose (1997) and Wu (2000a) observe that compared with the Pearl River Delta Region inward investments in Shanghai are characterized by multinational origins, high levels of technology, and higher-order enterprises such as headquarters, representative offices, management or sales offices of manufacturing firms which are located in sub-urban Shanghai or neighbouring provinces. These characteristics are derived from several advantages Shanghai enjoys compared with other big cities in China. Apart from its geographic location, Shanghai as a hinterland signifies the potential of a vast consumption market. The leaders of the central government believe that Shanghai will be the key to China's take-off, so gave Shanghai more political backup and more preferential policies than the other parts of China. Shanghai has a better-trained labour force, good infrastructure and relatively less corruption and bureaucracy that promote a more desirable business environment. However, evaluating Shanghai's development in the light of International Division of Labour it is found that this city is by no means comparable with cities at the top of the global hierarchy on two grounds.

First, Shanghai's fast economic growth during the reform period was mainly induced by vast capital investment rather than through increasing added value and upgrading the technological level. The impact of TNCs and FDI on Shanghai's economy is becoming increasingly prominent. Between 1990 and 2004, the accumulated FDI in Shanghai reached US 52.81 billion dollars with the annual ratio of the FDI to GDP being on the increase every year (Table 12.3). Chai (2000) concluded that the contribution rate of capital to local GDP growth was 65.6 per cent. A simple model

(ΔIFA/ΔGDP) suggested that the rate was at its peak in 1997 and has levelled since from 1990 to 2004, the average contribution is 43.3 per cent. It shows that the source of Shanghai's competitive advantage is based on investment rather than innovation. Such a characteristic makes economic growth in Shanghai vulnerable to the availability of capital. Once facing the 'bottleneck' of capital resources, the growth in economy cannot be sustained. Since the provision of goods and services in Shanghai remain low-to-medium-technology and at low-value-added level the utilization efficiency and rate of return of investment is relatively low. The waste and poor performance of capital will increase the possibility of capital crisis, which makes the economy vulnerable.

Second, although Shanghai has become the largest FDI destination in East Asia and has attracted some TNCs setting up their regional headquarters in this vicinity, it is the host city for subsidiary enterprises and branch organizations. They invest here primarily to tap into preferential policies, cheap land and resources, competitive human resources as well as the vast market in Shanghai's hinterland. Its indigenous entrepreneurship is not strong enough to compete in the international market.

The role of Shanghai municipal government under the open-door era

Castells (1998) argued that it is the 'bureaucratic entrepreneurs' that had led to the emergence of new capitalism in China. This argument is manifested in Shanghai's development in the 1990s. Although the market forces were apparently working and shaping this city's transformation since the 1978 reform, research findings have shown that state control did not diminish (Olds 1997, Han 2000, Wu 2000b and Yatsko 2000). Rather, reform created powerful local states that controlled enterprises and intervened in resource allocation (Han 2000, Wu 2000b). Heavy government intervention remained as a distinguished feature in Shanghai's development since the 1990s.

First, the industrial restructuring process is pushed ahead by local government. The municipal government recognized that a strong tertiary sector is critical for Shanghai to become the economic centre, and thus adopted a development principal which puts the tertiary sector on priority. The municipal government emphasizes the growth of commercial and financial sectors as well as the development of real estate, tourism and information services, to push ahead and guide the restructuring process. From 1990 to 1999, one-third of the 13,200 industrial enterprises were closed down; while another one-third was moved out from the city proper. For the first time, the contribution of the tertiary industry to the whole urban economy exceeded 50 per cent in 1999. The restructuring process has led to a redundancy of over 1 million people to take care of the retiree which is a precarious take for the municipal authority.

In order to attract foreign investment, Shanghai government does its best to improve the investment environment. With the land-use system reform in China, administrative allocation was gradually replaced by land leasing system. As the municipal government controls the land leasing, its role in urban development is thus enhanced. Government financed mega-infrastructure building and huge urban redevelopment projects with the revenue gained from land leasing.

More than ten huge infrastructure projects were finished in the period of 1990 and 1997, including subway project, new airport project and deep-water port project. At the same time, about 18 million square metre of old housing were demolished, accompanied by 436,200 families, which means about 1 million people, who had been relocated from the inner city. The striking numbers illustrate fully the efficiency of Shanghai municipal government in urban construction.

Government also intervenes directly in the economic activities of business enterprises. For example, about half of hi-tech business in Shanghai are government owned or half-government owned (Ning 2003). Government also involves in real estate development. There were instances of the government establishing official or quasi-official development enterprises as one of the actors in the market. For instance, when the development of Pudong was announced in 1990, the Pudong Development Corporation was set up by the government to oversee land development process. On the one hand, it acts as a developer looking after its own economic profits as an economic entity and competing with private sector in the market. On the other hand, it acted as a manager that should guarantee that public goods are provided. Conflict of interest is inevitable. It is noted that government would sometimes compromise the public interest to ensure its own economic gains. The detailed plan of Pudong District was changed several times for the above reason. Meanwhile, since the government would have to bear the business loss of official corporations, the soft budget constraints makes the latter tend to act unreasonably and without regard to commercial reality and principles.

Through reviewing the role played by the municipal government in the 1990s, it can be seen that the Shanghai government achieves tangible objectives and improves the physical environment efficiently. In contrast, the Shanghai government has not done enough work in building a modern city's software system, including the free-flow of economic and business information, less administrative burden for entrepreneurs, the rule of law, the availability of venture capital, consultation and business support services, well-regulated capital market, consistency in policy, etc. This point can be illustrated further using the development of business support service industry in Shanghai, as an example.

Traditionally, the role services play in the efficient functioning of economy is neglected in China owing to the ideological perception of 'production' as a material term and services as 'unproductive'. Shanghai had to transform from a 'consumptive' city into a 'productive' one, and focus on heavy industries. Professionals rarely provided business support services on the market. Industrial enterprises under the planned economic system are 'small and comprehensive' ('*xiao er quan*') social units and depended primarily on themselves to providing business support services. Rarely possessing specialized knowledge and skills, such services were of low quality, high transaction costs, impeding the development of enterprises and deteriorating the efficiency of the whole economy.

The general attitude towards services changed, since the introduction of market-oriented reforms, as Shanghai proposes to be an 'international economic, financial, and trade centre'. The contribution of the tertiary industry to the whole urban economy increases gradually, as shown earlier. However, a significant gap still exists between Shanghai and global metropolises in terms of the share of services to total value-added, and the quality of the services provided. The gap in business support services is especially larger than in services generally, and imposes much negative influence on its business environment.

Several important points account for the underdevelopment of business support services in Shanghai. First, due to its intangible and non-storable nature, the significance of business support services is not properly evaluated and fully understood. The government has been aware of the vital importance of technological level in economic upgrading. However, the major efforts are devoted into constructing hi-tech parks and attracting international hi-tech firms, while building up mature logistical network and support system has not gained proper emphasis.

Second, the development of business support services (consulting, marketing, quality control, R&D, information-related services, etc.) lies in the availability of specialized knowledge and skills, which cannot be acquired overnight by the introduction of market-oriented reforms but require a longer period of time and a more determined policy to build an efficient producer service sector (Stare 2001). Business support services were controlled by government previously and were opened to market provision for only a short history in China. The majority of local business support services in Shanghai is lack of professional knowledge, skills and experiences and thus fails to meet the growing requirements of firms.

Third, the introduction of market-oriented reform into the business support services is slower and later than other economic sectors. For example, telecommunication in China is not yet exposed to market competition now. Due to the absence of market competition and international rules and standards, China's telecommunication services charge very high price, which is not proportional to local average personal income. The range and quality of services and their adaptation to customer needs also fail to meet the market requirements. Although there are some foreign banks and insurance companies established in China, neither one of them is fully exposed to international competition at this stage. Their monopolistic operation is one of the key reasons for their substandard services. The situation begins to change gradually with China's accession to WTO membership.

Taking into account the increasing role it plays, promoting the development of business support services and other elements of the software system of a modern city would be an important strategy for Shanghai to improve its business environment. As international competition intensified, the importance of entrepreneurial culture and appropriate business environment are key attributes that transformed the Silicon Valley into the cradle of the New Economy. The software of business environment is what Shanghai needs in order to realize its planning and development objectives.

The case of software industries in Pudong[2]

At different stages of software development, industrial association and government management organization have different responsibilities and functions.

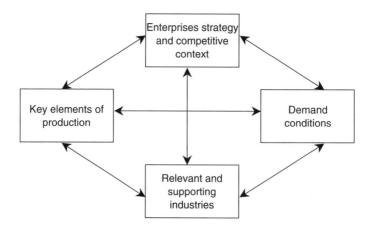

Figure 12.1 Analytical framework of competitiveness of industrial cluster.
Source: Ning (2003).

The relationship between software enterprises and the industrial association differs from that between software enterprises and government management organization. In general, software enterprises tend to maintain close relationship with business administrative department, intellectual property management department and industrial management department (Figure 12.1). These departments are responsible for the implementation of rules and regulations, cracking down piracy activities and protecting intellectual property and other legal rights thereby promoting a healthy development for the software industry.

The software enterprises

Software enterprises include software development and software servicing enterprises. In terms of the value system or value chain, it begins with the design and development of software and ends with the sales and servicing of software. Manufacturing and servicing enterprises occupy the core position in the chain. The other market relations are built around them. Software servicing is both the terminus and the starting point in the value chain of software industry. Software products are to serve the needs of the customers. The benefits associated with customer relationship form the last component of the values chain. The marketability of software products depends on the extent to which they are accepted by the consumers. At the same time, feedbacks from consumers provide the impetus for improvement and development of new products.

In terms of formation, the software enterprises in Pudong can be grouped into three categories. First, there are branches or joint ventures which are set up by domestic and foreign software corporations in the wake of the opening of Pudong. Second, there are enterprises formed by graduates who returned from studies abroad. Third, there are local enterprises based in Shanghai. They include enterprises established by government, associates of universities, research centres and collaborations between teachers and students. There are also small-scale enterprises formed by former employees of software corporations. Most of the 1,100 software enterprises registered in Pudong are categorized in the above mentioned three types. Among all, 457 are formed with foreign investment, 516 by local investment and 127 are privately owned. The technological support for these three categories of enterprises differs. Most foreign enterprises receive technological support from their parent corporations abroad. In particular, cooperatives set up by reputable multinational software companies stand to do better in terms of development of new products. Graduates from overseas, with their expertise and close overseas links, have better command of the updated technology. In the case of local enterprises, they depend primarily on local universities, research organizations and software parks and the training programmes offered by foreign software companies for support. On the whole, however, software enterprises do not devote a great deal of attention to the training and continued education for their employees.

In respect of the linkages of the enterprises, the relationship is mainly a vertical one. For enterprises that are branches or subsidiaries of foreign corporations, their relationship with their parent corporations is necessarily a vertical one in terms of capital agglomeration. As for those export-oriented software enterprises they are connected with overseas enterprise; their relationship with the overseas customers is a vertical one in terms of division of labour. In any of the vertical relationship, software enterprises in Pudong are unlikely to acquire the core technology, given that they only occupy a low position in the hierarchy of the New International Division of Labour (NIDL). Furthermore, software enterprises in Pudong are generally in small scale with a small clientele. Horizontal inter-links among the software enterprises are relatively uncommon and the division of labour is not clearly set.

The customer relationship

In terms of the relationship with their customers, software enterprises can be categorized into two types: First, an enterprise–customer chain that is associated with dealings within an enterprise. This refers to transactions between the production department of a software manufacturing enterprise and the customers that are carried out within the parent corporation. Given the globalization of the software industry, such transactions can take place between different countries. Within this type of enterprises, there are sub-groups. The first consists of corporation departments that deal with development of fit-in software, which forms the major business of the enterprises. There are many of these corporation departments in Pudong. Their annual turnovers are as high as several hundreds of million RMB. But because these software development departments are not separate entities, they are not entitled to the benefits and incentives offered by the state. The second type refers to enterprises that provide software development and servicing support to their parent headquarters. Considering the current trend of development, both types of enterprises have promising potentials. Specifically, with the gross output of the fit-in software exceeding that of the software enterprises, their development is a great help to the development of the software industry in Pudong. Further, with regard to subsidiaries in Shanghai that are established by domestic and foreign software corporations some of them focus on the R&D of hi-tech software while others concentrate on the development of less sophisticated data input system.

Second, an enterprise–customer chain is made up of transactions conducted outside the enterprises. Generally speaking, this involves independent software enterprises whose products and services are catered for the external market. Their clientele consists of corporate and individual consumers. There are two kinds of corporate customers. First, government is the major software consumer. The products required are mainly office software, management software and electronic administration software. Purchases by the government make up the major part of the Chinese software market. It is projected that the sales of office-use software may reach about 3 billion RMB in 2004. Notwithstanding this, the strength of the software enterprises in Shanghai does not lie in the production of office software. Second, enterprises are also the customers. The software used by enterprises fall into two main types. The first is general management software. The second is special software tailor-made for the enterprises. In terms of supply of management software for large enterprises, it is monopolized by Oracle and Sun from the United Sates and SAP from Germany. As for the management software for SMEs, the relatively low prices of their products have enabled the Chinese software suppliers to assume a large share of the market. One of the Shanghai enterprises even set up an R&D centre in Zhangjiang to research on and to develop products that serve the needs of SMEs. In respect of special software, they are mostly sectoral software that relate to finance, securities and stock, logistics, network security, transportation, education and games. This is a highly competitive area for the software enterprises in Shanghai and Pudong.

As for individual customers, the market demand for original and licensed software is small. The situation is slowly improving. In particular, the market for online games is developing, with the annual business turnover reaching 1 billion RMB. One of the software companies in Zhangjiang is the most influential online game developer in the national market. Another Shanghai enterprise, which is the major online game services provider in the country, has also set up a subsidiary in Zhangjiang for the development of online games. This is a classical example of consumer-led software development.[3]

The Yangtze River Delta, of which Shanghai forms the core, is one of the most vibrant regions in China with high consumption power. The demand for various types of software products is substantial. There is also a large pool of potential software consumers. By closely monitoring the needs and requirements of the customers, the software enterprises of Pudong will be able to develop and produce products that suit the needs of the customers, thereby maintaining their competitiveness in the market.

Servicing and supporting system of software industrial cluster

It is generally accepted that there is a strong government leadership under the economic management system of Shanghai. The government occupies key importance in promoting economic development. Given that Pudong New District is the pilot case in the economic development of Shanghai, the roles of the municipal government and the Pudong new district government are of equal importance. For the municipal government the policy of singling out Zhangjiang as the focus of development has caused the distribution of resources to be biased in favour of Pudong. Examples of this include the setting up of four state level development zones in Pudong, the setting up of R&D organizations and software infrastructure, all at the state level, in Zhangjiang, and the granting of preferential policies and treatments to Pudong New District. For the Pudong government, its role is reflected in the following areas.

First, the formulation of policy and plans for the industry. Acting on the policy of the central and municipal government to promote software industry, the Pudong government has formulated preferential policies and incentives that take into account the practical situation in Pudong New District. It has further devised a development plan to guide the development of the software industry in the district.

Second, the provision of financial support for the development of the software industry through the setting up of various scientific and technological research funds. The development of the Pudong software industrial cluster is dependent on a coordinated development of its components. Currently, it has built for itself a rather comprehensive servicing and supporting system, which includes training, technology support, product services, enterprise services, trade association and management organizations. Compared with software enterprise as a whole, the servicing and supporting system of the Pudong software industrial cluster is more comprehensive and has a better standard. This is an illustration of the proactive and leading role played by the government in the development process.

Since the mobility of human resources is high, it is possible for the Pudong software industrial cluster to recruit talents from Shanghai or other places within the country and even from other parts of the world. Training of personnel in Shanghai operates at three tiers. First, there are four pilot institutes (Fudan University, Jiaotong University, Tongji University and East-China Normal University) and two technical institutes. Second, there are a number of higher technical schools for training 'blue collar' technicians. Third, there is a vocational training school that aims to produce a large number of software technicians within a short time and at low costs.

In Zhangjiang, Pudong has established its own training centre to serve the enterprises in the software park. On the other hand, Tongji University offers software engineering courses and master programmes at the Lujiazui Park Branch since 2002. It also offers training courses and non-degree programmes for technical staff working in Pudong Software Park. Additionally, the computer school and microelectronic research centre of Fudan University will also be running courses and programmes in Pudong.

Pudong Software Park has a comprehensive technology supporting system. Within the system, it includes software assessment and testing centre, information centre, open laboratories and technology value-added services. Software enterprises often communicate with the customer through dealers and other intermediaries. They provide the enterprises with such services as electronic publication and translation as well as the provision of exhibition and conference centres.

The enterprise service system of Software Park is comprehensively organized. The services are provided by professional intermediaries that include audit firms, legal firms, core enterprise risk investment services system and software talent recruitment agencies. They provide corporate registration and legal services as well as other logistic arrangements for enterprises in the Park.

The most significant role of the software industrial association is the assessment of the qualification of software enterprises. The association also acts as the bridge between the government and the enterprises and serves to promote the flow of information on products and development of technology within the industry. However, due to the restriction of setting up association branches there is the only software association in Pudong. It can only perform some of the functions of the industrial association and is thus not very effective.

To this end, the urban management system would experience a de-regulation (diminishing the government direct control over market) and re-regulation process (regulating and promoting indigenous entrepreneurship with more market-oriented rules). That means the local government should disassociate itself from micro-economic activities and be responsible for macro adjustment and social development; exercise indirect control over enterprises and their economic activities; build up a simplified, unified and efficient administrative structure and set up an internationally acceptable standard of management.

Conclusion

Shanghai has accumulated rapid development and transformation and has upgraded its economy from basic factor-driven stage into investment-driven stage since the 1990s. China's accession into WTO will be another turning point for this city to revitalize the role it ever played in the international hierarchy. Appropriate government response would be vital for Shanghai to grasp the opportunity to upgrade its position.

Great government effort is the most marked characteristic in Shanghai's place-promotion process, which has successfully integrated Shanghai's economy into the global network and upgraded Shanghai's economy into investment-driven stage. However, such a role will not work to push Shanghai from the routine production site up to the core area in the International Division of Labour. This point has already been manifested by Shanghai's deficiency in building up the entrepreneurial culture and the software system. As the planned economy change towards a market-oriented one, a new administrative model that is compatible with market-oriented economic reform is of critical importance. The functions of local government should shift from direct intervention to the fostering of the market and guaranteeing its normal operation; from a producer and a controller to a referee and a manager who provide a favourable business environment in which indigenous entrepreneurship are facilitated and boosted.

As a new member of the WTO and the global trade leadership community, China has the chance to shape the global economy, not merely to be shaped by it (Frost 2001). Shanghai, the leading city in China, will be in the front line in participating in the International Division of Labour. WTO membership will bring in great external reinforcement to Shanghai's market-oriented reform, and also severe international competition. Transforming the role of government in such a turning point is vital for Shanghai to take advantage of the opportunities and tackle the challenges. Complying with WTO rules and its trade agreement will undoubtedly catalyse the de-regulatory and re-regulatory processes in China. However, WTO membership will bring rigorous competition into Chinese market as well. In short, local entrepreneurs are in a weak position compared with their foreign rivals, which means a great challenge for China.

Given that the competitive advantage of Shanghai in current development stage heavily rests on the availability of investment, the role of government is still substantial in its economic upgrading process. It can be important in such areas as channelling scarce capital into particular industries, promoting risk taking, stimulating and influencing the acquisition of foreign technology, etc. The enterprises, however, must begin to play a growing role as well. Government is the key actor in building up the entrepreneurial culture to nurture the growth of indigenous entrepreneurship. On the other hand, it should be cautious in distinguishing between direct control and indirect guidance, and avoiding over intervention and intervention deficiency.

Acknowledgements

This research is supported by the RGC project #10204049 awarded by the Hong Kong Research Grants Council. I am grateful for the research assistance of Sandy Lam, Carmen Chan, Hong Wen and Yao Xin, Ning Yuemin of East China Normal University for sharing with me the latest development of software industries in Shanghai and to three anonymous reviewers for their comments.

Notes

1 See Hong and Chan (2003) for a detailed discussion on the analytical background of global development.
2 This section is based on the field research and interviews conducted by the author in October 2003.
3 Personal Communication with Ning Yuemin, October 2004.

References

Borja, J. and Castells, M. (1997) *Local and Global: The Management of Cities in the Information Age*, London: Earthscan Publications Ltd.

Brotchie, J. F., Batty, M., Blakely, E., Hall, P. and Newton, P. (eds) (1995) *Cities in Competition: Production and Sustainable Cities for the 21st Century*, Melbourne, Australia: Longman.

Buchholz, R. A. (1992) *Business Environment and Public Policy: Implications for Management and Strategy* (4th Edition), Englewood Cliff, NJ: Prentice Hall.

Castells, M. (1989) *The Information City: Information Technology, Economic Restructuring, and Urban–Regional Process*, Oxford: Blackwell.

—— (1998) *End of Millennium*, Oxford: Blackwell.

Chai, J. M. (2000) 'Measuring the formation of World Cities: the case of Shanghai', unpublished PhD Dissertation, Hong Kong: The University of Hong Kong.

Chan, R. C. K. (2000) 'Shanghai: developing strategies and planning implications', Paper presented at international conference: *Re-inventing Global Cities*, The University of Hong Kong, Hong Kong.

Dicken, P. (1998) *Global Shift: Transformation the World Economy* (3rd Edition), London: Paul Chapman Publishing Ltd.

Eng, I. (1997) 'The rise of manufacturing towns: externally driven industrialization and urban development in the Pearl River Delta of China', *International Journal of Urban and Regional Research*, 21: 554–568.

Evans, P. (1995) *Embedded Autonomy: States and Industrial Transformation*, Princeton, NJ: Princeton University Press.

Frost, E. L. (2001) 'China, the WTO and globalization: what happens next?' Online. Available http://www.chinaonline.com (accessed 1 September 2004).

Han, S. S. (2000) 'Shanghai between state and market in urban transformation', *Urban Studies*, 37 (11): 2091–2112.

Hayter, R. (1997) *The Dynamics of Industrial Location: The Factory, the Firm and the Production System*, Chichester: Wiley.

Hong, W. and Chan, R. C. K. (2003) 'The role of government in creating competitive advantage in the globalized economy: the case of Shanghai, China', in Dawson, J., Mukoyama, M., Sang, C. C. and Larke, R. (eds) *The Internationalisation of Retailing in Asia*, London: RoutledgeCurzon, 169–188.

Markusen, A. (1996) 'Sticky places in slippery space: a typology of industrial districts', *Economic Geography*, 72 (3): 293–313.

Mascitelli, R. (1999) *The Growth Warriors: Creating Sustainable Global Advantage for America's Technology Industries*, Northridge, CA: Technology Perspectives.

Ning, Y. (2003) *A Study of Software Industrial Cluster in Pudong*, Shanghai, China Institute of Urban and Regional Research, East China Normal University.

Olds, K. (1997) 'Globalizing Shanghai: the "global intelligence Corps" and the building of Pudong', *Cities*, 14 (2):109–123.

Porter, M. E. (1990) *The Competitive Advantage of Nations*, New York: The Free Press.

Pounder, J. S. (1991) *Managing the Business Environment: Hong Kong and Beyond*, Hong Kong: Longman.

Rose, F. (1997) 'Shanghai: exception or rule? Consideration of urban development paths and processes in China since 1978', Paper presented to the South Asian Urbanization Conference, 26–29 August, London.

Schneider, M. and Kim, D. (1996) 'The effects of local conditions on economic growth, 1997–1990: the changing location of high technology activities', *Urban Affairs Review*, 32 (2): 131–156.

Shanghai Statistical Bureau (2004) *Statistical Yearbook of Shanghai*, Beijing: China Statistical Press.

Shanghai Statistical Bureau (2005) *2004 Shanghai Statistical Bulletin*, Online. Available http://www.stats.gov.cn/

Stare, M. (2001) 'Advancing the development of business support services in Slovenia with foreign direct investment', *The Service Industries Journal*, 21 (1): 19–34.

Storper, M. (1992) 'The limits to globalization: technology districts and international trade', *Economic Geography*, 68: 60–93.

—— (1998) 'Industrial policy for latecomers: products, conventions, and learning', in M. Storper, T. Thomadakis and L. Tsipouri (eds) *Latecomers in the Global Economy*, London: Routledge, 13–39.

Storper, M., Thomadakis, T. and Tsipouri, L. (eds) (1998) *Latecomers in the Global Economy*, London: Routledge.

Tang, Z. L. and Luan, F. (2000) '1990 nian dai shang hai de cheng shi kai fa yu yan biab (Urban development and restructuring of Shanghai city in the 1990's)', *Cheng Shi Gui Hua Hui Kan (Urban Planning Forum)*, 128: 32–37 (in Chinese).

Worthington, I. and Britton, C. (2003) *The Business Environment* (4th Edition), Essex: Prentice Hall, Pearson Education Limited.

Wu, F. L. (2000a) 'The global and local dimension of place-making: remaking Shanghai as a world city', *Urban Studies*, 37 (8): 1359–1377.

—— (2000b) 'Place promotion in Shanghai, PRC', *Cities*, 17 (5): 349–361.

Yatsko, P. (2000) *New Shanghai: The Rocky Rebirth of China' Legendary City*, New York Wiley.

Yeung, W. C. H. (1998) 'Capital, state and space: contesting the borderless world', *Transactions of the Institute of British Geographers*, NS 23: 291–309.

—— (1999) 'Grounding global flows: constructing an e-commerce hub in Singapore', Paper presented to the conference on '*Global networks, innovation and regional development*', UC Santa Cruz, 11–13 November 1999.

—— (2000) 'State intervention and neoliberalism in the globalizing world economy: lessons from Singapore's regionalization programme', *The Pacific Review*, 13 (1): 133–162.

Zhao, M. and Zhang, Z. Y. (1998) 'Metropolitan planning and governance in Asia and Pacific: the Shanghai case', unpublished paper, Tongji University, Shanghai, PRC.

13 Globalization and the growth of new economic sectors in the second-tier extended cities in the Yangtze River Delta

Wen Chen, Junbo Xiang, Wei Sun and Shengjin Chu

The second-tier extended metropolis in the Yangtze River Delta, including Suzhou, Wuxi and Changzhou near Shanghai, is becoming the most active and innovative of the new areas of industrial agglomeration. Manufacturing industries in these second-tier cities have been experiencing rapid growth due to increasing foreign direct investment (FDI). Nevertheless, the economic prospects of these cities are still constrained due to a lack of local R&D capacity and producer services and a continuing dependence upon those of Shanghai. This chapter analyses the impact of globalization on the new economic sectors in these cities, the changing industrial structure and the limitations of urban development and the problem of sustainability. It also analyses the conditions for high-tech industry and producer services in these areas. Furthermore, the chapter applies industrial organization theory to these cities and examines how they can cooperate with each other in terms of horizontal linkages. Finally, it discusses the future growth prospects of these industries.

While the primary metropolises suffer development problems such as traffic jams, high rents and a deteriorating environment, the second-tier cities within the metropolitan region, just ranking after the primary metropolises in size, have grown rapidly, like other active and innovative new areas of industrial agglomeration such as Silicon Valley in the United States (Markusen and DiGiovanna 1999).

Situated in the Yangtze River Delta to the north of Shanghai, the biggest metropolis in China, the region of Suzhou–Wuxi–Changzhou (Su–Xi–Chang for short) is the most developed region in China, with 13.65 million population, an area of 17,513 square kilometres and a GDP of 442.143 billion Ren Min Bi, accounting for, respectively, 1.05, 0.18 and 4.32 per cent of the figures for the whole nation (Map 13.1). Suzhou, Wuxi and Changzhou are three cities with over 1 million population. They are referred to as second-tier big cities. Since the 1990s, these metropolises have become the 'hot areas' for FDI and have gradually become big 'processing factories' for multinational corporations (MNC) in the global manufacturing commodity chain. However, shortages of technology and service systems may affect the sustainability of this region. Hence, the

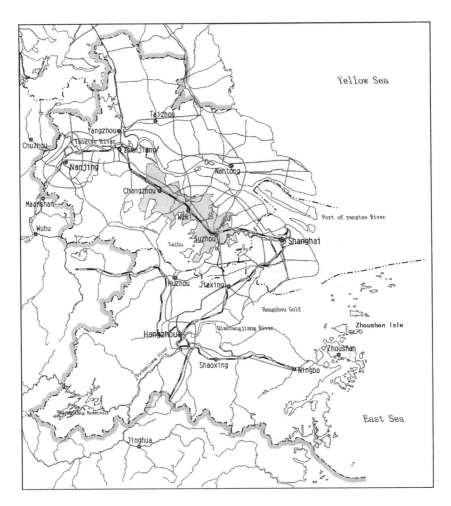

Map 13.1 Location of Su–Xi–Chang.

chapter analyses the development of the high-tech industry and producer services in these second-tier cities.

Rapid growth in the manufacturing sector

In the 1980s, township and village enterprises (TVEs) boomed in the region of Su–Xi–Chang, which developed the national well-known Southern Jiangsu Model (Zhu 1994) at the beginning of the Chinese reform period. The growth of TVEs pushed rapid growth in GDP. The GDP per capita increased about five times from 1978 to 1990 (Table 13.1). In the 1990s, along with the opening and development of Pudong, Shanghai, a significant amount of FDI swarmed into this

Table 13.1 GDP per capita in the cities of Su–Xi–Chang (yuan)

Area	1978	1984	1990	1996	1998	2000	2002
Suzhou	634	1,280	3,617	17,474	21,733	26,692	35,733
Wuxi	687	1,526	3,865	20,232	24,338	27,653	36,151
Changzhou	605	1,272	2,935	12,847	14,842	17,635	22,215

Source: Statistical Yearbook of Jiangsu, and Suzhou, Wuxi and Changzhou, 2003.

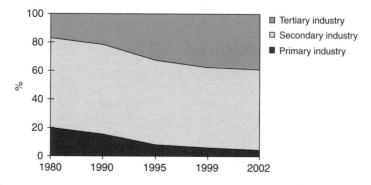

Figure 13.1 The change in economic sectors in Su–Xi–Chang.

Source: Statistical Yearbook of Jiangsu, and Suzhou, Wuxi and Changzhou, 2003.

region due to the proximity of the location to the Shanghai metropolises as well as to the advantageous developmental conditions and low manufacturing costs.

All of these changes have resulted in fast industrialization in this region. In 2002 the proportions of added value in the three economic sectors in GDP reached 4.47 : 56.78 : 38.75, with the agricultural and industrial proportions of GDP decreasing by about 15 per cent from 1980 to 2002; secondary industry dominated over the whole period accounting for 55 per cent and sometimes even over 60 per cent. The added value of the manufacturing sector has increased from 25 billion in 1980 to 194 billion in 2001, a 260-times growth (Figure 13.1). Thus, the contribution of secondary industry to GDP has ranked the first, above those of tertiary and primary industry, although the rate of contribution decreased from 1995 to 1999. This change is accompanied by an increase in GDP per capita.

Further analysis of growth change in the industrial structure has shown that while the textile industry still dominates the industrial sector, its percentage of local industrial output has decreased gradually since the 1990s, whereas electronic and electric machinery manufacturing has developed very fast, with its percentage of local industrial output increasing from 4 per cent at the beginning of the 1990s to 10 per cent at the end of the 1990s. The chemical industry also demonstrates growth (Table 13.2).

Since there are many manufacturing factories and industrial development zones in the region, people have begun to ask whether this region has become a 'world factory'. Although the proportion of manufacturing industry is very high producer services and technological innovation lag behind the development of

Table 13.2 Change in industrial sectors in local industry (in percentage)

	2001	1999	1995	1990
Textile	13.72	15.10	16.56	21.32
Electronic and communication manufacturing	11.32	9.90	3.24	4.35
Chemical processing	8.36	8.70	5.42	6.29
General machinery	7.16	7.30	5.09	10.16
Electric machinery	7.85	7.20	5.48	5.08
Black metal smelting	7.06	5.60	5.51	4.37
Clothing and fibre	4.87	4.90	4.03	n.a.
Metal produce	3.88	4.10	3.21	2.65

Source: Statistical Yearbook of China, Jiangsu, and Suzhou, Wuxi and Changzhou, 2002.

Table 13.3 Comparison of the high-tech industrial development

Indicators	Su–Xi–Chang			Nanjing			Shanghai		
	1994	1999	Annual growth rate (%)	1994	1999	Annual growth rate (%)	1994	1999	Annual growth rate (%)
Sales revenue of high-tech products (100 million yuan)	181.8	598.8	26.90	66.59	208.77	25.7	300	1,261	33.3
Expenditure of R&D (100 million yuan)	55.64	66.97	3.8	19.00	33.28	11.9	97.0	134	6.7
Sales revenue of new products (100 million yuan)	454.7	1,193.6	21.3	104.2	171.2	10.4	339.1	1,007.2	24.3

Source: State Statistical Bureau (1995, 2000): Science and Technological Statistical Yearbook of Jiangsu 1995 and 2000) and Shanghai Statistical Yearbooks 1995 and 2000.

manufacturing (Chen 1996, Chen *et al.* 2001). Hence, Lu (2001) argues that the region is just an industrial processing workshop for the world market.

Although the three cities have set up high-tech development zones and made successful progress, R&D inputs in technical innovation were less than 0.45 per cent of GDP. In the period from 1994 to 1999, the sales value of high-tech products and new products in the three cities increased by 26.6 and 21.3 per cent, respectively, lower than the respective figures for Shanghai, but higher than the figures for Nanjing (Table 13.3). However, most factories in the region process and assemble accessories into machines without any knowledge of the core industrial technologies of the products. Moreover, producer services have developed slowly because they are in the shadow of Shanghai, and the region's per capita value added has been about half of that of Shanghai (Table 13.4). The retail, trade and food services have dominated in the tertiary sector. The proportion of value-added financial services and insurance was 12 per cent in the tertiary sector, 2 per cent lower than 1997 and 18 per cent lower than in Shanghai (Table 13.5).

Table 13.4 Comparison of producer services in Shanghai, Suzhou and Wuxi in 2000 (yuan)

City	Service value added (100 million yuan)	Producer services value added (100 million yuan)	Producer services value added per capita (yuan)	The ratio of producer services in GDP (%)
Shanghai	2,304.27	1,143.18	8,650	25.0
Suzhou	104.00	45.44	4,102	13.5
Wuxi	191.34	38.56	3,413	9.0

Table 13.5 Comparison of tertiary industry between Shanghai and Su–Xi–Chang, 2000

	Proportion of tertiary industry value added in GDP (%)	Amount of tertiary industry added value (100 million yuan)	Proportion in tertiary industry (%)		
			Transportation storage and telecommu- nication	Wholesale retail trade and food- service	Finance and insurance
Su–Xi–Chang	37.92	1,267.37	15.19	38.61	11.59
Shanghai	50.63	2,304.27	13.68	21.06	29.78

Note
Producer services include the finance and insurance, real estate, education, research and tech service and the consultant.

The role of foreign investment

FDI, along with economic globalization, has played a great role in pushing rapid growth and industrial restructuring in this region. As the region has benefited from the opening up of Pudong its FDI has increased from US 1.2 billion dollars in 1989 to US 7.1 billion dollars in 2002. The FDI percentage of total investment in fixed assets rose from 1.08 to 8.25 per cent in the same period. For example, in Wuxi, FDI flows not only from Hong Kong, Macau and Taiwan but also from the European Union, the United States and Japan (Table 13.6).

Why, then, is this region attractive to FDI? The key factors include the location near Shanghai, the strong industrial base and a good social environment. First, situated at the junction of the sea and the Yangtze River this region is the core of Yangtze River Delta and has very convenient and close connections with Shanghai. Thanks to the improved comprehensive traffic system, the region is linked with the entire Yangtze River area, the whole country and the world. It is an 'opening' region with dense population and towns, as well as prosperous local economies. Second, it enjoys the advantages of a good environment for both living and investment including abundant water resources from the Taihu Lake and Yangtze River, a mild climate, a plain surface and fertile land, as well as a long history and culture, a cheap but educated labour force and a safe and comfortable society. All are attractive features for FDI. Moreover, the high level

Table 13.6 FDI by country and region in Wuxi and Suzhou (10,000 USD)

Country/region	Wuxi				Suzhou			
	1995	%	2000	%	1995	%	2001	%
Hong Kong	30,380	22.7	58,889	35.03	93,729	17.81	139,449	24.38
Japan	32,269	24.1	16,579	9.86	40,957	7.78	60,868	10.64
Taiwan	8,312	6.2	22,540	13.40	106,211	20.18	101,007	17.66
Singapore	10,862	8.1	7,208	4.29	102,983	19.57	37,818	6.61
Republic of Korea	2,361	1.8	1,278	0.76	21,705	4.12	17,488	3.06
United Kingdom	2,337	1.8	4,012	2.39	23,570	4.48	8,543	1.49
Germany	13,187	9.9	4,398	2.62	13,235	2.51	9,379	1.64
France	1,065	7.9	1,783	1.06	6,698	1.27	9,969	1.74
Italy	2,032	1.5	—	—	1,089	0.21	357	0.01
Latin America	142	0.1	26,692	15.88	832	0.16	10,562	1.85
Canada	1,967	1.5	74	0.04	60,981	11.59	53,162	9.29
United States	24,538	18.3	16,162	9.80	37,352	13.00	—	—

Source: Statistical Yearbook of Wuxi and Suzhou, 1996, 2001, 2002.

of per capita GDP, the strong manufacturing base and a large potential consumer market are all significant factors.

Many MNCs select the location and region that will strengthen their global competitiveness. According to a recent study in the region of Su–Xi–Chang (Zhu 2002) cheap production costs and land are still the dominant elements attracting the investors (Table 13.7). The next two factors are high expectations for the Chinese market and favourable government policies. However, many MNCs have paid attention to the quality of the investment environment. The survey shows that most foreign investors are satisfied with the investment environment including government performance: about 42.5 per cent of the interviewees rated government performance as excellent, 47.1 per cent as very good and only 10.3 per cent as good. This is why the region has continuously attracted FDI.

FDI has brought about a huge impact on regional economic growth and economic transformation. As the region under discussion is a leading region in terms of economic globalization, foreign firms and joint ventures have played a great role in regional economic internationalization. Different economic regions use their comparative advantages to cooperate and compete with each other. Making full use of FDI is a useful means of strengthening the competitive ability of Southern Jiangsu, which participates in the new international division of labour as well as occupying a share of the global market. In Suzhou, foreign firms and joint ventures have provided 78.9 per cent of export value. Suzhou ranked first in economic opening in 2001 among all the cities in the Yangtze River Delta, surpassing Shanghai (Table 13.8).

Moreover, FDI has improved the industrial structure. In particular, the agglomeration of electronics and electric machinery operations in the high-tech development zones of Suzhou, Wuxi, Changzhou and Kunshan economic zone has

Table 13.7 Options of FDI strategies and management in South Jiangsu

Investment purpose			Management strategies		
Option	*Rank*	*Average value*	*Option*	*Rank*	*Average value*
Utilizing local cheap work force and land	1	1.89	Decreasing production cost	1	1.76
Prospect for the Chinese future market development	2	1.53	Creating local production and management base	2	1.72
Entering local market right now	3	1.50	Realizing the new market development strategies	3	1.53
Obtaining production order	4	0.78	Enhancing production and technology	4	1.07
Developing regional production base for the world market	5	0.65	Advancing the sale and service system	5	0.99
Influenced by international investment in same sector	6	0.63	Tackling the international competition	6	0.72
Finding cheap nature resources and materials	7	0.56	Diversifying development approaches	7	0.36
Invited by local government	8	0.55	Enlarging material stock and product sale	8	0.34
Re-exporting products to overseas market	9	0.41	Introducing production technology	9	0.33
Invited by clients	10	0.28	Enhancing information collection, analysis and utilization	10	0.22

Source: Zhu (2002: 16).

Note
Within ten options, the foreign companies can choose three of them by the importance.

changed the original industrial structure, which specialized in light and textile industries. Also, the percentage of industrial output value of state-owned enterprises (SOEs) has decreased significantly. Most labourers work in non-SOE firms. In Suzhou, foreign firms and joint ventures have absorbed 319,000 labourers, which is 33.2 per cent of the whole (Figure 13.2).

In Suzhou, the former main industrial sector was based on traditional textile industries. Most factories were located in the crowded inner city. In order to protect the 5,000-year-old inner city, the government planned the Sino-Singapore Suzhou Industrial Park in the east of the city and the High and New Technological Development Zone on the west side as new industrial development space. Many new firms and sectors, including 70 per cent of information, electronics, new materials and high-tech manufacturing firms have clustered in these development zones. More than 50 MNCs, including Motorola and Philips, moved there.

Table 13.8 FDI and economic development in the Yangtze River Delta

| | Actual foreign investment (10,000 USD) | | | | | | The percentage of foreign oriented economic output in the local economic output | | | | | | | |
| | 1989 | | 1994 | | 2001 | | 1991 | | 1995 | | 1998 | | 2001 | |
	Amount	Rank	Amount	Rank	Amount	Rank	Value	Rank	Value	Rank	Value	Rank	Value	Rank
Shanghai	118,954	1	400,517	1	439,159	1	34.19	1	39.26	1	35.82	1	46.19	2
Nanjing	5,192	3	38,478	5	90,205	4	4.37	7	11.71	9	11.78	9	15.81	8
Suzhou	6,758	2	217,661	2	302,183	2	7.02	4	21.59	4	34.49	2	57.87	1
Wuxi	2,358	9	83,816	3	135,746	3	4.37	8	13.68	7	23.26	4	22.09	6
Changzhou	2,773	7	27,772	8	62,036	6	4.81	6	17.38	5	21.50	5	26.64	5
Yanghzou	833	10	13,581	10	9,968	14	1.50	10	14.77	6	17.05	8	12.28	9
Zhenjiang	2,459	8	17,343	9	32,637	8	3.05	9	9.43	10	11.58	10	10.81	10
Nantong	3,431	6	29,022	7	17,523	11	7.72	3	24.45	3	17.65	7	21.31	7
Taizhou	—	—	—	—	12,071	13	0.35	11	5.29	11	7.16	11	7.09	11
Hangzhou	4,839	4	41,998	4	50,324	7	—	—	—	—	—	—	—	—
Ningbo	3,493	5	37,406	6	87,446	5	13.54	2	31.03	2	29.36	3	39.38	3
Huzhou	267	13	3,800	13	20,972	10	—	—	—	—	—	—	—	—
Jiaxing	317	11	4,983	12	27,067	9	5.43	5	12.38	8	18.61	6	30.37	4
Shaoxing	314	12	11,166	11	15,777	12	—	—	—	—	—	—	—	—
Zhoushan	253	14	2,322	14	1,141	15	—	—	—	—	—	—	—	—
Yangtze Delta	—	—	—	—	—	—	14.93	—	21.89	—	25.29	—	34.31	—
Whole nation	—	—	—	—	—	—	17.56	—	21.61	—	19.76	—	23.35	—

Source: Statistical Yearbook of Jiangsu 2002, Shanghai and Zhejiang 2002.

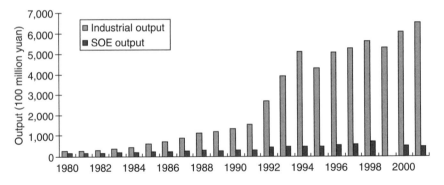

Figure 13.2 The growth of industrial output and SOE output.

The total value of FDI has reached US 3.4 billion dollars, dispersed across more than 300 projects. A high-tech industrial group has been formed, including electronics, information technology, integrated optical–mechanical–electronic products, biological medicine, new materials, and so on. This was the first development zone to come within the scope of the APEC. The Suzhou Industrial Park is supported by both the Chinese and the Singapore governments and was built as a technology-intensive industrial zone. It takes advantage of the global network to invite investment, and the mode of direct investment is attractive to MNCs and big syndicates. Using these development zones as a platform, many MNCs have developed their production bases in Suzhou. For instance, the Philips Consumer Electronics Ltd Co., Benque Electronic Communication Information Technology Ltd Co., Suzhou Luoji Electronic Ltd Co. and Renbao Computer Industrial Ltd Co. They manufacture colour TV sets, computers, monitors and mouses.

Wuxi New District strengthens cooperation between the municipal bureaus of industrial administration and large local enterprises to form joint organizations for attracting investment. The Bureau of Wuxi Electronic and Instrumental Industry, the Bureau of Mechanical Industry and the Little Swan Group all have several projects in the New District. Total investment has reached US 400 million dollars. The major, or 'pillar', industries in Wuxi are electronic, machinery and fine chemical industries. Considering this situation, Wuxi New District has paid more attention to its own pillar industries. A new group of pillar industries has formed quickly around the electronics and information technology industry, fine machinery industry, fine chemical industry, new materials industry, biological engineering and pharmaceuticals. These industries have had a strong impact on the industrial structure of the surrounding regions. MNCs such as the Japanese Sharp, Panasonic, Hitachi and Toshiba, and the German Siemens, Boshi and Byern all have joint ventures in this district.

Changzhou New District tries to develop various relationships to attract investment: using professionals in the city and staffs in the district, using old contacts and developing new ones, attracting domestic and foreign investment, and attracting

Table 13.9 FDI by sector in Su–Xi–Chang, 2001

Item	Number of projects			Value USD (10,000)		
	Suzhou	*Wuxi*	*Changzhou*	*Suzhou*	*Wuxi*	*Changzhou*
Farming, forestry, animal husbandry and fishery	21	11	11	4,181	3,607	279
Manufacturing and construction	1,228	2,336	1,295	683,474	165,348	57,094
Tertiary industry	113	191	107	35,359	7,418	2,663

Source: Statistical Yearbook of Changzhou, Wuxi, Suzhou, 2002.

direct as well as indirect investment. The expected result has been achieved and the foreign-oriented economy in Changzhou New District has developed to a new stage. New joint-venture enterprises have been established in this district by the Ensi Company of France and the Tongda Company of Hong Kong.

In southern Jiangsu, FDI projects are mainly in manufacturing (Table 13.9), especially in the field of processing. Most imported technologies are for conventional manufacturing. In the manufacturing enterprises established by MNCs, many core parts are imported from other countries. Local enterprises provide only a small part of the intermediate products for some FDI enterprises that need local support. However, the general level of use of FDI in the service sector is lower than that in manufacturing, partly due to the slow adoption of the open policy in the service market and the WTO. However, all these conditions have delayed the development of local producer services and technology innovation systems. This has inevitably brought about a negative effect on the local economy.

Firms would be unable to earn significantly more benefits without core advanced technology and might have to pay high transaction costs without good local producer services, even though they may have a big output value. As a result, the benefit of development quality does not coincide with a high level of GDP. The GDP increases by more than 10 per cent every year, but the income of the inhabitants of the region increases annually by just 5–6 per cent. Moreover, the expansion of the processing factories has occupied much land and polluted the environment. For every 100 million yuan GDP the amount of cultivated land decreases by about 7 hectares, used for construction; for every 100 million yuan industrial output the amount of waste water will increase by 100,000 tons.

The parts warehouse of Logitech in Suzhou is a typical example that illustrates the above point. One of Logitech's products is a wireless mouse called Wanda, which is sold to American consumers for around US 40 dollars. Of this, Logitech takes about US 8 dollars, while distributors and retailers take US 15 dollars. A further 14 dollars goes to the suppliers that provide Wanda's parts. A Motorola plant in Malaysia makes the mouse's chips and America's Aglient Technologies supplies the optical sensor. Even the solder comes from a US company, Cookson Electronics, which has a factory in China's Yunnan province near Vietnam.

Marketing is led from Fremont, California, where 450 staff earn far more than the 4,000 Chinese employed in Suzhou. China's take from each mouse comes to only US 3 dollars, including wages, power, transport and other overhead costs. Other products made in China rely less on US components and use Japanese, Korean or Taiwanese parts instead. But in many cases the outcome is the same: MNCs get the bulk of the profit.

The development of manufacturing by FDI has driven the fast growth of local GDP, however, the quality of life has not improved at the same time. Resources and environmental conditions have been deteriorating. The region urgently needs to change its economic development approach, that is, to look for the possibility of high-tech and producer service development.

Conditions for high-tech growth

Along with the opening up of Pudong, Shanghai has become the agglomeration centre for high-tech industries, as many MNCs have set up R&D centres in Shanghai to take advantage of its information and human resources. However, the second-tier extended cities near Shanghai, such as Suzhou, Wuxi and Changzhou, have the possibility of developing high-tech industry on an extensive scale, on the basis of both international experience and their own development conditions.

International experience shows that there are many high-tech and new industrial agglomeration areas in the world, such as San Jose (Silicon Valley), Route 128 in Boston and the Delta of North Carolina in the United States; the Silicon Valley Institute of Scotland and Gongbo Science City in Japan. These technopolises are not always primary metropolises but are located around or not far away from them. For instance, Silicon Valley, located along the Pacific Ocean part of California, is about 100 kilometres away from the San Francisco metropolis and just one hour's distance from the international airport of San Francisco. High-tech companies enjoy a suitable environment, better living conditions and convenient transportation. Another important factor affecting the distribution of these companies is that they are close to highly qualified universities, especially universities with higher level sciences, as Silicon Valley is close to the University of Stanford and Route 128 is near MIT. It is possible for them to maintain high-level research teams and keep updated with new technologies. Moreover, excellent outsourcing in the industrial chain, venture capital, mobile human resources, a social security system, start-up entrepreneurs and efficient services all contribute to the growth of the high-tech industry (Barnes and Gertler 1999, Sharksening 1999, Zhong 2001).

Su–Xi–Chang is 60–150 kilometres away from Shanghai with a convenient highway connection. There are three highways (Shanghai–Nanjing, Nanjing–Taicang, Nanjing–Hangzhou) connected with Shanghai, about 1–2 hours from Shanghai Pudong International Airport. A long history, diverse local culture, beautiful scenery and comfortable living conditions provide a suitable environment for the development of high-tech industry, while the large-scale manufacturing development led by TVEs and the growth of the foreign-oriented economy have stimulated strong demand for technology and investment support to high-tech industries. In sum, compared with the other regional-level cities, this area, in particular Suzhou and Wuxi, has high urban competitiveness (Table 13.10). Suzhou ranks sixth after Shanghai, Shenzhen, Beijing, Guangzhou and Dongguan. Among Chinese cities, this city is very suitable for high-tech development.

Furthermore, compared with Shanghai, industrial development in Su–Xi–Chang seldom has the same intense competitive pressure as is seen in the primary metropolises, where investment competes for a limited market and space. Also, some high-tech industries create the problems of environmental pollution, such as silicon garbage, which would be treated more easily in Su–Xi–Chang than in Shanghai. The Su–Xi–Chang region has a good foundation for high-tech industry development, since it has been designated as the National Torch Belt of High-tech Industry by the Ministry of Science and Technology.

However, with economic globalization, the knowledge economy and the entrance of the WTO all regions are facing more and more intense competition. On the other hand, the tendency towards technological modularity has created the possibility of separating R&D and technological manufacturing functions in different areas (Baldwin and Clark 1997).

The development result of Japanese local second-tier technopolises might offer a lesson for Su–Xi–Chang. In order to benefit from the economic agglomeration of Tokyo, the Japanese government set up several local technopolises in the 1970s. Oita and Kumamoto were invested in by certain large electronics enterprises, such as SONY, NEC and MRC, as new manufacturing bases. These bases promoted the growth of nearby cities rapidly at the beginning of the 1980s. However, due to the shortage of R&D and venture capital these 'technopolises without brains' (Markusen and Sasaki 1999) have weakened regarding the upgrading of manufacturing development and constrained regarding future development.

Nevertheless, other technopolises like Toyama could be regarded as successful examples of the transformation of traditional manufacturing into high-tech industry. Differing from the above technopolises, the local government there has paid more attention to technological development and R&D investment, and developed preferential policies on land prices, loans, tax returns, etc. These activities were useful for the transformation of the industrial structure and have accelerated the growth of localized high-tech enterprises thus strengthening Toyama's international competitiveness. Finally, the employment rate has a growth figure of 2.6 per cent, transportation 51.7 per cent and GDP 43.7 per cent. Fostering competition between adjacent regions and encouraging the utilization of local resources by the government are helpful for the establishment of a diverse and sustainable economy (Funaba *et al.* 1999).

The Japanese experience suggests that in Su–Xi–Chang the development of high-tech industry should be encouraged and innovation impetus should be fostered so as to keep the advantage of sustainable development. There are some obstacles restraining the development of high-tech industry in Su–Xi–Chang. The first is the lack of innovation, which can be divided into knowledge and technological innovation, knowledge dissemination and knowledge application

Table 13.10 Ranking of Chinese urban competitiveness in 2003

City	Intelligence	Capital	Science and technology	Facility	Location	Culture	Environment	Institution	Government management	Enterprise management	Open	Overall
Shanghai	2	1	2	1	1	4	2	4	1	7	7	1
Shenzhen	3	4	14	3	19	16	1	1	7	1	1	2
Beijing	1	2	1	2	2	5	23	14	4	10	10	3
Guangzhou	5	3	4	16	3	2	6	25	3	3	8	4
Dongguan	24	30	31	38	35	44	26	15	14	41	3	5
Suzhou	19	8	13	14	20	3	5	10	2	4	9	6
Tianjin	21	5	3	13	8	32	46	39	31	42	27	7
Ninbo	14	12	16	10	23	14	9	3	5	5	13	8
Hangzhou	4	6	10	15	10	6	22	12	15	6	14	9
Nanjing	8	7	5	5	7	11	15	22	32	22	19	10
Wuxi	35	27	22	7	18	13	3	19	6	11	18	11
Qindao	16	11	6	24	31	7	19	13	12	8	21	12
Jinan	9	13	8	46	30	33	10	23	11	16	29	13
Wuhan	10	26	7	33	4	31	24	40	23	44	25	14
Wenzhou	28	15	24	32	45	29	7	2	21	2	17	15

Source: Compiled from Ni (2004: 2).

systems. In the Su–Xi–Chang region, colleges and universities usually focus on education but not on technology innovation. Also, manufacturing enterprises prefer processing to innovation. The second obstacle is that the policy environment favours large foreign enterprises but has not promoted preferential policies for the integration of venture capital and innovative drive to facilitate the establishment of highly innovative firms. Thus, many small enterprises are stuck in general manufacturing at the entrance threshold.

Conditions for productive service development

Producer services is a new industry using new information technology based on information production, processing and distribution. Most, such as finance, information, logistics, etc., serve manufacturing efficiently. Producer services may stimulate technological and institutional innovation through a spill-over effect and positive externalities, which are the important conditions not only for increasing production returns, but also for the sustainable development of the cities (Hong and Chen 2000).

New tendencies such as the development of information networks, the diversified demands of the modern market, flexible production and industrial subdivision have created a close relationship between producer services and the manufacturing sector through industrial and spatial interaction. While local and just-in-time services create the regional network of distribution the possibility of investment in producer services in second-tier cities such as Su–Xi–Chang may be realized due to reduced information cost and individual demand. Producer services are undergoing specialization, such as the subdivision of finance creating several separated functions. Besides traditional deposits, loans and other financial services there are many new derivative services which could be distributed in different cities based on functional specialization. So the horizontal division of diversified supply of regional services gradually occurs in the functional connections between primary and second-tier cities. For example, within the north-east metropolitan area along the eastern coast of the United States, New York is an international financial centre, while Philadelphia and Boston are the same in being financial centres with outstanding performance in derivative and secondary finance (Baldwin and Clark 1997). Thus, diversified horizontal divisions are developed in the metropolitan area. The result is the development of a better industrial structure and a stronger innovative economy, and finally a strong and efficient global capital management/control base.

Development of producer services is needed in Su–Xi–Chang. First, they are all cities with over 1 million population (with 1.41, 1.56 and 1.05 million urban residents, respectively, in 2002). Since manufacturing costs will increase along with urban expansion it is necessary for these cities to adjust their industrial structures and avoid relying solely on manufacturing. Hence, 'retreating from secondary industry and developing towards tertiary industry' is the major policy for urban spatial adjustment in China. Also, the development of the manufacturing has not only magnified demand for producer services but also created an outlet for surplus capital, while the profit margin of manufacturing industries is in continuous decline (Chen *et al.* 2001).

Furthermore, with the trend towards specialization in the services market, the development of finance and trade in Shanghai is more and more inclined to the international market especially services for very large multinational and national enterprises. The goal of Shanghai is to become the international finance and trade centre of the Far East. However, second-tier cities such as Suzhou, Wuxi and Changzhou could focus on local finance, logistics and information services for local small and medium enterprises. Shanghai, the primary-tier city in the Yangtze Delta, aims to develop producer services and their specialization so as to facilitate the agglomeration of producer services systems and modern manufacturing systems in its metropolitan region and thereby to foster the economics of scale. From this viewpoint, the second-tier cities may have market potential for some of the producer services sectors.

Some security sales departments in Su–Xi–Chang have good performance due to the abundance of local capital and the scarcity of stock institutions and the profit of a single sales department in Wuxi may reach 30 million Ren Min Bi, far higher than in Shanghai. However, financial services in Su–Xi–Chang have developed slowly with small added value and at a low level. Why have producer services not grown faster in this region? The most important reason is the historical background. From 1949, central government required all cities to change 'from consumption city to production city', so as to improve manufacturing productivity. At present, local governments prefer to invest in manufacturing industries rather than in the service sector. Moreover, the shadow of the monopolized market of Shanghai's producer services has affected the growth of the service sector in the second-tier cities in Yangtze River Delta. Finally, the lack of a proper environment and support has also contributed to the underdevelopment of services.

Cooperation with Shanghai

For a long time, Su–Xi–Chang has maintained a very close economic and social connection with Shanghai, the primary metropolis in the region. At the beginning of the last century when modern industries appeared entrepreneurs in this region looked for investment from Shanghai. Up to the 1980s, the development of TVEs was mainly dependent on the trickle-down effect of Shanghai's industries and the service of Shanghainese 'Sunday engineers', who worked on Sundays in the TVEs. In the 1990s, the growth of FDI and multinational corporate production sites in this area took advantage of the spill-over effect from Shanghai, which has attracted investment. Therefore, it is often said that without Shanghai today's Suzhou, Wuxi and Changzhou would not be as they are. The prosperity of Su–Xi–Chang is dependent upon Shanghai.

While Suzhou, Wuxi and Changzhou are expanding quickly and becoming cities with over 1 million population it is natural to ask whether they should promote technological development, R&D and services or just remain as a manufacturing base. Traditionally, Shanghai is thought of as a regional and national, even international, financial and services centre. Su–Xi–Chang are modern manufacturing cities. There are vertical subcontract chains between Shanghai and Su–Xi–Chang. Therefore, encouraging R&D and services development in Su–Xi–Chang would break the established pattern of the regional division of labour. The industrial development of Su–Xi–Chang cannot be separated from the whole industrial system in the region. That is, the development of R&D and producer services in Su–Xi–Chang should be examined through the development of Shanghai metropolitan area.

Industrial production and producer services have developed industrial commodity chains. Along with economic globalization vertical chains have been developed in the global urban system with each city being characterized by its position in this global chain. At the top of the vertical chain are the global cities where the headquarters of the multinationals are located. These global cities have the capacity to manage and control the activity of whole regions and even of the world. In the middle of the chain are the second-tier big cities, mostly clustered into multinational manufacturing bases. At the bottom are a large number of cities whose economic destinies are dependent upon and controlled by the global metropolises and foreign capital.

Suppose that a city is just like a big firm: the relationships between cities could be like those between firms. We can see now how cities have created vertical and horizontal relationships (Krugman 1997). Vertical specialization is dominated by comparative advantage, which is formed by natural endorsement. The divisions between primary products and finished products and between low-tech products and high-tech products occur between developed countries or regions and developing countries or regions. According to this view of comparative advantages Shanghai has obvious comparative advantages in services and other high-order functions within the Yangtze River Delta. The nearby region should become factories behind Shanghai's front market; these factories are at the bottom of the vertical division of industry. This would reduce economic returns in Su–Xi–Chang and further hinder the agglomeration of high-quality productive elements in this region. Thus, at the end of day there would be only one winner, Shanghai, and all others would lose out.

However, in the market economy, regional trade between several sectors would result in vertical division among cities. Profit could attract more cities to develop high-order functions so as to break the monopoly. This turns monopoly into competition or oligarchic monopoly. In such a circumstance, consumer surpluses will increase along with a decrease in prices. Obviously, the benefit is greater than in the monopoly situation: competition and horizontal market division provide differential and specialized products as well as reducing the risks of growth (Tirole 1997). Hence, with diversified horizontal division between firms, the situation has changed. Horizontal division is division between the internal parts of production and technical processes. This means that products could benefit from the economy of scale in the same industrial sectors. The more similar the development structure and level are, the closer are the inter-regional connections. Thus, horizontal division may stimulate product specialization and create greater market choice and competition. The structure is improved, and innovation and market performance increase (Jin 1999).

Meanwhile, high-tech industry or producer services are dependent upon the economics of scale and incomplete competition (Krugman 1997). Due to the threshold and demand of the scale economy and monopoly profit it is impossible for these sectors to expand without limit. The vast initial input cost (capital) and the entrance threshold would limit the number of cities (oligarchies) able to supply these industrial products. Hence, the market construction of this special industrial distribution is similar to oligarchic monopoly competition. If Shanghai and other second-tier cities (a few oligarchies) within the Yangtze Delta metropolitan area are encouraged to engage wholly in high-tech and productive service production they will develop strong innovative management and service systems for the whole economy. Furthermore, regional relations could be improved and the level of development would be raised. Moreover, development has shown the benefit of horizontal links between manufacturing products distributed in Shanghai and other cities in the Yangtze River Delta, especially in electronics, machinery and chemical equipment. This has created strong competitive advantages in the domestic market (Chen 2000).

According to the above analysis, it is essential to stimulate the horizontal division between manufacturing industries in the region and the division of high-tech industries and producer services between the primary and second-tier big cities, so as to maintain sustainable development and advantages. There are not only vertical divisions of industrial development between Shanghai and Su–Xi–Chang but also horizontal divisions. The second-tier cities might be upgraded from the manufacturing/secondary level to the management and control level.

Future prospects for growth

In the 1980s, the cities of Suzhou, Wuxi and Changzhou ignored the construction of the regional technological innovation and producer services systems during the rapid development of their manufacturing industry. Many enterprises, particularly the TVEs, mainly depended on the supply of R&D and producer services from Shanghai for production and trading. This has led to a position of unsustainable future economic development in the region. Hence, it is necessary to transfer economic production to technology-based manufacturing.

Suzhou, Wuxi and Changzhou have the opportunities and advantages to develop high-tech producer services, not only based on the manufacturing market and economic capacities but also built upon their convenient location, good infrastructure and urban environment. The main problem is that the sectors have to be developed in the shadow of Shanghai. However, the high-tech and producer services in the region may in future form diversified competition and horizontal division with Shanghai (Ni 2004), which may in turn stimulate the development of technology, innovation and services, not only in the individual cities but also throughout the entire Yangtze River Delta, facilitating overall competitiveness and economic cooperation.

Nevertheless, the development of high-tech industry is a natural adjustment of industrial structure and sustainable development in Su–Xi–Chang. National and regional policies and measures including the law, tax, venture capital and the investment environment should be deployed to accelerate industrial development inside and outside of high-tech development zones. The Su–Xi–Chang region should be dedicated to the creation of innovative research and innovations to improve the start-up environment through providing governmental services and good living conditions and through the establishment of an investment system for small and medium enterprises.

The development of producer services in Su–Xi–Chang aims to set up producer services for the local population and enterprises in the region, so as to sustain or enhance innovation and agglomeration. The following development approaches may be considered. First, developing market services including services for small and medium enterprises the branches of multinationals and local residents; second, developing producer services including providing loan and derivative finance and insurance, regional logistics, R&D services and university and vocational education; third, fostering productive organizations including the development of small and medium service agents or foreign-invested companies and localized branches of MNCs; fourth, promoting institutional reform including changes in local culture and innovation systems, and the promotion of human capital development. These approaches are not exclusive and should be used to complement each other so as to serve the economic development of the second-tier large cities.

Acknowledgement

We would like to thank the support from the Chinese Academy of Sciences (Project No. KZCX3-SW-427) and National Science Foundation of China (Project No. 40371031).

References

Baldwin, C. and Kim B. Clark (1997) 'Managing in an age of modularity', *Harvard Business Review*, 75 (5): 84–93.

Barnes, T. J. and M. S. Gertler (eds) (1999) *The New Industrial Geography: Regions, Regulation and Institutions*, 1st edition, London: Routledge.

Chen, J. J. (2000) *Economic Development of Chinese High-speed Increase Region: A Study on the Model of Jiangsu and Zhejiang*, Shanghai: Shanghai People Press (in Chinese).

Chen, W. (1996) 'An approach to several problems of China's urbanization development', *The Journal of Chinese Geography*, 6 (2): 35–41 (in Chinese).

Chen, W., C. J. Zhou, J. S. Wang, J. B. Xiang (2001) 'The industrial choice and the spatial organization', *Economic Geography*, 21 (6): 679–683 (in Chinese).

Funaba, M., M. Sasaki, Y.-S. Lee and A. R. Markusen (1999) 'Japanese technopolis policy: view from four cities', in A. R. Markysen, Y.-S. Lee and S. DiGiovanna (eds) *Second Tier Cities, Rapid Growth beyond the Metropolis*, Minneapolis, MN: University of Minnesota Press.

Hong,Y. X. and W. Chen (2000) 'The new development and the urbanization mode', *Economic Research*, 12: 66–71 (in Chinese).

Jin, P. (1999) *Economy of Industrial Organization*, Beijing: Economic Management Press (in Chinese).

Krugman, P. (1997) *Development, Geography and Economic Theory*, Cambridge, MA: MIT Press.

Lu, Z. (2001) 'Will China become the world factory?', *Chinese Industrial Economy*, 11: 5–9 (in Chinese).

Markusen, A. R. and S. DiGiovanna (1999) 'Comprehending fast-growing regions', in A. R. Markusen, Y.-S. Lee and S. DiGiovanna (eds) *Second Tier Cities, Rapid Growth beyond the Metropolis*, Minneapolis, MN: University of Minnesota Press.

Markusen, A. R. and M. Sasaki (1999) 'Oita and Kumamoto: technopolises without brains', in A. R. Markusen, Y.-S. Lee and S. DiGiovanna (eds) *Second Tier Cities, Rapid Growth beyond the Metropolis*, Minneapolis, MN: University of Minnesota Press.

Ni, P. F. (2004) *Annual Report on Urban Competitiveness, Positioning: Way to Mutual Prosperity*, Beijing: Social Sciences Documentary Publisher.

Sharksening, A. (1999) *Regional Advantage – the Culture and Competition between Silicon Valley and Route 128*, Shanghai: Far Eastern Publisher (in Chinese).

State Statistical Bureau (1995) *Science and Technological Statistical Yearbook of Jiangsu 1995*, Beijing: China Statistics Press.

——(1995) *Shanghai Statistical Yearbook 1995*, Beijing: China Statistics Press.

——(1996) *Suzhou Statistical Yearbook 1996*, Beijing: China Statistics Press.

——(1996) *Wuxi Statistical Yearbook 1996*, Beijing: China Statistics Press.

——(2000) *Science and Technological Statistical Yearbook of Jiangsu 2000*, Beijing: China Statistics Press.

——(2000) *Shanghai Statistical Yearbook 2000*, Beijing: China Statistics Press.

——(2001) *Suzhou Statistical Yearbook 2001*, Beijing: China Statistics Press.

——(2001) *Wuxi Statistical Yearbook 2001*, Beijing: China Statistics Press.

——(2002) *Changzhou Statistical Yearbook 2002*, Beijing: China Statistics

——(2002) *China Statistical Yearbook 2002*, Beijing: China Statistics Press.

——(2002) *Jiangsu Statistical Yearbook 2002*, Beijing: China Statistics Press.

——(2002) *Shanghai Statistical Yearbook 2002*, Beijing: China Statistics Press.

——(2002) *Suzhou Statistical Yearbook 2002*, Beijing: China Statistics Press.

——(2002) *Wuxi Statistical Yearbook 2002*, Beijing: China Statistics Press.

——(2002) *Zhejiang Statistical Yearbook 2002*, Beijing: China Statistics Press.

——(2003) *Changzhou Statistical Yearbook 2003*, Beijing: China Statistics Press.

——(2003) *Jiangsu Statistical Yearbook 2003*, Beijing: China Statistics Press.

——(2003) *Suzhou Statistical Yearbook.2003*, Beijing: China Statistics Press.

——(2003) *Wuxi Statistical Yearbook 2003*, Beijing: China Statistics Press.

Tirole, J. (1997) *The Theory of Industrial Organization*, Beijing: Chinese People University Press.

Zhong, J. (2001) *Analysis of the System of Global Silicon Valley Mode*, Beijing: Chinese Social Science Publishing House (in Chinese).

Zhu, T. H. (1994) 'Approach to the south Jiangsu model', *Modern Theory*, 1: 16–21 (in Chinese).

Zhu, Z. Y. (2002) 'The enter mode and the management stratagem transformation of FDI: Example on Suzhou', *World Economy*, 10: 16–22 (in Chinese).

14 Political and economic implications of new public spaces in Chinese and Asian global cities

Steven W. Lewis

What role might public spaces play in the globalization of cities? Theories of the global city and the entrepreneurial city predict that integration into the labor, capital, and technological networks that comprise the global marketplace will cause urban residents to identify more and more with transnational political, economic, and social groups. And yet how these transformations in individual identification will occur is unclear. Many scholars examine the print and broadcast media looking to see how the state uses these in political campaigns to shape collective identity. Others look at the changing visual and textual rhetoric of the more traditional media of popular culture – film, literature, the visual, and performing arts – to see how domestic and international capital are calling on people to think beyond local and national communities (Ong 1999, Wang 2001, 2003). Left unexplored is the influence of new public spaces and the medium most common in them: advertising.

This chapter examines changes in the local political advertisements in the new public spaces of Chinese and Asian cities to explore how they may become locations with potential to shape the collective identities of the urban residents who move through them. As a first step toward uncovering these relationships, this study compares the public service advertisements (PSAs) in Beijing and Shanghai subway stations (1998–2002) with those in Hong Kong (2001–2002), Singapore and Taipei (1999–2002) to see what issues and policies are being promoted by local governments in these globalizing cities.[1] This study shows, first, that there seems to be a progression or development of themes that corresponds with the degree of local economic development and integration into the global economy. Second, there seems to be a visual and textual rhetoric in public service advertisements that corresponds with the role of the state in these societies. Third, and somewhat counter-intuitively, the PSAs do not present appeals to the commuters to think of themselves as competitors with other cities in a global economy. Fourth, the technology – formats, language, and the semiotics of visual and textual rhetoric – of public advertisements in subways affects their potential as media of discourse in these new public spaces. Finally, this discussion illustrates the need for inter-disciplinary research into the creation and influence of the advertising medium in these new public spaces.

In the first section, I argue that subway stations are new public spaces in Chinese cities that have a potentially large impact on the views and attitudes of China's rapidly urbanizing population. They are important as political symbols, as political arenas, as centers of economic exchange, and as locations for social interaction. As with shopping malls and cinemas they have become prominent new public spaces in Asia's global cities. I also argue that advertisements, the medium most common in these commercialized public spaces, may have a powerful, although as yet undetermined, long-term influence on the views and affinities of urbanites.

In the second section I compare the messages of subway advertisements across various Chinese and Asian global cities over time. Previous research shows that commercial advertisements in subway stations in these cities present imaginaries asking urbanites to join local, national, and transnational communities of consumers (Lewis 2003).[2] Here I examine public service advertisements in order to understand the evolving role of government in shaping the media of new public spaces in Asian globalizing cities. What are these local governments – with their unique histories and institutions of political economy – calling on urbanites to do? Are they asking them to identify with or compete with the citizens of other global cities? What other actors are asking citizens of these global cities to act in developing public goods, and what are their messages in these new public spaces? Finally, I conclude with a discussion of the limitations of this research and speculation about how this research may cause us to re-evaluate theories of the global city and the entrepreneurial city.

Subways as new public spaces

Subway stations in Chinese and Asian cities are not just transportation hubs. They are public spaces comprising a vast array of interconnected forms of political, economic, and social interaction. Many of the oldest subways in European, Russian, and American cities were constructed in the early twentieth century by governments and state-owned corporations in order to provide low-cost, efficient transportation for rapidly urbanizing and industrializing populations. As such, these 'public' subway stations themselves became political symbols through discussion of the associated public goods issues, especially taxation, efficiency, and safety, which arose in their development.

> [T]he most important thing about the evolution of the subway as a symbol is that it starts by expressing faith in the city's future and, once built, quickly becomes a handy rhetorical tool for expressing discontent with its present.
>
> (Brooks 1997)

They can be viewed popularly as symbols of distinctly local problems and achievements. Consider their portrayal as dangerous, crime-ridden subterranean spaces in popular paintings and art in London, Paris, and New York (Bobrick 1981), or as the playgrounds of youth gangs in such films and books as

The Warriors (Yurick 1965). On the other hand, when they are perceived to run smoothly and efficiently, they can become popular measures of successful local development. The quality of their operation, as with utilities and other local public goods, is an easily identifiable, individually observable daily metric of comfort (or discomfort) for hundreds of millions of commuters worldwide.

This political rhetoric establishing subways as symbols of urban development can be reinforced by the advertising campaigns of the transportation authorities and subway corporations themselves. Hong Kong's MRT proudly proclaims,

> [w]ith effective and efficient management in planning, design, operations, maintenance and continuous improvement of our railway services, we have achieved a world-class performance in safety, reliability, service quality and efficiency – becoming Hong Kong's fast track to a world-class city.[3]

Subways can thus be presented as unique symbols of modernity and economic development, the public valuation of which is their performance in comparison with subways in other "world-class cities."

But subways are also symbols of distinctly national political issues. Consider their extensive construction and use as civil defense shelters in times of war, particularly the Cold War. Or consider how they are viewed as important infra-structural features necessary for hosting international sporting events, including the Olympics and the World Cup. And if they tie into national government owned and operated railway systems their operation can become symbols of heated, partisan national political debate, as in Britain in recent years.

Subways can even figure prominently in public discourse about international trade and investment. European and Japanese trade negotiators have sought to claim political capital with their populations by successfully arranging large contracts for local manufacturers to provide subway trains to countries with which they have unpopular trade imbalances, China in particular. The American government, on the other hand, has been criticized for allowing domestic investors to reduce their income tax burden through the buying and leasing of subways and other public utilities in European cities.

And subways as physical spaces are sometimes high-profile political arenas. An individual with a sign, a billboard, or a megaphone can easily send a political message to a host of commuters and tourists streaming by. Striking workers, espe-cially subway employees, can quickly mobilize popular support if stranded com-muters believe that their cause is just or that they need to be accommodated in order to end disruptions in transportation. Subway stations can even serve as museums or performance halls when they display the messages of other media, including music (Tanenbaum 1995), graffiti (Miller 2002), and installation art (Seoul 2000). Commercial advertisements in subways can provoke political debate in other popular media, as in Hong Kong when the PRC Company Mengniu placed advertisements for milk using the picture of a Chinese astronaut and the phrase, in simplified characters, 'Strong Chinese People'. Coming at a time of heated debate about Mainland influence on political reforms in the former

British colony commentators criticized the advertisement as symptomatic of the denigration of Hong Kong's identity and local culture (IHT 2004).

Their prominence has also made subways and urban railways high-profile targets for violent political protest and terrorism. Consider the attempts to change government policies in the wake of subway and railway bombings in Spain, London, and Moscow in recent years. Or consider the broad debates on national policies on religious freedom and national security following the sarin gas attacks by Aum Shinrikyo in Tokyo in 1996.

Such attacks can at least temporarily capture the attention of national and international populations, but they also may shape profoundly the views of urbanites who see themselves as the targets of these attacks. Although research in this area is exploratory subways may figure prominently in the way city dwellers orient themselves psychologically in order to navigate through the complex living environments that are global cities (Garling 1995, Groat 1995, Shuffield 2002). More specifically, commuters may think of them as spaces that are uniquely public and private.

Interviews with the survivors of the Tokyo gas attacks reveal, counter-intuitively, that many felt such attacks on the national body politic were directed at them personally (Murakami 2001). These subway riders may have believed this because they had come to personalize these public spaces through the development of daily routines placing them at set boarding positions and at certain seats within certain cars at specific times. As Aum Shinrikyo members simultaneously released the deadly chemicals on many subway lines, a subway rider's idiosyncratic choice of time, train, and location within the train – upwind or downwind of the gas as it was released – thus largely determined his or her chances of survival.

As the interviews show, these blind and indiscriminate attacks by one group caused millions of survivors to re-evaluate the daily ordering of their lives. Bombing of a public square, a café, or a theater may cause many to wonder if they should frequent such places. But bombs in a few subway stations can impel the millions of survivors who are forced to pass through them daily to question their lifestyles: "Why didn't I pass through that station at that time that day?" Such impact is only possible in a society where people must commute to work through a location which is considered to be public (a symbolic target) and private (a personalized space). Clearly subways are a public space capable of creating these powerful individual psychological reflections for large segments of societies.

Subway stations in the global cities of Asia, however, may play an additional role in the development of public spaces. As with their earlier counterparts in Europe and the Americas, Tokyo and Beijing subways began as publicly financed projects of national and local governments. The first two subway lines in Beijing were constructed as underground civil defense shelters. Tokyo's oldest subway lines were established by semi-private companies. As such they have also figured prominently as political symbols of local and national development. Coming much later, Taipei's MRT was also a key battleground in an ongoing ideological debate between political parties and leaders, central, and local authorities (Lee 2005).

But railway stations and subways in many Asian global cities, including Beijing, Hong Kong, Shanghai, Singapore, and Taipei are also centers for retail trade and individual consumption. Following the lead of the powerful land development and railway company groups in Japan, subway corporations are promoting a new model of the subway station as a transportation hub below ground and commercial and residential living space above ground. Consider the residential and office skyscrapers, and the attached labyrinthine underground shopping arcades, built in suburban Tokyo: Ikebukuro, Shinjuku, and Shibuya. Even where urban railways were initially financed by the state and operated by government agencies – as in Taipei or Beijing – privatization in the 1990s has turned their newest stations into small-scale shopping malls. With rapid urbanization, and plans by more than 20 PRC cities to develop their own, subways will become a commercialized public space shared by hundreds of millions of urban Chinese.

Finally, subway stations are also potentially influential new public spaces of social interaction. These places may be particularly important for those parts of the urban population which have lost traditional public spaces – small parks, gardens, and recreational sites – to urban development. Where do children and the retired population spend their leisure time as these global cities are reworked into dynamic, accelerated work environments (Wang 2001)? The shopping malls of the new subway stations may become a significant social location for those not yet part of, or who are no longer members of, the working population.

Observant advertisers noticed that young women formed distinct consumption-oriented social groups in Taipei's MRT mall. They then developed advertisements using witty, cynical, and hip political puns in order to create a location and group-specific form of interactive, consumption-mediated political discourse. Young women who could decipher and interpret the language and imagery of these advertisements responded by returning again and again to these shopping malls. Advertisers succeeded because they were able to use the architecture of these new public spaces to develop a medium that could convey these appeals to such an imaginary "xinxing renlei" (new breeds of human) (Liao 2003). We must wonder if the state in the new global cities of Asia is capable of developing such sophisticated interactions with those urbanites who view these venues primarily as social spaces.

Public service advertisements in new public spaces

Governments can often control the capital, labor, and technologies of production of books, films, journals, and newspapers. The broadcast media – radio and television – can be controlled in similar fashion, and also because they represent classic public goods problems: with market failure their effective use requires coordination of a limited amount of airwaves. These media are more likely to be used by and to reflect the interests of that part of the nation-state that can most effectively control them, the central government. Subway advertisements, however, are capable of portraying the interests of local governments and corporations in addition to those of national and transnational actors. As with outdoor advertisements, we should observe variation in their content across localities as local governments use them to promote their distinct development goals (Lewis 2002).

In the context of decentralization, liberalization, and integration with the global economy, the governments of China's major cities increasingly must compete with the countryside, other Chinese cities, and those cities around the world that are also tied in to international networks of capital, people, and technology (Sassen 1991, 2002, Friedmann 2002). These governments must present many new images of their cities before many populations, near and far.

In order to make the transition from post-socialist city to global city they must attract new capital, people, and technologies. This includes changing the historical image of the city that already exists in the minds of domestic and foreign investors. Beijing has had to shed its portrayal as the home of an enormous bureaucracy, the headquarters of the military, and the location of such large sunset industry enterprises as Capital Iron and Steel. Likewise, Shanghai has had to rework its image as the outdated, over-milked cash cow of the central government, as the home of crowded tenements, and as the site of countless small-scale textile and clothing factories. The Beijing government is now keen to promote the information technology laboratories of Zhongguancun and Haidian District, while Shanghai proudly points to the financial, insurance, and service sector towers of Lujiazui. Both are intended to be beacons for new investors, both Chinese and foreign (Wu 2000a,b).

These city governments must struggle to find the fiscal resources to pay for the social costs of closing state-owned enterprises and downsizing government agencies. At the same time, they must build the communication, transportation, education, and technological infrastructure necessary to support new industries and economic sectors. China's local governments must therefore also make appeals to their citizens to pay their taxes and support such public goods. In doing so they make appeals to Beijingers and Shanghainese to think of themselves first and foremost as proud local citizens, inheritors of a glorious metropolitan heritage, and yet also as bold pioneers in the construction of new spaces that can compete with the great cities of the world. As with land and real estate developers, local governments have a need to use subway advertisements to refashion the way urbanites view their cities as their homes.

Millions of commuters in Asian cities descend daily to stand on platforms and await trains to carry them to and from their workplaces. As they wait they are compelled to look at large, back-lit billboards on the other side of the subway tracks. These billboards act as windows overlooking fantastic, exotic, and lush commercial landscapes: sports cars parked on beaches; fashion models posing on glaciers, polar bears hawking synthetic fibers; movie stars selling lipstick; three-person families playing in luxury condominiums; and skateboarders pushing cell phones. And yet in among these many commercial advertisements are a few billboards selling distinctly civic-oriented messages: athletes telling all to donate blood; stern text advising commuters to speak with civility in public spaces; the impoverished asking for medical assistance; politicians soliciting votes; and proud soldiers calling on compatriots to enlist. As with outdoor advertisements on the shopping and residential streets of Chinese cities, the public service advertisements in Chinese subways are not as common as the multitude of commercial advertisements. But they appear in many forms and carry diverse messages in these new public spaces.

I start with an examination to see if the content of public service advertisement[4] matches the stated and assumed (theoretical) goals of local governments in transition. Here, we would expect to find advertisements calling on citizens to support local governments as they try to brand themselves in the minds of potential investors and urban taxpayers. We might also expect to find a visual and textual rhetoric of competition, as these cities compete with each other to develop their own ties to global networks of capital, labor, and technologies. Related, we should also see the development of formats in public service advertisements – increasingly sophisticated use of images and text – over time as these cities become more tied in with the global economy. Finally, we should expect to see variation in the formats and sources of public service advertisements across these cities that share many aspects of a common culture and yet have very different political and economic systems. More specifically, we might expect to see a greater presence of non-governmental organizations in cities where they are allowed to incorporate and operate more freely – Singapore, Hong Kong, and Taipei – and less so in the PRC's Beijing and Shanghai.

Beijing

Murals depicting national historical figures and cultural and scientific achievements have stood across from the platforms in some of the oldest subway stations – most notably Jianguomen – in Beijing since their creation, seemingly blocking the placement of the new electric billboards. Nearby, on the pillars of these stations, have appeared more than 30 posters in small postings that also show off China's rich cultural heritage: well-known landscapes and famous couplets of poetry. On a few other pillars can be seen posters asking people – from a 1996 municipal government decree – to observe the norms of "socialist spiritual civilization" (shehui zhuyi jingshen wenming).

By 1998, when electric billboards had been introduced to many of these stations – sometimes crowded around the existing murals – they were reserved for the messages of commercial advertisements. Only in 1999 did the first public service advertisement appear on these larger billboards, and by 2000 there were many, with most tied in to specific multi-media campaigns of local and national government. A popular performance artist asks a stuffed panda, "Do you mind my smoking?" The panda replies, "Do you mind my extinction?" A young mother plays with her daughter in a field of flowers, a picture of what life could be like, if family planning laws were obeyed. A little girl embraces a gray-haired couple in a sun-drenched park with text advising all that respect for the elderly is everybody's responsibility. Famous athletes and entertainers smile, roll up their sleeves, and implore commuters to join them in donating blood. Figure 14.1 shows using

Figure 14.1 Advertisement in Beijing about preventing AIDS.

Figure 14.2 Advertisement in Beijing about the subway policemen.

national celebrities to promote public awareness of social problems in China:
Actor Pu Cunxin, AIDS Ambassador, calls on commuters to fight AIDS in a
Ministry of Public Health public service advertisement appearing in Beijing
subways in 2004. The advertisement reads: "Preventing AIDS is the responsibility
of all of Society; Love and Cherish Life and Resist AIDS." Figure 14.2 shows local
government personifying and localizing public order in Chinese subway stations
for a global commuter: The Qianmen subway station transit police provide emer-
gency contact information in Chinese and English in a 2004 announcement.

More focused advertisements ask commuters to call the local consumer rights association to report fraudulent products. A couple – with one child – relaxes on the vast green of a park as accompanying text from the State Drug Administrations asks viewers to report fake medicines. Many others show athletes in training, a call to support the capital's campaign to attract the 2008 Olympics and to host the Special Olympics.

In 2000, advertisements promoting local economic development began to appear. Large, formal red characters ask commuters to support reforms and economic development. Underneath, the distant image of skyscrapers is tied to several smaller symbols of modernity in the foreground, of subways, highways, subway stations, and satellite dishes. The text of a similar advertisement tells commuters to "liberate your thinking, seek truth from facts, and commit your support for the policies of reform and opening up" (jiefang sixiang, shishi qiushi, jianding buyi de tuijin gaige kaifang) with images below of skyscrapers, and somewhat incongruously for landlocked Beijing, a large ocean ship next to a thundering sea.

A 2002 advertisement, in much the same style, has the bronze statue of a dragon gazing at a glittering forest of office towers, with text above telling commuters to implement the "three represents" (sange daibiao) of Jiang Zemin and to make the capital into a modern city through hard work and struggle. Finally, a smaller poster on a pillar promotes, in Chinese and in English, the "Sixth Major Cities Summit," to be held in Beijing in 2000. Here a smaller version of the Temple of Heaven stands before three towering, mirrored skyscrapers, with doves flying overhead.

Shanghai

Built in the mid-1990s, the subway stations in Shanghai have more space for retail shops and for advertisements than their counterparts in Beijing. A few stations have murals, but here in East China the lit billboards predominate. Public service advertisements appeared in 1998 in Shanghai, earlier than Beijing, with simple textual ones proscribing the "seven do nots" (qi bu guifan) of civilized behavior,[5] advertising the China Welfare Lottery, and promoting investment in the Caohejing High-Technology Development Zone (in English and Chinese, above a photo of modern office blocks: "We Always Aim High – Shanghai Caohejing Hi-Tech Park"). In 1999, the same man and the same panda from the anti-smoking campaign in Beijing asked Shanghai commuters to give up smoking. Shanghai also had one bright red billboard with facial photographs of "model enterprise" workers, including both Chinese and foreign employees of "advanced enterprises" in the city.

As in Beijing, 2000 saw the introduction of many more policy-oriented public service advertisements in the subways. Over a picture of a forest, characters implore commuters to "Respect the Flora, Protect the Environment: Make our Home Even More Beautiful" (aihu luhua, baohu huanjing: rang women jiayuan geng meili). Text over a picture of flowers and a baby asks for blood donations.

Figure 14.3 Advertisement in Shanghai about "civilized behavior."

In one of the few advertisements using national political symbols, a host of colorfully dressed people, representing China's nationalities, parade in front of The Gate of Heavenly Peace in Beijing and the Great Wall. Characters above ask the peoples of the world to unite peacefully. And in leading by example, simple red characters on a white background announce that the workers of the subway will provide excellent service in order to create a civilized space for commuters. Figure 14.3 shows local subway companies using images of metropolitan vistas to promote civic pride and civil behavior in subway stations: in 2004 Shanghai's subway company presents images of the Shanghai Concert Hall, a towering river bridge, the Bund, and the skyscrapers of Lujiazui, above a cartoon family, asking commuters to, "Make Beautiful Shanghainese Through Orderly Subway Transit." Local subway companies and local governments use images of civilized behavior to promote public order in Chinese subway stations: in 2004 Shanghai's subway company and the Huangpu District Committee for the Construction of Spiritual Civilization show pictures of orderly queuing and giving up seats to mothers bearing children with the slogan, "Make Beautiful Shanghainese Through Orderly Subway Transit" (Figure 14.4). Local government also use national and local pride to promote local development through presenting an image of the city as a financial hub of the nation to its commuters. The Office of Coordination and

Figure 14.4 Advertisement in Shanghai showing how to become a "civilized person."

Cooperation of the Shanghai Municipal People's Government tells commuters, above images of the skyscrapers of the Lujiazui Financial Zone in Pudong District, "Circulating Into the Whole Country, Serving the Whole Country." This 2004 advertisement is also an example of the recycling of images in Chinese public service advertisements (Figure 14.5, see also the photograph of Lujiazui in Figure 14.3).

Another scene of skyscrapers and the East China Television Tower in Shanghai has multi-colored Chinese characters and English words together overhead: "Love wo ni ta: zhenqing shan shi zhong" (Love Myself, You and Him/Her: Start off True and See it Through). Other advertisements ask people to support the Special Olympics and to go to the Art Museum for public events. One advertisement has simple red characters asking viewers to pay their taxes because it is the "civilized thing to do" (yi fa na shui: shi xiandai wenming de biaozhi). Finally, over the aerial photograph of a green plain and a river next to a cluster of glittering skyscrapers characters remind Shanghainese, "We have all come from the same level to advance toward tomorrow."

Some public service advertisements announce public events as a reflection of the ways Shanghai leaders want their citizens to view their place in the world, as well as the way they want foreigners to view Shanghai. The 2001 Asia-Pacific Economic Cooperation (APEC) organization meeting in Shanghai prompted the placement of two billboard advertisements. In one, over the drawing of the top half of a pacific ocean globe, with lotus flowers below, text in Chinese characters

Figure 14.5 Advertisement in Shanghai about Shanghai's role in serving the whole nation.

(jiaqiang hezuo zoujin yatai diqu jingji fazhan) above and English below (Promote Economic Development in the Asia-Pacific Region Through Cooperation) heralds the meeting. In another, using only English words (Welcome to APEC China 2001), there is an aerial view of the towers of Lujiazui, but looking eastward from Puxi to Pudong, with only the tops of the historic colonial buildings of the Bund visible at forefront in the bottom.

The year 2002 brought new political or public education campaigns from the Shanghai government. Large characters in front of a picture of trees in bloom advises, "Take nature into our hearts, sow beauty throughout the world" (ba lu bo zai xinli, ba mei sa xiang renjian). The Shanghai State Administration of Industry and Commerce (SSAIC) and the Shanghai Consumer Protection Association place a uniformed male SSAIC officer standing behind a primly dressed woman wearing a telephone headset, and telling commuters to call the Consumer Protection Hotline if they have any problems. Another example of the privatization of public service advertisements through the piggy-backing of commercial with public message, this advertisement at bottom has a separate panel advertising the credit card services of the Shenzhen Bank of Development (Lewis 2002). And there is an advertisement promoting Shanghai as a venue for events of global importance. In front of an ocean red with the sunset, a male child reaches up toward a blue globe with the Shanghai Expo 2010 logo. Below, there are characters (qipan: zhongguo 2010 shanghai shibo hui) (Hope: the China 2010 Shanghai World Expo), and also English text "Bring Our Wishes Into Reality."

Finally, in 2002, there are three political advertisements created by and bearing the logo of the Shanghai Subway Corporation. On a wall, a small poster of "Famous Words from Famous People" (mingren mingyan) has the image of a traditional calligraphy brush and inkstone, with characters written in a clear hand-written style, attributed to the reform leader Deng Xiaoping: "I am a son of China. I deeply love my motherland and my people" (wo shi zhongguo ren de erzi.

Wo shenjing de aizhe wode zuguo he renmin – Deng Xiaoping). The second advertisement, also a small wall poster, asks people to celebrate national politics. At top, Chinese characters announce, "Welcome the Great Achievements of the 16th Communist Party Congress" and, unusual for a Chinese advertisement, there is a line immediately below with the pinyin romanization for each of these characters (yi youyi chengji yingjie dang de shiliuda). In the background, in an example of the recycling of political advertisements, is a hammer and sickle floating over a scene of the Great Wall, with a multitude of people in various ethnic costumes and clothing. These are the same people and background vista used in the 2000 advertisement asking peoples of the world to unite peacefully.

The third advertisement, a large backlit billboard, further recycles this visual rhetoric, taking the remaining pieces of the 2000 advertisement – the Gate of Heavenly Peace in Beijing and the Great Wall, but without any figures of people – and adding Chinese characters above, "Be patriotic and law-abiding; be polite and trustworthy; be cooperative and friendly; be frugal and independent; be committed and selfless (ai guo zun fa; ming li cheng xin; tuan jie you shan; qin jian zi qiang; jing ye feng xian) in an excerpt from the "Implementing measures for the construction of civic morality" (gongmin daode jianshe shishi gangyao).

Singapore

Singapore's public service advertisements are produced by the Singapore government, a few non-local governmental organizations, and the Singapore Metropolitan Rail Transit (SMRT) corporation (formed in 1987 with the construction of the first subway line). Advertisements use only English text and images of people to educate Singaporeans about government services and to promote national military service.

In one of the few public service advertisements to depict Singapore as a place, a seated woman and a man standing behind her look at a computer screen, with the glittering skyscrapers and highways of Singapore beneath the purple sky of a setting sun. English text tells the citizens, "Prosperity: Committed to defend, confident of victory." The same text appears in another military service advertisement, this time with the image of a mother clutching a baby and gazing out over the verdant parks and residential towers of the city. Another national service advertisement, from 2002, has a close-up image of a navy frog man climbing out of the ocean toward the viewer, covered in black wet suit, wearing face goggles and toting a machine gun: "Smothered in a numbing dark night sea. Perfect."

A final government advertisement, from 2000, promotes the Singapore 21 omnibus government social policy campaign, begun in 1997, with images of four Asian children imploringly looking up at the viewer. Text announces the five key elements of the campaign to promote family planning, education, racial tolerance, public service, and civic morality, "Singapore 21: Together we make the difference; Every Singaporean Matters; Opportunities for all; Strong Families: Our Foundation and Our Future; The Singapore Heartbeat; Active Citizens: Making a Difference to Society."[6]

Non-governmental organizations also make appeals to Singapore citizens. The Singapore Trade Development Board advertises a campaign to protect intellectual property rights with the image of a young, beautiful woman staring straight at the viewer, "Stop Piracy! Protect our *Creative Works* and your *Future*." Student organizations use close-up images of a beautiful woman and a battered woman to increase awareness of violence against women, and a civil organization uses smiling faces of the physically and mentally handicapped to encourage employers to hire the disabled. The face of a red panda sits beneath large red English text, "ENDANGERED SPECIES." Finally, in a 2000 advertisement, a photograph of the smiling face of a little girl lies placed over the head of a body lying in a dark alley, "She wasn't born a heroin addict."

Appeals to Singaporeans as individuals to change their public behavior are left to the SMRT, which does so mainly through cartoons, many with a lion mascot (and in English, Malay, and Thai), advising commuters to be courteous to fellow commuters and to move efficiently through these public spaces. The only Chinese character advertisements are a series of SMRT advertisements with abstract shapes and vibrant colors, with large calligraphic characters and common English text translations. Four advertisements draw on the Analects of Confucius (lun yu):

> If one learns from others but does not think, one will be bewildered. If, on the other hand, one thinks but does not learn from others, one will be in peril (xue er bu si ze wang; si er bu xue ze dai).
>
> (2:15)

> The rule of virtue can be compared to the Pole Star which commands the homage of the multitude of stars without leaving its place (wei zheng yi de, pi ru bei chen zhong xing gong zhi).
>
> (2:1)

> If one sets strict standards for oneself and makes allowances for others when making demands on them, one will stay clear of ill will (gong zi hou, er bo ze yu ren, ze yuan yuan yi).
>
> (15:15)

> There are nine things the gentleman turns his thought to: to seeing clearly when he uses his eyes, to hearing acutely when he uses his ears, to looking cordial when it comes to his countenance, to appearing respectful when it comes to his demeanour, to being conscientious when he speaks, to being reverent when he performs his duties, to seeking advice when he is in doubt, to the consequences when he is enraged, and to what is right at the sight of gain. (jun zi you jiu si, shi si ming, ting si cong, se si wen, mao si gong, yan si zhong, shi si jing, fen si nan, jian de si yix.)
>
> (16:10)[7]

Taipei

Taipei's new subway stations had few public service advertisements in 1999, mainly comprising small posters in posting in the stairwells and entrances. The Taipei Municipal Government used these to promote several campaigns. In one, a group of faceless, abstract white figures seem to be walking into a haze of gray miasma, with a knife, a gun, and blood-spatters inside: "The dark side... it's hard to come back from; Keep gangs from infiltrating school campuses; The Taipei municipal government cares about you" ("hei" le... jiu hen nan "bai" hui lai; fangzhi bangpai shenru xiaoyuan; taipeishi zhengfu guangxin nin). In another, a large hand reaches toward the viewer, grasping a red circle with a line drawn down across, and large English characters, "Anti-Corruption," with Chinese characters above, "Put on some repellent... fight the corruption virus!" (fangtan chengxu qidong zhong... jujue tanwu bingdu ruqin!). Other local government advertisements promote the consumption of local fruits and vegetables, local tourism, and protection of animals.

Non-governmental organizations place advertisements asking philosophical or spiritual questions, often with ties to morality and ethics. The Love the Earth More Foundation uses simple text and the picture of a globe to ask commuters to slow down and to contemplate, "What is life for?" The Child Care Foundation uses the image of a galaxy of stars and simple Chinese characters to implore commuters to find charity in their hearts.

The Taibei MRT Company puts up the only posters placing Taipei as a location. Several use photographs of Taipei streets, skyscrapers, and public monuments (the Chiang Kai-Shek Memorial Hall) to portray the city as a clean, dynamic modern metropolis.

The year 2000 brought many more campaigns from the national and local government. A young man in white naval uniform stands in front of a missile cruiser plowing through the sea, with simple white characters above declaring, "See all under heaven, command the four seas; join the navy and have it all" (zongheng tianxia, sihai chengxiong; jiaru haijun, yici yongyou). A beautiful young woman clad in black leather points a handgun at the viewer, with English characters, "AIDS Terminator" beside her, and Chinese characters, "I'll terminate AIDS, starting with you!" (zhongjie aizi, cong ni wo zuoqi!). Another advertisement uses smiling cartoon couples and simple text advising commuters to not to be afraid of contracting AIDS from simple physical contact. A hand inserting a car key into the mouth of a bottle warns citizens to avoid driving while drunk. A woman lying on a couch and staring out the window mournfully tells citizens to avoid abusive relationships in marriage. A cartoon of woman reading a book advises citizens to promote literacy. The Ministry of Finance uses simple characters over photographs of foreign currency to announce that economic growth depends upon stability in financial markets (jinrong you anding, jingji geng chengzhang).

Many more advertisements of private religious foundations and groups advise commuters to behave with morality. The year 2001 saw a proliferation of governmental advertisements on the same issues as 1999 and 2000, and new advertisements protecting copyrights, promoting traffic safety and relief for earthquake victims.

Political parties also ran advertisements of candidates, commonly with a photograph of the candidate standing in front of a field of colors similar to those of the political party, and also frequently making reference to Taiwan's position in the world. One candidate, Zhang Youru, announces that she is 29 years old and that she will "bring the world back to Taiwan" (wo ba shijie daihui taiwan). In a 2002 advertisement, Zhongshan and Datong candidate Lin Jinzhang holds forth a fist and declares that he will make Taipei into a "world-class capital city" (dazau taibei wei shijie diqiu guo shoudu).

In 2002, famous actors urge giving up cigarettes. The Aboriginal Affair Commission uses close-up images of two young men, one wearing a white Western-style business shirt and the other a colored uniform, standing in front of an ocean vista to promote equal opportunity in hiring: "Give aboriginal people a chance at work" (gei yuanzhumin yifen gongzuo jihui). The health commission advises people to look for the symptoms of hepatitis and psychological depression. And as in previous years, there are few non-governmental organizations – a few advertisements from the Taiwan Red Cross – other than those of religious groups. Overall, most advertisements use only a small amount of English.

Hong Kong

Hong Kong, in contrast to Taipei, Singapore, Beijing, and Shanghai, has both many advertisements from governmental agencies and also many international non-governmental organizations. Many advertisements use English and Chinese, and there was only one advertisement in 2001 and 2002 that had an image of cityscape, an MTR corporation advertisement putting the image of the Sphinx over an MTR stop set amidst a forest of luminous skyscrapers.

The World Wildlife Fund, UNICEF, Oxfam, Medecins Sans Frontier, World Vision Hunger, and Greenpeace have advertisements in the Hong Kong subways. Most use simple images of impoverished non-Asian children and Chinese characters. Government agencies use English and Chinese to promote awareness of medical services, breast cancer awareness, equal opportunity in hiring, adoption services, pension benefits, and various anti-crime campaigns. A group of young Asian people stroll arm in arm down the street behind the close up image of a cellphone, asking people to call the Independent Commission on Anti-Corruption to report graft, with playful Chinese characters above, "Give us a call if you need to: the choice of a smart new generation" (ying da jiu da: xin renlei zhishi) and English words below, "3G Power: Go Get the Grafters." In another, over a photograph of three tough young men selling CDs and VCDs on the ramp of the ferry terminal, the Intellectual Property Department of the HKSAR advises commuters not to buy pirated goods.

Conclusions and future research

What are local governments calling on urbanites to do? The surveys of public service advertisements across these Asian "Chinese" cities show important variations in themes and formats that might affect the nature of discourse in these new public spaces.

First, there seems to be a progression or development of themes that corresponds with the degree of local economic development and integration into the global economy. The Beijing and Shanghai governments are still trying to establish themselves as important economic centers in the minds of investors and citizens, as reflected in the many advertisements presenting an image of the developed city to the citizens themselves. Their subways have many advertisements with visual and textual rhetoric calling on citizens to support economic reforms in order to make their urban homes into advanced (shining, skyscrapered, highwayed, and subwayed) cities. Although both local governments and real estate development companies use images of the city, the Shanghai and Beijing governments do not seem to present nostalgic images of the city in their public service announcements. National monuments – the Great Wall, the Forbidden City – appear in advertisements for national campaigns on racial harmony and supporting the Communist Party, but the Shanghai's colonial Bund and Beijing's hutongs are replaced by skyscrapers in the development-oriented advertisements of these governments.

Other advertisements use simple text to remind viewers that development requires support for collectively beneficial state policies, including taxation and family planning. Hong Kong, Taipei, and Singapore have few government advertisements that present an image of the city to the citizens, or that call on citizens to support economic development more generally. Only individual political candidates in Taipei, the Ministry of Finance in Taiwan, and the Ministry of Defense in Singapore seem to create these types of images and use this textual rhetoric. The Hong Kong and Taipei municipal governments have many advertisements promoting awareness of public goods – crime prevention, anti-corruption initiatives, equal opportunity among races, protection of intellectual property rights, and consumer rights – but these are advertisements directing commuters to contact government agencies for information and services. As such, they are not directly calling on citizens to re-imagine visually and geographically the urban space that they live and work within.

Second, there seems to be a visual and textual rhetoric in public service advertisements (PSA) that reflects the role of the state in these societies. Because the Chinese Communist Party does not allow competition from other political parties, or political and social organizations, local governments are the only actors capable of addressing civic morality and ethics in public service advertisements. Beijing and Shanghai have many PSAs calling on citizens to behave with social responsibility and civic morality, even detailing what that entails in lists as part of the "socialist spiritual civilization" campaigns of the 1990s. Unlike commercial advertisements appealing to consumers to think of themselves as members of a transnational, Chinese middle class (Lewis 2003), there are as yet no public service advertisements in the PRC appealing to Chinese commuters to think of themselves as actors in solving distinctly transnational, global, or even international social or economic problems. This stands in sharp contrast with Hong Kong, where many international and local NGOs call on commuters to contribute to solving poverty, violence, and environmental problems in other parts of the world. These are less common in Singapore and Taipei, which also seem to be focused more on developing the civic identity of commuters for local or national goals. Taipei's subways, however, present many advertisements for religious organizations and political parties that suggest a much more diverse range of actors who can influence civic identity. Related, the subway corporations themselves are likely to be influential actors in public debates about the norms of appropriate public behavior. In all of these cities, the subway corporations present the few advertisements that focus on the behavior of the individual in public. Most are directed at promoting consideration for others in navigating the crowded subway stations, but some, as seen in the advertisements using Confucian sayings in Singapore, might provoke individual reflection on the role of the individual in society. Clearly the role of these transportation companies in shaping public debates about civic behavior should be examined more closely.

Third, and somewhat counter-intuitively, the public service advertisements do not present appeals to Chinese commuters to think of themselves as competitors with other cities in a global economy. Beijingers and Shanghainese are called upon to consider their local and national history and identity as they develop, but they are not asked to think of themselves as being superior to the citizens of other cities or nations. This may be so for many organizational and technical reasons. China's local governments, and the subway corporations, are promoting foreign investment and participation in China's economic development. The subway corporations themselves are often joint-ventures of capital and technology, with some, as in the case of Hong Kong's MRT, consultants in the development of urban transportation systems in other countries. Additionally, the format of advertising may not allow for more sophisticated arguments that simultaneously promote local development while criticizing the development of other cities and nations. These might be possible only in media that can command more sustained attention from viewers: publications, broadcast, and film.

The overwhelming influence of commercialization in these new public spaces in Asia might also be important in explaining the lack of images of competition. These public service advertisements must also compete with commercial advertisements – much greater in number – that ask commuters to think of themselves as global consumers. Only PSAs by international NGOs contain images of other parts of the world. Such images are common in commercial advertisements. Chinese smokers are told to think of cigarette smoking as a cosmopolitan behavior because Kent uses the New York City skyline as background in its advertisements. Toyota has images of Tokyo, Paris, and New York landmarks in its advertisements, juxtaposing them with popular scenes in Beijing and Shanghai. Commercial actors are busy trying to establish global affinities, and local governments in China might find it difficult to go against this tide in portraying any negative aspects of foreign competitors.

Fourth, the technology – formats, language, and the semiotics of visual and textual rhetoric – of public advertisements in subways affects their potential as media of discourse in these new public spaces. Some survey research suggests that commuters do indeed pay much attention to these subway platform advertisements, in much the same way that they can clearly recall the advertisements in other locations where the architecture 'forces' them to be viewed, including elevators and other transit centers (China Advertising Information Net 2000,

AFP 2003). Other survey research suggests that commuters find advertisements in the subways entertaining, to the degree that they disapprove when they are vandalized in political protests (AP 2004). If this is true in general, then public service advertisements are a medium that can benefit from innovation and technological developments. The progression from simple textual advertisements in Beijing and Shanghai subway stations in 1998 to ones in 2000 that also incorporate photographic images may thus reflect not only an increase in technical sophistication but also more investment in the capital necessary to implement these new formats. As with outdoor advertisements in general, local governments in Chinese cities appear to be adapting to the development of these media in new public spaces by incorporating new technologies and resources (Lewis 2002).

Privatization has facilitated this process, as local governments have drawn upon new regulations by the State Administration for Industry and Commerce requiring commercial advertisers to dedicate 3 percent of advertising space and time for public service advertisements (Xinhua 2003), thereby developing a 'piggy-back' situation where advances in the development of commercial advertising can benefit public sector advertising. This political condition, without potentially devastating commercial implications, thus provides an incentive for advertising firms to be exploratory and innovative in designing public service advertisements that can even be used to compete with PSAs from other countries in advertising industry competitions (Hess 2003). The fact that PSAs in subways may be designed to compete with advertisements from other countries may also explain why more and more PSAs in these cities use English and Chinese: they appeal to distinctly international panels of judges. This use of native and international language may have long-term influence on the nature of discourse in these new public spaces.

Finally, this discussion illustrates the need for inter-disciplinary research on the nature of advertising production and distribution in these new public spaces in Asia's global cities, as well as the influence they may have on the attitudes and affinities of millions of commuters. Because this medium is the product of the complex interaction of political, economic, and social actors across national boundaries, explaining its creation and influence in these public spaces will require the theoretical approaches and methodological tools of social scientists, humanities scholars, and industry practitioners.

Notes

1 Researchers from the Transnational China Project have thus far collected more than 4,000 images of advertisements from the subways of Asian cities: Beijing (1998–2003), Fukuoka (2001–2003), Hong Kong (2001–2003), Kaohsiung (1999–2000), Seoul (2000), Shanghai (1998–2003), Singapore (1999–2003), Taipei (1999–2003), and Tokyo (2000–2003). Coding of many of the Chinese-language advertisements is ongoing, with at least two coders identifying some basic content in each advertisement, using categories commonly used in comparative marketing/advertising studies: product category, form (photographic image, drawing, or text), product origin, brand, or product name, corporate name, use of human figures in images (including number, gender, and ethnicity of figures), and text of advertisement (English translation). Product categories include cosmetics and fashion, entertainment, food and drink, household

appliances, industrial products, information technology, medicine, miscellaneous (including public service), personal care, and services. A digital archive of these images for researchers and students is being prepared online and is available at http://www.ruf.rice.edu/~tnchina/

2 These surveys were sponsored by the Transnational China Project of the Baker Institute for Public Policy at Rice University and supported by the Henry Luce Foundation. The author thanks the following scholars for comments on previous versions of this chapter: Ackbar Abbas, Anne Chao, Lingchei Letty Chen, Craig Clunas, Stephanie Hemelryk Donald, Harriet Evans, Megan Ferry, Katie Hill, Michael Keane, Helena Kolenda, Stefan Landsberger, Anru Lee, Benjamin Lee, Ping-hui Liao, Maurizio Marinelli, David Meyer, Richard Smith, Wanning Sun, David Tse, Jing Wang, and Jianying Zha. The author also thanks the following scholars and students for their help in collecting and codifying the images of these surveys: Dieqin Chen, Bryan Ho, David Ho, Tze-yu Hsu, Yen-Ming Mark Lai, Chung Kang Lee, Tai Wei Lim, Michelle Lin, Takamichi Mito, Joe Ng, Christopher Pound, Shisha van Horn, Ting Wang, Sheng-Peng Wu, Arthur Jiantao Yan, Yue Yuan, and Jieming Zhu.

3 See "Vision" section of the MTR website, available May 2004 at Online. Available http://www.mtr.com.hk/eng/railway/railway.html

4 In these surveys, public service advertisement are identified as those promoting a non-commercial civic activity or service.

5 The Shanghai Seven Do Nots:

1 Do not spit (bu suidi tutan).
2 Do not litter (bu luan reng laji).
3 Do not destroy public property (bu sunhuai gongwu).
4 Do not destroy the flowers (bu pohai luhua).
5 Do not jaywalk (bu luanchuan malu).
6 Do not smoke in public spaces (bu zai gonggong changsuo xiyan).
7 Do not curse (bu shuo cuhua luanhua zanghua).

Although only appearing on small posters in the entrances to subways, Beijing has its "Ten Things to Avoid in Promoting Civic Morality" (jin shehui gongde shi buzuo):

1 Do not curse (bu shuo cuhua luanhua zanghua).
2 Do not spit (bu suidi tutan).
3 Do not displace rubbish (bu luandao laji).
4 Do not litter (bu luan reng feiqi wu).
5 Do not put up structures (bu sida luanjian).
6 Do not jaywalk (bu luanchuan malu).
7 Do not illegally park vehicles (bu luan tingfang cheliang).
8 Do not destroy public property (bu sunhuai gongwu).
9 Do not loiter and use public spaces (bu luan zhan gonggong yongdi).
10 Do not smoke in public spaces (bu zai gonggong changsuo xiyan).

6 For a copy of the Singapore 21 report see online, available at http://www.singapore21.org.sg/s21_reports.pdf

7 There are, of course, many translations of the Analects; these are based on Lau (1979).

References

AFP (2003) "Advertising Creeps into Previously Unused Spaces in China," Agence France Press, November 3.

AP (2004) "Activists Target Paris Subway Ads," Associated Press, March 8.

Bobrick, B. (1981) *Labyrinths of Iron: A History of the World's Subways*, New York: Newsweek Books.

Brooks, M. W. (1997) *Subway City: Riding the Trains, Reading New York*, New Brunswick, NJ: Rutgers University Press.

China Advertising Information Net (*zhongguo guanggao xiaoxi wang*) (2000) Effectiveness Survey of Beijing Subway Advertisements (*Beijing ditie guanggao xiaoguo diaocha*) (in Chinese), Online. Available http://www.chinaad114.com/document/bjdt.htm

Friedmann, J. (2002) *The Prospect of Cities*, Minneapolis, MN: University of Minnesota Press.

Garling, T. (ed.) (1995) *Readings in Environmental Psychology: Urban Cognition*, London: Academic Press.

Groat, L. (ed.) (1995) *Readings in Environmental Psychology: Giving Places Meaning*. London: Academic Press.

Hess, N. (2003) "D'Arcy Beijing: hot and cold advertising," *Graphis*, 345: 36–49.

IHT (2004) "Selling chinese milk and patriotism," *International Herald Tribune*, March 9.

Lau, D. C. (1979) *Confucius: The Analects*. London: Penguin.

Lee, A. R. (2005) "Heteroglossia and the subway: reading Taipei's MRT in the context of global cities," *Tamkang Review*, 36: 1.

Lewis, S. W. (2002) "What can I do for Shanghai? Selling spiritual civilization in Chinese cities," in S. H. Donald, M. Keane, and Y. Hong (eds) *Media in China: Consumption, Content and Crisis*, London: RoutledgeCurzon, 139–151.

——(2003) "The media of new public spaces in global cities: Subway advertising in Beijing, Hong Kong, Shanghai and Taipei," *Continuum: Journal of Media and Culture*, 17: 261–272.

Liao, P. H. (2003) "Image consumption and trans-local discursive practice: decoding advertisements in the Taipei MRT Mall," *Postcolonial Studies*, 6: 159–174.

Miller, I. (2002) *Aerosol Kingdom: Subway Painters of New York City*, Jackson, MS: University Press of Mississippi.

Murakami, H. (2001) *Underground*, New York: Vintage International.

Ong, A. (1999) *Flexible Citizenship: The Cultural Logics of Transnationality*, Durham, NC: Duke University Press.

Sassen, S. (1991) *The Global City: New York, London, Tokyo*, Princeton, NJ: Princeton University Press.

—— (2002) (ed.) *Global Networks, Linked Cities*, London: Brunner Routledge.

Seoul Sirip Misulgawan (2000) *Media_City Seoul 2000: Media Art 2000, Escape: City Vision, Clip City: Subway Project, Public Furniture*, Seoul: The Organizing Committee.

Shuffield, J. (2002) "The subway as intermediary public space," unpublished manuscript (Department of Urban Planning, Columbia University), Online. Available http://www.columbia.edu/~jws150/subway.html

Tanenbaum, S. J. (1995) *Underground Harmonies: Music and Politics in the Subways of New York*, Ithaca, NY: Cornell University Press.

Wang, J. (2001) "Culture as leisure and culture as capital," *Positions*, 9: 69–104.

—— (2003) "Framing Chinese Advertising: some industry perspectives on the production of culture," *Continuum: Journal of Media & Cultural Studies*, 17: 247–260.

Wu, F. L. (2000a) "Place promotion in Shanghai, PRC," *Cities*, 17: 349–361.

—— (2000b) "The global and local dimensions of place-making: remaking Shanghai as world city," *Urban Studies*, 37: 1359–1377.

Xinhua (2003) "Media required to reserve three percent of ad time, space for public service ads," January 29.

Yurick, S. (1965) *The Warriors*, New York: Holt, Rinehart & Winston.

15 Globalization and grassroots practices

Community development in contemporary urban China

Yuan Ren

Globalization is a process in which productive factors such as goods, services and labour forces in various countries flow across spatial constraints and are distributed through the market system. Different countries and regions adjust their economic structure according to a new international division of labour. Globalization is not only an economic process but also an impetus to impel all countries and different regions to change their social structure, political structure and cultural values. As China adopted open policies after the 1980s and decided to compete in the global export market, it changed the economic model from that of a planned economy towards a market-oriented economy, and started down the road towards reducing its welfare function, similar to the shrinking of the welfare state. Therefore, community development at grassroots level serves more social functions during the period of socioeconomic reform, revealing the nature of global–local forces. The force of globalization penetrates deeply into local societies, promoting community development and social transitions. It changes and reconstructs the socioeconomic structure, and makes community building a global trend. On the other hand, local socio-cultural and socio-political factors exist and strongly influence the community development process with local characteristics.

Urban community development started in the 1980s after the adoption of the 'open door' policy. In the planned economy system, the administration of urban and rural areas in China had followed the administrative model of 'omnipotent government', in which the upper levels of governments control almost all social resources and carry out top-down vertical control of the development of lower levels (Wu 2002). The upper levels of governments convey their orders to grassroots through various channels and utilize a pyramidal system for the implementation and carrying-out of policies through 'ordering–obeying' methods. The capacity for community building was almost destroyed under such a socioeconomic institution. For over 20 years since the beginning of the open door policy continuous transformation and globalization has provided communities with the space and momentum for growth. The construction and functional adjustment of grassroots power, reforms to the social management system, increase in individual consciousness and expansion of the public domain have triggered urban community development. The administratively integrated society has gradually become disaggregated. Social functions have been translated from the *danwei* system to society. At the same time, during the process of economic reform and change in social structure, a series of new urban phenomena has emerged, such as the process of rapid ageing, urbanization and population mobility, urban housing demolition and urban regeneration, improvement in the quality of life, etc. (Tang 2000, Xu 2001, Cheng 2002). These problems could not be solved within the traditional planned administrative system and community development is required to play a great role in addressing these public problems and in taking responsibility for the provision of social functions.

There are three stages in community development in urban China (NDRC and FaCS 2003).

1 From the mid-1980s to the mid-1990s, urban community development was in the start-up stage of community development that was dominated by departments of civil affairs. Community services had changed from their traditional disadvantaged recipients to all community residents, and a series of services were developed, moving from the specific to the general and from single items to multiple items.

2 From the mid-1990s to the late 1990s, urban community development entered the exploratory stage, which advanced in different ways including community planning, community health, community services, community sports, community education, etc. In this stage there was an emphasis on joint participation by multiple departments and comprehensive administration.

3 Since the late 1990s, the reform stage of community development had begun starting to focus on reforms in administrative systems and on the construction of social organizations in urban communities.

The key components needing exploration for the reform of the urban community administrative system were to break down the barriers among different departments, to mobilize various social forces and resources, to jointly participate in the construction of communities and to facilitate the construction of structural systems for community democracy and community autonomy. Community development oriented towards society building has been gradually increasing in recent years.

The practice of community development reveals a process of continuous reform in the administrative system, grassroots democracy, improvement of the social system and transition of the social structure. Community development in China is in accordance with the global trend, while at the same time its practice has local characteristics. This chapter examines community development in China from the viewpoint of global–local relations. Community development has become a global trend, although it is shaped by the different focuses and characteristics of its practice in different countries, in the context of their special historic and socio-cultural backgrounds, and is influenced by the different socio-economic institutions in these societies. Local grassroots practices of community building also prove that community development is in essence a local bottom-up process continuously enriched in contents and connotations through mutual exchange of their learnings and public life. The author concludes by discussing the typical characteristics of contemporary community development in China, and suggests new directions towards better social governance in the future.

Community development as a global trend

The concepts of community and community development vary at different historical stages and in different countries and regions. Community development is defined as a process within which residents, the government and relevant social organizations can integrate the utilization of community resources in order to identify and resolve community issues and to improve the community environment and quality of life in communities. It is also a process of creating a sense of identity and a common awareness among residents, enhancing community participation, mutual support and self-governance and promoting overall social progress. Community development is a development process in terms of social organization, social participation, capacity building and social capital, through bottom-up efforts, and has become a widely accepted idea with global influence.

Community development brings the local residents, the government, enterprises and non-governmental organizations together in forms of cooperation, and enables grassroot communities to achieve self-operation through partnership and joint development, helping to promote social and public welfare. The development of communities aims to achieve better social governance in which the government, society and market cooperate together (Lin 2002). Community development in the Western societies always has a government subsidy of some kind, and government, market and community jointly serve different functions within a social governance structure.

Features of community development in China

Community development in China started in the 1980s. The street offices and neighbourhood committees were adjusting their administrative model under the planned economy system to the reforms of market-oriented system. Community development was then still at its starting point and at the stage of exploring towards social governance. Its path of development and the process of exploration have been unavoidably affected by the traditional administrative system that was shaped in the planned economy.

Street office and neighbourhood committee

The concept of community in China emphasizes common interests and concrete services. MacIver (1958) concluded that a community refers to any area where people live together. Any villages, townships, cities and counties can be considered a community. Although location is a basic factor in defining community, the community concept in Western society is mainly considered to be groups with common interests and common demands. Therefore, a community is defined on the basis of a common point such as social class, occupation, hobbies, social needs, etc., even including the idea of an electronic community. However, in China emphasis has always been strongly placed on the location feature of community to identify where 'people live together'.

From the 1980s, academia and the government mostly use the 'Street Office' (SO) and 'Neighbourhood Committee' (NC) as the basic location units for analysing and advancing community development, because at the first stage of community development the government was able to rely only on traditional local organizations to distribute administrative resources and organize residents' autonomy. A working system for community development was shaped, based on location structure (Lei 2001). Most community organizations grow on or are embedded in location units, for example, community service centres, community schools, community hospitals, community sports centres, etc. This makes location units very important for community development in urban China. In recent years, some new organizations have been set up outside of the SO/NC location framework, for example, estate owner committees, which are difficult to integrate into the SO/NC framework. Meanwhile, social services, including education, health care, household shopping and so on, are being spatially re-organized among SO/NCs and beyond the SO/NC structure shaping new community space and new location structures for community building. This process is gradually changing the binary SO/NC location structure of community development. While in general, current local community development is still developing within the SO/NC location framework location is the key feature for advancing community development in China.

Establishment of community management

Most societies pay attention to the promotion of community development through community planning, services, construction, organization and community mechanisms, etc. However, in respect of specific practices, community development in China places more emphasis on community administration and the establishment of a system of community operation. (Wu and Gu 1996, Xi 1996, Tang 2000). For example, the Shanghai Model is famous for its 'Two Tiers of Government with Three Levels of Administration' and the Shenyang Model, the Jianghan Model and some newly emerged models have all focused on the establishment of an institution for community management. In contrast, community development in most Western societies is more focused on work programmes that consist of a range of procedures and activities; community development is largely based on the implementation of these programmes and working plans. For example, community development in Australia is closely linked to a range of nationwide and local-level community development projects.

Evolving out of the planned economy

Community development in urban China was born from the planned economy, in which the upper levels of government controlled all resources and carried out a top-down vertical administration. Government conveyed its commands to the grassroots level through various lines via lower levels of government and these commands were then implemented with an 'ordering–obeying' method. In the context of economic transformation from the planned economy towards the socialist market economy, the space for community development has been expanding. This is because it is difficult to address various urban issues under the traditional planned administrative system so that urban community development has emerged as a resolution of public affairs in the context of the transitional background. The planned economy plays a role of the starting point of community development, and it influences the contents, orientation and processes of community development. In the West, the market economy is well established and it is possible to determine what the market failings are so that community development is often a means by which society steps in to provide goods that the market cannot. Community development originated from the human rights movement in the 1960s and the 1970s. In the context of power delegation and social reforms, an emphasis has been placed on reforms and actions from the bottom-up so as to empower the people to make decisions on public affairs affecting their lives.

The role of government in community development

Community development in Western societies also emerged as a means of solving 'market dysfunction' and 'government dysfunction' through promoting participation and independent operation. Meanwhile, the relationship between government and community in China is really complicated.

1 Community development first appeared in opposition side to the 'welfare state', and was, to a large extent, non-government and even anti-government. However, communities have grown within the planned economy in China, and acquired resources from the governmental system. The relationship between the government and community building is harmonious.

2 Although in Western societies most community developments acquire subsidies and support from government, the fundamental principle for community building remains that the government should not directly control local communities by mandatory means. Government intervention and its 'top-down' activity might hinder or be dangerous for healthy community development. Communities mainly achieve their self-development by relying on social forces. However, the structure of traditional administrative integration in China means that social resources and forces can hardly be found outside the government system (Wu 1997). The establishment and development of communities are achieved through administrative push from the government. Governments use their administrative forces to promote social development, and as a result, the functions of government are gradually being extended from the administrative system. These overflowing functions have gradually contributed to the de-administration process of continuous disintegration between the government and the society. Community building with

administrative strengths has become a typical Chinese local path with its own characteristics.

3 Community development in Western countries tends to address the issues of 'state welfarism' and 'market individualism' by means of 'welfare pluralism' and 'public corporatism', respectively.

China faces the inadequate function of both government and market, and needs community building to make up for the deficiencies of the government in the newly emerged social spaces. Social security and relief are typical examples. This does not mean that the Chinese government provides too much social security and needs communities to take responsibility for social and public welfare in order to address the low efficiency and dysfunction of the operation of the government. Instead, it means that the government has a very weak role and needs communities to take responsibility for social and public welfare so as to top up the deficiency of the government and make up for the inadequate supply of social welfare. This further confirms that community development in China has very strong local features. The government's role is not weakened in community building but rather strengthened: government and community work together to advance social development in current urban China.

Diversity in grassroots practices in community development

Various places have explored new methods of community development at the grassroots level, showing the bottom-up process and practice features of community development. There are some typical community development models in different Chinese cities (Ren and Zhang 2003). Different models in urban community development have their own unique features. Some major models are examined (Table 15.1).

Qingdao Model

The Qingdao Model was the earliest to start in China. Beginning in 1987, the community service in the Shinan District in Qingdao city pioneered the process, and the model has always focused on community services. In 1996, community services were undertaken on a full scale. A large-scale shuffling of neighbourhood committees was implemented and 786 neighbourhood committees in four districts in the city were reduced to 562. Community assistants were employed in these neighbourhood committees. The municipal party commission and the municipal government released guides concerning the enhancement of community services. All street offices in central districts set up community service centres and the rate of community facility implementation reached 82.4 per cent.

The Qingdao Model is committed to comprehensively promoting the integration of five components, that is, residents' services, community management, community safety, community culture and community security.

Table 15.1 Comparisons of major urban community development models in China

Items for comparison	Qingdao Model	Shanghai Model	Shenyang Model	Jianghan Model	Baibuting Model
Key features	Headed by community services to increase community functions	Takes street offices as the working unit, and promotes community development with administrative force	Promotes the system of community democracy with organizational construction	Changes government functions, and identifies power and responsibility between government and community	Without street offices, communities conduct autonomous management under district government
Organizational system	Four levels of community services system from municipal, district, street office and neighbourhood committee; three systems of community services in management, help and facilities	Two layers of government and three layers of management; some street office set up community development committees	Congress of community members' representatives (decision-making); community consultation committee (consultation); community committee (implementation); community party branches (leadership), and various associations	Congress of community members' representatives (decision-making); community consultation committee (consultation); community committee (implementation); community party branches (leadership), and various associations	Community party committee, congress of community members' representatives, community administrative centre, community service centre
Resource allocation	Government input, acceleration of industrialization of community services, advocating resource sharing within community and work units, joint contribution and joint construction	Government input, establishment of estates			Autonomous management jointly by community committee, community services network and estate owners committee
Development method	Governmental promotion and society's participation	Government promotion	Government promotion and democratic autonomy	Government promotion	Governmental and market promotion

1   There is a focus on convenience for people and enhancing community service functions. Community services continue to be used as the access point and breakthrough point for promoting community building. In general, community service centres have been set up at the municipal level, district level and street office level in the city, and dedicated community service teams and community volunteer teams have been established. There are over 11,000 dedicated community service members in the city and 700 community voluntary service organizations which have 32,000 members. A community service management system, service assistance system and facilities service system have been established, improving the mutual independent and interconnected service network at different city levels. There are more than 1,600 community service facilities run by district and street offices, with more than 8,000 service points in the city. There are over 100 service items in eight community services series.

2   The Qingdao Model focuses on enhancing public management functions. It expanded beneficial provision from work units, and shaped a service system combining professional management and self-management by community residents.

3   The Qingdao Model also focuses on ensuring a good quality of life for residents and enhancing the stabilizing function of communities. Safety patrols and crime prevention teams comprised of police officers, community safety guards and housing area guards were formed, and a grassroots safety prevention network was set up.

4   There was a focus on raising the morality of residents and enhancing community culture and educational functions. Qingdao organized and undertook community learning activities. Most street offices and big-scale communities set up comprehensive cultural and educational centres. Cultural and educational facilities in many secondary and primary schools have been encouraged to open to the public.

5   In the wake of the reform of the planned economy, the Qingdao Model focuses on enhancing the function of community social security. Qingdao established community assistance teams, serving as safety networks and providing basic social relief, and raising community functions to develop their communities. Generally speaking, the practice of community development in Qingdao changed urban management into services. Cities with models similar to the Qingdao Model went even further, continuously enriching community service as an important component of community building.

Shanghai Model

In 1996, the Shanghai Municipal Party Commission and municipal government held a city working meeting where they put forward a new framework of 'two levels of governments with three levels of management' to be explored in Shanghai, a leading large city in China. In terms of form, they regarded the street office as a level of management and used the new framework as the guiding principle for community development in Shanghai.

The specific feature of the Shanghai Model is based on a vertical management system from city government to district government and street office level. Through this vertical chain, the local government's power is expanded, and their management functions play leading roles in community development, eliminating the drawback of line management that does not reach to the bottom of the city, and reinforcing the functions of local units as grassroots modules, by conferring on street offices the administrative and management functions for the overall coordination, organization, leadership, supervision and inspection of community affairs. For example, in the Wuliqiao street office, which is a famous success of community development in Shanghai, four working committees were established: the public administration committee, the community development committee, the community safety and general governance committee and the finance and economics committee. The public administration committee carries out the overall management of municipal and cityscape work under its jurisdiction. The community development committee manages and coordinates social development and the improvement of social welfare. The community safety and general governance committee mainly assists street office party and street office executives in public safety and social order. The finance and economics committee is responsible for budgets and final accounts for their street offices, conducting the overall management and coordination of business enterprises. The structure of the four working committees enables street offices to extend their functions. Street offices, as the main stakeholders of the region, coordinating and cooperating with work units in the local area, can integrate their joint strengths to ensure the good management of community affairs.

The Shanghai Model pays attention to the shift of social management from party and government to the lower levels of society, which is closely linked with urban management reform. Shanghai positioned the community on the street office level. Based on the administrative resources shaped in street offices, local party and government offices, communities are being developed. During the continuous interactions between street offices and the neighbourhood committees, various undertakings and social organizations are being developed within communities. This community development model has strong characteristics of administrative promotion, which has been described as a process of 'administrative community building'. Through this governmental push, Shanghai has put a great deal of human resources and materials into improving community environments, constructing various service facilities in communities, creating modern communities, building community consciousness and linking community development with the performance evaluation of local officials. Based on such great strength, community development in Shanghai has been developed in an unprecedented way, and a large number of civilized communities, modern estates, model street offices and model neighbourhood committees have emerged. Many of these practices were followed in the Shijiazhuang, Tianjin and Xicheng districts in

Beijing, which followed this model, although there were still some differences in the definition of the boundaries of community functions.

Shenyang Model

In 1999, the Community Department of the Ministry of Civil Affairs held a conference in Shenyang city, at which it was represented that the Shenyang Model had been formed as a paradigmatic model for community development. Currently, there are 112 street offices and 1,289 communities in Shenyang city, where 1,289 community service centres and over 5,000 community associations and organizations have been established and 3,000 teams of community volunteers have been developed.

The Shenyang Model started its exploration at the end of the 1990s. The first major work was to re-zone communities, in which process urban communities were positioned as smaller than sub-district and larger than the previous neighbourhood committees, readjusting the scope of a community according to physical boundaries. Most communities cover 1,000 households, with large ones covering 2,000–3,000. The re-zoning of communities is a good step towards overcoming the disadvantages of community organizations having previously become government attachments. In actual practice, there were different patterns in the re-zoning of communities in Shenyang according to different characteristics of local communities.

The core of the Shenyang Model is the accomplishment of community autonomy via the restructuring of grassroots organizations. The construction target of the Shenyang Model is to create a grassroots society that adopts self-education, self-service, self-management and self-supervision by community members, based on fully functioning neighbourhood committees, with the participation of various social forces. In order to accelerate democratic autonomy in the communities, Shenyang has established, correspondingly, four parts for community functions, including decision-making, implementation, consultation and community executives. A congress of community member representatives serves the function of decision-making, which is the organization of power utilization for community autonomy. A community committee serves the function of implementation, carrying out most public affairs from above. The community committee is responsible to the congress of community member representatives. The community consultations committee comprising of congressmen, members of the political consultative committee, well-known persons, representatives of residents and representatives of work units inside local area, serves the function of consultation. Their function is to consult with and make suggestions for local community matters and supervise the work of community development. The communist party organization within the community serves the function of the executive, and always provides the core leadership for the community. By imitating the organizational structure of the central government, the Shenyang Model has improved local autonomy and made clear the functional distribution among different organizations within the community. Shenyang's experience has had a strong demonstration effect, which is regarded as a mechanism for fostering civil politics. It must be said that, in extent, the Shenyang Model has been widely advocated and widely imitated. Besides Liaoning taking the typical Shenyang Model, Haikou, Wuhan, Harbin, Xi'an, Hefei and many other cities are beginning to reform local grassroots communities according to the Shenyang Model.

Jianghan Model

Having studied the Shanghai Model and Shenyang Model, the community development model in Jianghan District in Wuhan city identified further rights and responsibilities of government and community. The core features here are to change the functions of government and establish an urban grassroots management system combining a new governmental administrative mechanism and mechanism of community autonomy. This model is referred to as the Jianghan Model, and its preliminary form was shaped after 2000. Chen (2001) described it as a mechanism of symbiosis, mutually complementary and a 'win–win' for government and community, and evaluated it as a community governance model in which there was integration of governments carrying out implementations according to law and communities carrying out autonomy according to law, an integration of an administrative mechanism and an autonomy mechanism, and a mutual complementing of governmental and community functions.

The Jianghan Model adjusts the relationships between government and community via a proactive change of functions by governments, so as to achieve community autonomy. The main contents of the Jianghan Model are the following:

1   *Smoothing relationships*. Clearly understanding that the relationships between neighbourhood committees, street offices and government departments are based on guiding, assistance, service and supervision, and not traditional top-down administrative relationship shaped by command and obedience.
2   *Identifying functions*. The relationships of 'guiding and assistance, service and supervision' could only be put into effect along clear divisions of corresponding functions. Jianghan District analysed the work of administrative departments and communities. Some of their responsibilities are to be undertaken by district government assisted by local community staff, and some are to be undertaken by community organizations with guidance from upper levels of government. For example, the Chunman street office itemized 40 functions, and clearly stipulated that 19 of these functions are to be undertaken by various departments of the upper government, whereas 13 should be undertaken by government and assisted by community neighbourhood committees, while the remaining 5 might be carried out by community organizations themselves.
3   *Ensuring the autonomous rights of community neighbourhood committees*. Neighbourhood committees no longer need to find the agreement of responsibilities with street offices. Government departments and street offices must, according to law, support communities in exercising the powers of appointing social workers, decision making in public affairs, autonomous power in finance, democratic management, refusal of the unreasonable levying of charges, and

meanwhile must guide and assist the community to independently conduct services convenient for residents, such as community education and management, community safety and security, community environmental improvement, and the prevention of government from infringing upon community autonomy.

4 *Government subsidy for community assistance in administrative affairs.* In order to ensure that administrative matters are jointly undertaken by government and assisted by the local community, government should ensure that staff members are deployed to the community, that work and tasks are carried out for the community, that working funds are allocated to the community, that service commitment to the community is made, and that assessment and supervision are carried out by the community. For example, in Jianghan District, 112 professional family-planning social workers were publicly employed in the community, and their salaries are paid by the district government.

5 Power follows responsibility and budgets follow services. Public affairs and social benefit in the community must have corresponding subsidies from the government's budget. Jianghan District pioneered an exploratory reform of separating powers and responsibilities between government and community in nine government functions, and created inspiring experiences.

Baibuting Model

Baibuting ward in Wuhan city occupies a total area of 500 acres with a total planned construction area of 3 million square metres, where 30,000 households and a permanent population of 100,000 reside. It is a new estate built on a suburban area of the city, with rampant weeds, flood-prone land, polluted water and very few community service facilities. At the beginning of community development, a 'people-centred' philosophy was put forward and used to formulate '4321' guiding policies including the following:

1 Satisfying 4 needs:

   (a) the need for enterprise development (developers)
   (b) the need to raise residents' living standards
   (c) the need for social stability
   (d) the needs of the state.

2 Achieving 3 returns:

   (a) return to enterprises
   (b) return to communities
   (c) return to the state.

3 Developing 2 accelerations:

   (a) the acceleration of community in developing a spiritual civilization
   (b) a material civilization.

4 Fulfilling 1 target:

   (a) enabling residents to live and work in peace and contentment.

Baibuting community achieved great success and received an excellent community award in Wuhan city, and another award in Hubei Provinces.

The major feature of the Baibuting Model is that it does not set up a street office for community development. The community conducts work directly under leadership from the district government. Baibuting regards the entire estate as one community, and elects one community committee. With support from Jiang'an District Party Commission and District government, they set up a community party working committee, which has organized more than 500 party members in the community and established a general branch, 4 branches, 18 party teams and a party working committee to undertake leadership and supervisory functions. A community congress of residents' representatives makes democratic decisions and undertakes the democratic management of important matters in the community. In community administrative affairs the centre provides various policy-dictated services, for example, military service formalities, marriage, business registration, taxation, social security, household registration, family planning, etc. Baibuting community actively promotes community services and explores re-employment for laid-off workers. Because there is no street office, administrative expenses are greatly reduced. Cultural and educational facilities that have been built include a cultural and arts centre incorporating a reading room, reading boards, an etiquette school, a university for the elderly, a cultural corridor and a sports centre incorporating a soccer field, basketball field, tennis court, croquet ground, playground for children and ping pong room, etc. Similar to the Baibuting Model is Fushanhou in Qingdao city, which is also a community development model with no street office in a newly built residential estate. These kinds of explorations are in their infancy and have yet to be systematically appraised.

In general, the differences in the features of these community development models are determined by the specific features and conditions in different cities, and this has reflected the different focuses in practice at different stages. Different grassroots practices in community development have their own specific features. Looking at the local practices of community building in most cities, some models are quite mature, and some are in formation; more often, they are a mixture of different models. Various community development models are generally intermingled with each other, and then continuously create fresh vibrant contents. The previous so-called models are also changing. For example, the Qingdao Model of community development was widely advocated by many other cities, yet now the Qingdao Model is learning new practices from the Shenyang Model and other models, and absorbing new ideas for community development. The Shanghai Model emphasized 'Two Layers Government and Three Layers Management', but when community development has reached a new stage, the model will have to keep pace by making appropriate changes and creating new contents and features in its practice. Because of the richness of community development practices, it is very difficult for us at this current stage to make a firm judgement on the organizational system and operational structure of urban community development. Urban community development in China still lacks systematic, well-established and uniform institutions, and remains a matter of exploration at grassroots level. Urban community development is learning by doing local exploration, development through path-dependency and achieving rich experiences through grassroots practices.

The Chinese path in community development

Chinese society has its own unique history and cultural background. The characteristic features of its community development, therefore, reflect these. Its starting point, specific connotations and development process are obviously localized and different from those of community building in western societies. The transition from a highly centralized planned economy system to the socialist market economic system, along with the transformation of society, have gradually resulted in a modern structure of administration and provided the historical context for community development in China. Community development, as an important pillar of modern society, has to a large extent been established by the government with administrative power, either consciously or unconsciously. The practice in China shows that community development can be promoted very efficiently, in that the government transforms the resources within its administrative system into social resources. Under circumstances where social and market forces are not well developed, the government's role is of great significance. The grassroots administrative structure and communities overlap with each other, making the local administrative units a good working carrier for community building. Actually, such an empowerment of the grassroots community from within the administrative system is favourable for the gradual growth of non-administrative forces and mechanisms, and for the promotion of the development of the intrinsic organization of social forces. Community development is ongoing with support from administrative forces. The non-administrative social forces and the de-administration process occurred under the existing administrative structure. This seems to be a paradox. But it precisely explains what forces have pushed Chinese society forward under the planned system towards social transformation. This very fact has contributed to the local features of urban community development in China, which is different from most Western societies. It has also pointed out an effective path towards a smooth transition in societies with strong traditions of administrative management.

The current non-administrative social forces and spaces in the communities have to some extent developed and played the role of a 'sub-government', or an implementer for the government. However, its social role is still not clear, and in addition, weakened social functions, underdeveloped social mechanisms, the low participation of residents and the administrative framework of community building still affect the development of the community's social system. The dominant role is still that of the administrative forces. It is a special phenomenon that has emerged during the transformation process out of the traditional planned economy system and has determined the characteristic features of urban community development in China at its current stage, which is clearly very different from the practice of community building in Western societies. In spite of these factors, when we look at the development of urban grassroots societies from a historical perspective we might find that grassroots communities under the planned economy system were almost in a 'vacuum' and that a social system has truly emerged and gradually developed. Community development has brought about social resources, social organizations, social participation and social institutions, and has gradually played a more and more important role.

Therefore, local community development in urban China reveals a double dimension.

1   Urban community development has emerged from within the administrative system and structure. It is unavoidably dependent on the administrative system. The traces of 'administrative dominance' and 'administrative promotion' can still be found in the objectives, directions, structure, functional design and operational mechanisms of community development. There are very distinctive features of community building through administrative promotion by the government.

2   Urban community development is essentially the expansion of social space and the self-organization and operation of social forces. It is a process in which social forces emerge and grow up, and where urban social systems are established. It shapes a picture of ongoing social reform at the grassroots level.

'Administrative promotion' and 'socializing development' are top-down and bottom-up forces, respectively. The former is promoted from within the administrative system while the latter grows outside of the system. These two forces do not repel each other; rather, they integrate, promote each other and interconnect with each other. The society has grown from within the administrative system. The momentum of administrative promotion helps to shape the final outcome of social development. As a result, the society has gradually emerged from an invisible state within the administrative system and has operated and expanded on its own. The above characteristic features have determined the unique path of community development in urban China.

If community development in China at its current stage could be characterized by administrative promotion, then further community development by means of promoting the development of social organizations and by facilitating the participation of social forces will be an important driving force for a better established social system. This might constitute a new wave of community building going forward, with a special feature of society building. Drawing on experiences from Western societies, the following practical experiences and characteristic features are of particular value to the furthering of community development in China.

1   Community development requires the strengthening of a full range of social services, which are largely specialized social services that require specialized

professionals such as medical practitioners, legal workers and other specialists to provide their services to the communities with their specialized knowledge, methods and skills.

2   Community development requires the full development of non-governmental social organizations and their involvement in community-based public affairs. These organizations might become an important social force that provides a range of public services to the residents of the communities and facilitates the flow of resources and volunteers.

3   Full play should be given to the market mechanism in the development of communities, so as to vigorously encourage various enterprises to participate in the development of social and public welfare, and promote the use of non-governmental capital in community development. Community services could also be regarded as an essential part of urban social services. It is also necessary to promote the development of social enterprises and the establishment of community public funds.

4   Community programmes need to be vigorously promoted with standardized management and operations. In line with specific public needs, community programmes such as childcare, care of the aged, environmental protection, parenting skills, adult education, violence prevention, women's development, employment and so on should be vigorously promoted. Usually, government prepares a guiding programme for these programmes and specifies the use of public funds, and various social organizations and groups are expected to submit detailed proposals. Some of the guiding programmes have very strict requirements and specify detailed requirements for the qualifications of the applicant. Others are relatively flexible and encourage the creative participation of grassroots communities in the projects, so as to improve the efficiency of services through competition. Standardized assessments and appraisals are to be introduced for community programmes in order to provide a basis for the further promotion of community programmes in the future.

5   A favourable legal and institutional environment for community development is to be established. The legal system for community development is relatively well established in Western societies. In addition to legislation for community development, the planning standards and specific laws and regulations related to various public affairs in communities have also played an important role in improving community development.

6   Take community development as the starting point for better social development and political democracy. The vigorous social participation of the vast number of residents in the public affairs of communities and the development of social democracy has constituted the practice of democratic participation and self-management. Thus, community development also has provided the basis for the political democracy of a country. Community development in China is still very inadequate or even draws a blank in some of the above aspects, and needs to draw on successful practices in Western societies.

Globalization has a deep influence on all aspects of urban life. At the macro-level, globalization makes a city and region acquire a position in the global industrial system, and embeds cities within the global urban system. At the micro-level, globalization changes citizens' livelihoods, strengthens individuals' global linkage and changes individual human values and social beliefs. Meanwhile, at the urban grassroots level, community development becomes a basic place to show the global–local nexus, and the globalization process also has its influence on local community development.

1   Globalization may strengthen empowerment and shape good partnership among government, market and society.
2   Global migration has increased in the wake of globalization and capital mobility. With the booming of foreign enterprises and joint venture enterprises, international CEOs and high-ranking white-collar workers have been rapidly increasing in large cities in China. Shanty slums, old housing estates and high standard new high-rise communities simultaneously shape the multiple features of local communities.
3   Globalization advances industrial structural adjustment and market competition, aggravating urban unemployment and making the local community play a more important role in the provision of social security and social services.
4   Globalization is not only an industrial restructuring process; it brings about the deeper involvement of international capital in the social services sector. For example, some international companies have become involved in community gym, bodybuilding and similar fields; these ongoing involvements also bring international management experience into community services.
5   International social NGOs and Non-Profit Organizations (NPOs) are involved more deeply in addressing urban affairs in the context of globalization. For example, more and more international social programmes have been set up in different cities for practical urban affairs and social problems, mostly focusing on social protection for disadvantaged people. Thus, international cooperation in social fields extends global linkages in social development, strengthening the NGOs' development and better functioning.

The question of how globalization affects local community development in urban China remains open. For example, is there a relation between the predominance of laid-off workers from state-owned enterprises in a city and the type of community development the city undertakes? Is there a relationship between a city's approach to community development and the amount of foreign investment a city attracts, and the way it attracts and channels it? What is the relationship between the community development movement and the growth of migrant communities? What are the characteristics of international communities, and how has the evolution of socio-geographic stratification developed? All these questions are connected to the globalization of urban development. In general, grassroots strength will inevitably grow and shape multiple features of community development in China as well as the communities themselves.

Acknowledgements

I greatly appreciate comments from Fulong Wu, Xiangming Chen and two anonymous reviewers.

References

Chen, W. (2001) 'Government and community: the case of Jianghan District in Wuhan', *Journal of Central China Normal University* (Humanities and Social Sciences) (Hua Zhong Shi Fan Da Xue Xue Bao), 3: 7–12 (in Chinese).

Cheng, Y. S. (2002) *Research on Urban Community Development in China* (*Zhong Guo cheng Shi She Qu Fa Zhan Yan Jiu*), Shanghai: East China Normal University Press (in Chinese).

Lei, J. Q. (2001) *Urban Grassroots Community Organizations in Transition: Research on the Grassroots Community Organizations and Community Development in Beijing* (*zhuang Xing Zhong De Cheng Shi Ji Ceng She Qu Zu Zhi: Bei Jing Shi Ji Ceng She Qu Zu Zhi Yu She Qu Fa Zhan Yan Jiu*), Beijing: Beijing University Press (in Chinese).

Lin, S. L. (2002) *Community Democracy and Administration: Case Studies* (*She Qu Min Zhu Yu Zhi Li: An Li Yan Jiu*), Beijing: Social Science Literature Press (in Chinese).

Maclver, R. M. (1958) *Community: A Sociological Study*, New York: Macmillan Press.

NDRC and FaCS (2003) *Australia–China Joint Research on Community Development: Community Development and Community Employment Joint Report*. Australian Government Department of Family and Community Services International Studies Asian Occasional Papers, Commonwealth of Australia, ISSN1448–7667.

Ren, Y. and Zhang, Z. G. (2003) 'Comparative studies on community development models in urban China', *Social Science Research* (*She Hui Ke xue Yan Jiu*), 6: 97–110 (in Chinese).

Tang, Z. X. (2000) *An Outline of Urban Community Building in China* (*Zhong Guo Cheng Shi She Qu Jian She Gai Lun*), Tianjin: Tianjin People Press (in Chinese).

Wu, D. (1997) *Community Development: Grand Program on Hot Soil* (*She Qu Jian She: Re Tu Shang De Hong Wei Gong Cheng*), Shanghai: Dangdai China Press (in Chinese).

Wu, D. L. and Gu, Y. C. (1996) *Urban Community Development in China* (*Zhong Guo Cheng Shi She Qu Jian She*), Knowledge Publishing House (in Chinese).

Wu, F. (2002) 'China's changing urban governance in the transition towards a more market-oriented economy', *Urban Studies*, 39 (7):1071–1093.

Xi, C. Q. (1996) *Community Research: Community Building and Community Development* (*She Qu Yan Jiu: She Qu Jian She Yu She Qu Fa Zhan*), Huaxia Press (in Chinese).

Xu, Y. X. (2001) *Theory on Community Development* (*She Qu Fa Zhan Lun*), Shanghai: East China Polytechnic University (in Chinese).

Index

Abu-Lughod, J. 4
actual foreign investment 259
administrative forces 296
'administrative promotion' 306
aesthetic fusion 109
air traffic 88
American style suburban housing 181
American Victorian 215
apartment complexes 196
Appadurai, A. 3
architectural styles 191, 205, 209,
    216, 223
Artificial mountains 221
Asian financial crisis 35
Asian Game Village 191
Asian global cities 271
Asia-Pacific Trans-shipment Centre
    147, 153
'Asia's world city' 87

Bahia Praia Grande 110, 115
Baibuting Model 303
Beauregard, R. 204
Beaverstock, J. V. 86
Beijing 63, 277; advertisement in 278;
    foreign housing project, distribution of
    199; as an 'internationalised metropolis'
    63–83; Master plan for 67, 69, 198;
    municipal government 176; Olympics
    76–77
'border' 9
border trade 31
boundary effects 139
Boxer, C. 111
Business environment 234

Capital Iron and Steel Works 68
Capital Land 179
capital valorization 10

Castells, M. 10
CBD 96; segregation in 95
Central Taichung Science Park 160
Changzhou New District 260
Chen, X. M. 23
China's new urbanism 184; and
    globalization 1–15; materiality of
    globalization 14
Chinese element 221
Chineseness 218
Chinese path 305
Chinese urbanization 57
circulation of vital energy 219
city: building 6; development 10;
    discourse 8; government 174;
    landscapes 11; marketing of
    Taipei; -region development 155–158
cityscapes 190; to exploit
    globalization 190
civic behavior 280
civic pride 280
'civilization clash' 11
'civilization mix' 11, 209, 213, 222
'closer economic partnership arrangement'
    (CEPA) 9
colonialism 110
commercialization, influence of 288
commodity housing 195
'common interest development' 201
community 192; 'construction' 4;
    management 295
community development 13, 201, 292;
    models 204; role of government in
    296; three stages in 293
commuters in Asian cities 276
competitive advantage, national 232;
    creating, role of government in 234
competitive market 200
conservation 80

consumerism 181
cross-border: ethnic ties 24, 40; integration 9, 125; regions 125
cross-boundary: activities 132; housing purchasing 132; movement of population and vehicles 130; shopping 132; vehicular trips 131
cultural: 'globalization' 211; heritage 117; 'industry' 159; 'politics' 10; transnationalism 184; values 110
culture dominance 184
Cyberport 8

danwei 168, 170; -built housing 171; -originated large developers 173
decentralization 32
Dehong 34
Democratic Progressive Party 148
de-regulation 248
derivative by-product 14
design 192
'development fever' 175
development trajectory 65
discourses 12, 108, 289
'Disneylandization' 11, 223
domestic politics 9
Dreamed Westernality 217

East lake Villas 196
e-business 71
econometric analysis 50
economic sectors, new 252
'economic villas' 194
Edmonds, R. L. 111
e-government 71
English, importance of 99
ethnic ties 34
Evans, P. 233

FDI 7, 57, 184, 252; by sector in Su-Xi-Chang 261
fengshui 213
Filipino maids 98
finance 89
'floating population' 49, 76
Fontainebleau 11, 208; Villas 214
Forbidden City 74, 197
'force of industrialization' 5
foreign: designers 183; domestic helpers 97; experts 196; 'housing' 195, 204; housing projects 196; investment 256, 308; investors 177
Forrest, R. 101–102

Fraser, D. 203, 214
French architecture 215
French aristocratic style 214, 216
Friedmann, J. 1, 70, 85
frontier cities 26, 40

gated communities 11, 190, 196, 210
Gaubatz, P. R. 22
Gini coefficient 101
global: city immigrants 103; city-regions 126; discourses 204; -local economic nexus 22; -local force 292; '-local nexus' 1; sub-society 104; urban hierarchy 6
'global cities', typologies of 2
'glocalization' 2
'glurbanization' 6
golden ghettos 210
governance 12, 81
government-firm relationship 235
Grand Canal 65
grassroots democracy 293
grassroots governance 13
'great city' 7
Greater Mekong Subregion (GMS) 25
'Greater PRD' 127–128
Greater Tumen Subregion (GTS) 25
'great transformation' 4
Great Wall 74
'Green Olympics' 77
Guangzhou 137
Guangzhou-Foshan metropolitan cluster 137
guidebooks 118

Hall, P. 70
Hannerz, U. 192
health problems 76
hegemonic convergence 191
'hidden' land market 170
High and New Technological Development Zone 258
high-tech growth 262
high-tech industrial development 149
Hills, P. 78, 101
HKSAR Government's Central Policy Unit 140
Ho, Stanley 120
homeowners' association 202
Hong Kong 8, 86, 286; sectoral and spatial changes in 91
horizontal division 267
housing commodification 199, 202

housing enclaves 214
Hsinchu city 155, 157
Hsinchu Science Park 150
Hsing, Y.-T. 22
Huang, Y. Q. 11
Hunchun BECZ 29, 40
Hunchun China-Russia Free Market and Trade Zone 29
Hunchun Export Processing Zone 29
Huntington, S. 11
hutong (alleys) 67
Hypo Real Estate Bank International 179

identity crisis 223
immigration 96, 99; policy 161
income polarisation 100
industrial output, growth of 260
industrial parks 147, 153, 161
Inner Harbour 113
international division of labour 233
'internationalised metropolis' 63
'internationalization' 7
internationalization of China's real estate development 180
international schools 201
'investment risks' 167, 184

Japanese local second-tier technopolises 263
Jessop, B. 2, 12
Jianghan Model 302
Jiang Zemin 279
Jilin 27, 32

Keppel Land 179
Kinship-based social networks 35
Knox, P. 205

land: 'contestation over the meaning of the place' 184, 191; development 10; efficient land use 174; leasing system 200; politics 10; -related regulations 178; supply 169
landscape: of modernity 117; 'restless' formation and reformation of 205
'LA school' 190
'Le Château' 212
lifestyles 203; new lifestyle 181, 195
Li Ka-Shing 75, 179
Lin, G. C. S. 2
local: economies 12; governance 202; institutions 202; land market 184;

milieu 205; or national goals 287; politics 10; R&D capacity 252
local society 103, 104, 138; continuity of 13
Logan, J. R. 2, 184
Louis XIV 217
Lujiazui Financial Zone 281
Luxury, harmonious relationship with the universe 224

Ma, L. J. C. 2
Macau 8, 99, 108
McDonalds 75
manufacturing sector 253
market forces 142
materializations of globalization 14
May 4 Movement 66
mega-Guangzhou 137
Mekong River 38
metis culture 119
Mies 215
MNCs 14
'modernity' 10
'modernization' 3, 5, 7
monopoly 267
multi-nucleated city-region 135
multi-nucleated pattern 138

Nangang Software Park 153–154
'nation state' 6
neighbourhood committee 294
Neihu Technology Park 153–154
'neoliberal' policies 13
New Territories 102
New World Group 179
Ng, M. K. 78, 101
'No.121 Document' 178
non-agricultural population 7
North Korea 27

'Open City' 69
'Open Door' policy 69
Orange County 191–192
'ordering–obeying' method 296
'ordinary' cityscapes 190, 204
'ordinary city' 6
Oriental Plaza 75
Orum, A. M. 23
Outer Harbour 110, 119

Panyu 137
'people-centred' philosophy 303
'place embeddedness' 235

place-promotion 248
politics of scale 2
Porter, J. 111
Porter, M. E. 233
Portman 215
post-socialist cities 13, 203
Praia Grande Bay 121
PRD–Hong Kong cross-boundary
   city-region 127
primary land market 169
private estates 210
private rental 200
producer services 12
productive service development 265
property management companies 202
property rights 200
proud local citizens 276
public service advertisements 271, 275
public space 12; new public space
   271–289
Pudong 243; New District 247; Software
   Park 248
Purple Jade Villas 191

Qingdao Model 297

R&D centre 246
'regime of accumulations' 3, 8
regional competition 138
regional headquarters 90
regional services 265
relocation projects 81
'removing Chinese-ness' 159
re-regulation 248
residential districts 194
Rua Praia Grande 109
'rural Dutch style' 215

SARS 82
Sassen, S. 1, 21, 23, 85, 126
Scott, A. J. 126
Second Opium War 66
secured compound 201
segregation and suburbanisation 101
sense of 'community' 202
SEZ 56
Shanghai 237, 279; advertisement in 280,
   282; Model 299; municipal government
   241; Real Estate Group 177;
   nostalgia 8
Shenzhen 9, 137
Shenzhen Model 301
Siheyuan (courtyard) 80
'Silk Alley' 76

Singapore 283
Sino-Singapore Suzhou Industrial
   Park 258
Sinyi new CBD 150
Skidmore, Owings & Merrill (SOM) 182
Smart, A. 1
social forces, current
   non-administrative 305
'socialism and post-socialism' 5
'socialist spiritual civilization' 277
'socializing development' 306
social structure 96
software enterprises 244; customer
   relationship 245; linkages of 245
software industrial cluster 247
software industries 243
Software Park 248
SOHO 148
Southern Jiangsu 261
South Korean investment 35
'space of flow' 10, 70
spaces of globalization 3
spatial concentration of jobs 93
spatial differentiation 104
spatial segregation 102
Special Administrative Region 103
Special Economic Zones (SEZs) 48
state danwei 171
state land tenure 168
state-level open cities 33
state socialism 5
status symbol 201
Storper, M. 235
street office 294
'structural' competitiveness 12
subjective geography 110
subregional economy dynamics 7
subways 272
Suzhou-Wuxi-Changzhou (Su-Xi-Chang)
   252, 253, 262–263; cooperation with
   Shanghai 266
symbols of modernity 273

Taipei 9, 147, 285; County mayor 157;
   culture and marketing 158; high-tech
   corridor 151; MRT Company 285;
   Taipei 101 147, 150
Taoist paradise 221
Taoyuan city 157
Taylor, P. 65
technology-based manufacturing 268
technopolises 263
telecommunications 89
temporality 4, 6; of globalization 4

territorial governing system 172
tetsudoin 124
'Third World city' 2
'three-links' 150, 158
'three represents' 279
Tomson Golf Villas 210
tourist guidebooks 108
tourist industry 120
tourist literature 116
townhouse 190–191, 194
township and village enterprises
 (TVEs) 50
'transborder subregions' 6, 40
'transitional economies' 3
'trans-local' 1
Transnational Corporations
 (TNCs) 231
transnational sphere 13
transnational symbols 13
transport infrastructure 25, 36
Tumen River 29; development 32

urban: competitiveness 264; forms 14;
 influence of globalization 308; models
 in urban community development 297;
 political and economic implications 12;
 politics, new 167; redevelopment 181;
 'Renaissance' 13
urbanism 1, 6; new urbanism 14, 184
urbanization 6, 47; globalization as 6;
 impact of openness 53

vertical division 267
villa compounds 196
villas 195

Wang Qishan 81
Webster, C. 11–12, 190
Welfare State, Shrinking of 292
Western Development Policy 57
'Westernization' 3, 6
Westernized landscape 11
Western lifestyles 203
Western 'modernity' 182
Wolff, G. 1
Wong, H. 101
work-unit 13
'world factory' 254
World Health Organisation
 (WHO) 81
WTO 2, 5
Wuxi New District 260

Xijiang River 112

Yanbian 27, 32
Yangtze River Delta 268
Yangtze River Region 229
Yanji 34
Yan Mingfu 63
Yunnan 30–31

Zukin, S. 11

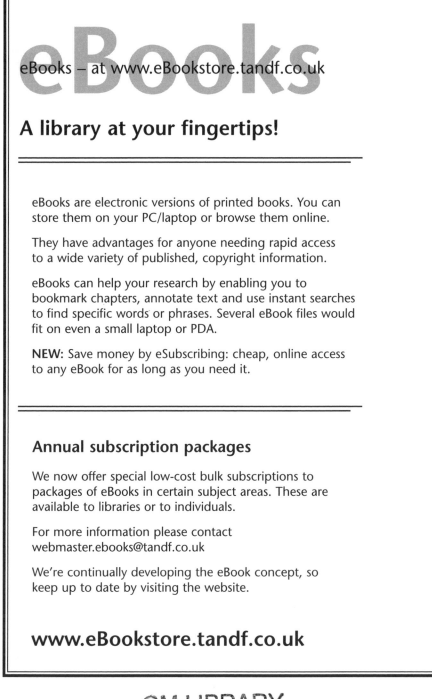